ALL·IN·ONE

CEH™ Certified Ethical Hacker

EXAM GUIDE

ALL·IN·ONE

CEH™ Certified Ethical Hacker

EXAM GUIDE

Matt Walker

New York • Chicago • San Francisco • Lisbon
London • Madrid • Mexico City • Milan • New Delhi
San Juan • Seoul • Singapore • Sydney • Toronto

The McGraw·Hill Companies

Cataloging-in-Publication Data is on file with the Library of Congress

CEH™ Certified Ethical Hacker All-in-One Exam Guide

34567890 QFR QFR 1098765432

ISBN: Book p/n 978-0-07-177230-3 and CD p/n 978-0-07-177231-0
of set 978-0-07-177229-7

MHID: Book p/n 0-07-177230-8 and CD p/n 0-07-177231-6
of set 0-07-177229-4

Sponsoring Editor Timothy Green	**Technical Editor** Brad Horton	**Production Supervisor** James Kussow
Editorial Supervisor Jody McKenzie	**Copy Editor** Bart Reed	**Composition** Apollo Publishing Services
Project Editor Emilia Thiuri, Fortuitous Publishing Services	**Proofreader** Louise Watson	**Illustration** Lyssa Wald
	Indexer Jack Lewis	**Art Director, Cover** Jeff Weeks
Acquisitions Coordinator Stephanie Evans		

This book is dedicated to my children:
Faith, Hope, Christian, and Charity.
They are the world to me.

ABOUT THE AUTHOR

Matt Walker, an IT Security and Education professional for over 20 years, has served as the Director of the Network Training Center and the Curriculum Lead/Senior Instructor for the local Cisco Networking Academy on Ramstein AB, Germany. After leaving the U.S. Air Force, Matt served as a Network Engineer for NASA's Secure Network Systems (NSS), designing and maintaining secured data, voice, and video networking for the Agency. Soon thereafter, Matt took a position as Instructor Supervisor and Senior Instructor at Dynetics, Inc., in Huntsville, Alabama, providing onsite certification awarding classes for ISC2, Cisco, and CompTIA, and after two years came right back to NASA as the IT Security Manager for UNITeS, SAIC, at Marshall Space Flight Center. He has written and contributed to numerous technical training books for NASA, Air Education and Training Command, the U.S. Air Force, as well as commercially, and he continues to train and write certification and college-level IT and IA Security courses. Matt holds numerous commercial certifications, including CEHv7, CPTS, CNDA, CCNA, and MCSE. Matt is currently the IT Security Manager for Lockheed Martin at Kennedy Space Center.

About the Technical Editor

Brad Horton currently works as an Information Security Specialist with the U.S. Department of Defense. Brad has worked as a security engineer, commercial security consultant, penetration tester, and information systems researcher in both the private and public sectors.

This has included work with several defense contractors, including General Dynamics C4S, SAIC, and Dynetics, Inc. Mr. Horton currently holds CISSP, CEH, CISA, and CCNA trade certifications. Brad holds a bachelor's degree in Commerce and Business Administration from the University of Alabama, a master's degree in Management of Information Systems from the University of Alabama in Huntsville (UAH), and a graduate certificate in Information Assurance from UAH. When not hacking, Brad can be found at home with his family or on a local golf course.

The views and opinions expressed in all portions of this publication belong solely to the author and/or editor and do not necessarily state or reflect those of the Department of Defense or the United States Government. References within this publication to any specific commercial product, process, or service by trade name, trademark, manufacturer, or otherwise, do not necessarily constitute or imply its endorsement, recommendation, or favoring by the United States Government.

About the Contributing Editor

Angie Walker is currently an Information Systems Security Engineer for Harris Corporation, located in Melbourne, Florida. Among the many positions she has filled over the course of her 20-plus years in Information Technology and Information Assurance are Chief Information Security Officer for the University of North Alabama, Manager of the Information Systems Security (ISS) office for the Missile Defense Agency (MDS) South, and lead for the MDA Alternate Computer Emergency Response Team (ACERT). She served as Superintendent of the United States Air Forces in Europe (USAFE) Communications and Information Training Center, Superintendent of the 385 Communications Squadron on Ali Al Saleem AB, Kuwait, and Senior Information Security Analyst for Army Aviation Unmanned Aircraft Systems. Angie holds several industry certifications, including CISSP, Network+ and Security+, and a master's degree in Information Systems Management. She has developed and taught courseware worldwide for the U.S. Air Force, as well as several computer science courses for the University of Alabama in Huntsville and Kaplan University in Fort Lauderdale, Florida.

CONTENTS AT A GLANCE

CONTENTS

ACKNOWLEDGMENTS

First and foremost, I'd like to thank Timothy Green and McGraw-Hill Professional for making this all happen. Saying Tim is a busy man is somewhat akin to mentioning Mount Everest is kind of tall, and getting a hold of him sometimes means scheduling a midnight satellite link during the first quarter of the vernal equinox, so it was a true pleasure to hear his voice asking me to write another book. CEH, and the field it covers, is a passion of mine, and I can't thank Tim and company enough for giving me this opportunity. I've tried with all that's in me to provide something they can be proud of. I hope we've succeeded.

Speaking of the McGraw-Hill team, I can't begin to continue without mentioning my utmost appreciation for, and undying gratitude to, Stephanie Evans—my editing consultant, acquisition coordinator, feng shui guide, and taskmaster throughout the entire process. Writing a book is sometimes a manic-depressive, bipolar enterprise—one day you're excited and thrilled with the process (eager to see things through and happy with the prospect of nose to the grindstone, knowing you're putting out a good product that's going to help people) and the next you're sick of looking at computer screens and formatting text, praying for an end to the madness. To make it through something like that, you have to have someone to provide encouragement when you're down, instruction for questions along the way, and of course to beat you with a rubber hose to keep you on schedule.

Stephanie was a guiding light throughout the entire process, and one of the reasons I made it through. I could probably cobble together a pretty darned good book from our e-mail conversations along the path alone, but suffice it to say she did a great job. She's incredibly talented, intelligent, funny, and one heck of a writer. Just don't go sailing with her....

I also need to provide a special note of thanks to our technical editor, Brad Horton. I've known Brad since 2005, when we both served time in "the vault" at Marshall Space Flight Center, and I am truly blessed to call him friend. Brad is, without doubt, the singularly most talented technical mind I have ever met in my life. He is a loving husband to his beautiful wife, a great father to his son, one-of-a-kind pen tester, a fantastic team lead, and even plays the piano and other musical instruments like a pro. I hate him.

This book simply could not have been possible without Brad. His insights as a pen-test lead for the past few years were laser sharp, and provided great fodder for more discussion. Want proof he's one of the best? I'd be willing to bet none of you reading this book have ever actually relished a full critique of your work. *But I do.* Brad's edits are simultaneously witty, humorous, and cutting to the core. If someone had bet me four or five years ago that I'd not only enjoy reading critiques of my work, but would be looking forward to them, I would be paying off in spades today. You're one of the absolute bests, my friend... for a government worker, anyway.

Finally, there is no way this book could have been started, much less completed, without the support of my lovely and talented wife, Angie. In addition to the unending encouragement throughout the entire process, Angie was the greatest contributing editor I could have ever asked for. Having someone as talented and intelligent as her sitting close by to run things past, or ask for a review on, was priceless. Not to mention she's adorable. Her insights, help, encouragement, and work while this project was ongoing sealed the deal. I can't thank her enough.

INTRODUCTION

Welcome, dear reader! I sincerely hope you've found your way here to this introduction happy, healthy, and brimming with confidence—or, at the very least, curiosity. I can see you there, standing in your bookstore flipping through the book, or sitting in your living room, clicking through virtual pages at some online retailer. And you're wondering whether you'll buy it or not—whether *this* is the book you need for your study guide. You probably have perused the outline, checked the chapter titles—heck, you may have even read that great author bio they forced me to write. And now you've found your way to this—the introduction. Sure, this intro is supposed to be designed to explain the ins and outs of the book—to lay out its beauty and crafty witticism in such a way that you just can't resist buying it. But I'm also going to take a moment and explain the realities of the situation, and let you know what you're really getting yourself into.

This isn't a walk in the park. Certified Ethical Hacker (CEH) didn't gain the reputation and value it has by being easy to attain. It's a tough, challenging examination that tests more than just simple memorization. It's worth has elevated it as one of the top certifications a technician can attain, and is now a part of DoD 8570's call for certification on DoD networks. In short, this certification *actually means something* to employers, because they know the effort it takes to attain it. If you're not willing to put in the effort, maybe you should pick up another line of study. Like cake decorating. Or Sudoku.

All that said, I can think of a couple of groups who will be interested in this book. The first group is easy to spot. There you are, with your eyes bright and shining, the glow of innocent expectation on your faces. Either you're new to the career field or you're curious and want to expand your knowledge. In either case, step over here to the entrance sign with me. Come on, you've seen one before—it's just like the one out in front of the roller coaster reading, "You must be this tall to enter the ride." However, this one's just a little different. Instead of your height, I'm interested in your knowledge, and I have a question or two for you. Do you know the OSI Reference Model? What port does SMTP use? How about Telnet? What transport protocol (TCP or UDP) do they use and why?

Why am I asking these questions? Because, dear reader, I'm trying to save you some agony. Just as you wouldn't be allowed on a roller coaster that could potentially fling you off into certain agony and/or death, I'm not going to stand by and let you waltz into something you're not ready for. If any of these questions I asked seem otherworldly to you, you need to spend some time studying the mechanics and inner workings of networking before attempting this certification. As brilliantly written as this little tome is, it—nor any other book—is a magic bullet.

Don't get me wrong—*go ahead and buy it*—you'll want it later. All I'm saying is you need to learn the basics before stepping up to this plate. I didn't bother to drill down into the basics in this book because it would have been 20,000 pages long and scared you off right there at the rack without you even picking it up. Instead, I want you to go learn the "101" stuff first so you can be successful with this book. It won't take long, and it's not rocket science. (Heck, this yahoo from Alabama figured it out—how tough can it be for you?) However, it's gotta be done. There is plenty in here for the beginner, though, trust me. I wrote it in the same manner I learned it: simple, easy, and hopefully fun. This stuff isn't necessarily *hard*, you just need the basics out of the way first. I think you'll find, then, this book perfect for your goals.

As for the second group—those of you who have already put your time in and know the basics—I think you'll find this book pleasantly surprising. You're obviously aware by now that technology isn't magic, nor is it necessarily difficult or hard to comprehend—it's just learning how something works so you can use it to your advantage. I tried to attack ethical hacking in this manner, making things as light as possible and laughing a little along the way. Combine this book with some hands-on practice, and I don't think you'll have any trouble at all with the exam.

There is, of course, one primary goal and focus of this book—to help you achieve the title of Certified Ethical Hacker by passing the Version 7 exam. I believe this book provides you with everything you'll need to pass the test. However, I'd like to think this little book has more to it than that. Hopefully, I also succeeded in another goal that's just as important: helping you to actually become an *employed* ethical hacker. No, there is no way someone can simply pick up a book and magically become a seasoned IT Security professional just by reading it, but I sincerely hope I've provided enough real-world insight that you can safely rely on keeping this book around on your journey out there in the real world.

How to Use This Book

This book covers everything you'll need to know for EC-Council's Version 7 of the Certified Ethical Hacker examination. Each chapter covers specific objectives and details for the exam, as defined by EC-Council. I've done my best to arrange them in a manner that makes sense, and I hope you see it the same way.

Each chapter has several components designed to effectively communicate the information you'll need for the exam:

- The certification objectives covered in each chapter are listed first, right off the bat. These identify the major topics within the chapter, and help you to map out your study.

- Sidebars are included in each chapter and are designed to point out information, tips, and stories that will be helpful in your day-to-day responsibilities. Not to mention they're just downright fun sometimes. Please note, though, that although these entries provide real-world accounts of interesting pieces of information, they are sometimes used to reinforce testable material. Don't just discount them as simply "neat"—some of the circumstances and tools described in these sidebars may prove the difference in correctly answering a question or two on the exam.

- Exam Tips are exactly what they sound like. These are included to point out a focus area you need to concentrate on for the exam. No, they are not explicit test answers. Yes, they will help you focus your study.

- Specially called out Notes are part of each chapter, too. These are interesting tidbits of information that are relevant to the discussion and point out extra information. Just as with the sidebars, don't discount them.

- Some chapters have step-by-step exercises designed to provide a hands-on experience and to reinforce the chapter information. As your system and circumstances are no doubt different from mine, these may, from time to time, need a little adjustment on your end. For additional information on the exercises—and any of the tools listed in the book, for that matter—visit your favorite search engine. I guarantee you'll find more than enough videos and tutorials already created to whet your appetite.

The Examination

Before I get to anything else, let me be crystal clear: *This book will help you pass your test.* I've taken great pains to ensure everything EC-Council has asked you to know before taking the exam is covered in the book, and I think it's covered pretty darn well. The only cautionary note I'd place here is to not use this book as your sole source of study. This advice goes for any book for any certification: You simply cannot expect to pick up a single book and pass a certification exam. You need practice. You need hands-on experience. And you need to practice some more.

Yes, I'm fully confident this book is a great place to start, and a good way to guide your study. Just don't go into this exam without performing some (a lot of) hands-on practice with the tools. There is simply no substitute for experience, and I promise you, come test time, you'll be glad you put your time in.

Speaking of the test, these tidbits should help you:

- Be sure to pay close attention to the Exam Tips in the chapters. They are there for a reason. And retake the exams—both the end-of-chapter exams and the CD exams—until you're sick of them. They will help, trust me.

- The exam is 150 questions, all multiple choice, and you are allowed to mark, and skip, questions for later review. Go through the entire exam, answering the ones you know beyond a shadow of a doubt. On the ones you're not sure about, *choose an answer anyway* and mark the question for further review (you don't want to fail the exam because you ran out of time and had a bunch of questions that didn't even have an answer chosen). At the end, go back and look at the ones you've marked. Only change your answer if you are absolutely, 100-percent sure about it.

- You will, with absolute certainty, see a couple of types of questions that will blow your mind. One or two will come totally out of left field. I've taken the CEH exam three times—from version 5 to the current version 7 (which this book is written for)—and every single time I've seen questions that seemed so far out of the loop I wasn't sure I was taking the right exam. When you see them, don't panic. Use deductive reasoning and make your best guess. Almost every single question on this exam can be whittled down to at least 50/50 odds on a guess. The other type of question you'll see will use some very bad grammar in regard to the English language. Just remember this is an international organization and sometimes things don't translate so easily.

- On code questions on the exam (where code snippets are shown for you to answer questions on), pay attention to port numbers. Even if you're unsure about what generated the log or code, you can usually spot the port numbers pretty quickly. This will definitely help you on a question or two. Additionally, don't neglect the plaintext on the right side of the code snippet. It can very often show you what the answer is.

And finally, dear reader, thank you for picking this book up. I sincerely hope your exam goes well, and wish you the absolute best in your upcoming career. Here's hoping I see you out there, somewhere and sometime!

Ethical Hacking Basics

In this chapter you will learn about
- Identifying basic elements of information security
- Understanding security, functionality, and ease of use
- Defining and profiling an ethical hacker
- Defining classifications of hackers and terms associated with hacking
- The five stages of ethical hacking
- Defining the types of system attacks
- Understanding U.S. federal laws related to cyber crime
- Understanding various international laws related to cyber crime

In my youth I spent a lot of time working in a body shop owned by a neighbor just down the road. We fixed cars that had been involved in accidents, did plenty of custom work on vehicles at customer request, and painted one bodacious flame job on a 1974 Volkswagen Beetle. I remember how excited I was that first day of work, greatly looking forward to picking up a paint gun and blasting a beautiful scene on someone's car. I also remember how deflating it was seconds later when my boss held up a paint gun in one hand and some masking tape and a sander in the other. "See this?" he said, holding up the paint gun. "When you learn how to use these correctly," he said, shaking the tape and sander, "then I'll teach you how to use the paint gun."

Sorry to disappoint you, but this chapter is a lot like that tape and sander. I know you're excited. I know you can't wait. I can close my eyes and see you there, trembling with excitement and eager to get to the first few keystrokes that will turn you into a *hacker*—but you're going to have to learn some of the basics first. And most of it isn't any more exciting or sexy than masking tape.

This chapter is about all the bedrock and highly essential (but inanely boring and mundane) information you'll need to know—not only to become a successful ethical hacker, but also to pass the exam. Just as with any certification you attempt, there are any number of definitions and terms you'll need to know, including just what an *ethical hacker* is supposed to be. There are also numerous rules, regulations, and laws you'll need to know—both those applying within the United States and those relevant to international law. Granted, none of this is as exciting as cracking into some high-level network, but it is essential.

Introduction to Ethical Hacking

Ask most people to define the term "hacker," and they'll instantly picture a darkened room, several monitors ablaze with green text scrolling across the screen, and a shady character in the corner furiously typing away on a keyboard in an effort to break or steal something. Unfortunately, a lot of that *is* true, and a lot of people worldwide actively participate in these activities for that very purpose. However, it's important to realize there are differences between the good guys and the bad guys in this realm. It's the goal of this section to help define the two groups for you, as well as to help provide some background on the basics.

Whether for noble or bad purposes, the art of hacking remains the same. Using a specialized set of tools, techniques, knowledge, and skills to bypass computer security measures allows someone to "hack" into a computer or network. The *purpose* behind their use of these tools and techniques is really the only thing in question. Whereas some use these tools and techniques for personal gain or profit, the good guys practice them in order to better defend their systems and, in the process, provide insight on how to catch the bad guys.

Security Basics: CIA

Before we get into what a hacker is and how you become one, let's take a few moments and talk about some security basics you'll need to know. First and foremost, ask any true security professional what "CIA" stands for, and they won't respond with "Central Intelligence Agency," as you might expect. Instead, you'll get a knowing smile and a response including the holy trinity of IT security: Confidentiality, Integrity, and Availability. Whether you're an ethical hacker or not, these three items constitute the hallmarks of security we all strive for. You'll need to be very familiar with two aspects of each term in order to achieve success as an ethical hacker as well as on the exam: what the term itself means and which attacks are most commonly associated with it.

Confidentiality

Confidentiality, addressing the secrecy and privacy of information, refers to the measures taken to prevent disclosure of information or data to unauthorized individuals or systems. Confidentiality for the individual is a must, considering its loss could result in identity theft, fraud, and loss of money. For a business or government agency, it could be even worse. The use of passwords within some form of authentication is by far the most common logical measure taken to ensure confidentiality, and attacks against passwords are, amazingly enough, the most common confidentiality attacks.

For example, your logon to a network usually consists of a user ID and a password, which is designed to ensure only you have access to that particular device or set of network resources. If another person were to gain your user ID and password, they would have unauthorized access to resources, and could masquerade as you throughout their session. Although authentication (using passwords, for example) is by far the most common method used to enforce confidentiality, numerous other options are available to ensure confidentiality, including options such as encryption, biometrics, and smart cards.

EXAM TIP Be careful with the terms "confidentiality" and "authentication." Sometimes these two are used interchangeably, and if you're only looking for one, you may miss the question altogether. For example, a MAC address spoof (using the MAC address of another machine) is called an *authentication* attack. Authentication is definitely a major portion of the confidentiality segment of IT security.

Integrity

Integrity refers to the methods and actions taken to protect the information from unauthorized alteration or revision—whether the data is at rest or in transit. In other words, integrity measures ensure the data sent from the sender arrives at the recipient with no alteration. For example, imagine a buying agent sending an e-mail to a customer offering the price of $300. If an attacker somehow altered the e-mail and changed the offering price to $3,000, the integrity measures have failed and the transaction will not occur as intended—if at all. Oftentimes, attacks on the integrity of information are designed to cause embarrassment or legitimate damage to the target.

Integrity in information systems is often ensured through the use of a hash. A *hash* function is a one-way mathematical algorithm (such as MD5 and SHA-1) that generates a specific, fixed-length number (known as a hash value). When a user or system sends a message, it generates a hash value to also send to the recipient. If even a single bit is changed during the transmission of the message, instead of showing the same output, the hash function will calculate and display a greatly different hash value on the recipient system. Depending on the way the controls within the system are designed, this would result in either a retransmission of the message or a complete shutdown of the session.

 EXAM TIP "Bit flipping" is one form of an integrity attack. In bit flipping, the attacker isn't interested in learning the entirety of the plaintext message. Instead, bits are manipulated in the ciphertext itself to generate a predictable outcome in the plaintext once it is decrypted.

Availability

Availability is probably the simplest, easiest to understand segment of the security triad, yet it should not be overlooked. It refers to the communications systems and data being ready for use when legitimate users need them. Many methods are used for availability, depending on whether the discussion is about a system, network resource, or the data itself, but they all attempt to ensure one thing—when the system or data is needed, it can be accessed by appropriate personnel.

Attacks against availability all fall into the "denial of service" realm. *Denial of service (DoS)* attacks are designed to prevent legitimate users from having access to a computer resource or service, and can take many forms. For example, attackers could attempt to use all available bandwidth to the network resource, or they may actively attempt to destroy a user's authentication method. DoS attacks can also be much simpler than that—unplugging the power cord is the easiest DoS in history!

NOTE Many in the security field add other terms to the security triad. I've seen several CEH study guides refer to the term "authenticity" as one of the "four elements of security." However, it's not used much outside the certification realm. This is useful to keep in mind, though, come test time.

The Security, Functionality, and Ease of Use Triangle

Another important triad to remember in security is the Security, Functionality, and Ease of Use triangle. To effectively understand this topic, consider a common example used in almost every class and book I've ever seen on the subject. Suppose a security professional named Joe was charged with securing access to a building. Joe looks at it from a pure security perspective, and wants to do everything he can to restrict access. So, he puts in guard posts. And eyeball scanners. And passcodes with a lockdown feature only the guards can unlock. Voice recognition, smart cards, and a key, cut only from on-site security, round out his plan.

After the first day, Joe would most likely be fired. Why? Imagine working in the building Joe "secured." You left your key at home? You're done—you can't come to work, and will have to wait several days for a new key to be cut. Got an important meeting with customers (assuming they can even get in the building) and you forgot your passcode? You're done—your delay in the lockdown center waiting on the guards to release you prevented you from making the meeting. Didn't pass the eyeball scanner? Goodness knows what Joe has in store for you.

The Security, Functionality, and Ease of Use triangle is simply a graphic representation of a problem that has faced security professionals for an eternity—the more secure something is, the less usable and functional it becomes. Want to completely secure a computer? Leave it in the box and never turn it on. Want to make the system easy for Mom to use? Better be prepared for the inevitable security breach when she clicks on the link promising <fill in the blank>.

Why is it represented as a triangle? The objective is simple, as you can see in Figure 1-1. If you start in the middle and move the point toward Security, you're moving further and further away from Functionality and Ease of Use. Move the point toward Ease of Use, and you're moving away from Security and Functionality. Simply put, as security increases, the system's functionality and ease of use decrease. As a security professional, and a student preparing for the CEH exam, you'll need to remember this axiom and apply as much common sense as possible in your designs.

Figure 1-1
The Security,
Functionality, and
Ease of Use Triangle

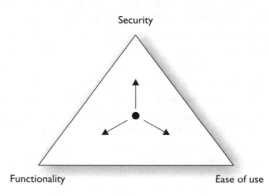

Defining the Ethical Hacker

So what makes someone an "ethical" hacker? Can such a thing even exist? Considering the art of hacking computers and systems is, in and of itself, a covert action, most people might believe the thought of engaging in a near-illegal activity to be significantly *un*ethical. However, the purpose and intention of the act itself has to be taken into account.

For comparison's sake, law enforcement professionals routinely take part in unethical behaviors and situations in order to better understand, and to catch, their criminal counterparts. Police and FBI agents must learn the lingo, actions, and behaviors of drug cartels and organized crime in order to infiltrate and bust the criminals, and to do so sometimes forces them to engage in criminal acts themselves. Ethical hacking can be thought of in much the same way. In order to find and fix the vulnerabilities and security holes in a computer system or network, you sometimes have to think like a criminal and use the same tactics, tools, and processes they might employ.

In CEH parlance, and as defined by several other entities, there is a distinct difference between a hacker and a cracker. An *ethical hacker* is someone who employs the same tools and techniques a criminal might use, with the customer's full support and approval, in order to help secure a network or system. A *cracker*, also known as a *malicious hacker*, uses those skills, tools, and techniques for either personal gain or destructive purposes or, in purely technical terms, to achieve a goal outside the interest of the system owner. Ethical hackers are employed by customers to improve security. Crackers either act on their own or, in some cases, act as hired agents to destroy or damage government or corporate reputation.

Espionage Hacking

We would be remiss if we simply counted individuals in the realm of the dark side of hacking. In truth, many state-sponsored groups are actively targeting government and commercial networks and systems in an effort to promote their own nation's interests and to control political advantage. Although governments around the world still play the spy game the way they always have, there's no escaping the reality of the modern world. The James Bond–like super-agent has given way to a different kind of spy—one who maneuvers a digital landscape instead of the cloak-and-dagger physical realm, although with the same smoothness, tact, and sleek moves as Mr. Bond.

Examples of attacks against United States government systems are, unfortunately, widespread and easy to discover. Over the past couple of years, attacks on Department of Homeland Security (DHS) systems, Department of Defense (DoD) networks, and several Silicon Valley technology firms have been well documented. The results of a recent congressional investigation showed that the U.S. Department of Homeland Security networks were the victim of cyber attacks initiated by foreign entities, with terabytes of information being ferreted away to "Web hosting services that connect to Chinese Web sites." Here's just one article on the subject: http://articles.cnn.com/2007-09-24/us/homelandsecurity .computers_1_dhs-unisys-homeland-security?_s=PM:US.

> The truly scary news, though, isn't the number of attacks every year—easily in the millions—it's that these millions of attacks are only the ones we know about. In the DHS attacks just referenced, the congressional staff noted incidents were not noticed until months after the initial attacks, and even then it's only "when hackers are sloppy that you find out." This one episode alone, among the hundreds reported in the press every year, serves notice that the ethical hacking field is here to stay.

While we're on the subject, another subset of this community uses its skills and talents to put forward a cause or a political agenda. These people hack servers, deface websites, create viruses, and generally wreak all sorts of havoc in cyberspace under the assumption that their actions will force some societal change or shed light on something they feel to be political injustice. It's not some new anomaly in human nature—people have been protesting things since the dawn of time—it has just moved from picket signs and marches to bits and bytes. In general, regardless of the intentions, acts of "hactivism" are usually illegal in nature.

Hacker Classification: The Hats

In addition to the definitions already given, the hacking community in general can be categorized into three separate classifications: the good, the bad, and the undecided. In the world of IT security, this designation is given as a hat color, and if you've ever watched an old Western movie, you can probably guess where this is going:

- **White hats**   Considered the good guys, these are the ethical hackers, hired by a customer for the specific goal of testing and improving security, or for other defensive purposes. White hats are well respected and don't use their knowledge and skills without prior consent.

- **Black hats**   Considered the bad guys, these are the crackers, illegally using their skills for either personal gain or malicious intent. They seek to steal or destroy data, and to deny access to resources and systems. Black hats do *not* ask for permission or consent.

- **Gray hats**   The hardest group to categorize, these hackers are neither good nor bad. Generally speaking, there are two subsets of gray hats—those that are simply curious about hacking tools and techniques, and those that feel like it's their duty, with or without customer permission, to demonstrate security flaws in systems. In either case, hacking without a customer's explicit permission and direction is a crime.

 NOTE   Lots of well-meaning hacker types have found employment in the security field by hacking into a system and then informing the victim of the security flaw(s) so that they may be fixed. However, many more have found their way to prison attempting the same thing. Regardless of your intentions, do not practice hacking techniques without approval. You may think your hat is gray, but I guarantee the victim sees only black.

One final class of hacker borders on the insane. Some hackers are so driven, so intent on completing their task, they are willing to risk everything to pull it off. Whereas we, as ethical hackers, won't touch anything until we're given express consent to do so, these hackers are much like hactivists and feel that their reason for hacking outweighs any potential punishment. Even willing to risk jail time for their activities, so-called *suicide hackers* are the truly scary monsters in the closet.

Ethical Hacking Steps and Stages

You've probably noted by now an over-arching thought stated repeatedly throughout this first chapter. And yes, it *is* that important, so we'll state it again here: To be an ethical hacker you must work within the confines of an agreement made between you and a customer. This agreement isn't simply a smile, a conversation, and a handshake just before you flip open a laptop and start hacking away. No, instead it is a carefully laid-out plan, meticulously arranged and documented to protect both the ethical hacker and the client.

In general, an ethical hacker will first meet with the client and sign a contract. The contract defines not only the permission and authorization given to the security professional (sometimes called the "get out of jail free card"), but also confidentiality and scope. No client would ever agree to having an ethical hacker attempt to breach security without first ensuring the hacker will not disclose any information found during the test. Usually, this concern results in the creation of a Non-Disclosure Agreement (NDA).

Additionally, clients almost always want the test to proceed to a certain point in the network structure, and no further—"you can try to get through the firewall, but do not touch the file servers on the other side…because you may disturb my MP3 collection." They may also want to restrict what types of attacks you run. For example, the client may be perfectly okay with you attempting a password hack against their systems, but may not want you to test every DoS attack you know. Oftentimes, however, even though you're hired to test their security and you know what's really important in security and hacking circles, the most serious risks to a target are not allowed to be tested due to the "criticality of the resource." If the test designed to improve security actually blows up a server, it may not be a winning scenario; however, sometimes the data that is actually at risk makes it important enough to proceed. This really boils down to cool and focused minds during the security testing negotiation.

 NOTE   A common term you'll see referenced in your CEH study is *tiger team*, which is nothing more than a group of people, gathered together by a business entity, working to address a specific problem or goal. Ethical hackers are sometimes part of a tiger team, set up to thoroughly test all facets of a security system. Whether you're hired as a part of the team or as an individual, pay attention to the rules of engagement.

Companies and government agencies ask for penetration tests for a variety of reasons. Sometimes rules and regulations force the issue. For example, many medical facilities need to maintain compliance with the Health Insurance Portability and

Accountability Act, and will hire ethical hackers to complete their accreditation. Sometimes the organization's leadership is simply security conscious and wants to know just how well existing security controls are functioning. And sometimes it's simply an effort to rebuild trust and reputation after a security breach has already occurred. It's one thing to tell customers you've fixed the security flaw that allowed the theft of all those credit cards in the first place. It's another thing altogether to show the results of a penetration test against the new controls.

With regard to your exam, and to your future as an ethical hacker, there are two processes you'll need to know: how to set up and perform a legal penetration test, and how to proceed through the actual hack. A *penetration test*, also known as a *pen test*, is a clearly defined, full-scale test of the security controls of a system or network in order to identify security risks and vulnerabilities, and has three major phases. Once the pen test is agreed upon, the ethical hacker begins the "assault" using a variety of tools, methods, and techniques, but generally follows the same five stages to conduct the test. For the CEH exam, you'll need to be very familiar with the pen test stages and the five stages of a typical hack.

There are three main phases to a pen test—*preparation, assessment,* and *conclusion*—and they are fairly easy to define and understand. The preparation phase defines the time period during which the actual contract is hammered out. The scope of the test, the types of attacks allowed, and the individuals assigned to perform the activity are all agreed upon in this phase. The assessment phase (sometimes also known as the security evaluation phase) is exactly what it sounds like—the actual assaults on the security controls are conducted during this time. Lastly, the conclusion (or post-assessment) phase defines the time when final reports are prepared for the customer, detailing the findings of the tests (including the types of tests performed) and many times even providing recommendations to improve security.

Once an ethical hacker is within the assessment phase of the pen test, it's time to begin the attack. Although there are many different terms for these phases, and some of them run concurrently and continuously throughout a test, EC Council has defined the standard hack as having five separate phases, shown in Figure 1-2. Whether the attacker is ethical or malicious, these five phases capture the full breadth of the attack.

Figure 1-2
Phases of ethical
hacking

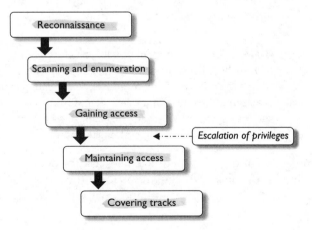

EXAM TIP   Keep the phases of hacking in mind throughout your study. You'll most likely see several questions asking you to identify not only what occurs in each step, but which tools are used in each one.

Reconnaissance is probably going to be the most difficult phase to understand for the exam—mainly because many people confuse some of its steps as being part of the next phase (scanning and enumeration). *Reconnaissance* is nothing more than the steps taken to gather evidence and information on the targets you wish to attack. It can be passive in nature or active. *Passive reconnaissance* involves gathering information about your target without their knowledge, whereas *active reconnaissance* uses tools and techniques that may or may not be discovered, but put your activities as a hacker at more risk of discovery.

For example, imagine your pen test has just started and you know nothing about the company you are targeting. Passively, you may simply watch the outside of the building for a couple of days to learn employee habits and see what physical security measures are in place. Actively, you may simply walk up to the entrance or guard shack and try to open the door (or gate). In either case, you're learning valuable information, but with passive reconnaissance you aren't taking any action to signify to others that you're watching. Examples of actions that might be taken during this phase are social engineering, dumpster diving, and network sniffing—all of which are addressed throughout the remainder of this study guide.

In phase 2, *scanning and enumeration,* security professionals take the information they gathered in recon and actively apply tools and techniques to gather more in-depth information on the targets. This can be something as simple as running a ping sweep or a network mapper to see what systems are on the network, or as complex as running a vulnerability scanner to determine which ports may be open on a particular system. For example, whereas recon may have shown the network to have 500 or so machines connected to a single subnet inside a building, scanning and enumeration would tell me which ones are Windows machines and which ones are running FTP.

Not Just by the Book

Sometimes the phases of a test blend into one another. Instead of being held to a book definition, a good pen tester knows when to strike while the iron is hot and opportunity presents itself.

On one test I was a part of long ago, I stationed myself in front of the building, merely to take notes on the physical security measures in place. I noticed, after a few moments, that the great majority of people at the entrance gate would hold the door for others coming through—it was raining, after all, and they wanted to be polite. On a whim, I jumped out of my car and walked across the street, just as an employee was swiping his card at the gate. He not only held the gate open for me, but directed me to the executive's personal conference room and unlocked the door for me.

Phase 1? I was already well on my way to completion of phase 4 (at least for physical security anyway) and hadn't even spent 30 minutes on the job.

Phase 3, as they say, is where the magic happens. This is the phase most people delightedly rub their hands together over, reveling in the glee they know they will receive from bypassing a security control. In the *gaining access* phase, true attacks are leveled against the targets enumerated in phase 2. These attacks can be as simple as accessing an open and nonsecured wireless access point and then manipulating it for whatever purpose, or as complex as writing and delivering a buffer overflow or SQL injection against a web application. The attacks and techniques used in the phase will be discussed throughout the remainder of this study guide.

In phase 4, *maintaining access*, hackers attempt to ensure they have a way back into the machine or system they've already compromised. Back doors are left open by the attacker for future use—especially if the system in question has been turned into a *zombie* (a machine used to launch further attacks from) or if the system is used for further information gathering—for example, a sniffer can be placed on a compromised machine to watch traffic on a specific subnet. Access can be maintained through the use of Trojans, rootkits, or any number of other methods.

 EXAM TIP Some study guides will also sneak in another phase of hacking called "escalation of privileges" between phases 3 and 4. This defines the actions taken by a hacker to promote his access to root or administrative levels. If you see this on the exam, be prepared—actions taken here span the gap between the gathering access and maintaining access phases. You'll have to use your best judgment in answering the question.

In the final phase, *covering tracks*, attackers attempt to conceal their success and avoid detection by security professionals. Steps taken here consist of removing or altering log files, hiding files with hidden attributes or directories, and even using tunneling protocols to communicate with the system. If auditing is even turned on and monitored, and often it is not, log files are an indicator of attacks on a machine. Clearing the log file completely is just as big an indicator to the security administrator watching the machine, so sometimes selective editing is your best bet. Another great method to use here is simply corrupting the log file itself—whereas a completely empty log file screams an attack is in progress, files get corrupted all the time and, chances are, the administrator won't bother to try to rebuild it. In any case, good pen testers are truly defined in this phase.

A couple of insights can, and should, be gained here. First, contrary to popular belief, hackers do not just randomly assault things hoping to find some overlooked vulnerability to exploit. Instead, they normally follow a specific, organized method to thoroughly discover every aspect of the system they're targeting. Good ethical hackers performing a pen test ensure these steps are very well documented, taking exceptional and detailed notes and keeping items such as screenshots and log files for inclusion in the final report. Second, keep in mind that security professionals performing a pen test do not normally repair or patch any security vulnerabilities they find—it's simply not their job to do so. The ethical hacker's job is to discover security flaws for the customer, not to fix them.

NOTE Sometimes what CEH covers and what happens in the "real world" are at odds. In this case, you should probably know that a hacker who is after someone in particular may not bother sticking to a set method in getting to what they want. Hackers in the real world will take advantage of the easiest, quickest, simplest path to the end goal, and if that means attacking before enumerating, then so be it.

Hacking Terminology and Attacks

In this section, we'll cover some of the more mundane stuff—the definitions, terms, and other notes you'll need to know to be successful on the exam. Of course, it's a necessity to know the lingo on the actual job as well, but when you're itching to put fingers on keyboard to begin hacking, it's sometimes maddening to read through. Trust me, though, this stuff is essential.

Ethical Hacking Testing Types

In performing a pen test, an ethical hacker must attempt to reflect the criminal world as much as possible. In other words, if the steps taken by the ethical hacker during the pen test don't adequately mirror what a "real" hacker would do, then the test is doomed to failure. For that reason, most pen tests have individuals acting in various stages of knowledge about the *target of evaluation (TOE)*. These different types of tests are known by three names—black box, white box, and gray box.

In *black box* testing, the ethical hacker has absolutely no knowledge of the TOE. It's designed to simulate an outside, unknown attacker, takes the most amount of time to complete and, usually, is by far the most expensive option. For the ethical hacker, black box testing means a thorough romp through the five stages of an attack, and removes any preconceived notions of what to look for. The only true drawback to this type of test is it focuses solely on the threat outside the organization, and does not take into account any trusted users on the inside.

White box testing is, amazingly enough, the exact opposite of black box testing. In this type, pen testers have full knowledge of the network, system, and infrastructure they're targeting. This, quite obviously, makes the test much quicker, easier, and less expensive, and is designed to simulate a knowledgeable internal threat, such as a disgruntled network admin or other trusted user.

The last type, *gray box* testing, is also known as *partial knowledge* testing. What makes this different from black box testing is the assumed level of elevated privileges the tester has. Whereas black box testing is generally done from the network administration level, gray box testing assumes only that the attacker is an insider. Because most attacks do originate from inside a network, this type of testing is very valuable and can demonstrate privilege escalation from a trusted employee.

Attack Types

Once the ethical hacker is engaged, several different categories or labels are placed on the actual type of attack being used. EC Council broadly defines all these in four categories:

- **Operating system attacks**   Generally speaking, these attacks target the common mistake many people make when installing operating systems—accepting and leaving all the defaults. Things like administrator accounts with no passwords, all ports left open, and guest accounts (the list could go on forever) are examples of settings the installer may forget about. Additionally, operating systems are never released fully secure—they can't be, if you ever plan on releasing them within a timeframe of actual use—so the potential for an old vulnerability in newly installed operating systems is always a plus for the ethical hacker.

- **Application-level attacks**   These are attacks on the actual programming codes of an application. Although most people are very cognizant of securing their OS and network, it's amazing how often they discount the applications running on their OS and network. Many applications on a network aren't tested for vulnerabilities as part of their creation and, as such, have many vulnerabilities built into them. Applications on a network are a goldmine for most hackers.

- **Shrink-wrap code attacks**   These attacks take advantage of the built-in code and scripts most off-the-shelf applications come with. The old refrain "Why reinvent the wheel?" is very often used to describe this attack type. Why spend time writing code to attack something when you can buy it already "shrink wrapped"? These scripts and code pieces are designed to make installation and administration easier, but can lead to vulnerabilities if not managed appropriately.

- **Misconfiguration attacks**   These attacks take advantage of systems that are, on purpose or by accident, not configured appropriately for security. Remember the triangle earlier, and the maxim "As security increases, ease of use and functionality decrease"? This type of attack takes advantage of the administrator who simply wants to make things as easy as possible for the users. Perhaps to do so, the admin will leave security settings at the lowest possible level, enable every service, and open all firewall ports. It's easier for the users, but creates another goldmine for the hacker.

Elements of Risk and More Hacking Terminology

Risk analysis and management are major parts of the IT security career field. Basically the goal is to identify what risks are present, quantify them on a measurement scale (see Figure 1-3 for a sample risk analysis matrix), and then come up with solutions to miti-

Figure 1-3
Risk analysis matrix
example

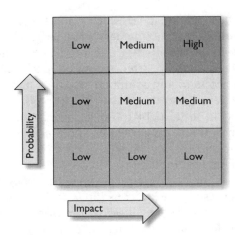

gate, eliminate, or accept the risks. To fully accomplish this task, you'll need to be aware of the three basic elements of risk—asset, threat, and vulnerability. Combine them with the probability of an attack and what the impact of a successful attack would be, and you've got an easy way to identify high, medium, and low risks.

An *asset* is an item of economic value owned by an organization or an individual. Identification of assets within the risk analysis world is the first and most important step. After all, if you don't know what you have, how can you possibly secure it? Assets can be anything from physical devices (such as desktops, servers, printers, switches, and routers) to databases and file shares.

NOTE When it comes to assets, don't neglect the "intangibles." Public image and reputation are just as important as trade secrets and proprietary information.

A *threat* is any agent, circumstance, or situation that could cause harm or loss to an IT asset. Threats can take on many forms, and may not always be readily identifiable. For example, you probably already think of malicious hackers and viruses as threats, but what about bad weather? A hurricane, tornado, flood, or earthquake could cause just as much damage to your assets as a hacker could ever dream of doing. Ethical hackers are, obviously, much more concerned with the virtual threat agent techniques, but security professionals designing an entire program need to be cognizant of as many threats as possible.

A *vulnerability* is any weakness, such as a software flaw or logic design, that could be exploited by a threat to cause damage to an asset. The goal of pen testers is to discover these vulnerabilities and attempt to exploit them. The key thing to remember about vulnerabilities is that their existence does not necessarily equate to a risk. For example, given physical access to any computer system, a hacker could easily (usually) successfully hack the device—so the vulnerability (physical access) exists. However, if your server is locked in an airtight room, buried in an underground silo, with multiple guards and physical security measures in place, the probability of it being exploited is reduced to near zero.

Other hacking terminology you may run into or read includes the different types and designations of various hackers (including phreakers, script kiddies, and whackers), the differences in attack vectors (an *inside attack* generates from inside the network boundary, whereas an *outside attack* comes from outside the border), and things like daisy chaining. To avoid a 100-page chapter of endless definitions, and to attempt to assist you in maintaining your sanity in studying for this exam, I'm going to recommend you peruse the glossary at the end of this book for more information. You'll see these terms used throughout the book anyway, and most of them are fairly easy to figure out on your own, but don't discount the definitions you'll find at the end. Besides, we worked *really hard* on the glossary—it would be a shame if it went unnoticed.

 EXAM TIP Definition questions should be no-brainers on the exam. Learn the hacker types, the stages of a hack, and other definitions in the chapter—don't miss the easy ones.

Legal Hacking: Laws and Guidelines You Need to Know

So we've spent some time defining what an ethical hacker is, how to become one (for one thing, pass the CEH exam!), and learning some of the lingo of the trade. This next section deals with the laws and legality every ethical hacker needs to know and work under. Yes, I know, you didn't pick this book up as part of your bar examination study to become a lawyer. However, you do need to be very cognizant of the laws regarding cyber crime, both inside the United States and around the world—not only because it will help the subset of our chosen profession that uses statutes against criminals, but also to ensure you stay out of jail yourself.

The good news here is you don't need to commit this entire section to memory. Laws and legality may not appear on the exam any more—the CEH objectives no longer call for them—but they're included in this chapter as a reference for you. I know you're probably wondering, then, why you should bother with reading it—after all, you picked this book up in order to study for an exam. The answer, my friend, is that being an ethical hacker is about a lot more than just passing an exam. Some laws can be confusing in their real-world implementation, and if you don't pay attention you can wind up in jail. For example, a computer attack could originate in China, be launched from Singapore through a computer in Alabama (yes, there are some there), and exploit a system in England. Whose laws take precedence? Who is liable for the attack? How much culpability do the carriers hold? Who will prosecute? We'll examine a couple of relevant laws and acts, and do our best to list and describe those others you'll need to know.

U.S. Cyber Crime Laws

On October 29, 1969, a U.S. Defense Department team successfully established a link between three separate nodes—and the ARPANET was born. From this humble beginning, packet switching technology, a new protocol stack called TCP/IP, and the Internet were born. Early on in computing, most crimes were nothing more than any other—physical theft or destruction of the devices. However, as time moved on and more and more data became available and accessible on networks, it wasn't long before criminals discovered an entirely new realm in which to play.

For example, in 1978 a group of players at the Flagler Dog Track in Florida found a way to fake winning dog race tickets using a computer system. After more than a few fraudulent tickets made their way past the booth, the owners became suspicious and, finally, caught the cheaters. However, the technology was so new, no one knew what statute to charge them under. As a result, the first law regarding computer use and abuse in the United States was created: the Florida Computer Crimes Act.

 NOTE All computer crimes fall into one of two major categories: crimes where a computer or network was used in the commission of a crime, and those where the computer or network itself was the target of the crime. In either case, the penalties for computer crimes are getting more and more severe as time, and our understanding, moves on.

Since that time, computer law has grown and become more specific, just as the use of computers and networking in crimes has become more sophisticated. Although a large number of U.S. statutes and laws need to be learned, we will simply concentrate on the most relevant to your professional future. Hacking specifically is addressed under law in United States Code Title 18: Crimes and Criminal Procedure, Part I: Crimes, Chapter 47: Fraud and False Statements, Sections 1029 and 1030. Other regulations and laws are also described in this section.

18 U.S.C § 1029 and 1030

Section 1029, "Fraud and related activity in connection with access devices," has several subsections and statutes defined. Basically, the law gives the U.S. government the authority to prosecute criminals who traffic in, or use, counterfeit access devices. In short, the section criminalizes the misuse of any number of credentials, including passwords, PIN numbers, token cards, credit card numbers, and the like. If a person creates or sells devices that fake credentials, or if they traffic the credentials created by the fake machines, Section 1029 provides punishment under the law.

Section 1030, "Fraud and related activity in connection with computers," is a little different. This statute actually targets hackers themselves, and criminalizes unauthorized access to computer systems or data. Section 1030 also addresses and criminalizes the spread of viruses and malware. Full texts of both sections of the U.S. Code referenced here can be found at the U.S. Department of Justice website at www.justice.gov/criminal/cybercrime/1029NEW.htm and www.justice.gov/criminal/cybercrime/1030NEW.htm.

The SPY Act

In 2007, the Securely Protect Yourself Against Cyber Trespass Act passed the U.S. Congress and became law. Dealing mainly with spyware, the act makes it unlawful for any person who is not the owner, or authorized user, of a computer used for a financial institution, the U.S. government, or in any interstate or foreign commerce or communication to engage in "unfair or deceptive acts," including the following:

- Taking unsolicited control of the system
- Modifying computer settings
- Collecting personally identifiable information
- Inducing the owner or authorized user to disclose personally identifiable information
- Inducing the unsolicited installation of computer software
- Removing or disabling a security, antispyware, or antivirus technology

In short, the act criminalizes the collection of personal information (through the use of a keystroke logger, or any other means) without the user's consent. It also prevents an outsider from redirecting a web browser to another site, taking control of a system without authorization, and using a system to send unsolicited information to others (spam). The full text of the SPY Act, in both its original House and Senate versions, can be found at the U.S. Library of Congress site at http://thomas.loc.gov/cgi-bin/query/z?c109:H.R.29.

Freedom of Information Act (5 U.S.C. § 552) and the Privacy Act of 1974

I once took a U.S. history class in college while I was serving in the military. The instructor was a naturalized citizen who grew up, if memory serves me here, in either Oman or Yemen, and he brought a unique perspective to the history of my nation. I remember one class in particular, he was railing on about how many nations' citizens have no idea what their governments are up to and how the lack of basic information on government activities could be very dangerous. This served as his lead-in to a discussion of just how open the U.S. government is with its citizens. One instance of that is the Freedom of Information Act (FoIA).

NOTE FoIA doesn't necessarily help you in hacking, but it does provide a cover for a lot of information. Anything you uncover that could have been gathered through FoIA is considered legal. The Privacy Act, though, defines the information that is not available to you. Dissemination and storage of privacy information needs to be *very* closely controlled to keep you out of hot water.

FoIA was originally signed in 1966 and serves the people's right to know certain pieces of information not deemed to be classified. For the most part, FoIA can be used by any U.S. citizen to get any and every piece of information they want from the government. As a matter of fact, the act doesn't state what information one is allowed to get—it rather states the nine instances in which one can't ask for it. These instances are generally things such as military and law enforcement information, classified secrets, and information pertaining to trade secrets or inter-agency litigation.

With all the uproar, protest, and eventually celebration over freedom of information, many also began looking at the downside of too much information being made available. What about items of personal information regarding individuals? If government agencies, or other entities, collected this information and made it available to anyone, the individual's safety—financially or otherwise—may be put at risk. Additionally, citizens of the United States have an expectation of privacy, which has been thoroughly debated and argued in more court cases than we have time to review here. This thought process brought about the Privacy Act of 1974.

The Privacy Act basically states government agencies cannot disclose personal information about an individual without that person's consent. It also defines what personal information is and lists 12 exemptions for the release of this information (generally with regard to law enforcement issues). Loads of information on FoIA, including its full text, can be found on the U.S. Department of Justice site at www.justice.gov/oip/.

Federal Information Security Management Act (FISMA)

Mention FISMA to a group of security professionals, and you're liable to get groans of disgust and anguish (from the groups charged with writing the security plan), followed by grumbling of reserved admiration (or at least acceptance). FISMA basically is an effort to ensure the security of government systems by promoting a standardized approach to security controls, implementation, and testing. The act requires government agencies to create security plans for their systems, and to have them "accredited" at least once every three years. It also requires periodic assessments of the security controls in place, which is where the ethical hacker comes into play—*somebody* has to make sure the controls for authentication on the network actually work the way the security plan *says* they do.

FISMA is a giant program with far too many facets and details to cover in this book. The key thing to remember is that it creates a framework for government security program creation, maintenance, and testing. In your real-world work as a security testing professional, you'll need to become *very* familiar with everything FISMA-related. More information on FISMA can be found on the National Institute of Standards and Technology (NIST) site at http://csrc.nist.gov/groups/SMA/fisma/index.html.

USA PATRIOT Act of 2001

Still one of the more controversial laws in our current system, the USA PATRIOT Act, signed into law in October of 2001, dramatically increased the government's ability to monitor, intercept, and maintain records on almost every imaginable form of communication (telephone, networking, e-mail, and medical and financial records are all addressed). The original goal of the act, in response to the September 11th terrorist attacks on the United States, was to better equip the government to prevent future terrorist activity. As a side effect, it has also served to increase observation and prevention of hacking attempts on many systems. The things hackers used to be able to do without fear of discovery, hiding behind privacy laws, are now part of history, and it has forced hackers to be much more thorough in hiding their attempts.

More information on the USA PATRIOT Act can be found on the U.S. Department of Justice website at www.justice.gov/archive/ll/highlights.htm.

 NOTE   I'd be willing to bet, if you were aware of this law already, you probably referred to it as the "Patriot Act," believing, like most of us, that the term "patriot" in the title was, indeed, a word. You might be interested to know it's not actually a word, but an acronym. USA PATRIOT stands for *Uniting and Strengthening America by Providing Appropriate Tools Required to Intercept and Obstruct Terrorism*. I was unaware any government had that kind of creative prowess.

Other U.S. Laws of Relevance

We could continue romping through the U.S. Code, ferreting out every individual law that might remotely touch on hacking, data, communication, computers, or networks, but you'd lose interest and I would blow my chapter page count before we ever even got to the good stuff. Suffice it to say there are a lot of laws, and although they're all relevant to your job as an ethical hacker, it's impossible for you to know them all—unless, of course, you want to be an ethical hacking *lawyer*. For the rest of us, Table 1-1 lists a few other laws of relevance, with some quick details you need to know about each.

International Cyber Crime Laws

Ethical hackers need to be cognizant that U.S. law isn't the only legal guideline in our chosen profession. Many times data and systems regarding a crime either can reside physically in foreign countries or may traverse them somehow. Although the prospect of learning *all* foreign law regarding the subject is daunting, rest assured you won't need to be an international law expert to fulfill your duties on a pen test

Law Title	Details
Federal Managers Financial Integrity Act (1982)	Requires financial institutions to ensure the protection of records and data by mandating ongoing evaluations of their security measures.
Computer Fraud and Abuse Act (1984)	Protects systems and data owned by the federal government, defining classified systems and providing punishment for theft and/or malicious code regarding these systems.
Electronic Communications Privacy Act 18 U.S.C. § 2510 (1986)	Protects wire, oral, and electronic information while in transit. Later, a second title protected data in storage as well.
Cyber Security Enhancement Act (2002)	In addition to various funding and requirements levied by NIST, this act also strengthens sentencing guidelines for hackers whose activities cause death or bodily harm to others.
Government Paperwork Elimination Act (GPEA, 2003)	Requires the government to use electronic forms, filing, and signatures as much as possible and practical.

Table 1-1   Relevant U.S. Laws Regarding Cyber Crime

team. Some of the more pertinent international laws you may want to at least read are listed here:

- **Cyber Crime Law in Mexico**   Section 30-45-5: Unauthorized computer use
- **Cyber Crime Law in Brazil**   Art. 313-A: Entry of false data into the information system. Art. 313-B: Unauthorized modification or alteration of the information system
- **Cyber Crime Law in Canada**   Canadian Criminal Code Section 342.1
- **Cyber Crime Law in the United Kingdom**   Computer Misuse Act 1990 and Police and Justice Act 2006
- **Cyber Crime Law in Europe**   Section 1: Substantive Criminal Law
- **Cyber Crime Law in Belgium**   Computer Hacking Article 550(b)
- **Cyber Crime Law in Denmark**   Penal Code Section 263
- **Cyber Crime Law in France**   Chapter III: Attacks on Systems for Automated Data Processing, Article 323-1 and Article 323-2
- **Cyber Crime Laws in Germany**   Penal Code Section 202a: Data Espionage and Penal Code. Section 303a: Alteration of Data

- **Cyber Crime Law in Greece**   Criminal Code Article 370C § 2
- **Cyber Crime Law in Italy**   Penal Code Article 615: Unauthorized access into computer or telecommunication systems. Criminal Code Article 138a
- **Cyber Crime Law in Norway**   Penal Code § 145, § 145b, and § 151b
- **Cyber Crime Laws in Switzerland**   Article 143b and Article 144b
- **Cyber Crime Law in Australia**   The Cybercrime Act 2001
- **Cyber Crime Law in India**   The Information Technology Act, 2000
- **Cyber Crime Law in Japan**   Law No. 128 of 1999
- **Cyber Crime Law in Singapore**   Chapter 50A: Computer Misuse Act
- **Cyber Crime Laws in Korea**   Chapter VI: Stability of the Information and Communications Network: Article 48, Article 49, and Chapter IX Penal Provisions: Article 61
- **Cyber Crime Law in Malaysia**   Computer Crimes Act 1997
- **Cyber Crime Law in Hong Kong**   Telecommunication Law

Don't fret—you won't need to memorize every nuance and verse of every foreign law related to cyber crime. The intent of this section is simply to make you aware that as an ethical hacker, you'll need to know the various laws that may affect your activities. Take note of where you'll be testing and what you expect to find; then check the laws of that country to ensure you aren't getting yourself into trouble.

Chapter Review

To be a successful ethical hacker, you don't just need the knowledge of tools and techniques, but also the background information that provides a secure foundation for your career. Some of the basics include the security triad of Confidentiality, Integrity, and Availability. Confidentiality, addressing the secrecy and privacy of information, refers to the measures taken to prevent disclosure of information or data to unauthorized individuals or systems. The use of passwords is by far the most common logical measure taken to ensure confidentiality, and attacks against passwords are, amazingly enough, the most common confidentiality attacks. Integrity refers to the methods and actions taken to protect the information from unauthorized alteration or revision—whether the data is at rest or in transit. Integrity in information systems is often ensured through the use of a hash (a one-way mathematical algorithm such as MD5 or SHA-1). Availability refers to the communications systems and data being ready for use when legitimate users need it. Denial of service (DoS) attacks are designed to prevent legitimate users from having access to a computer resource or service, and can take many forms.

Another security basic is the Security, Functionality, and Ease of Use triangle, which is simply a graphic representation of a problem that has faced security professionals for an eternity—the more secure something is, the less usable and functional it becomes. As security increases, the system's functionality and ease of use decrease.

Defining an ethical hacker, as opposed to a cracker (or malicious hacker), basically comes down to the guidelines one works under—an ethical hacker only works with explicit consent and approval from a customer. Ethical hackers are employed by customers to improve security. Crackers either act on their own or, in some cases, are employed by malicious entities to destroy or damage government or corporate reputation. In addition, some hackers who use their knowledge to promote a political cause are referred to as "hactivists."

Hackers are generally classified into three separate groups. *White hats* are the ethical hackers hired by a customer for the specific goal of testing and improving security, or for other defensive purposes. *Black hats* are the crackers illegally using their skills for either personal gain or for malicious intent—and they do *not* ask for permission or consent. *Gray hats* are neither good nor bad—they are simply curious about hacking tools and techniques, or feel like it's their duty, with or without customer permission, to demonstrate security flaws in systems. In any case, hacking without a customer's explicit permission and direction is a crime.

A penetration test, also known as a pen test, is a clearly defined, full-scale test of the security controls of a system or network in order to identify security risks and vulnerabilities. The three main phases in a pen test are preparation, assessment, and conclusion. The preparation phase defines the time period when the actual contract is hammered out. The scope of the test, the types of attacks allowed, and the individuals assigned to perform the activity are all agreed upon in this phase. The *assessment* phase (sometimes also known as the *security evaluation* phase) is when the actual assaults on the security controls are conducted. The *conclusion* (or post-assessment) phase defines the time when final reports are prepared for the customer, detailing the findings of the test (including the types of tests performed) and many times even providing recommendations to improve security.

The act of hacking itself consists of five main phases. Reconnaissance involves the steps taken to gather evidence and information on the targets you wish to attack. It can be passive in nature or active. Scanning and enumeration takes the information gathered in recon and actively applies tools and techniques to gather more in-depth information on the targets. In the gaining access phase, true attacks are leveled against the targets enumerated in phase 2. In phase 4, maintaining access, hackers attempt to ensure they have a way back into the machine or system they've already compromised. Finally, in the final phase, covering tracks, attackers attempt to conceal their success and avoid detection by security professionals.

Three different types of tests are performed by ethical hackers. In black box testing, the ethical hacker has absolutely no knowledge of the target of evaluation (TOE). It's designed to simulate an outside, unknown attacker. In white box testing, pen testers have full knowledge of the network, system, and infrastructure they are testing and it is designed to simulate a knowledgeable internal threat, such as a disgruntled network admin or other trusted user. In gray box testing, the attacker has limited knowledge about the TOE. It is designed to simulate privilege escalation from a trusted employee.

Lastly, there are multiple laws, both inside and outside the United States, for the ethical hacker to study and be aware of. You should know not only what each law specifically addresses, and what punishments it may levy, but also what each law means to an ethical hacker and how our business is done.

Questions

1. Which element of security ensures a data message arrives at its destination with no alteration?

   A. Confidentiality

   B. Integrity

   C. Availability

   D. Authentication

2. A hacker grows frustrated in his attempts against a network server and performs a successful denial of service attack. Which security element is being compromised?

   A. Confidentiality

   B. Integrity

   C. Availability

   D. Authentication

3. As security in the enterprise increases,

   A. ease of use increases and functionality decreases.

   B. functionality increases and ease of use decreases.

   C. ease of use decreases and functionality increases.

   D. functionality decreases and ease of use decreases.

4. An ethical hacker is hired to test the security of a business network. The CEH is given no prior knowledge of the network and has a specific framework in which to work, defining boundaries, Non-Disclosure Agreements, and the completion date. Which of the following is a true statement?

   A. A white hat is attempting a black box test.

   B. A white hat is attempting a white box test.

    C. A black hat is attempting a black box test.

    D. A black hat is attempting a gray box test.

5. When an attack by a hacker is politically motivated, the hacker is said to be participating in

    A. black hat hacking.

    B. gray box attacks.

    C. gray hat attacks.

    D. hactivism.

6. Two hackers attempt to crack a company's network resource security. One is considered an ethical hacker, whereas the other is not. What distinguishes the ethical hacker from the "cracker"?

    A. The cracker always attempts white box testing.

    B. The ethical hacker always attempts black box testing.

    C. The cracker posts results to the company's security experts.

    D. The ethical hacker always obtains written permission before testing.

7. In which stage of an ethical hack would the attacker actively apply tools and techniques to gather more in-depth information on the targets?

    A. Active reconnaissance

    B. Scanning and enumeration

    C. Gaining access

    D. Passive reconnaissance

8. Which type of attack is generally conducted as an inside attacker with elevated privileges on the resource(s)?

    A. Gray box

    B. White box

    C. Black box

    D. Active reconnaissance

9. Which attacks take advantage of the built-in code and scripts most off-the-shelf applications come with?

    A. OS attacks

    B. Bit-flipping

    C. Misconfiguration

    D. Shrink-wrap

10. A number of laws are relevant to ethical hacking. Within the United States, which federal statute specifically addresses hacking under U.S. law?

    A. United States Code, Title 18

    B. SPY Act

    C. PATRIOT Act

    D. Freedom of Information Act

11. Which act attempts to ensure a standard level of security in U.S. federal systems?

    A. United States Code, Title 18

    B. PATRIOT Act

    C. FISMA

    D. FoIA

12. As part of a pen test, an ethical hacker discovers a file listing government workers' social security numbers. His dissemination of this document is best governed by which act?

    A. Freedom of Information Act

    B. Privacy Act

    C. PATRIOT Act

    D. FISMA

Answers

1. B. The security triad element of integrity ensures data stays in the form it was originally intended—during transit and at rest.

2. C. The security triad element of availability ensures communications systems and data are ready for use when legitimate users need them.

3. D. Per the Security, Functionality, and Ease of Use triangle, as security increases, functionality and ease of use decrease.

4. A. In this example, an ethical hacker was hired under a specific agreement, making him a white hat. The test he was hired to perform is a no-knowledge attack, making it a black box test.

5. D. Hackers who use their skills and talents to forward a cause or a political agenda are practicing hactivism.

6. D. The ethical hacker always obtains written permission before testing, and never performs a test without it!

7. **B**. The second of the five phases of an ethical hack attempt, scanning and enumeration, is the step where ethical hackers take the information they gathered in recon and actively apply tools and techniques to gather more in-depth information on the targets.

8. **B**. A white box attack is intended to simulate an internal attacker with elevated privileges, such as a network administrator.

9. **D**. Most software inevitably comes with built-in code and script vulnerabilities, and attacks taking advantage of this are known as shrink-wrap attacks.

10. **A**. United States Code, Title 18 defines most of the U.S. law concerning hacking and computer crime.

11. **C**. The Federal Information Security Management Act provides a green light to an ethical hacker with regard to a lot of information, because it makes this information readily available to the public.

12. **B**. The Privacy Act protects information of a personal nature, including social security numbers.

Cryptography 101

In this chapter you will learn about
- An overview of cryptography and encryption techniques
- Cryptographic algorithms
- How public and private keys are generated
- An overview of MD5, SHA, RC4, RC5, and Blowfish algorithms
- The digital signature and its components
- The method and application of digital signature technology
- An overview of digital certificates
- Cryptanalysis and code-breaking methodologies
- Listing the cryptography attacks

You really have to wonder exactly when mankind started keeping secrets from one another. Was it in ancient Greece, where men in the cradle of civilization used tattoos on slaves to send messages to one another? Maybe in ancient Egypt, with messages carved into stone to protect the royals' communications from the rest of the court? Or perhaps it was in caves in Aboriginal Australia, with one cave dweller wanting to let his friend know about the fruit tree discovery without alerting others? Regardless of who gets to claim it first, trying to keep secrets from one another has been around for a very, very long time.

From cavemen working out a succession of knocks and beats to the secure e-mail I just sent my boss a few minutes ago, we've been trying to keep things secret since the dawn of time. And, since the dawn of time, we've been trying to figure out what the other guy was saying—trying to "crack his code." The implementation and study of this particular little fascination of the human psyche—securing communication between two or more parties—is known as *cryptography*. For you budding ethical hackers out there reading this book, the skill you're looking to master, though, is *cryptanalysis*—the study and methods used to crack encrypted communications.

Cryptography and Encryption Overview

I debated long and hard over just how much history to put into this discussion on cryptography, but finally came to the conclusion I shouldn't put in any—even though it's *really* cool and interesting. After all, you're probably not concerned with how the ancient Romans tried to secure their communications, or who the first purveyors of *steganography*—hiding messages inside an image—were (toss-up between the Greeks and the Egyptians, depending on your persuasion). What you are, and should be, concerned with is what cryptography actually is and why you should know anything about it. Excellent thoughts. Let's discuss.

Cryptography is the science or study of protecting information, whether in transit or at rest, by using techniques to render the information unusable to anyone who does not possess the means to decrypt it. The overall process is fairly simple: Take *plaintext* (something you can read) data, apply a cryptographic method, and turn it into *ciphertext* (something you can't read)—so long as there is some provision to allow you to bring the ciphertext back to plaintext. What is not so simple is the actual process of encrypting and decrypting. The rest of this chapter is dedicated to exploring some of the mathematical procedures, known as *encryption algorithms*, used to encrypt and decrypt data.

 NOTE   Don't be confused by the term plaintext. Yes, it can be used to define text data in ASCII format. However within the confines of cryptography, plaintext refers to *anything* that is not encrypted—whether text or not.

It's also important to understand what functions cryptography can provide for us. In Chapter 1, we discussed the hallowed trinity of security—confidentiality, integrity, and availability. When it comes to cryptography, confidentiality is the one that most often is brought up. Encrypting data helps to provide confidentiality of the data, because only those with the "key" can see it. However, some other encryption algorithms and techniques also provide for integrity (hashes that ensure the message hasn't been changed) as well as a new term we have yet to discuss here: non-repudiation. *Non-repudiation* is the means by which a recipient can ensure the identity of the sender and that neither party can deny having sent or received the message. Our discussion of PKI later will definitely touch on this. This chapter is all about defining what cryptography methods we have available so that you know what you're up against as an ethical hacker.

Encryption Algorithms and Techniques

Cryptographic systems can be as simple as substituting one character for another (the old Caesar Cipher simply replaced characters in a string: *B* for *A, C* for *B*, and so on) or as complex as applying mathematical formulas to change the content entirely. Modern-day systems use encryption algorithms and separate keys to accomplish the task. In its simplest definition, an *algorithm* is a step-by-step method of solving a problem. The problem, when it comes to the application of cryptography, is how do you render something unreadable, then provide a means to recover it? Encryption algorithms were created for just such a purpose.

 NOTE Encryption of bits takes, generally, one of two different forms: substitution or transposition. Substitution is exactly what it sounds like—bits are simply replaced by other bits. Transposition doesn't replace bits at all; it changes their order altogether.

Encryption algorithms—mathematical formulas used to encrypt and decrypt data— are highly specialized and, sometimes, very complex. The good news for you, as a CEH candidate, is you don't need to learn the minutiae of how these algorithms actually accomplish their task. You will need to learn, however, how they are classified and some basic information about each one. For example, a good place to start might be the understanding that modern-day systems use encryption algorithms that are dependent on a separate key—meaning that without the key, the algorithm itself should be useless in trying to decode the data. There are only two methods by which these keys can be used and shared: symmetric and asymmetric. Before we get to that, though, we need to have a quick discussion about how ciphers work.

Block and Stream Ciphers

All encryption algorithms on the planet have basically two methods they can use to encrypt data. If you think about it, they make perfect sense. In one method, bits of data are encrypted as a continuous stream. In other words, readable bits in their regular pattern are fed into the cipher and are encrypted one at a time, usually by an XOR operation (exclusive-or). Known as *stream ciphers,* these work at a very high rate of speed.

XOR Operations

XOR operations are at the very core of a lot of computing. An XOR operation requires two inputs. In the case of encryption algorithms, this would be the data bits and the key bits. Each bit is fed into the operation—one from the data, the next from the key—and then XOR makes a determination: If the bits match, the output is a 0; if they don't, it's a 1 (see the following XOR table).

First Input	Second Input	Output
0	0	0
0	1	1
1	0	1
1	1	0

For example, say you had a stream of data bits that read 10110011 and a key that started 11011010. If you did an XOR on these bits, you'd get 01101001. The first two bits (1 from data and 1 from the key) are the same, so the output is a zero.

> The second two bits (0 from data and 1 from the key) are different, outputting a one (1). Continue that process through and you'll see the result.
>
> In regard to cryptography and pure XOR ciphers, keep in mind that key length is of utmost importance. If the key chosen is actually smaller than the data, the cipher will be vulnerable to frequency attacks. In other words, because the key will be used repeatedly in the process, its very frequency makes guessing it (or using some other cryptanalytic technique) easier.

In the other method, data bits are split up into blocks and fed into the cipher. Each block of data (usually 64 bits at a time) is then encrypted with the key and algorithm. These ciphers, known as *block ciphers,* use methods such as substitution and transposition in their algorithms and are considered simpler, and slower, than stream ciphers.

 EXAM TIP   When it comes to encryption algorithm questions on the exam, you'll need to know two main points—what the key length is and what type of cipher (block or stream) it is.

Symmetric Encryption

Also known as *single key* or *shared key, symmetric encryption* simply means one key is used both to encrypt and decrypt the data. So long as both the sender and the receiver know/have the secret key, communication can be encrypted between the two. In keeping with the old acronym K.I.S.S. (Keep It Simple, Stupid), the simplicity of symmetric encryption is its greatest asset—as you can imagine, this makes things very easy and very fast. Bulk encryption needs? Symmetric algorithms and techniques are your best bet.

But symmetric key encryption isn't all roses and chocolate—there are some significant drawbacks and weaknesses. For starters, key distribution and management in this type of system is difficult. How do you safely share the secret key? If you send it over the network, someone can steal it. Additionally, because everyone has to have a specific key from each partner they want to communicate with, the sheer number of keys needed presents a problem.

Suppose you had two people you wanted to safely communicate with. This creates three different lines of communication that must be secured; therefore, you'd need three keys. If you add another person to the mix, there are now six lines of communication, requiring six different keys. As you can imagine, this number jumps up exponentially the larger your network becomes. The formula for calculating how many key pairs you will need is

N (N – 1) / 2

where N is the number of nodes in the network. See Figure 2-1 for an example.

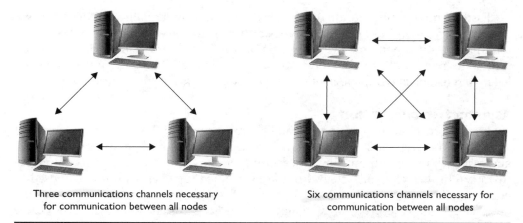

Three communications channels necessary
for communication between all nodes

Six communications channels necessary for
communication between all nodes

Figure 2-1   Key distribution in symmetric encryption systems

Here are some examples of symmetric algorithms:

- **DES**   A block cipher that uses a 56-bit key (with 8 bits reserved for parity). Due to the small key size, this encryption standard became quickly outdated and is not considered a very secure encryption algorithm.

- **3DES**   A block cipher that uses a 168-bit key. 3DES (called *triple* DES) can use up to three keys in a multiple-encryption method. It's much more effective than DES, but is much slower.

- **AES (Advanced Encryption Standard)**   A block cipher that uses a key length of 128, 192, or 256 bits, and effectively replaces DES. Much faster than DES or 3DES.

- **IDEA (International Data Encryption Algorithm)**   A block cipher that uses a 128-bit key, and was also designed to replace DES. Originally used in PGP 2.0 (Pretty Good Privacy), IDEA was patented and used mainly in Europe.

- **Twofish**   A block cipher that uses a key size up to 256 bits.

- **Blowfish**   A fast block cipher, largely replaced by AES, using a 64-bit block size and a key from 32 to 448 bits. Blowfish is considered public domain.

- **RC (Rivest Cipher)**   Encompasses several versions from RC2 through RC6. A block cipher that uses a variable key length up to 2,040 bits. RC6, the latest version, uses 128-bit blocks, whereas RC5 uses variable block sizes (32, 64, or 128).

And there you have it—symmetric encryption is considered fast and strong, but poses some significant weaknesses. It's a great choice for bulk encryption, due to its speed, but key distribution is an issue because the delivery of the key for the secured channel must be done offline. Additionally, scalability is a concern because the larger the network gets, the number of keys that must be generated goes up exponentially.

Lastly, symmetric encryption does a great job with confidentiality, but does nothing to provide for another very important security measure—non-repudiation. Non-repudiation is the method by which we can prove the sender's identity, as well as prevent either party from denying they took part in the data exchange. These weaknesses led to the creation and implementation of the second means of encryption—asymmetric.

Asymmetric Encryption

Asymmetric encryption came about mainly because of the problem inherent in using a single key to encrypt and decrypt messages—just how do you share the key efficiently and easily without compromising the security? The answer was, of course, to simply use two keys. In this key pair system, both are generated together, with one key used to encrypt a message and the other to decrypt it. The encryption key, also known as the *public key*, could be sent anywhere, to anyone. The decryption key, known as the *private key*, is kept secured on the system.

For example, suppose two people wish to secure communications across the Internet between themselves. Using symmetric encryption, they'd need to develop some offline method to exchange the single key used for all encryption/decryption (and agree on changing it fairly often). With asymmetric encryption, they both generate a key pair. User A sends his public key to User B, and User B sends his public key to User A. Neither is concerned if anyone on the Internet steals this key because it can only be used to encrypt messages, not to decrypt them. This way, data can be encrypted by a key and sent without concern, because the only method to decrypt it is the use of the private key belonging to that pair.

 EXAM TIP Asymmetric encryption comes down to this—what one key encrypts, the other key decrypts. It's important to remember the public key is the one used for encryption, whereas the private key is used for decryption. Either can be used for encryption or decryption within the pair (as you'll see later in this chapter), but in general remember public = encrypt, private = decrypt.

In addition to addressing the concerns over key distribution and management, as well as scalability, asymmetric encryption also addresses the non-repudiation problem. For example, consider the following scenario. There are three people on a network—Bob, Susan, and Badguy—using asymmetric encryption. Susan wishes to send an encrypted message to Bob and asks for a copy of his public key. Bob sees this request, and so does Badguy. Both send her a public key that says "Bob's Public Key." Susan is now confused, because she does not know which key is the real one. So how can they prove to each other exactly who they are? How can Bob send a public key to Susan and have her, with some semblance of certainty, know it's actually from him?

The answer, of course, is for Bob to send a message from his system encrypted with his private key. Susan can then attempt to decrypt the message using both public keys. The one that works must be Bob's actual public key because it's the only key in the world that could open a message encrypted with his private key. Susan, now happy with the knowledge she has the correct key, merrily encrypts the message and sends it on.

Bob receives it, decrypts it with his private key, and reads the message. Meanwhile, Badguy weeps in a corner, cursing the cleverness of the asymmetric system. This scenario, along with a couple of other interesting nuggets and participants, illustrates the public key infrastructure framework we'll be discussing later in this chapter.

NOTE It's important to note that although signing a message with the private key is the act required for providing a digital signature and, in effect, confidentiality and non-repudiation, this is only valid if the keys are good in the first place. This is where key management and the CA process comes into play—without their control over the entire scenario, none of this is worthwhile.

Here are some examples of asymmetric algorithms:

- **Diffie-Hellman** Developed for use as a key exchange protocol, Diffie-Hellman is used in Secure Sockets Layer (SSL) and IPSec encryption. Can be vulnerable to man-in-the-middle attacks, however, if the use of digital signatures is waived.

- **Elliptic Curve Cryptosystem (ECC)** Uses points on an elliptical curve, in conjunction with logarithmic problems, for encryption and signatures. Uses less processing power than other methods, making it a good choice for mobile devices.

- **El Gamal** Not based on prime number factoring, this method uses the solving of discrete logarithm problems for encryption and digital signatures.

- **RSA** An algorithm that achieves strong encryption through the use of two large prime numbers. Factoring these numbers creates key sizes up to 4,096 bits. RSA can be used for encryption and digital signatures and is the modern de facto standard.

Asymmetric encryption provides some significant strengths in comparison to its symmetric brethren. Asymmetric encryption can provide both confidentiality and non-repudiation, and solves the problems of key distribution and scalability. In fact, the only real downside to asymmetric—its weaknesses that you'll be asked about on the exam—is its performance (asymmetric is slower than symmetric, especially on bulk encryption) and processing power (usually requiring a much longer key length, it's suitable for smaller amounts of data).

Hash Algorithms

Last in our discussion of algorithms are the hashing algorithms—which really don't encrypt anything at all. A hashing algorithm is a *one-way* mathematical function that takes an input and typically produces a fixed-length string (usually a number), or hash, based on the arrangement of the data bits in the input. Its sole purpose in life is to provide a means to verify the integrity of a piece of data—change a single bit in the arrangement of the original data and you'll get a different response.

NOTE The "one-way" portion of the hash definition is very important. Although a hash does a great job of providing for integrity checks, it's not designed to be an encryption method. There isn't a way for a hash to be reverse-engineered.

For example's sake, suppose you have a small application you've developed and you're getting ready to send it off. You're concerned that it may get corrupted during transport and want to ensure the contents arrive exactly as you've created them. To protect it, you run the contents of the app through a hash, producing an output that reads something like this: EF1278AC6655BBDA93425FFBD28A6EA3. After e-mailing the link to download your app, you provide the hash for verification. Anyone who downloads the app can run it through the same hash program—and if the two values match, the app was downloaded successfully. If even a single bit was corrupted during transfer, the hash value would be wildly different.

Exercise 2-1: Hashing

Numerous hash programs can be downloaded for free online. This exercise is shown only as an example of one such application; many others work just as well, if not better, than this one. Here are the steps to follow:

1. Install Digital Volcano MD5 Hash and open the application.

2. Open Notepad and create a text file named test.txt. Type **CEH is a good certification!** Save and close the file.

3. In Digital Volcano MD5 Hash, click the Select File(s) button (see Figure 2-2).

Figure 2-2
MD5 Hash screen

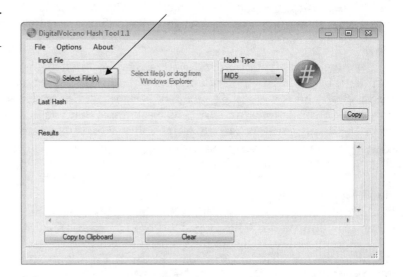

4. Navigate to your test.txt file within the window and click Open. The hash for the file appears in the MD5 screen.

5. Open test.txt again and change "good" to "great." Save and close the file.

6. Follow step 3 again. Note the difference in the hash values displayed in the MD5 window (see Figure 2-3).

Figure 2-3
Hash values

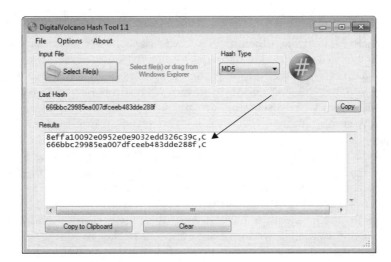

Here are some examples of hash algorithms:

- **MD5 (Message Digest algorithm)**   Produces a 128-bit hash value output, expressed as a 32-digit hexadecimal. Created by Ronald Rivest, MD5 was originally very popular for ensuring file integrity. However, serious flaws in the algorithm, and the advancement of other hashes, have resulted in this hash being rendered obsolete (U.S. CERT, August 2010). Despite its past, MD5 is still used for file verification on downloads and, in many cases, to store passwords.

- **SHA-1**   Developed by the NSA (National Security Agency), SHA-1 produces a 160-bit value output, and was required by law for use in U.S. government applications. In late 2005, however, serious flaws became apparent and the U.S. government began recommending the replacement of SHA-1 with SHA-2 after the year 2010 (see FIPS PUB 180-1).

- **SHA-2**   Actually holds four separate hash functions that produce outputs of 224, 256, 384, and 512 bits. Although it was designed as a replacement for SHA-1, SHA-2 is still not as widely used.

NOTE Rumors of SHA-3 being right around the corner have slowed the deployment of SHA-2. Although theoretically SHA-1 can be cracked, there haven't been any proven cases of it. Combined with the fact that the U.S. government has stated it wants everyone on SHA-3 by 2012, businesses and contractors have been slow to change.

A note of caution here: Hashing algorithms are not impervious to hacking attempts, as is evidenced by the fact that they become outdated (cracked) and need replacing. The attack or effort used against hashing algorithms is known as a collision or a collision attack. Basically, a collision occurs when two or more files create the same output—which is not supposed to happen. When a hacker can create a second file that produces the same hash value output as the original, he may be able to pass off the fake file as the original, causing goodness knows what kinds of problems. Collisions, no matter which hash we're discussing, are always a possibility. By definition, there are only so many combinations the hash can create given an input (MD5, for example, will only generate 2^128 possible combinations). Therefore, given the computation speed of modern computing systems, it isn't infeasible to assume you could re-create one.

For instance, one of the more common uses for a hash algorithm involves passwords. The original password is hashed; then the hash value is sent to the server (or whatever resource will be doing the authentication), where it is stored. When the user logs in, the password is hashed with the same algorithm and key—if the two match, then the user is allowed access. Suppose a hacker were to gain a copy of this hashed password and begin applying a collision attack to the value—that is, he compares data inputs and the hash values they present until the hashes match. Once the match is found, access is granted and the bad guy now holds the user's credentials. Granted, this can be defined as a brute-force attack (and when we get to password attacks later on, you'll see this), but it is included here to demonstrate the whole idea—given a hash value for an input, you can duplicate it over time using the same hash and applying it to different inputs.

Sure, this type of attack takes a *lot* of time, but it's not unheard of. As a matter of fact, many of your predecessors in the hacking field have attempted to speed things up for you by creating *rainbow tables* for just such a use. Because hackers must lead boring lives and have loads of time on their hands, lots of unscrupulous people sat down and started running every word, phrase, and compilation of characters they could think of into a hash algorithm. The results were stored in the rainbow table for use later. Therefore, instead of having to use all those computational cycles to hash your password guesses on your machine, you can simply compare the hashed file to the rainbow table. See? Isn't that easy?

NOTE You can find some pretty good information (and a very detailed exercise) on rainbow tables and how to use them at www.ethicalhacker.net/content/view/94/24/. We toyed with including an exercise here but avoided it for two reasons: First, it's a very long process. Second, it's not tested heavily on the exam. You should practice with rainbow tables for your real-world expertise, but stick with us for the exam goodies.

To protect against collision attacks and the use of rainbow tables, you can also make use of something called a salt. No, not the sodium chloride on your table in the cute little dispenser. This salt is much more virtual. A *salt* is a collection of random bits that are used as a key in addition to the hashing algorithm. Because the bits, and length, are random, a good salt makes a collision attack very difficult to pull off. Considering that every time a bit is added to the salt it adds a power of 2 to the complexity of the number of computation involved to derive the outcome, you can see why it's a necessity in protecting password files.

 EXAM TIP   When it comes to questions on the exam regarding hashes, remember two things. First, they're used for integrity (any deviation in the hash value, no matter how small, indicates the original file has been corrupted). Second, even though hashes are one-way functions, a sufficient collision attack may break older versions (MD5).

Steganography

While not an encryption algorithm in and of itself, steganography is a great way to send messages back and forth without others even realizing it. *Steganography* is the practice of concealing a message inside another medium (such as another file or an image) in such a way that only the sender and recipient even know of its existence—let alone the manner in which to decipher it. Think about it: In every other method we've talked about so far, anyone monitoring the wire *knows* you're trying to communicate secretly— they can see the ciphertext and know something is up. With steganography, you're simply sending a picture of the kids fishing. Anyone watching the wire sees a cute picture and a lot of smiles, never knowing they're looking at a message saying, for instance, "People who eavesdrop are losers."

Steganography can be as simple as hiding the message in the text of a written correspondence or as complex as changing bits within a huge media file to carry a message. For example, you could let the recipient know that each letter starting a paragraph is relevant. Or you could simply write in code, using names of famous landmarks to indicate a message. In another example, if you had an image file you could simply change the least meaningful bit in every byte to represent data—anyone looking at it would hardly notice the difference in the slight change of color or loss of sharpness. In a sound file it may even be less noticeable.

Before you get all excited, though, and go running out to put secret messages in your cell phone pics from last Friday night's party, you need to know that there are a variety of tools and methods in place to look for, and prevent, steganographic file usage. Although there are legitimate uses for it—digital watermarks (used by some companies to identify their applications) come to mind—most antivirus programs and spyware tools actively look for steganography. There are more "stego" tools available than we could possibly cover here in this book, and they can be downloaded from a variety of locations—just be careful.

Steganography Tool

One steganography tool available for download and play is gifshuffle (open source, available at www.darkside.com.au/gifshuffle/index.html). It is used to conceal messages in GIF images. By shuffling bits in the color map, gifshuffle leaves the image visibly unchanged. The syntax for use of this tool is

```
gifshuffle [ -CQS1 ] [ -p passwd ] [ -f file | -m message ] [ infile.gif
[ outfile.gif ]]
```

where **C** compresses the data for concealment, **Q** runs the tool in quiet mode (no reporting during progress), **S** provides reporting on space available, and **1** retains compatibility with earlier versions.

For example, the following command will conceal the message "I love CEH" in the file CEH.gif, with compression, and encrypted with "ethical" as the password. The resulting text will be stored in hacker.gif:

```
gifshuffle -C -m "I love CEH" -p "ethical" CEH.gif hacker.gif
```

To extract the message, you would use the following command:

```
gifshuffle -C -p "ethical" hacker.gif
```

PKI, the Digital Certificate, and Digital Signatures

So, we've spent some time discussing encryption algorithms and techniques as well as covering the theory behind it all. But what about the practical implementation? Just how does it all come together?

Well, there are a couple of things to consider in an overall encryption scheme. First is the protection of the data itself—the encryption. This is done with the key set—one for encrypting, one for decrypting. This may be a little bit of review here, but it's critical to realize the importance of key generation in an asymmetric encryption scheme. As we've already covered, two keys are generated for each party within the encryption scheme, and the keys are generated *as a pair*. The first key, used for encrypting message, is known as the public key. The second key, used for decrypting messages, is known as the private key. Public keys are shared; private keys are not.

No pun intended here, I promise, but the key to a successful encryption system is the infrastructure in place to create and manage the encryption keys. Imagine a system with loose controls over the creation and distribution of keys—it would be near anarchy! Users wouldn't know which key was which, older keys could be used to encrypt and decrypt messages even though the user was gone, and the storage of key copies would be a nightmare. In a classic (and the most common) asymmetric encryption scheme, a public and a private key, at a minimum, have to be created, managed, distributed, stored, and, finally, revoked.

Second, keep in mind that there's more to it than just encrypting and decrypting messages—there's the whole problem of non-repudiation to address. After all, if you're not sure which public key actually belongs to the user Bill, what's the point of having an encryption scheme in the first place? You may wind up using the wrong key and encrypting a message for Bill that the bad guy can read with impunity—and Bill can't even open! There are multiple providers of encryption frameworks to accomplish this task, and most follow a basic template known as *public key infrastructure,* or *PKI*.

The PKI System

A friend of mine once told me that the classic PKI infrastructure is an example of "beautifully complex simplicity." PKI is basically a structure designed to verify and authenticate the identity of individuals within the enterprise taking part in a data exchange. It consists of hardware, software, and policies that create, manage, store, distribute, and revoke keys and digital certificates (which we'll cover in a minute). The system starts at the top, with a (usually) neutral party known as the *Certificate Authority (CA)*. The CA acts as a third party to the organization, much like a notary public—when it stamps something as valid, you can trust, with relative assuredness, that it is. Its job is to create and issue digital certificates that can be used to verify identity. The CA also keeps track of all the certificates within the system and maintains a *Certificate Revocation List (CRL),* used to track which certificates have problems and which have been revoked.

 NOTE There always seems to be a lot of confusion when it comes to understanding PKI, and I think I know why. Most newcomers to the field want to think of PKI as an encryption algorithm itself. PKI is simply a framework by which keys are distributed and, most importantly, people can verify their identities through certificates.

The way the system works is fairly simple. Because the CA provides the certificate and key (public), the user can be certain the public key actually belongs to the intended recipient—after all, the CA is vouching for it. It also simplifies distribution of keys—Bill doesn't have to go to every user in the organization to get their keys; he can just go to the CA.

For a really simple example, consider user Joe, who just joined an organization. Joe needs a key pair to encrypt and decrypt messages. He also needs a place to get the public keys for the other users on the network. With no controlling figure in place, he would simply create his own set of keys and distribute them in any way he saw fit. Other users on the network would have no real way of verifying his identity, other than, basically, to take his word for it. Additionally, Joe would have to go to each user in the enterprise to get their public key.

Trust Models

The term *trust model* is used in describing how entities within an enterprise deal with keys, signatures, and certificates, and there are three basic models. In the first, called *web of trust*, multiple entities sign certificates for one another. In other words, users within this system trust each other based on certificates they receive from other users on the same system.

The other two systems rely on a more structured setup. A *single authority system* has a CA at the top that creates and issues certs. Users trust each other based on the CA itself. The *hierarchical trust system* also has a CA at the top (which is known as the root CA), but makes use of one or more intermediate CAs underneath it— known as *registration authorities (RAs)*—to issue and manage certificates. This system is the most secure because users can track the certificate back to the root to ensure authenticity without a single point of failure.

User Bob, on the other hand, joins an organization using a PKI structure with a local person acting as the CA. Bob goes to his security officer (the CA) and applies for encryption keys. The local security guy first verifies Bob is actually Bob (driver's license and so on) and then asks how long Bob needs the encryption keys and for what purpose. Once he's satisfied, the CA creates the user ID in the PKI system, generating a key pair for encryption and a digital certificate for Bob to use. Bob can now send his certificate around, and others in the organization can trust it because the CA verifies it. Additionally, anyone wanting to send a message to Bob goes to the CA to get a legitimate copy of Bob's public key. Much cleaner, much smoother, and much more secure. As an aside, and definitely worth pointing out here, the act of the CA creating the key is important, but the fact that he signs it digitally is what validates the entire system. Therefore, protection of your CA is of utmost importance.

Digital Certificates

I know this may seem out of order, since I've mentioned the word "certificate" multiple times already, but it's nearly impossible to discuss PKI without mentioning certificates, and vice versa. As you can probably tell so far, a digital certificate isn't really involved with encryption at all. It is, instead, a measure by which entities on a network can provide identification. A digital certificate is an electronic file that is used to verify a user's identity, providing non-repudiation throughout the system.

The certificate itself, in the PKI framework, follows a standard used worldwide. The X.509 standard, a part of a much bigger series of standards set up for directory services and such, defines what should and should not be in a digital certificate. Because of the standard, any system complying with X.509 can exchange and use digital certificates to establish authenticity.

The contents of a digital certificate are listed next. To see them in action, try the steps listed afterward to look at a certificate from McGraw-Hill Professional:

- **Version**   This identifies the certificate format. Over time, the actual format of the certificate has changed slightly, allowing for different entries. The most common version in use is 1.

- **Serial Number**   Fairly self-explanatory, the serial number is used to uniquely identify the certificate itself.

- **Subject**   Whoever or whatever is being identified by the certificate.

- **Algorithm ID (or Signature Algorithm)**   Shows the algorithm that was used to create the digital signature.

- **Issuer**   Shows the entity that verifies the authenticity of the certificate. The issuer is the one who creates the certificates.

- **Valid From and Valid To**   These fields show the dates the certificate is good through.

- **Key Usage**   Shows for what purpose the certificate was created.

- **Subject's Public Key**   A copy of the subject's public key is included in the digital certificate, for obvious purposes.

- **Optional fields**   These fields include Issuer Unique Identifier, Subject Alternative Name, and Extensions.

Exercise 2-2: Viewing a Digital Certificate

Any site using digital certificates will work—this one is simply used as an example. Here are the steps to follow:

1. Open Internet Explorer and go to www.mhprofessional.com.

2. Select any book pictured on the front page and click ADD TO CART.

3. Click the CHECKOUT button. Once the page loads, you should see the protocol in the URL change from "http" to "https." You should also see a lock icon appear on the right side of the address bar (see Figure 2-4).

Figure 2-4
IE address bar
lock icon

Figure 2-5
IE View Certificates
button

Website Identification ✕

VeriSign has identified this site as:

www.mhprofessional.com

This connection to the server is encrypted.

Should I trust this site?

View certificates

4. Click the lock icon and choose View Certificates (see Figure 2-5).

5. Click the Details tab so you can view the contents of the digital certificate. Clicking the Certification Path tab shows the certificate being tracked and verified back to a root CA at VeriSign (see Figure 2-6).

Figure 2-6
Viewing a digital
certificate

| General | Details | Certification Path |

Show <All>

Field	Value
Version	V3
Serial number	22 59 59 a6 3c 18 c1 51 ...
Signature algorithm	sha1RSA
Signature hash algorithm	sha1
Issuer	VeriSign Class 3 Secure ...
Valid from	Monday, November 22, 2...
Valid to	Wednesday, November 2...
Subject	www.mhprofessional.co...

Edit Properties...   Copy to File...

Learn more about certificate details

OK

EXAM TIP Know what is in the digital certificate and what each field does. It's especially important to remember the public key is sent with the cert.

So how does the digital certificate work within the system? For example's sake, let's go back to user Bob. He applied for his digital certificate through the CA and anxiously awaits an answer. The cert arrives and Bob notices two things: First, the certificate itself is encrypted. Second, the CA provided a copy of its own public key. Confused, he asks his security person what this all means.

Bob learns this method is used to deliver the cert to the individual safely and securely, and also provides a means for Bob to be *absolutely certain* the cert came from the CA and not from some outside bad guy. How so? The cert was encrypted by the CA before he sent it using the CA's private key. Because the only key in existence that could possibly decrypt it is the CA's own public key, which is readily available to anyone, Bob can rest assured he has a valid cert. Bob can now use his certificate, containing information about him that others can verify with the CA, to prove his identity.

Digital Signatures

Lastly, we come to the definition and description of the digital signature. The only real reason this is ever a confusing topic is because instructors spend a lot of time drilling into student's heads that the public key is for encryption and that the private key is for decryption. In general, this is a true statement (and I'm willing to bet you'll see it on your exam that way). However, remember that the keys are created in pairs—what one key does, the other undoes. If you encrypt something with the public key, the private key is the only one that can decrypt it. But that works in reverse, too—if you encrypt something with your private key, your public key is the only thing that can decrypt it.

Keeping this in mind, the digital signature is an easy thing to understand. A digital signature is nothing more than an algorithmic output that is designed to ensure the authenticity (and integrity) of the sender—basically a hash algorithm. The way it works is simple:

1. Bob creates a text message to send to Joe.

2. Bob runs his message through a hash and generates an outcome.

3. Bob then encrypts the outcome with his private key and sends the message, along with the encrypted hash, to Joe.

4. Joe receives the message and attempts to decrypt the hash with Bob's public key. If it works, he knows the message came from Bob.

When it comes to PKI, asymmetric encryption, digital certificates, and digital signatures, remembering a few important facts will solve a lot of headaches for you. Keys are generated in pairs, and what one does, the other undoes. In general, the public key (shared with everyone) is used for encryption, and the private key (kept only by the owner) is used for decryption. Although the private key is created to decrypt messages sent to the owner, it is also used to prove authenticity through the digital signature (encrypting with the private key allows recipients to decrypt with the readily available public key). Key generation, distribution, and revocation is best handled within a framework, often referred to as PKI. PKI also allows for the creation and dissemination of digital certificates, which are used to prove the identity of an entity on the network and follow a standard (X.509).

Encrypted Communication and Cryptography Attacks

So we've learned a little bit about what cryptography is and what encryption algorithms can do for us. In this section, we need to cover the final two pieces of the CEH cryptography exam objective: how people communicate securely with one another, using these encryption techniques, and what attacks allow the ethical hacker to disrupt or steal that communication.

Data Encryption: At Rest and While Communicating

Data at rest (DAR) is a term being bandied about quite a bit lately in the IT Security world. Most people attribute DAR as being one of a couple of things. First, the data files and folders can be encrypted themselves. More than a few products and applications are available out there for doing just this. Microsoft builds Encrypted File Systems (EFS) into its operating systems now for data at rest encryption. Others range from free products (such as TrueCrypt) to using PKI within the system (such as Entrust products). Another method of data at rest encryption is to encrypt the entire drive at the sector level. This prevents access to the hard drive at all, except by an authorized user with the correct passphrase. You can find more information on this, along with an exercise in using TrueCrypt, in Chapter 7.

It's one thing to protect your data at rest, but it's another thing altogether to figure out how to transport it securely and safely. Encryption algorithms—both symmetric and asymmetric—were designed to help us do both, mainly because when all this (networking and the Internet) was being built, no one even thought security would be an issue.

Want proof? Name some application layer protocols in your head and think about how they work. SMTP? Great protocol, used to move e-mail back and forth. Secure? Heck no—it's all in plaintext. What about Telnet and SNMP? Same thing, and maybe even worse (SNMP can do bad, bad things in the wrong hands). FTP? Please, don't even begin to tell me that's secure. So how can we communicate securely with one another? The list provided here isn't all-inclusive, but it does cover the major communications avenues you'll need a familiarity with for your exam:

- **Secure Shell (SSH)** SSH is, basically, a secured version of Telnet. SSH uses TCP port 22, by default, and relies on public key cryptography for its encryption. Originally designed for remote sessions into Unix machines for command execution, it can be used as a tunneling protocol as well. SSH2 is the successor to SSH. It's more secure, efficient, and portable, and includes a built-in encrypted version of FTP (SFTP).

- **Secure Sockets Layer (SSL)**   Encrypts data at the transport layer, and above, for secure communication across the Internet. It uses RSA encryption and digital certificates, and can be used with a wide variety of upper-layer protocols. SSL uses a six-step process for securing a channel, as shown in Figure 2-7. It is being largely replaced by TLS (Transport Layer Security).

- **Transport Layer Security (TLS)**   Using an RSA algorithm of 1024 and 2048 bits, TLS is the successor to SSL. The handshake portion allows both client and server to authenticate to each other.

- **Internet Protocol Security (IPsec)**   A network layer tunneling protocol which can be used in two modes—tunnel (entire IP packet encrypted) and transport (data payload encrypted). IPsec is capable of carrying nearly any application.

- **Point-to-Point Tunneling Protocol (PPTP)**   Widely used for VPNs, it relies on PPP (point-to-point protocol) for encryption and security, using RC4 encryption.

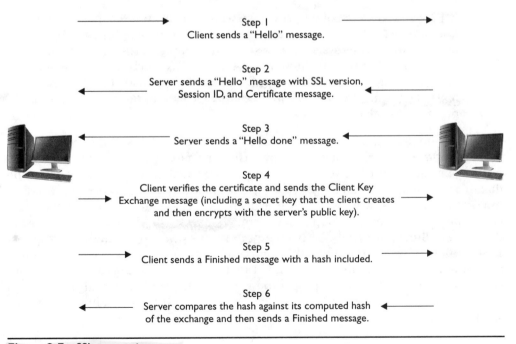

Step 1
Client sends a "Hello" message.

Step 2
Server sends a "Hello" message with SSL version,
Session ID, and Certificate message.

Step 3
Server sends a "Hello done" message.

Step 4
Client verifies the certificate and sends the Client Key
Exchange message (including a secret key that the client creates
and then encrypts with the server's public key).

Step 5
Client sends a Finished message with a hash included.

Step 6
Server compares the hash against its computed hash
of the exchange and then sends a Finished message.

Figure 2-7   SSL connection steps

Cryptography Attacks

For the ethical hacker, all this information has been great to know, and *is* very important, but it's not enough just to know what types of encryption are available. What we need to know, what we're *really* interested in, is how to crack that encryption so we can read the information being passed. A variety of methods and tools is available, and although we can't cover all of them, we will cover many of the relevant ones:

- **Known plaintext attack**   In this attack, the hacker has both plaintext and corresponding ciphertext messages—the more, the better. The plaintext copies are scanned for repeatable sequences, which are then compared to the ciphertext versions. Over time, and with effort, this can be used to decipher the key. A variant of this is known as *chosen-plaintext*, where the attacker encrypts multiple plaintext copies himself in order to gain the key.

- **Ciphertext-only attack**   In this attack, the hacker gains copies of several messages encrypted in the same way (with the same algorithm). Statistical analysis can then be used to reveal, eventually, repeating code, which can be used to decode messages later on. A variant of this is known as *chosen-cipher attack*, where the same process is followed (statistical analysis without a plaintext version for comparison), but it's only for portions of gained ciphertext.

- **Replay attack**   Most often performed within the context of a man-in-the-middle attack. The hacker repeats a portion of a cryptographic exchange in hopes of fooling the system into setting up a communications channel. The attacker doesn't really have to know the actual data (such as the password) being exchanged, he just has to get the timing right in copying and then replaying the bit stream. Session tokens can be used in the communications process to combat this attack.

Along with these attacks, a couple of other terms are worth discussing here. *Man-in-the-middle attack* is usually listed by many security professionals and study guides (depending on the test version you get, it may even be listed as such). Just keep in mind that this term simply means the attacker has positioned himself between the two communicating entities. Once there, he can launch a variety of attacks (interference, fake keys, replay, and so on). Additionally, the term *brute force attack* is apropos to discuss in this context. Brute force refers to an attempt to try every possible combination against a target until successful. Although this can certainly be applied to cracking encryption schemes—and most commonly is defined that way—it doesn't belong *solely* in this realm (for example, it's entirely proper to say using 500 people to test all the doors at once is a brute force attack, as is sending an open request to every known port on a single machine).

NOTE An inference attack may not be what you think it is. *Inference* actually means you can derive information from the ciphertext without actually decoding it. For example, if you are monitoring the encrypted line a shipping company uses and the traffic suddenly increases, you could assume the company is getting ready for a big delivery.

What's more, a variety of other encryption-type attack applications is waiting in the wings. Some applications, such as Carnivore and Magic Lantern (more of a keylogger than an actual attack application), were created by the U.S. government for law enforcement use in cracking codes. Some, such as L0phtcrack (used mainly on Microsoft Windows against SAM password files) or John and Ripper (a Unix/Linux tool for the same purpose), are aimed specifically at cracking password hashes. Others might be aimed at a specific type or form of encryption (for example, PGPcrack is designed to go after PGPO-encrypted systems). You'll learn more about these applications and attacks throughout the rest of this book.

Regardless of the attack chosen or the application used to try it, it's important to remember that, even though they may be successful, attempts to crack encryption take a very, very long time. The stronger the encryption method and the longer the key used in the algorithm, the longer the attack will take to be successful. Additionally, it's not acceptable security practice to assign a key and never change it. No matter how long and complex the key, given a sufficient amount of time a brute force attack will crack it. However, that amount of time can be from a couple of minutes for keys shorter than 40 bits to 50 or so years for keys longer than 64 bits. Obviously, then, if you combine a long key with a commitment to changing it out within a reasonable time period, you can be relatively sure the encryption is "uncrackable." Per the U.S. government, an algorithm using at least a 256-bit key cannot be cracked (see AES).

 NOTE A truism of hacking really applies here: Hackers are generally about the "low-hanging fruit." The mathematics involved in cracking encryption usually make it not worthwhile.

Chapter Review

Cryptography is the science or study of protecting information, whether in transit or at rest, by using techniques to render the information unusable to anyone who does not possess the means to decrypt it. Plaintext data (something you can read) is turned into ciphertext data (something you can't read) by the application of some form of encryption. Encrypting data provides confidentiality because only those with the "key" can see it. Integrity can also be provided by hashing algorithms. Non-repudiation is the means by which a recipient can ensure the identity of the sender and that neither party can deny having sent or received the message.

Encryption algorithms—mathematical formulas used to encrypt and decrypt data—are highly specialized and very complex. There are two methods in which the algorithms actually work, and two methods by which these keys can be used and shared. In stream ciphers, bits of data are encrypted as a continuous stream. In other words, readable bits in their regular pattern are fed into the cipher and are encrypted one at a time. These work at a very high rate of speed. Block ciphers combine data bits into blocks and feed them into the cipher. Each block of data, usually 64 bits at a time, is then encrypted with the key and algorithm. These ciphers are considered simpler, and slower, than stream ciphers.

Symmetric encryption, also known as single key or shared key, simply means one key is used both to encrypt and decrypt the data. It is considered fast and strong, but poses some significant weaknesses. It's a great choice for bulk encryption, due to its speed, but key distribution is an issue because the delivery of the key for the secured channel must be done offline. Additionally, scalability is a concern because as the network gets larger, the number of keys that must be generated goes up exponentially. DES, 3DES, AES (Advanced Encryption Standard), IDEA (International Data Encryption Algorithm), Twofish, and RC (Rivest Cipher) are examples.

Asymmetric encryption comes down to this: What the one key encrypts, the other key decrypts. It's important to remember the public key is the one used for encryption, whereas the private key is used for decryption. *Either can be used for encryption or decryption within the pair*, but in general remember public = encrypt, private = decrypt. Asymmetric encryption can provide both confidentiality and non-repudiation, and solves the problems of key distribution and scalability. The weaknesses include its performance (asymmetric is slower than symmetric, especially on bulk encryption) and processing power (asymmetric usually requires a much longer key length, so it's suitable for smaller amounts of data). Diffie-Hellman, Elliptic Curve Cryptosystem (ECC), El Gamal, and RSA are examples.

A hashing algorithm is a one-way mathematical function that takes an input and produces a single number (integer) based on the arrangement of the data bits in the input. It provides a means to verify the integrity of a piece of data—change a single bit in the arrangement of the original data and you'll get a different response. The attack or effort used against hashing algorithm is known as a collision or a collision attack. A collision occurs when two or more files create the same output—which is not supposed to happen. To protect against collision attacks and the use of rainbow tables, you can also make use of something called a salt. A *salt* is a collection of random bits used as a key in addition to the hashing algorithm. MD5, SHA-1, and SHA2 are examples of hash algorithms.

Steganography is the practice of concealing a message inside another medium (such as another file or an image) in such a way that only the sender and recipient even know of its existence—let alone the manner in which to decipher it.

PKI is a structure designed to verify and authenticate the identity of individuals within the enterprise taking part in a data exchange. It can consist of hardware, software, and policies that create, manage, store, distribute, and revoke keys and digital certificates. The system starts at the top, with a (usually) neutral party known as the Certificate Authority (CA) that creates and issues digital certificates. The CA also keeps track of all the certificates within the system, and maintains a Certificate Revocation List (CRL), used to track which certificates have problems and which have been revoked.

A *digital certificate* is an electronic file that is used to verify a user's identity, providing non-repudiation throughout the system. The certificate itself typically follows the X.509 standard, which defines what should and should not be in a digital certificate. Version, Serial Number, Subject, Algorithm ID (or Signature Algorithm), Issuer, Valid From and Valid To, Key Usage, Subject's Public Key, and Optional are all fields within a digital certificate. A *digital signature* is nothing more than an algorithmic output that is designed to ensure the authenticity (and integrity) of the sender.

Cipher attacks fall into a few categories and types. Known plaintext attacks, ciphertext-only attacks, and replay attacks are examples. Man in the middle is usually listed as a type of attack by many security professionals and study guides (depending on the test version you get, it may even be listed as such). Just keep in mind that man in the middle simply means the attacker has positioned himself between the two communicating entities. Brute force refers to an attempt to try every possible combination against a target until successful.

Questions

1. You want to ensure your messages are safe from unauthorized observation, and you want to provide some means of ensuring the identities of the sender and receiver during the communications process. Which of the following best suits your goals?

    A. Steganography

    B. Asymmetric encryption

    C. Hash

    D. Symmetric encryption

2. The DES encryption key is _____ bits long.

    A. 32

    B. 56

    C. 64

    D. 128

3. The 3DES encryption key is _____ bits long.

    A. 56

    B. 64

    C. 168

    D. 192

4. Joe and Bob are both ethical hackers and have gained access to a folder. Joe has several encrypted files from the folder, and Bob has found one of them unencrypted. Which of the following is the best attack vector for them to follow?

   A. Cipher text only

   B. Known plaintext

   C. Chosen ciphertext

   D. Replay

5. Which is a symmetric algorithm?

   A. SHA-1

   B. Diffie-Hellman

   C. ECC

   D. DES

6. Which of the following is used to distribute a public key within the PKI system, verifying the user's identity to the recipient?

   A. Digital signature

   B. Hash value

   C. Private key

   D. Digital certificate

7. A hacker feeds plaintext files into a hash, eventually finding two or more that create the same fixed-value hash result. This anomaly is known as a

   A. collision.

   B. chosen plaintext.

   C. hash value compromise.

   D. known plaintext.

8. What is the standard format for digital certificates?

   A. X.500

   B. X.25

   C. XOR

   D. X.509

9. Which of the following statements is true regarding encryption algorithms?

   A. Symmetric algorithms are slow, are good for bulk encryption, and have no scalability problems.

   B. Symmetric algorithms are fast, are good for bulk encryption, and have no scalability problems.

    C. Symmetric algorithms are fast, are good for bulk encryption, but have scalability problems.

    D. Symmetric algorithms are fast, but have scalability problems and are not suited for bulk encryption.

10. Within a PKI system, Joe encrypts a message for Bob and sends it. Bob receives the message and decrypts the message using

    A. Joe's public key.

    B. Joe's private key.

    C. Bob's public key.

    D. Bob's private key.

11. Which "public domain" algorithm uses a 64-bit block and an encryption key of up to 448 bits?

    A. DES

    B. 3DES

    C. Blowfish

    D. SHA-2

12. Which symmetric algorithm uses variable block sizes (from 32 to 128 bits)?

    A. DES

    B. 3DES

    C. RC

    D. MD5

13. Which hash algorithm produces a 160-bit output value?

    A. SHA-1

    B. SHA-2

    C. Diffie-Hellmann

    D. MD5

Answers

1. **B.** Asymmetric encryption protects the data and provides for non-repudiation.

2. **B.** The DES key is 56 bits long, with an additional 8 bits of parity.

3. **C.** The triple DES encryption key is 168 bits.

4. **B.** In a known plaintext attack, the hacker has both plaintext and ciphertext messages—the plaintext copies are scanned for repeatable sequences, which are then compared to the ciphertext versions. Over time, and with effort, this can be used to decipher the key.

5. **D.** DES is the only symmetric algorithm listed.

6. **D.** A digital certificate contains, among other things, the sender's public key, and it can be used to identify the sender.

7. **A.** When two or more plaintext entries create the same fixed-value hash result, a collision has occurred.

8. **D.** X.509 provides the standard format for digital certificates.

9. **C.** Symmetric algorithms are fast, are good for bulk encryption, but have scalability problems.

10. **D.** Bob's public key is used to encrypt the message. His private key is used to decrypt it.

11. **C.** Blowfish uses a 64-bit block and an encryption key of up to 448 bits.

12. **C.** Rivest Cipher (RC) uses variable block sizes (from 32 to 128 bits).

13. **A.** SHA-1 produces a 160-bit output value.

Reconnaissance: Information Gathering for the Ethical Hacker

In this chapter you will learn about
- Defining footprinting
- Describing the information-gathering methodology
- Understanding the use of whois, ARIN, and nslookup
- Describing DNS record types
- Defining and describing Google hacking
- Using Google hacking

Have you ever read *The Art of War* by Sun Tzu? If you haven't, let me warn you: It's not something you're liable to snuggle up on the bed with and read breathlessly, wondering how it's going to end. It is, though, a masterpiece of insight into military strategy that is as applicable today as it was when it was written by the Chinese general a couple of thousand years ago. I'm not sure if, when he wrote it, Sun Tzu had any idea that his book would have this kind of staying power, but the fact that it is, to this day, still considered mandatory reading for military leaders shows that he knew a thing or two about waging war. And because our chosen field in information technology is, in effect, a battlefield, what better resource to turn to?

Two (or several) thousand years ago, moving an army out across any distance at all was a time-consuming and very costly endeavor. In addition to all the associated costs—food, support personnel, and so on—if the journey was long and the timeframe short, the army could very well wind up arriving too tired to actually engage in the battle. And as we all know, you can't call a timeout in war for a water break. Sun Tzu's answer to this was intelligence. He had a firm belief that if you put as much time and effort into learning everything you could about your enemy as you did actually fighting them, your victory was as good as ensured. In Sun Tzu's time, this intelligence was gathered manually, using spies on foot to watch, listen, and report back on what the enemy was doing and thinking. Sun Tzu said spies were "as important to an army as water."

In the virtual battlefield we find ourselves in, Sun Tzu's assertions are just as valid. You want to be successful as an ethical hacker? Then you'd better learn how to gather information about your targets *before you ever even try to attack them*. This chapter is all about the tools and techniques to do that. And for those of you who relish the thought of spy-versus-spy and espionage, although most of this is done through virtual means, you can still employ human spies and good old legwork to get it done. First, though, we should take at least a few moments to make sure we know just what attack vectors and vulnerabilities are out there.

Vulnerability Research

I know what some of you out there are saying already. I can virtually hear you now, screaming at the pages and telling me that vulnerability research isn't a part of footprinting (which we'll define in a minute). And, frankly, I'll agree with you; you're right, it's definitely *not* part of footprinting as it is defined in CEH. However, I have two main goals in this book: to help you pass the test and to help you *actually become an ethical hacker*. Passing a test demonstrates knowledge. Applying it day in and day out is another thing altogether. This section isn't about running vulnerability scanners against machines you've already footprinted—that comes later on as a separate step. This is about keeping abreast of current, relevant knowledge that will make you an effective hacker.

For those of you who picked this book up and are just now getting involved in ethical hacking, vulnerability research is a vital step you need to learn and master. After all, how can you get ready to attack systems and networks if you don't know what vulnerabilities are already defined? Additionally, I just believe this is the perfect time to talk about the subject. For *everyone* reading this book, vulnerability research is covered in detail on the exam, so pay close attention.

We already touched on vulnerability research a little bit in Chapter 1, and we'll definitely brush up on it some more in Chapter 11, but we need to spend at least a little bit of time going over it right here. Much of vulnerability research is simply remaining aware of what is out there for your use. In all seriousness, vulnerability research is a nonstop endeavor that many entities have taken it upon themselves to do. Therefore, because the proverbial wheel has already been invented, just roll with it. However, keep in mind that even though all this work is already being done for you, it's still your responsibility to keep on top of it.

Most of your vulnerability research will come down to a lot of reading, most of it from websites. What you'll be doing in your ongoing research is keeping track of the latest exploit news, any zero-day outbreaks in viruses and malware, and what recommendations are being made to deal with them. Sure, keep up with the news and read what's going on—but just remember, by the time it gets to the front page of *USA Today* or FoxNews.com, it's probably already been out in the wild for a long, long time.

For example, Adobe had a few serious vulnerabilities come about in 2010, and the company didn't come out with an update or patch for quite some time. The recommended fix action required some manual intervention on the administrator's part, and many folks simply didn't do it—they just sat around waiting for a patch from Adobe. It was literally a month before I ever saw this mentioned in a "legit" newspaper, and even then it was just a blip, buried far below the latest exposé on some starlet heading back to rehab. A smart ethical hacker who knew what to look for could attempt to exploit it, and reading just a few websites would be all you'd need to do to have a leg up on the competition. Here are a few of the sites to keep in your favorites list:

- National Vulnerability Database (nvd.nist.gov)
- Exploit-Database (exploit-db.com)
- Securitytracker (www.securitytracker.com)
- Securiteam (www.securiteam.com)
- Secunia (www.secunia.com)
- Hackerstorm Vulnerability Research Tool (www.hackerstorm.com)
- HackerWatch (www.hackerwatch.org)
- SecurityFocus (www.securityfocus.com)
- Security Magazine (www.securitymagazine.com)
- SC Magazine (www.scmagazine.com)

Other sources you may consider are in—how can I put this—the *seedy* side of the Internet. These are sites and boards where code, ideas, tools, and more are exchanged between people looking for vulnerabilities in any and every thing you can think of. I considered putting a list together here, but decided against it. I don't want you getting yourself in trouble in your efforts to find things out there that might not have been shouted from the virtual rooftops yet. My best advice to you in this regard is to find someone who has been in security for a while, and ask him to take you under his wing. He will keep you from going somewhere you'll regret down the road. Remember, a lot of people out there doing vulnerability research aren't just unethical, they're criminal. Just know that you need to be careful.

 NOTE One great place to meet IT security professionals—to learn about what to look for, where to find it, and places not to go—is at professional organization gatherings. For one example, the ISSA (Information Systems Security Association) has chapters all across the United States, and attending their meetings is generally free or costs very little. You can find chapter locations on the association's website (www.issa.org).

Exercise 3-1: Researching Vulnerabilities

You can use any of the sites listed earlier, among other locations, to find information on vulnerabilities. This exercise just explores one of them—the free Hackerstorm Open Source Vulnerability Database (OSVDB) tool. Here are the steps to follow:

1. Create a folder on your C:\ drive named Hackerstorm (just to store everything).

2. Go to www.hackerstorm.com and click the OSVDB Free Tool tab at the top.

3. Click Download GUI v.1.1, saving the file to the Hackerstorm folder you created. Unzip the files to the folder.

4. Click Download XML dB, save the file to the Hackerstorm folder you created, and unzip the files to the folder. Choose "Yes to All" when prompted about overwriting files.

5. In the C:\Hackerstorm folder, double-click the START.html file. The home screen of the free OSVDB search screen appears (see Figure 3-1).

6. Click the OSVDB Search button at the bottom. Scroll through the vendors on the left, choose Mozilla Organization, and then click the View button.

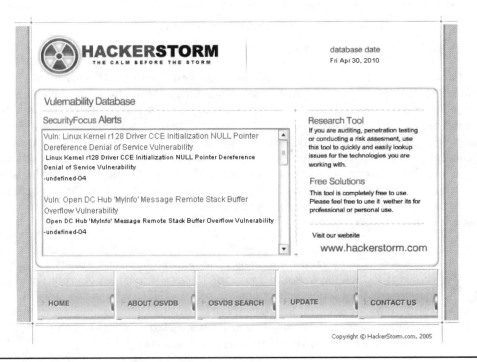

Figure 3-1   Hackerstorm Vulnerability Database tool

7. On the next screen, click View All. Scroll through the vulnerabilities listed, and choose one of them by clicking it. By clicking the Description, Solution, Details, References, and Credits buttons at the bottom of the screen, you can view all sorts of information about a particular vulnerability (see Figure 3-2).

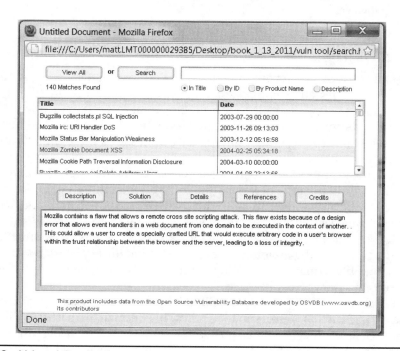

Figure 3-2 Vulnerability details

The database for this tool is updated daily, so you can download it and keep track of up-to-date vulnerability news at the click of a mouse. Again, it's not the only tool out there, but it's a good place to start.

We will be revisiting vulnerability research later on, when we get to the pen test itself. Vulnerability research tools range from "old-school" point-and-shoot applications, such as Nessus, to highly specialized gadgets you can even put on a cell phone. It's important for you to know vulnerability research isn't considered a part of footprinting, per se, but it is an integral part of what you'll need to know before you even get around to mapping out a network. Again, we're not talking about finding a vulnerability in the target you've already footprinted and enumerated—that comes much later in the phases of hacking. We're simply talking about maintaining a solid knowledge base, and knowing what's available out there for (and against) you; keeping an eye on what's out there is expected of any security professional. We'll get into vulnerability scan tool usage later in the book.

NOTE In a purely philosophical point of contention here, it's relevant for the new hacker to consider a Sun Tzu tactic: Define victory before engaging in battle. Keep in mind that *any* activity taken without purpose introduces risk. Therefore, if you're not sure why you should footprint/enumerate something, then *don't do it.*

Footprinting

Gathering information about your intended target is more than just a beginning step in the overall attack—it's an essential skill you'll need to perfect as an ethical hacker. I believe what most people desiring to learn more about this career field wonder comes down to two questions: what kind of information am I looking for, and how do I go about getting it? Both are excellent questions (if I do say so myself) and both will be answered in this section.

You were already introduced to the term *reconnaissance* in Chapter 1, so I won't bore you with the definition again here. I do think it's important, though, that you understand there *may* be a difference in definition between reconnaissance and *footprinting*, depending on which security professional you're talking to. For many, recon is more of an overall, over-arching term for gathering information on targets, whereas footprinting is more of an effort to map out, at a high level, what the landscape looks like. They are interchangeable terms in CEH parlance, but if you just remember that footprinting is part of reconnaissance, you'll be fine.

During the footprinting stage, you're looking for any information that might give you some insight into the target—no matter how big or small. Of particular importance are things such as the high-level network architecture (what routers are they using and what servers have they purchased?), the applications and websites (are they public-facing?), and the physical security measures (what type of entry control systems present the first barrier, and what routines do the employees seem to be doing daily?). Of course, anything providing information on the employees themselves is always great to have, because the employees represent a gigantic target for you later in the test. Although some of this data may be a little tricky to obtain, most of it is relatively easy to get and is right there in front of you, if you just open your virtual eyes.

First up, let's cover a couple of terms: active footprinting versus passive footprinting. An *active footprinting* effort is one that requires the attacker to touch the device or network, whereas *passive footprinting* can be undertaken without communicating with the machines. For example, passive footprinting might be perusing websites or looking up public records, whereas running a scan against an IP you find in the network would be active footprinting. When it comes to the footprinting stage of hacking, the vast majority of your activity will be passive in nature. As far as the exam is concerned, you're considered passively footprinting when you're online, checking on websites, and looking up DNS records, and you're actively footprinting when you're gathering social engineering information by talking to employees.

EXAM TIP *Footprinting* is defined as the process of gathering information on computer systems and networks. It is the very first step in information gathering and provides a high-level blueprint of the target system or network. It is all about gathering as much information as possible—usually easy-to-obtain, readily-available-to-anyone information.

Footprinting, like everything else in hacking, follows a fairly organized path to completion. You should start with information you can gather from the "50,000-foot view"—using the target's website and web resources to collect other information on the target. For example, let's consider the term *competitive intelligence* (especially since it's a direct objective within CEH and you'll definitely see it on the exam). Competitive intelligence refers to the information gathered by a business entity about its competitor's customers, products, and marketing. Most of this information is readily available and can be acquired through a host of different means. It's not only legal for companies to pull and analyze this information, it's expected—and it's sometimes valuable to you as an ethical hacker. More than a few methods to gain competitive intelligence may be useful to you.

The company's own website is a great place to start. Think about it: what do people want on their company's website? They want to provide as much information as possible to show potential customers what they have and what they can offer. Sometimes, though, this information becomes information overload. Just some of the open source information you can pull on almost any company from its site includes company history, directory listings, current and future plans, and technical information. Directory listings become very useful in social engineering (covered in Chapter 7), and you'd probably be surprised how much technical information businesses will keep out on their sites. Designed to put customers at ease, sometimes sites inadvertently give hackers a leg up by providing details on the technical capabilities and makeup of the network.

NOTE Sometimes company websites have all sorts of internal links, providing information to employees and business partners. An easy way to map out these links for further exploration is to use Netcraft or a link extractor, from a company like iWEBTOOL or Webmaster Alpha.

Another absolute goldmine of information on a potential target is the job boards. Go to CareerBuilder.com, Monster.com, Dice.com, or any of the multitude of others out there, and you can quite literally find everything you'd want to know about the company's technical infrastructure. For example, a job listing that states "candidate must be well versed in Windows 2003 Server, MS SQL 2000, and Veritas Backup services" isn't representative of a network infrastructure made up of Linux servers. The technical job listings flat-out tell you what's on the company's network—and often-times what versions. Combine that with your already astute knowledge of vulnerabilities and attack vectors (which we covered earlier in this chapter), and you're well on your way to a successful pen test!

While we're on the subject of using websites to uncover information, don't neglect the innumerable options available to you—all of which are free and perfectly legal. Social networking sites can provide all sorts of information for you. Sites such as LinkedIn (www.linkedin.com)—where professionals build relationships with peers—can be a great place to profile for attacks later on. Facebook and Twitter are also great sources of information, especially when the company has had layoffs or other personnel problems recently—disgruntled former employees are always good for some relevant company dirt. And, just for some real fun, check out http://en.wikipedia.org/wiki/Robin_Sage to see just how powerful social networking can be for determined hackers.

Finally, two other web footprinting options are worth noting here. First, copying a website directly to your system can definitely help speed things along, and tools such as BlackWidow, Wget, and TeleportPro are all viable options. Second, information relevant to your efforts may have been posted on a site at some point in the past, but has since been updated or removed. Sites such as www.archive.org and Google Cache provide insight into information your target may have thought they'd safely gotten rid of—but as the old adage says, once posted, always available.

NOTE *Anonymous* and *pseudonymous footprinting* are two new terms making the rounds in the ethical hacking community. Anonymous footprinting refers to footprinting efforts that can't be traced back to you. Pseudonymous footprinting is closely related; however, the idea is to have any tracing efforts lead to a different person.

The list of information-gathering options in the footprinting stage is nearly impossible to complete. The fact is, there are opportunities everywhere for this kind of information gathering. Don't forget to include search engines in your efforts—you'd be surprised what you can find through a search on the company name (or variants thereof). Other competitive intelligence tools include Google Alerts, Yahoo! Site Explorer, SEO for Firefox, SpyFu, Quarkbase, and DomainTools.com (see Figure 3-3). The list, literally, goes on forever.

Figure 3-3
Easy footprinting
tools

Footprinting Example

Without giving away too much information (I'll use fake names and such where needed), I decided to see what information I could gather in less than five minutes, simply from a company website. No other searching—just the main website and the links contained within. I looked up a local business, simply by going to Google Maps and looking around. Once I found my "target," I opened their web page and started hunting around. What did I find?

I found that this company has multiple military and space program contracts and ties. I also learned they are part of a larger parent company and recently bought out one of their biggest competitors, AnyCompany, Inc., including all their assets and contracts. This included a large Linux infrastructure and probably (just guessing here) resulted in a few layoffs—Facebook and Twitter, here I come! I also know they have a major product release coming up. As far as contact information, I not only found a directory listing, with names, e-mail addresses, and desk phone numbers, but also came across this one little entry I thought was really neat: "After Hours Contact," listing the names and personal numbers for the techs.

Is any of this information dangerous? Will it, alone, result in a huge security gap for the company? And did I break any laws or ethical guidelines in obtaining it? Of course not. This is stuff they want their customers—potential and current—to know. But with this beginning, some tool usage, and a crafty mindset, I think you can see how I would already be ahead of the game in targeting this business. Had they hired me to test their systems, I'd already have this portion down and in the report.

Take some time to research these on your own. Heck, type **footprinting tool** into your favorite search engine and check out what you find (I just did and got over 141,000 results), or you can peruse the lists compiled in the back of this book. Go out and gather some information of your own on a target of your choosing, and see what kind of information matrix you can build, organizing it however you think makes the most sense to you. Remember, all these opportunities are perfectly legal (most of the time, anyway—never rely on a certification study book for legal advice), and anyone can make use of them at any time, for nearly any purpose. You've got what you need for the exam already here—now go play and develop some skill sets.

EXAM TIP   Have you ever looked at an e-mail header? You can really get some extraordinary detail out of it, and sometimes sending a bogus e-mail to the company and watching what comes back sure can help you pinpoint a future attack vector!

Footprinting with DNS

I hate getting lost. Now, I'm not saying I'm always the *calmest* driver, and that I don't complain (loudly) about circumstances and other drivers on the road, but I can honestly say nothing puts me on edge like not knowing where I'm going while driving—especially when the directions given to me don't include the road names. I'm certain you know what I'm talking about—directions that say, "Turn by the yellow sign next to the drugstore and then go down half a mile and turn right onto the road beside the walrus hide factory. You can't miss it." Inevitably I do wind up missing it, and cursing ensues.

Thankfully, negotiating the Internet isn't reliant on crazed directions. The road signs we have in place to get to our favorite haunts are all part of the Domain Naming Service (DNS), and they make navigation easy. DNS, as you're no doubt already aware, provides a name-to-IP-address (and vice versa) mapping service, allowing us to type in a name for a resource as opposed to its address. This also provides a wealth of footprinting information for the ethical hacker—so long as you know how to use it.

DNS Basics

As we established in the introduction (you *did* read it, right?), there are certain things you're just expected to know before undertaking this certification and career field, and DNS is one of them. So, no, I'm not going to spend pages of material here on DNS. But we do need to take at least a couple of minutes to go over some basics—mainly because you'll see this stuff explicitly on the CEH exam. The simplest explanation of DNS I can think of follows.

The DNS system is made up of servers all over the world. Each server holds and manages the records for its own little corner of the world, known in the DNS world as a *namespace.* Each of these records gives directions to or for a specific type of resource. Some records provide IP addresses for individual systems within your network, whereas others provide addresses for your e-mail servers. Some provide pointers to other DNS servers, which are designed to help people find what they're looking for.

 NOTE Port numbers are always important in discussing anything network-wise. When it comes to DNS, 53 is your number. Name lookups generally use UDP, whereas zone transfers use TCP.

Big, huge servers might handle a namespace as big as the top-level domain ".com," whereas another server further down the line holds all the records for "mcgraw-hill. com." The beauty of this system is that each server only has to worry about the name records for its own portion of the namespace and to know how to contact the server "above" it in the chain for the top-level namespace the client is asking about. The entire system looks like an inverted tree, and you can see how a request for a particular resource can easily be routed correctly to the appropriate server. For example, in Figure 3-4, the server for anyname.com in the third level holds and manages all the records for that namespace, so anyone looking for a resource (such as their website) could ask that server for an address.

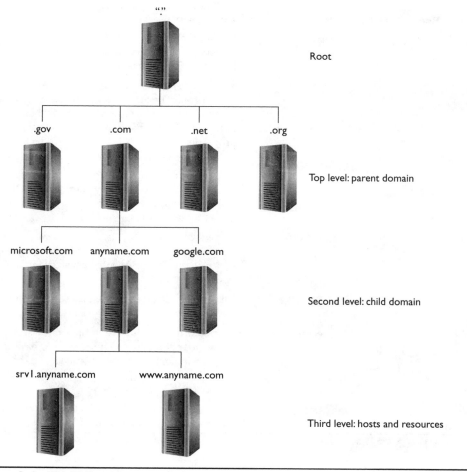

Figure 3-4 The DNS system

The only downside to this system is that the record types held within your DNS system can tell a hacker all she needs to know about your network layout. For example, do you think it might be important for an attacker to know which server in the network holds and manages all the DNS records? What about where the e-mail servers are? Heck, for that matter, wouldn't it be beneficial to know where all the public-facing websites actually reside? All this can be determined by examining the DNS record types, which I've so kindly listed in Table 3-1.

 EXAM TIP Know the DNS records well and be able to pick them out of a lineup. You will definitely see a DNS zone transfer on your exam and will be asked to identify information about the target from it.

DNS Record Type	Label	Description
SRV	Service	Defines the host name and port number of servers providing specific services, such as a Directory Services server.
SOA	Start of Authority	This record identifies the primary name server for the zone. The SOA record contains the host name of the server responsible for all DNS records within the namespace, as well as the basic properties of the domain.
PTR	Pointer	Maps an IP address to a host name (providing for reverse DNS lookups). You don't absolutely need a PTR record for every entry in your DNS namespace, but these are usually associated with e-mail server records.
NS	Name Server	This record defines the name servers within your namespace. These servers are the ones that respond to your clients' requests for name resolution.
MX	Mail Exchange	This record identifies your e-mail servers within your domain.
CNAME	Canonical Name	This record provides for domain name aliases within your zone. For example, you may have an FTP service and a web service running on the same IP address. CNAME records could be used to list both within DNS for you.
A	Address	This record maps an IP address to a host name, and is used most often for DNS lookups.

Table 3-1 DNS Record Types

These records are maintained and managed by the authoritative server for your namespace (the SOA), which shares them with your other DNS servers (name servers) so your clients can perform lookups and name resolutions. The process of replicating all these records is known as a *zone transfer*. Considering the importance of the records kept here, it's obvious administrators need to be very careful about which IP addresses are actually allowed to perform a zone transfer—if you allowed just any IP to ask for a zone transfer, you might as well post a network map on your website to save everyone the trouble. Because of this, most administrators restrict the ability to even ask for a zone transfer to a small list of name servers inside their network.

An additional note is relevant to the discussion here, even though we're not in the attacks portion of the book yet. Think for a moment about a DNS lookup for a resource on your network: Say, for instance, a person is trying to connect to your FTP server to upload some important, sensitive data. The user types in **ftp.anycomp.com** and hits ENTER. The DNS server closest to the user (defined in your TCP/IP properties) looks through its cache to see if it knows the address for ftp.anycomp.com. If it's not there, the server works its way through the DNS architecture to find the authoritative server for anycomp.com, who must have the correct IP address. This response is returned to the client and ftp-ing begins happily enough.

NOTE When it comes to DNS, it's important to remember there are two real servers in play within your system. *Name resolvers* simply answer requests. *Authoritative servers* hold the records for a given namespace, given from an administrative source, and answer accordingly.

Suppose you were an attacker, and you *really* wanted that sensitive data yourself. One way to do it might be to change the cache on the local name server to point to a bogus server instead of the real address for ftp.anycomp.com. Then the user, none the wiser, would connect and upload the documents directly to your server. This process is known as *DNS poisoning*, and one simple mitigation is to restrict the amount of time records can stay in cache before they're updated. There are loads of other ways to protect against this, which we're not going to get into here, but it does demonstrate the importance of protecting these records—and how valuable they are to an attacker.

The SOA record itself provides loads of information, from the host name of the primary server in the DNS namespace (zone) to the amount of time name servers should retain records in cache. The record itself contains the following information:

- **Source Host**   Host name of the SOA server.
- **Contact Email**   E-mail address of the person responsible for the zone file.
- **Serial Number**   Revision number of the zone file. (This increments each time the zone file changes.)
- **Refresh Time**   The amount of time a secondary DNS server will wait before asking for updates.
- **Retry Time**   The amount of time a secondary server will wait to retry if the zone transfer fails.
- **Expire time**   The maximum amount of time a secondary server will spend trying to complete a zone transfer.
- **TTL**   The minimum "time to live" for all records in the zone. (If not updated by a zone transfer, they will perish.)

I think, by now, it's fairly evident why DNS footprinting is an important skill for you to master. So now that you know a little about the DNS structure and the records kept there (be sure to review them well before your exam—you'll thank me later), it's important for us to take a look at some of the tools available for your use as an ethical hacker. This next section won't cover every tool available—and you won't be able to proclaim yourself an expert after reading it. However, we will hit on these tools throughout the remainder of this book, and you will need to know the basics for your exam.

Exercise 3-2: Demonstrating DNS Attack Results

In this exercise, we're not actually going to change DNS records on a server, or steal anything from anyone. We're going to use the *hosts* file built into Windows to demonstrate DNS lookup problems. Before the system checks its own cache or a local DNS server, it looks, by default, in a file called "hosts" for a defined entry. This exercise will show how easy it is for a target's machine to be redirected to a site they did not intend to go to (if the entries on the local name server had been changed the same way, the user would see the same results). Here are the steps to follow:

1. Open the browser of your choice and go to www.google.com. The DNS entry for this site is now in your cache. You can view it by typing **ipconfig /displaydns**. Type **ipconfig /flushdns** to clear all entries. Close your browser.

2. Use Explorer and navigate to C:\Windows\System32\drivers\etc (if you happen to be using a 64-bit version of Windows XP or 7, try C:\Windows\SysWOW64\System32\Drivers\etc).

3. Open the hosts file in Notepad. Save a copy before you begin.

4. In the hosts file, enter **209.191.122.70 www.google.com** underneath the last line in the file (the last line will show 127.0.0.1 or ::1, or both). Save the file and exit.

5. Open a new browser session and try to access www.google.com. Your browser, instead, displays Yahoo!'s search engine. Updating the hosts file provided a pointer to Yahoo!'s address, which preempted the lookup for Google.

NOTE Be sure to clear the entry you added to the hosts file. The copy you made earlier is just in case something really goes wrong, you have a backup.

DNS Footprinting Tools: whois, nslookup, and dig

In the dawn of networking time, when dinosaurs roamed outside the buildings and cars had a choice between regular and unleaded gas, setting up the DNS system required not only a hierarchical design, but someone to manage it. Put simply, someone had to be in charge of registering who owned what name, and which address range(s) went with it. For that matter, someone had to hand out the addresses in the first place.

IP address management started with a happy little group known as the IANA (Internet Assigned Numbers Authority), which finally gave way to the ICANN (Internet Corporation for Assigned Names and Numbers). ICANN manages IP address allocation and a host of other goodies. So, as companies and individuals get their IP addresses (ranges), they simultaneously need to ensure the rest of the world can find them in DNS. This is done through one of any number of domain name registrants worldwide (for example, www.networksolutions.com, www.godaddy.com, and www.register.com). Along with those registrant businesses, five Regional Internet Registries (RIRs) provide overall management of the public IP address space within a given geographic region. These five registrant bodies are:

- **ARIN (American Registry for Internet Numbers)**   North and South America as well as sub-Saharan Africa

- **APNIC (Asia-Pacific Network Information Center)**   Asia and Pacific

- **RIPE (Réseaux IP Européens) NCC**   Europe, Middle East, and parts of Central Asia/Northern Africa. If you're wondering, the name is French.

- **LACNIC (Latin America and Caribbean Network Information Center)** Latin America and the Caribbean

- **AfriNIC (African Network Information Center)**   Africa

Obviously, because these registries manage and control all the public IP space, they should represent a wealth of information for you in footprinting. Gathering information from them is as easy as visiting their sites (ARIN's is www.arin.net) and inputting a domain name. You'll get all sorts of information back, including the network's range, organization name, name server details, and origination dates.

You can also make use of a tool known as *whois*. Originally started in Unix, whois has become ubiquitous in operating systems everywhere, and has generated any number of websites set up specifically for that purpose. It queries the registries and returns all sorts of information, including domain ownership, addresses, locations, and phone numbers.

To try it out for yourself: Use your favorite search engine and look up **whois**. You'll get literally millions of hits on everything from use of the command line in Unix to websites performing the task for you. For example, the second response on my search returned www.whois.sc—a site I've used before. Open the site and type in **mcgraw-hill.com** (the site for McGraw-Hill, my publisher). Notice the administrative, technical, and registrant contact information displayed, and how nicely McGraw-Hill ensured they were listed as a business name instead of an individual—way to go, guys! Additionally, notice the three main DNS servers for the namespace listed at the bottom:

```
Domain Name......... mcgraw-hill.com
   Creation Date........ 1994-05-07
   Registration Date.... 2011-03-07
   Expiry Date.......... 2012-05-09
   Organisation Name.... The McGraw-Hill Companies, Inc.
   Organisation Address. 1221 Avenue of the Americas
   Organisation Address.
   Organisation Address. New York
   Organisation Address. 10020-1095
   Organisation Address. NY
   Organisation Address. UNITED STATES
```

```
Admin Name...........  .  .
   Admin Address....... The McGraw-Hill Companies Inc.
   Admin Address....... 148 Princeton-Hightstown Rd.
   Admin Address....... Hightstown
   Admin Address....... 08520-1450
   Admin Address....... NJ
   Admin Address....... UNITED STATES
   Admin Email......... hostmaster@mcgraw-hill.com
   Admin Phone......... +1.6094265291
   Admin Fax...........

Tech Name........... Hostmaster .
   Tech Address........ The McGraw-Hill Companies Inc.
   Tech Address........ 148 Princeton-Hightstown Rd.
   Tech Address........ Hightstown
   Tech Address........ 08520-1450
   Tech Address........ NJ
   Tech Address........ UNITED STATES
   Tech Email.......... hostmaster@mcgraw-hill.com
   Tech Phone.......... +1.6094265291
   Tech Fax.............
   Name Server......... CORP-UKC-NS1.MCGRAW-HILL.COM
   Name Server......... CORP-HTS-NS1.MCGRAW-HILL.COM
   Name Server......... CORP-55W-NS1.MCGRAW-HILL.COM
```

Other well-known websites for DNS or whois footprinting include www.geektools. com, www.dnsstuff.com, www.samspade.com (which is still listed as a potential tool for CEH purposes but is, for all intents, defunct), and www.checkdns.net. If you do a search or two on some local business domains, I'd bet large sums of cash you'll find individuals listed on many of them. Additionally, a lot of whois outputs will give you phone numbers, e-mail addresses, and all sorts of information.

 EXAM TIP You're going to need to be familiar with whois output, paying particular attention to registrants' and administrative names, contact numbers for individuals, and the DNS server names.

Another useful tool in the DNS footprinting toolset is an old standby—a command-line tool people have used since the dawn of networking: nslookup. This is a command that's part of virtually every operating system in the world, and it provides a means to query DNS servers for information. Syntax for the tool is fairly simple:

```
nslookup [-options] {hostname | [-server]}
```

The command can be run as a single instance, providing information based on the options you choose, or you can run it in interactive mode, where the command runs as a tool, awaiting input from you.

For example, on a Microsoft Windows machine, if you simply type **nslookup** at the prompt, you'll see a display showing your default DNS server and its associated IP address. From there, nslookup sits patiently, waiting for you to ask whatever you want (as an aside, this is known as *interactive mode*). Typing a question mark shows all the options and switches you have available. For example, the command

```
set query=MX
```

tells nslookup all you're looking for are records on e-mail servers. Entering a domain name after that will return the IP addresses of all the mail servers DNS knows about for that namespace.

Nslookup can also provide for something known as a *zone transfer*. As stated earlier, a zone transfer differs from a "normal" DNS request in that it pulls every record from the DNS server instead of just the one, or one type, you're looking for. To use nslookup to perform a zone transfer, first make sure you're connected to the SOA server for the zone and then try the following steps:

1. Enter **nslookup** at the command line.

2. Type **server <IPAddress>**, using the IP address of the SOA. Press ENTER.

3. Type **set type=any** and press ENTER.

4. Type **ls -d *domainname*.com**, where *domainname*.com is the name of the zone, and then press ENTER.

You'll either receive an error code, because the administrator has done her job correctly, or you'll receive a copy of the zone transfer, which looks something like this:

```
anycomp.com.          SOA hostmaster.anycomp.com (845968 11620 3600 1782000
3600)
anycomp.com.          NS      DN1234.anycomp.com
anycomp.com.          NS      DN5678.anycomp.com
anycomp.com.          A       172.16.55.12
anycomp.com.          MX      30      mailsrv.anycomp.com
mailsrv                       A       172.16.101.5
www                           A       172.16.101.10
fprtone                       A       172.16.101.15
fprttwo                       A       172.16.101.16
```

The areas in bold are of particular importance. "3600" defines the TTL for the zone. If you remember our discussion on DNS poisoning earlier, it may be helpful to know the longest a bad DNS cache can survive here is one hour (3600 seconds). Also notice the MX record saying, "The server providing our e-mail is named mailsrv.anycomp. com," followed by an A record providing its IP address. Important information for an attacker to know, wouldn't you say?

 TIP After finding the name servers for your target, type **nslookup** at the command prompt, to get into interactive mode, and then change to your target's name server (by typing **server *servername***). Performing DNS queries from a server inside the network might provide better information than relying on your own server.

Another option for viewing this information is the "dig" command utility. Native to Unix systems, but available as a download for Windows systems (along with BIND 9), dig is used to test a DNS query and report back the results. Basic syntax for the command looks like

```
dig @server name type
```

where *server* is the name or IP of the DNS name server, *name* is the name of the resource you're looking for, and *type* is the type of record you wish to pull.

There are literally dozens and dozens of switches you can add to the syntax to pull more explicit information. To see all the switches available, use the following at the command line:

```
dig -h
```

Dig output is broken into different sections, each with its own header. For discussion's sake, consider the following output (I've numbered each line for easy reference):

```
Dig @152.115.100.100 www.anycomp.com any
1  ; <<>> DIG 9.2.1 <<>> @152.115.100.100 www.anycomp.com any
2  ;; global options:  printcmd
3  ;; Got answer:
4  ;; ->>HEADER<<- opcode: QUERY, status: NOERROR, id: 41
5  ;; flags: qr aa rd ra; QUERY: 1, ANSWER: 3, AUTHORITY: 2, ADDITIONAL: 2
6  ;; QUESTION SECTION:
7  ;www.anycomp.com.              IN       ANY
8  ;; ANSWER SECTION:
9  www.anycomp.com.       86400   IN       A        207.217.96.28
10 www.anycomp.com.       86400   IN       A        207.217.96.29
11 www.anycomp.com.       86400   IN       MX       10 Mailsrv.anywhere.net.
12 ;; AUTHORITY SECTION:
13 anycomp.com.           86400   IN       NS       DNSRV2.anywhere.net.
14 anycomp.com.           86400   IN       NS       DNSRV1.anywhere.net.
15 ;; ADDITIONAL SECTION:
16 DNSRV2.anywhere.net.     151304   IN       A        207.217.77.12
17 DNSRV1.anywhere.net.     151305   IN       A        207.217.126.11
18 ;; Query time: 400 msec
19 ;; SERVER: 147.100.100.34#53(147.100.100.34)
20 ;; WHEN: Mon Dec 09 23:04:49 2002
21 ;; MSG SIZE  rcvd: 140
```

Some highlights from the output warrant attention. Line 1 displays the dig version used (9.2.1 in this case). "NOERROR" in line 4 indicates, amazingly enough, the command completed successfully with no errors. Line 6 starts the question section, and relays the query used in line 7. Line 8 starts the answer section, and displays everything found below it (lines 9–11). The "AUTHORITY" and "ADDITIONAL" sections display information on the DNS entries found during the query.

EXAM TIP You need to know the nslookup and dig syntax and output very well. Be sure you know how to get into interactive mode with nslookup and how to look for specific information once there. You'll definitely see it on your exam.

Determining Network Range

Although we've spent a lot of time in DNS footprinting so far, discovering and defining the network range is another important footprinting step to consider. Knowing where the target's IP addresses start and stop greatly limits the time you'll need to spend figuring out specifics later on. One of the easiest ways to do this—at least on a high level—is to make use of ARIN. For example, suppose you knew the IP address of a WWW server (easy enough to discover, as you just learned in the previous sections). If you simply enter that IP address in www.arin.net, the network range will be shown. As you can see in Figure 3-5, entering the IP address of www.mcgraw-hill.com gives us the entire network range. As an aside, ARIN provides a lot of other useful information as well: Figures 3-6 and 3-7 show the Administrative and Technical Point of Contact (POC) for the IP range given.

Network	
NetRange	198.45.24.0 - 198.45.24.255
CIDR	198.45.24.0/24
Name	MMSPC-9
Handle	NET-198-45-24-0-1
Parent	NETBLK-MMSPC (NET-198-45-16-0-1)
Net Type	Reassigned
Origin AS	
Organization	Macmillan/McGraw-Hill School Publishing Company (MSP)
Registration Date	1993-01-08
Last Updated	2004-08-03
Comments	
RESTful Link	http://whois.arin.net/rest/net/NET-198-45-24-0-1

Function	Point of Contact
Tech	MW1053-ARIN (MW1053-ARIN)
Tech	JGE8-ARIN (JGE8-ARIN)

See Also	Related organization's POC records.
See Also	Related delegations.

Figure 3-5 Network range from ARIN

Point of Contact	
Note	ARIN has attempted to validate the data for this POC, but has received no response from the POC since 2010-07-12
Name	Weyman , Mike
Handle	MW1053-ARIN
Company	The McGraw-Hill Companies Inc.
Street	148 Princeton-Hightstown Rd N-1
City	Hightstown
State/Province	NJ
Postal Code	08520-1450
Country	US
Registration Date	1996-03-10
Last Updated	2004-04-01
Comments	
Phone	+1-609-426-5291 (Office)
Email	mike_weyman@mcgraw-hill.com
RESTful Link	http://whois.arin.net/rest/poc/MW1053-ARIN

Figure 3-6 Administrative POC

Point of Contact	
Name	Gervasio , John
Handle	JGE8-ARIN
Company	The McGraw-Hill Companies
Street	148 princeton Hightstown Rd BLDG N1
City	Hightstown
State/Province	NJ
Postal Code	08520-1450
Country	US
Registration Date	2003-10-13
Last Updated	2011-03-08
Comments	
Phone	+1-609-426-5017 (Office)
Email	john_gervasio@mcgraw-hill.com
RESTful Link	http://whois.arin.net/rest/poc/JGE8-ARIN

Figure 3-7 Technical POC

Chapter 3: Reconnaissance: Information Gathering for the Ethical Hacker

73

Another tool available for network mapping is *traceroute*. traceroute (or tracert *hostname* on Windows systems) is a command-line tool that tracks a packet across the Internet and provides route path and transit times. It accomplishes this by using ICMP ECHO packets to report information on each "hop" (router) from the source to the destination. The TTL on each packet increments by one after each hop is hit and returns, ensuring the response comes back explicitly from that hop and returns its name and IP address. Using this, an ethical hacker can build a picture of the network. For example, consider a traceroute command output from my laptop here in Satellite Beach, Florida, to a local surf shop just down the road (names and IPs changed to protect the innocent):

```
C:\>tracert xxxxxx.com
Tracing route to xxxxxx.com [xxx.xxx.xxx.xxx] over a maximum of 30 hops:
   1     1 ms      1 ms      1 ms   192.168.1.1
   2    11 ms     13 ms      9 ms   10.194.192.1
   3     9 ms      8 ms      9 ms   ten2-3-orld28-ear1.noc.bhn.net [72.31.195.24]
   4     9 ms     10 ms     38 ms   97.69.193.12
   5    14 ms     17 ms     15 ms   97.69.194.140
   6    25 ms     13 ms     14 ms   aels0-orld71-cbr1.noc.bhn.net [72.31.194.8]
   7    19 ms     21 ms     42 ms   72-31-220-0.net.bhntampa.com [72.31.220.0]
   8    37 ms     23 ms     21 ms   72-31-208-1.net.bhntampa.com [72.31.208.1]
   9    23 ms     22 ms     27 ms   72-31-220-11.net.bhntampa.com [72.31.220.11]
  10    19 ms     19 ms     19 ms   66.192.139.41
  11    20 ms     27 ms     20 ms   orl1-ar3-xe-0-0-0-0.us.twtelecom.net [66.192.243
.186]
  12     *         *         *      Request timed out.
  13    21 ms     27 ms     31 ms   ssl7.cniweb.net [xxx.xxx.xxx.xxx]
Trace complete
```

A veritable cornucopia of information is displayed here. Notice, though, the entry in line 12, showing timeouts instead of information you're used to seeing. This indicates, usually, a firewall that does not respond to ICMP requests—useful information in its own right. Granted, it's sometimes just a router that ditches all ICMP requests, or even a properly configured layer 3 switch, but it's still interesting knowledge (we'll get into firewall hacking later on in the book). To test this, a packet capture device will show the packets as Type 11, Code 0 (TTL Expired) or Type 3, Code 13 (Administratively Blocked).

 EXAM TIP There can be significant differences in traceroute from a Windows machine to a Linux box. Windows uses the command tracert, whereas Linux uses traceroute. Also keep in mind that Windows is ICMP only, whereas Linux can use other options (UDP and TCP).

All this information can easily be used to build a pretty comprehensive map of the network between my house and the local surf shop down the road on A1A. As a matter of fact, large numbers of tools save you the time and trouble of writing down and building the map yourself. These tools take the information from traceroute and build images, showing not only the IPs and their layout, but also the geographic locations you can find them at. McAfee's Visual Trace (NeoTrace to some) is one such example; others include Trout and VisualRoute. Most of these tools have trial versions available for download. Take the plunge and try them out—you'll probably be amazed at the locations where your favorite sites are actually housed!

Google Hacking

When I was a child, a research paper for school actually meant going to a library and opening (gulp!) *books*. In today's information-driven society, that's almost a thing of the past. Now my children can simply open a search engine and type in whatever they're looking for. No more racing through the card catalog, flipping through encyclopedias and stacking up 20 books on a table to go through: that paper on major exports from European nations or the feeding habits of the three-toed sloth is only a click away. And while most of us know that already, what you may not know is, just by manipulating that search string a little bit, you can turn a search engine into a fairly powerful footprinting and hacking tool.

This very useful tactic in footprinting a target was popularized mainly in late 2004 by a guy named Johnny Long. Mr. Long was part of an IT security team at his job, and while performing pen tests and ethical hacking, he started paying attention to how the search strings worked in Google. See, the search engine has always had additional operators that were designed to allow you to fine-tune your search string. What Mr. Long did was simply apply that logic for a more nefarious purpose.

Suppose, for example, instead of just looking for a web page on boat repair or searching for an image of a cartoon cat, you decided to tell the search engine, "Hey, do you think you can look for any systems that are using Remote Desktop Web Connection?" Or how about, "Can you please show me any MySQL history pages, so I can try and lift a password or two?" Amazingly enough, search engines can do just that for you, and more. The term this practice has become known by is *Google hacking*.

Google hacking involves manipulating a search string with additional specific operators to search for vulnerabilities. Advanced operators for Google hack search strings are listed in Table 3-2.

Innumerable websites are available to help you with Google hack strings. For example, from the Google Hacking Database (a site operated by Mr. Johnny Long and Hackers for Charity, http://www.hackersforcharity.org/ghdb/), try this string from wherever you are right now:

```
allinurl:tsweb/default.htm
```

Basically we're telling Google to go look for web pages that have TSWEB in the URL (indicating a remote access connection page), and we only want to see those that are running the default HTML page (default installs are common in a host of different areas, and usually make things a lot easier for an attacker). I think you may be surprised by the results—I even saw one page where an admin had edited the text to include the logon information.

Operator	Syntax	Description
cache	**cache:**URL [string]	Searches through Google's cache for information on a specific site (version) or for returns on a specific word or phrase (optional string). For example, the following will display Google's cache version of the page: `cache:www.mcgraw-hill.com`
filetype	**filetype:**type	Searches only for files of a specific type (DOC, XLS, and so on). For example, the following would return all Microsoft Word documents: `filetype:doc`
index of	**index of** /string	Displays pages with directory browsing enabled, usually used with another operator. For example, the following will display pages that show directory listings containing "passwd": `"intitle:index of" passwd`
intitle	**intitle:**string	Searches for pages that contain the string in the title. For example, the following will return pages with the word "login" in the title: `intitle: login` For multiple string searches, you can use the allintitle operator. Here's an example: `allintitle:login password`
inurl	**inurl:**string	Displays pages with the string in the URL. For example, the following would display all pages with the word "passwd" in the URL itself: `inurl:passwd` For multiple string searches, use allinurl. Here's an example: `allinurl:etc passwd`
link	**link:**string	Displays linked pages based on a search term.
related	**related:**webpagename	Shows web pages similar to webpagename.
site	**site:**domain or web page string	Displays pages for a specific website or domain holding the search term. For example, the following would display all pages with the text "passwds" in the site anywhere.com: `site:anywhere.com passwds`

Table 3-2 Google Search String Operators

NOTE Google hacking is such a broad topic it's impossible to cover all of it in one section of a single book. This link, among others, provides a great list to work through: http://it.toolbox.com/blogs/managing-infosec/google-hacking-master-list-28302. Take advantage of any of the websites available and learn more as you go along. What you'll need exam-wise is to know the operators and how to use them.

As you can see, Google hacking can be used for a wide range of purposes. For example, you can find free music downloads (pirating music is a no-no, by the way, so don't do it):

```
"intitle:index of" nameofsong.mp3
```

You can also discover open vulnerabilities on a network. For example, the following provides any page holding the results of a vulnerability scan using Nessus (interesting to read, wouldn't you say?):

```
"intitle:Nessus Scan Report" "This file was generated by Nessus"
```

Combine these with the advanced operators, and you can *really* dig down into some interesting stuff. Again, none of these search strings and "hacks" are illegal—you can search for anything you want (assuming, of course, you're not searching for illegal content—again, don't take your legal advice from a certification study book). However, actually exploiting them without prior consent will definitely land you in hot water.

Google Dorks

The success of Google hacking depends on a lot of things, but the most important is simply the ignorance of administrators and users who set up various web-facing sites and appliances. And before you get all upset with me, please keep in mind I use the term *ignorance* as it was *originally* intended—not a measure of intelligence, but simply a lack of knowledge on a particular subject. I, for instance, am ignorant about the electrical wiring on a boat. I still think I'm a fairly sharp guy, I just don't know anything about it—no one has ever taught me.

In the world of Google hacking, attackers rely on administrators and users simply not knowing what they're presenting to the outside world. For example, do a quick web search on **default passwords**. You'll see that if a person installs a Linksys WRT45G wireless router and accepts the defaults, the administration page could be accessed by using the default password (user ID "admin"; password blank). Would that necessarily indicate the user, who's never been trained in router setup, or even networking at all, was less intelligent than anyone else? No, of course not. It does indicate, though, that this person has never been told about it and probably has no idea what is being shown to the world.

Google hackers refer to people who ignorantly provide this type of information or access over the Internet as "Google dorks." I don't know that I actually agree with that, because I tend to see people as either informed or ignorant, not intelligent or dumb (or "dorky" for that matter). Hopefully the ethical hacking community does as well. If not, your pen test presentation to your very first customer, if he or she is made to feel stupid due to a blaring security vulnerability found by a simple web search, will probably be your last.

Other Tips and Tools

Finally, no chapter on footprinting would be complete without covering a few additional tools and tips we haven't touched on yet. And some of them really require no technical skills at all. For example, how much information might you gain simply by asking people for it? In the world of hacking, social engineering is probably as productive, if not more so, as any other measure. Don't believe me? Just take a look at the statistics on hacking and read your newspapers. Most attacks occur simply because someone responded to an e-mail or gave up their information over the phone.

NOTE Even though all the methods we've discussed so far are freely available publicly, and you're not breaking any laws, I'm *not* encouraging you to footprint or gauge the security of any local business or target. As ethical hackers, you should get proper permission up front, and even passively footprinting a business can lead to some hurt feelings and a lot of red tape. Again, always remain ethical in your work.

I daresay if you picked a local business and tried to footprint it, you would get just as much information by talking to the employees as you would combing through their website and digging up whois information. It's frankly amazing how much information people are willing to part with just because you're a nice guy, or the emotionally upset customer with a problem, or the IT guy trying to help them out. We'll delve much more into social engineering later in the book. Just keep in mind, while you're footprinting a network, not to forget the people working there—they may very well make your job a lot easier than it should be!

Other options to help in footprinting are things like e-mail tracking and web spiders. E-mail tracking applications range from easy, built-in efforts on the part of your e-mail application provider (such as a read receipt and the like within Microsoft Outlook) to external apps and efforts (from places such as www.emailtrackerpro.com and www.mailtracking.com). Simply appending ".mailtracking.com" to the end of an e-mail address can provide a host of information about where the e-mail travels and how it gets there.

Exercise 3-3: Using MailTracker to Footprint E-mail

In this exercise, we'll simulate using an e-mail-tracking program (mailtracker.com) to footprint information via e-mail. Follow these steps:

1. Got to www.mailtracker.com and register for an account. (Note: You may want to create an e-mail account on a free provider somewhere to use for this test.)

2. Log in to www.mailtracker.com after registering. The screen should show no e-mails to track.

3. Open your email application and send an e-mail to a friend, appending **.mailtracker.com** to the end of the address (for example, sending to matt@matt.com would look like matt@matt.com.mailtracker.com).

4. Go back to mailtracker.com and click the Refresh Display button at the top. The e-mail you sent should appear in the list. After it is opened, you can click the e-mail and review header information and details of its path to the recipient.

Web spiders are applications that crawl through a website, reporting back information on what they find. Most search engines rely on web spidering to provide the information they need in responding to web searches. However, this benign use can be used by a crafty ethical hacker. As mentioned earlier, using sites such as www.news.netcraft.com and www.webmaster-a.com/link-extractor-internal.php can help you map out internal web pages and other links you may not notice immediately—and even those the company doesn't realize are still available. One way web administrators can help to defend against standard webcrawlers is to use "robots.txt" files at the root of their site, but many sites remain open to spidering.

Two other tools of note in any discussion on social engineering and general footprinting are Maltego (which you can purchase) and SEF (Social Engineering Framework). Maltego (www.paterva.com/web5/) is "an open source intelligence and forensics application" designed explicitly to demonstrate social engineering (and other) weaknesses for your environment. SEF (http://spl0it.org/projects/sef.html) has some great tools that can automate things such as extracting e-mail addresses out of websites and general preparation for social engineering. SEF also has ties into Metasploit payloads for easy phishing attacks.

Regardless of which methods you choose to employ, footprinting is probably the most important phase of hacking you'll need to master. Spending time in this step drastically increases the odds of success later on, and is well worth the effort. Just maintain an organized approach and document what you discover. And don't be afraid to go off script—sometimes following the steps laid out by the book isn't the best option. Keep your eyes, ears, and mind open. You'll be surprised what you can find out.

Chapter Review

Vulnerability research, although not necessarily a footprinting effort, per se, is an important part of your job as an ethical hacker. Research should include looking for the latest exploit news, any zero-day outbreaks in viruses and malware, and what recommendations are being made to deal with them. Some tools available to help in this regard are the National Vulnerability Database (nvd.nist.gov), Securitytracker (www.securitytracker.com), Hackerstorm Vulnerability Database Tool (www.hackerstrom.com), and SecurityFocus (www.securityfocus.com).

Footprinting is defined as the process of gathering information on computer systems and networks. It is the very first step in information gathering and provides a high-level blueprint of the target system or network. Footprinting follows a logical flow—investigating web resources and competitive intelligence, mapping out network ranges, mining whois and DNS, and finishing up with social engineering, e-mail tracking, and Google hacking.

Competitive intelligence refers to the information gathered by a business entity about their competitors' customers, products, and marketing. Most of this information is readily available and is perfectly legal for you to pursue and acquire. Competitive intelligence tools include Google Alerts, Yahoo! Site Explorer, SEO for Firefox, SpyFu, Quarkbase, and DomainTools.com.

The DNS system provides ample opportunity for footprinting. DNS is made up of servers all over the world, with each server holding and managing records for its own namespace. DNS lookups generally use UDP port 53, whereas zone transfers use TCP 53. Each of these records gives directions to or for a specific type of resource. DNS records are:

- **SRV (Service)**   Defines the host name and port number of servers providing specific services, such as a Directory Services server.
- **SOA (Start of Authority)**   Identifies the primary name server for the zone. The SOA record contains the host name of the server responsible for all DNS records within the namespace, as well as the basic properties of the domain.
- **PTR (Pointer)**   Maps an IP address to a host name (providing for reverse DNS lookups).
- **NS (Name Server)**   Defines the name servers within your namespace.
- **MX (Mail Exchange)**   Identifies the e-mail servers within your domain.
- **CNAME (Canonical Name)**   Provides for domain name aliases within your zone.
- **A (Address)**   Maps an IP address to a host name, and is used most often for DNS lookups.

The SOA record itself provides information on Source Host (hostname of the SOA server), Contact E-mail (e-mail address of the person responsible for the zone file), Serial Number (revision number of the zone file), Refresh Time (the number of seconds a secondary DNS server will wait before asking for updates), Retry Time (the number of seconds a secondary server will wait to retry if the zone transfer fails), Expire Time (the maximum number of seconds a secondary server will spend trying to complete a zone transfer), and TTL (the minimum time to live for all records in the zone).

IP address management started with the IANA (Internet Assigned Numbers Authority), which finally gave way to the ICANN (Internet Corporation for Assigned Names and Numbers). ICANN manages IP address allocation, and any number of domain name registrants worldwide assist with DNS registry. Along with those registrant businesses are five Regional Internet Registries (RIRs) that provide overall management of the public IP address space within a given geographic region:

- **ARIN (American Registry for Internet Numbers)** North and South America as well as sub-Saharan Africa
- **APNIC (Asia-Pacific Network Information Centre)** Asia and Pacific
- **RIPE (Réseaux IP Européens)** Europe, Middle East, and parts of Central Asia/Northern Africa
- **LACNIC (Latin America and Caribbean Network Information Center)** Latin America and the Caribbean
- **AfriNIC (African Network Information Center)** Africa

Gathering information from them is as easy as visiting their site (ARIN's is www. arin.net) and inputting a domain name.

DNS information for footprinting can also be garnered through the use of whois. Whois originally started in Unix and has generated any number of websites set up specifically for its purpose. It queries the registries and returns all sorts of information, including domain ownership, addresses, locations, and phone numbers. Well-known websites for DNS or whois footprinting include www.geektools.com, www.dnsstuff.com, and www.samspade.com.

Nslookup is a command that's part of virtually every operating system in the world, and provides a means to query DNS servers for information. Syntax for the tool is as follows:

```
nslookup [-options] {hostname | [-server]}
```

The command can be run as a single instance, providing information based on the options you choose, or you can run it in interactive mode, where the command runs as a tool, awaiting input from you. Nslookup can also provide for a zone transfer, using ls -d. A zone transfer differs from a "normal" DNS request in that it pulls every record from the DNS server instead of just the one, or one type, you're looking for.

Native to Unix systems, but available as a download for Windows systems (along with BIND 9), dig is another tool used to test a DNS query and report back the results. Basic syntax for the command is

```
dig @server name type
```

where server is the name or IP of the DNS name server, name is the name of the resource you're looking for, and type is the type of record you wish to pull.

Determining network range is another important footprinting task for the ethical hacker. If you simply enter an IP address in www.arin.net, the network range will be shown. Additionally, traceroute (or tracert hostname on windows systems) is a command-line tool that tracks a packet across the Internet and provides route path and transit times. McAfee's Visual Trace (NeoTrace to some), Trout, and VisualRoute are all examples of applications that use this information to build a visual map, showing geographical locations as well as technical data.

Don't forget the use of the search engine in footprinting! Google hacking refers to manipulating a search string with additional specific operators to search for vulnerabilities. Operators for Google hacking are:

- **cache:** Syntax: cache:URL [string]. This searches through Google's cache for information on a specific site (version) or for returns on a specific word or phrase (optional string).

- **filetype:** Syntax: filetype:type. This searches only for files of a specific type (DOC, XLS, and so on).

- **index of:** Syntax: index of /string. This displays pages with directory browsing enabled, usually used with another operator.

- **intitle:** Syntax: intitle:string. This searches for pages that contain a string in the title. For multiple string searches, use the allintitle operator (allintitle:login password, for example).

- **inurl:** Syntax: inurl:string. This displays pages with a string in the URL. For multiple string searches, use allinurl (allinurl:etc/passwd, for example).

- **link:** Syntax: link:string. This displays linked pages based on a search term.

- **site:** Syntax: site:domain_or_web_ page string. This displays pages for a specific website or domain holding the search term.

Social engineering, e-mail tracking, and web spidering are also footprinting tools and techniques. Social engineering involves low- to no-tech hacking, relying on human interaction to gather information (phishing e-mails, phone calls, and so on). E-mail trackers are applications used to track data on e-mail whereabouts and trails. Web spiders are used to crawl sites for information, but can be stopped by adding "robots.txt" to the root of the website.

Questions

1. You've been hired to test security for a business headquartered in Venezuela. Which regional registry would be the best place to go for network range determination?

   A. APNIC

   B. RIPE

   C. ARISK

   D. ARIN

2. While footprinting a network, you successfully perform a zone transfer. Which DNS record in the zone transfer indicates the company's e-mail server?

   A. MX

   B. EM

   C. SOA

   D. PTR

3. Which footprinting tool uses ICMP to provide information on pathways between sender and recipient?

   A. whois

   B. EDGAR

   C. NMAP

   D. traceroute

4. An SOA record gathered from a zone transfer is shown here:

   ```
   @   IN   SOA      DNSRV1.anycomp.com.   postmaster.anycomp.com. (
                          4                ; serial number
                          3600             ; refresh    [1h]
                          600              ; retry      [10m]
                          86400            ; expire     [1d]
                          3600 )           ; min TTL    [1h]
   ```

   What is the name of the authoritative DNS server for the domain, and how often will secondary servers check in for updates?

   A. DNSRV1.anycomp.com, 3600 seconds

   B. DNSRV1.anycomp.com, 600 seconds

   C. DNSRV1.anycomp.com, 4 seconds

   D. postmaster.anycomp.com, 600 seconds

5. You are footprinting DNS information using dig. What command syntax should be used to discover all mail servers listed by DNS server 199.55.77.66 in the anycomp.com namespace?

   A. dig @www.anycomp.com MX 199.55.77.66

   B. dig MX @www.anycomp.com 199.55.77.66

   C. dig MX @199.55.77.66 www.anycomp.com

   D. dig @199.55.77.66 www.anycomp.com MX

6. Which footprinting tool or technique can be used to find names and addresses of employees or technical points of contact?

   A. whois

   B. nslookup

    C. dig

    D. traceroute

7. Which Google hack would display all pages that have the phrase "SQL" and "Version" in their titles?

    A. inurl:SQL inurl:version

    B. allinurl:SQL version

    C. intitle:SQL inurl:version

    D. allintitle:SQL version

8. Which of the following is *not* a footprinting tool?

    A. nmap

    B. traceroute

    C. nslookup

    D. dig

9. Which DNS record type maps an IP address to a host name, and is used most often for DNS lookups?

    A. NS

    B. MX

    C. A

    D. SOA

10. You have an FTP service and an HTTP site on a single server. Which DNS record allows you to alias both services to the same record (IP address)?

    A. NS

    B. SOA

    C. CNAME

    D. PTR

Answers

1. **D.** ARIN is the correct registry for the North/South American region.

2. **A.** MX records define a server as an e-mail server. An associated A record will define the name-to-IP for the server.

3. **D.** traceroute sends an ICMP Echo Request packet with a single hop count (TTL) to the first hop. The ICMP Echo reply provides information back to traceroute. Then the next ICMP packet goes out with TTL of 2. The process repeats until the destination is reached.

4. **B.** The SOA always starts defining the authoritative server—in this case DNSRV1—followed by e-mail contact and a host of other entries. Retry time defines the interval in which secondary servers will wait to check in for updates—in this case, 600 seconds.

5. **D.** Dig syntax is dig *@server name type* (where server is the name or IP of the DNS name server, name is the name of the resource you're looking for, and type is the type of record you wish to pull). In this case, the server IP is 199.55.77.66, the resource is www.anycomp.com, and the type is MX.

6. **A.** Whois provides information on the domain registration, including technical and business POCs' addresses and emails.

7. **D.** The Google search operator allintitle allows for the combination of strings in the title. The operator inurl only looks in the URL of the site.

8. **A.** Nmap is a scanning and enumeration tool. All others listed are footprinting tools.

9. **C.** "A" records provide IP-address-to-name mappings.

10. **C.** CNAME records provide for aliases within the zone.

Scanning and Enumeration

In this chapter you will learn about

- Describing the CEH scanning methodology, scan types, and the objectives of scanning
- Describing the use of various scanning and enumeration tools
- Describing scan types, such as ping sweep, SYN, Stealth, XMAS, NULL, and many more
- Describing TCP communication (three-way handshake and flag types)
- Understanding OS fingerprinting through banner grabbing
- Listing scanning countermeasures
- Understanding enumeration and its techniques
- Describing NULL sessions and its countermeasures
- Describing SNMP enumeration and their countermeasures
- Describing the steps involved in performing enumeration

If this were a movie instead of a book, we'd be watching our hero begin a career in ethical hacking instead of reading about how to do it ourselves. Deciding to become a hacker (maybe this would be during the opening credits), he'd spend the first few scenes researching vulnerabilities and keeping track of the latest news—checking in on websites and playing around with tools in his secret lab. Very soon thereafter, he would get his first break and sign a written contract allowing him to test a client—a client holding a secret that could change the very fabric of modern society (this *is* a movie, after all).

Before we're even halfway through the buttered popcorn, he has completed some footprinting work and has tons of information on potential targets. Some of it seems harmless enough, while some is so bizarre he's not even sure what it is. He leans in, looking at the multitude of monitors all around him (while foreboding music leads us all to the edge of our seats). The camera zooms in for a close-up, showing his eyes widening in wonder. The crescendo of music hits as he says, "OK...so what do I do *now?*"

Welcome to Chapter 4, where you learn what to do with all those targets you identified in the last chapter. You know how to footprint your client; now it's time to learn how to dig around what you found for relevant, salient information. As somewhat of an interesting side note here (and a brief glimpse into the "real" world of pen testing versus exam study), it's important for you to consider which targets are worth scanning and which aren't. If you know some targets are easy, don't risk discovery by scanning them. If you know an army of nerds is arrayed against you, maybe social engineering is a better option. In any case, scanning can be viewed as a necessary evil, but needs to be approached with caution and respect.

When it comes to your CEH study, which is what all this is supposed to be about, you'll need to stick with the flow and move through the steps as designed. So, after footprinting, you'll need to scan for basics—the equivalent of knocking on all your neighbors' doors to see who is home and what they look like. Then, when you find a machine up and about, you'll need to get to know it really well, asking some rather personal questions—but don't worry, systems don't get upset. We'll go over all you'll need to know for the exam regarding scanning and enumeration, and play with some pretty fun tools along the way.

Scanning for Targets

Our first step after footprinting a target is to get started with scanning. While in the footprinting stage, we were gathering all sorts of information; with scanning, however, we're talking about a much more focused effort. In short, *scanning* is the process of discovering systems on the network and taking a look at what open ports and applications may be running. With footprinting, we wanted to know how big the network was and some general information about its makeup; in scanning, we'll actually go into the network and start touching each device—to find out more about it.

When it comes to scanning, there are three major types—network scanning, port scanning, and vulnerability scanning—as well as a basic set of steps for the ethical hacker to follow. It's important to remember, though, that just as the steps of the overall hacking process can blend into one another, these steps are simply a general guideline and are not a hard-and-fast set of rules to follow. When you're out on the job, situations and circumstances will occur that might force you to change the order of things. Sometimes the process of completing one step will seamlessly blend directly into another. Don't fret—just go with the flow and get your job done. The steps for a scanning methodology are:

1. *Identify live systems.* Something as simple as a ping can provide this. This gives you a list of what's actually alive on your network subnet.

2. *Discover open ports.* Once you know which IP addresses are active, find what ports they're listening on.

3. *Identify the OS and services.* Banner grabbing and OS fingerprinting will tell you what operating system is on the machines and which services they are running.

4. *Scan for vulnerabilities.* Perform a more focused look at the vulnerabilities these machines haven't been patched for yet.

Identifying Active Machines

In your first step after footprinting, you'll want to find out which IP addresses are actually "alive." The simplest and easiest way to do this is to take advantage of a protocol that's buried in the stack of every TCP/IP-enabled device on the planet—ICMP (Internet Control Message Protocol). As I'm sure you're already aware, IP is what's known as a connectionless, "fire and forget" protocol. It creates a packet by taking data and appending a header, which holds bunches of information, including a "From" and "To" address, and allows the sender to fire packets away without regard, as quickly as the stack on the machine will allow. This is done by relying on other layer protocols for transport, error correction, and so on.

However, some shortfalls needed to be addressed at the network layer. IP itself has no error messaging function, so ICMP was created to provide for it. It allows for error messaging at the network layer, and presents the information back to the sender in one of several ICMP types. Table 4-1 lists some of the more relevant message type codes. The most common of these are Type 8 (Echo Request) and Type 0 (Echo Reply). An ICMP Type 8 packet received by a host tells the recipient, "Hey! I'm sending you a few packets. When you get them, reply back with the same number so I know you're there." The recipient will respond with an ICMP Type 0, stating, "Sure, I'm alive. Here are the data packets you just sent me as proof!"

ICMP message types you'll need to know for your exam are listed in Table 4-1. Because ICMP is built into each TCP/IP device, and the associated responses provide detailed information about the recipient host, it makes a good place to start when network scanning. For example, consider an Echo Request (Type 8) sent to a host that returns a Type 3. The code could tell us whether the host is down (Code 7), the network route is missing or corrupt in our local route tables (Type 0), or a filtering device, such as a firewall, is preventing ICMP messages altogether (Type 13).

This process, called a *ping,* has been part of networking since its inception, and combining pings to each and every address within a subnet range is known as a *ping sweep.* A ping sweep is the easiest method available to identify active machines on the network; just keep in mind it's not necessarily the only, or even best, way to do it. Although ICMP is a part of every TCP/IP stack, it's not always enabled. As a matter of fact, many administrators will disable ping responses on many network systems and devices, and will configure firewalls to block them.

ICMP Message Type	Description and Important Codes
0: Echo Reply	Answer to a Type 8 Echo Request
3: Destination Unreachable	Error message indicating the host or network cannot be reached. Codes: 0—Destination network unreachable 1—Destination host unreachable 6—Network unknown 7—Host unknown 9—Network administratively prohibited 10—Host administratively prohibited 13—Communication administratively prohibited
4: Source Quench	A congestion control message
5: Redirect	Sent when there are two or more gateways available for the sender to use, and the best route available to the destination is not the configured default gateway. Codes: 0—Redirect datagram for the network 1—Redirect datagram for the host
8: ECHO Request	A ping message, requesting an Echo reply
11: Time Exceeded	The packet took too long to be routed to the destination (Code 0 is TTL expired).

Table 4-1   Relevant ICMP Message Types

 EXAM TIP   Know ICMP very, very well. Pay particular attention to Type 3 messages and the associated codes, especially Code 13, which lets you know a poorly configured firewall is preventing the delivery of ICMP packets.

Additionally, not only will a great many devices not respond to the ping, the actual ping sweep itself is very noisy and the systems will alert anyone and everyone as to what's going on. Network intrusion detection systems (NIDS) and host-based IDS (HIDS) will both easily and readily pick up on a ping sweep. With this in mind, be very cautious and deliberate with your sweep—slow and random are your friends here. Remember, hacking isn't a race, it's a test of will, patience, and preparation.

In addition to the ping command on its own, several applications will provide a ping sweep for you. Angry IP Scanner is one of the more prevalent tools available (just be careful with it, because a lot of antivirus programs consider it a virus). Some other tools of note include, but are not limited to, Pinger, WS_Ping, SuperScan, and Friendly Pinger. Sample use of a ping sweep tool is covered in Exercise 4-1.

A Wolf in Ping's Clothing

When you send a ping, the actual payload of the packet itself can range greatly in value amount. The Request for Comment (RFC) that created and still governs ping never got around to identifying what data is supposed to go into the payload, so it's usually just enough ASCII code to build the packet up to sufficient length. This was by design, to allow traffic experts to test and monitor how the network would respond to varying packet lengths and such.

Unfortunately, just like other great inventions and applications on the network, it can be hijacked and used for illicit purposes. The payload of an ICMP packet could wind up being the perfect covert channel for hackers to communicate with each other, using the payload area to simply embed messages. Most people—even security types—wouldn't even bother with a ping packet or two crossing their paths, never knowing what information was being funneled away right beneath their noses.

There are a few Intrusion Detection System (IDS) signatures that do look for this. For example, a lot of ping utilities designed to take advantage of this have default signatures that any decent IDS can pick up on; in nmap, a "0 byte field" can trigger it, for example. Windows and other operating systems have specific defaults that are supposed to be found in the packet, and their alteration or omission can also trigger a hit. But none of this changes the fact that it's still a cool hack.

Exercise 4-1: Using a Ping Sweep Tool

A couple of notes are necessary before you begin this exercise. First, for some odd reason, Angry IP Scanner is considered a virus by many antivirus (AV) programs out there. To be safe, you should create a folder explicitly for your hack tools and exclude it from your AV scans and auto-protect (or kill the AV protection on your test machine altogether). Second, Angry IP Scanner is bound by the connection limitations of the machine on which you run it. Most laptop or desktop Windows XP or Windows 7 machines will only allow 10 concurrent sessions. Therefore, you'll only be able to run a sweep on 10 IPs at a time. For this exercise, I'm assuming you are on a home network set with the default 192.168.1.x /24 subnet. Simply adjust the IP range if your particular subnet differs.

Here are the steps to follow:

1. Install Angry IP Scanner by simply copying the executable to a folder location on your system.

2. Double-click the ipscan executable. You may see several additional screens, such as the one shown in Figure 4-1, identifying issues and providing tips. Click Yes to view information and/or continue.

Figure 4-1
Angry IP Scanner
installation
information window

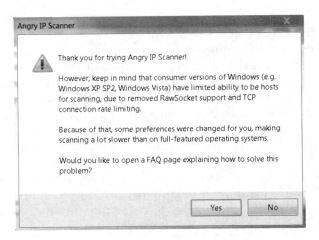

3. Within the main window, set the IP range to your network specification. Angry IP Scanner should automatically default to the correct IP range and subnet mask for you, but you can change the range if you wish.

4. Click the Select Fetchers icon just to the right of the Start button (see Figure 4-2).

5. Add all available fetchers by selecting them in the right column and clicking the double arrows in the center to move them over to the left column. When you're done, click OK.

6. Click the Start button. Angry IP Scanner will display the results in column format. Double-click any live system for more details (see Figure 4-3).

One last quick note on scanning for active machines before we move forward: Remember that at the opening of this section I mentioned that the scanning steps may bleed into one another? As I mentioned earlier, identifying active machines on the network using a ping sweep is not the only method available. Sometimes it's just as easy to combine the search for active machines with a port scan—especially if you're trying to be sneaky about it.

 NOTE If you want to be legitimately sneaky, there are tons of methods available. Check out the details here for a fun option: www.aldeid.com/index.php/Tor/Usage/Nmap-scan-through-tor.

Figure 4-2
The Fetchers icon

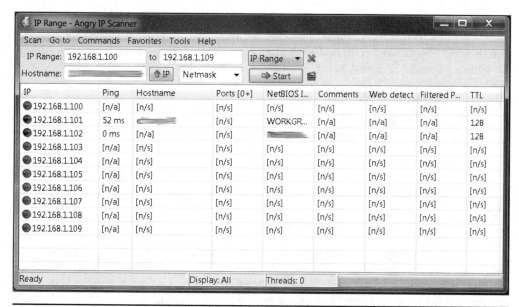

Figure 4-3 Ping sweep results

Port Scanning

Remember all that time you spent in Networking 101, or some other class with a silly name, learning the basics of computing? Remember the OSI Reference Model and all those steps computers take to talk to one another? And remember how you thought at the time, "Why are we bothering with this? When are we going to get to real networking?" Well, congratulations, this is where all that time and effort pays off. Very quickly, let's take a walk down memory lane, for reminder's sake, so we can fully understand our next topic—port scanning.

As you'll recall, when a recipient system gets a *frame*, it checks the physical address to see who the message is intended for. If the address is indeed correct, it opens the frame, checks to make sure it's valid, and ditches the header and trailer, passing the remainder up to the network layer. There, the layer 3 address is verified in the *packet* header, along with a few other assorted goodies, and the header is stripped off. The remaining PDU, now called a *segment*, is passed on to layer 4. At the transport layer, a whole host of important stuff happens—end-to-end delivery, segment order, reliability, and flow control are all layer 4 functions—including the salient issue in our discussion here: port numbering.

Why the heck do we even need port numbers in networking? Well, consider where we are at right now in this communications process. The recipient has verified the frame and packet belongs to it, and knows it has a segment available for processing. But how is it supposed to know which application-layer entity is supposed to process it? Maybe it's an FTP datagram. Or maybe a Telnet request. Or maybe even e-mail. Without *something* to identify which upper-layer protocol to hand this information to, the system sits there like a government mid-level manager, paralyzed by indecision.

A port number, inside the transport-layer protocol header (TCP or UDP), identifies which upper-layer protocol should receive the information contained within. Systems use them to identify to recipients what they're trying to accomplish. The port numbers range from 0 to 65,535 and are split into three different groups:

- **Well-known**: 0–1023
- **Registered**: 1024–49151
- **Dynamic**: 49152–65535

NOTE Ever wonder why port numbers go from 0 to 65,535? If you've ever taken a Cisco class and learned any binary math, the answer is rather evident: The field in which you'll find a port number is 16 bits long. Sixteen bits give you 65,536 different combinations, from 0 all the way up to 65,535.

Of particular importance to you on the CEH exam are the well-known port numbers. No, you don't need to memorize all 1,024 of them, but you do need to know a good many of them. The ports listed in Table 4-2 are absolutes—you simply must memorize them, or quit reading and studying for your exam here.

Port scanning is the method by which systems on a network are queried to see which ports they are listening to. Assuming you know which well-known port number is associated with which upper-layer protocol, you can tell an awful lot about what a system is running just by knocking on the port doors to see what is open. A system is said to be listening for a port when it has that port open.

For example, assume you have a server hosting a website and an FTP service. When the server receives a message, it needs to know which application is going to handle the message. At the same time, the client that made the request needs to open a port on which to hold the conversation (anything above 1023 will work). Figure 4-4 demonstrates how this is accomplished—the server keeps track of which application to use via the port number in the destination port field of the header, and answers to the source port number.

Port Number	Protocol	Transport Protocol	Port Number	Protocol	Transport Protocol
20/21	FTP	TCP	110	POP3	TCP
22	SSH	TCP	135	RPC	TCP
23	Telnet	TCP	137–139	NetBIOS	TCP and UDP
25	SMTP	TCP	143	IMAP	TCP
53	DNS	TCP and UDP	161/162	SNMP	UDP
67	DHCP	UDP	389	LDAP	TCP and UDP
69	TFTP	UDP	443	HTTPS	TCP
80	HTTP	TCP	445	SMB	TCP

Table 4-2 Important Port Numbers

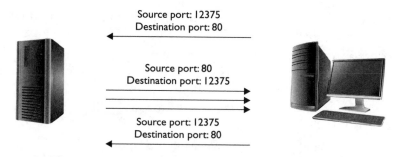

Figure 4-4 Port numbers in use

Exercise 4-2: Examining Open Ports

This exercise is designed simply to show you the open ports you have on your Windows machine right now. If you're using something other than a Windows machine, open one up in a VM or borrow one from your friend. Many tools are available for this, but we'll stick with just two—CurrPorts and Fport. Here are the steps to follow:

1. Download and install CurrPorts
    (http://currports.softlate.com/?gclid=CI23uYCBwqgCFYjsKgodgEs7vQ).
    It's a stand-alone executable, so ignore any of the additional add-on offers
    and just download the application.

2. Navigate to the folder Currports installed in and double-click the CurrPorts
    icon to launch the program. The CurrPorts window opens and runs
    immediately, displaying all ports on your machine (see Figure 4-5).

Process Na... /	Proces...	Protocol	Local Port	Local Por...	Local Address	Remote ...	Remote ...
AppleMobileD...	1380	TCP	27015		127.0.0.1		
AppleMobileD...	1380	TCP	27015		127.0.0.1	1585	
AppleMobileD...	1380	UDP	55997		127.0.0.1		
AppleMobileD...	1380	UDP	55998		127.0.0.1		
cvpnd.exe	1592	TCP	62514		127.0.0.1		
cvpnd.exe	1592	UDP	62514		127.0.0.1		
firefox.exe	5092	TCP	1594		192.168.1.103	443	https
firefox.exe	5092	TCP	1597		192.168.1.103	443	https
firefox.exe	5092	TCP	1598		192.168.1.103	80	http
firefox.exe	5092	TCP	1599		192.168.1.103	80	http
firefox.exe	5092	TCP	1600		192.168.1.103	80	http
firefox.exe	5092	TCP	1601		192.168.1.103	80	http
firefox.exe	5092	TCP	1602		192.168.1.103	80	http
firefox.exe	5092	TCP	1603		192.168.1.103	80	http
firefox.exe	5092	TCP	1611		192.168.1.103	80	http
firefox.exe	5092	TCP	11537		127.0.0.1	11538	
firefox.exe	5092	TCP	11538		127.0.0.1	11537	

59 Total Ports, 9 Remote Connections, 1 Selected   NirSoft Freeware. http://www.nirsoft.n

Figure 4-5 CurrPorts screen

3. Select a port and go to File | Properties. Note the process ID, port number, and other information listed. Close the Properties window.

4. To close a suspicious connection, select the offender and choose File | Close Selected TCP Connections, or File | Kill Processes of Selected Ports. (Note: Be careful you don't close something that's actually valuable and legitimate!)

5. Download and install Fport (the download is a ZIP file—simply extract it in the C:\ drive).

6. Open a command prompt and navigate to C:\fport\.

7. Type **fport.exe**. The running processes and ports will be shown, much like this:

```
C:\>fport
FPort v2.0 - TCP/IP Process to Port Mapper
Pid Process Port Proto Path
392 svchost -> 135 TCP C:\WINNT\system32\svchost.exe
8 System -> 139 TCP
8 System -> 445 TCP
508 MSTask -> 1025 TCP C:\WINNT\system32\MSTask.exe
392 svchost -> 135 UDP C:\WINNT\system32\svchost.exe
8 System -> 137 UDP
8 System -> 138 UDP
8 System -> 445 UDP
224 lsass -> 500 UDP C:\WINNT\system32\lsass.exe
212 services -> 1026 UDP C:\WINNT\system32\services.exe
```

Switches are available with Fport to sort by port, application, PID, or process.

So, now that we know what ports are, how they're used, and why it's so important to scan for them on our target subnet, the question becomes, "How do we do it?" The answer is, of course, by using several different methods and with several different tools. We can't possibly cover them all here, but we'll definitely spend some time on those you'll see most often on your exam. Regardless, all port scanners work by manipulating transport layer protocol flags in order to identify active hosts and scan their ports. So, in order to learn about port scanners and how they get their job done, we first need to cover what a TCP flag is and how the communications process works.

TCP and UDP Communication

When two TCP/IP-enabled hosts communicate with each other, as you no doubt already know, two methods of data transfer are available at the transport layer: connectionless and connection-oriented. Connectionless communication is fairly simple to understand: The sender doesn't care whether the recipient has the bandwidth (at the moment) to accept the message, nor does the sender really seem to care whether the recipient gets the message at all. Connectionless communication is "fire and forget." In a much faster way of sending datagrams, the sender can simply fire as many segments as it wants out to the world, relying on other upper-layer protocols to handle any problems. This, obviously, comes with some disadvantages as well (no error correction, re-transmission, and so on).

At the transport layer, connectionless communication is accomplished with UDP. UDP, as you can tell from the segment structure shown in Figure 4-6, is a low-overhead, very simple, and very fast transport protocol. Generally speaking, the application protocols that make use of this transport method are moving very small amounts of data (sometimes just a single packet or two), and usually are moving them inside a network structure (not across the Internet). Examples of protocols making use of UDP are TFTP, DNS, and DHCP.

 NOTE Although it's true TFTP can be used to move a fairly significant amount of data, it's usually almost always used inside a single network segment—thus greatly reducing the opportunity for packet loss. DNS and DHCP use UDP because most of their communication consists of single packets.

Connection-oriented communication using TCP, although a lot slower than connectionless, is a much more orderly form of data exchange and makes a lot more sense for transporting large files or communicating across network boundaries. Senders will reach out to recipients, before data is ever even sent, to find out if they're available and if they'd be willing to set up a data channel. Once data exchange begins, the two systems continue to talk with one another, making sure flow control is accomplished, so the recipient isn't overwhelmed and can find a nice way to ask for retransmissions in case something gets lost along the way. How does all this get accomplished? Through the use of header flags, and something known as the three-way handshake. Figure 4-7 shows the TCP segment structure.

Figure 4-6
UDP segment
structure

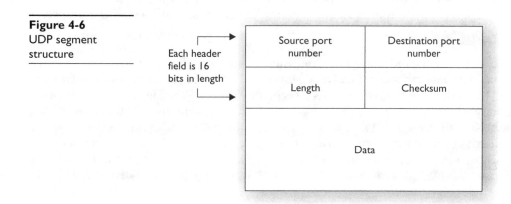

Figure 4-7
TCP segment
structure

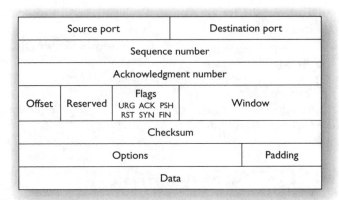

Taking a look at Figure 4-7, you can see that six flags can be set in the TCP header. Depending on what the segment is intended to do, some or all of these flags may be put into use. The TCP header flags are:

- **URG (Urgent)**   When this flag is set, it indicates the data inside is being sent out of band.

- **ACK (Acknowledgment)**   This flag is set as an acknowledgment to SYN flags. This flag is set on all segments after the initial SYN flag.

- **PSH (Push)**   This flag forces delivery of data without concern for any buffering.

- **RST (Reset)**   This flag forces a termination of communications (in both directions).

- **SYN (Synchronize)**   This flag is set during initial communication establishment. It indicates negotiation of parameters and sequence numbers.

- **FIN (Finish)**   This flag signifies an ordered close to communications.

To fully understand these flags and their usage, consider what happens during a normal TCP data exchange. First, a session must be established between the two systems. To do this, the sender forwards a segment with the SYN flag set, indicating a desire to synchronize a communications session. This segment also contains a sequence number—a theoretically random number that helps maintain the legitimacy and uniqueness of this session. As an aside, the generation of these numbers isn't necessarily all that random after all, and plenty of attack examples point that out. For study purposes, though, just remember what the sequence number is and what its purpose is.

EXAM TIP Know the TCP flags and the three-way handshake very, very well. You'll definitely be asked questions on what flags are set at different points in the process, what responses a system provides given a particular flag receipt, and what the sequence numbers look like during a data exchange.

When the recipient gets this segment, it responds with the SYN and ACK flags set, and acknowledges the sequence number by incrementing it by one. Additionally, the return segment contains a sequence number generated by the recipient. All this tells the sender, "Yes, I acknowledge your request to communicate and will agree to synchronize with you. I see your sequence number and acknowledge it by incrementing it. Please use my sequence number in further communications with me so I can keep track of what we're doing." The three-way handshake is illustrated in Figure 4-8.

When this segment is received by the original sender, it generates one more segment to finish off the synchronization. In this segment, the ACK flag is set, and the recipient's own sequence number is acknowledged. At the end of this three-way handshake, a communications channel is opened, sequence numbers are established on both ends, and data transfer can begin.

Lastly, there are two other fields of great importance while we're on the subject. The source and destination port fields, in TCP or UDP communication, define the protocols that will be used to process the data. Better stated, they actually define a channel on which to work, and that channel has been generally agreed upon by default to support a specific protocol, but you get the point.

Knowing the TCP flags and the communications setup process, I think it's fairly obvious how a hacker (with a tool capable of crafting segments and manipulating flags) could manipulate, disrupt, manufacture, and even hijack communications between two systems. Now that you know a little more about this process, we can focus on how to put it all into use. For now we're concentrating on port scanning and how manipulating TCP flags can assist us, and that's where nmap comes into play.

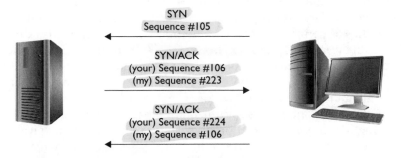

Figure 4-8 The three-way handshake

nmap

Without a doubt, the most widely used scanning and enumeration tool on the planet is *nmap*, so you'll need to be very familiar with it for the exam. nmap can perform many different types of scans (from simply identifying active machines to port scanning and enumeration) and can also be configured to control the speed at which a scan operates—in general, the slower the scan, the less likely you are to be discovered. It comes in both a command-line version and a GUI version (now known as Zenmap), works on multiple OS platforms, and can even scan over TCP and UDP. And the best thing of all? It's free.

nmap syntax is fairly straightforward:

```
nmap <scan options> <target>
```

The target for nmap can be a single IP address, multiple individual IPs separated by spaces, or an entire subnet range (using CIDR notation). For example, to scan a single IP, the command might look like

```
nmap 192.168.1.100
```

whereas scanning multiple IPs would look like

```
nmap 192.168.1.100 192.168.1.101
```

and scanning an entire subnet would appear as

```
nmap 192.168.1.0/24
```

Starting nmap without any of the options runs a "regular" scan and provides all sorts of information for you. But to get really sneaky and act like a true ethical hacker, you'll need to learn the option switches—and there are a bunch of them. Table 4-3 lists some of the more relevant nmap switches you'll need to know.

As you can see, quite a few option switches are available for the command. The "s" commands determine the type of scan to perform, the "P" commands set up ping sweep options, and the "o" commands deal with output. The "T" commands deal with speed and stealth, with the serial methods taking the longest amount of time. Parallel methods are much faster because they run multiple scans simultaneously. Again, the slower you run scans, the less likely you are to be discovered. The choice of which one to run is yours. For a full and complete rundown of every switch and option, visit nmap's man page, or check with the originator's documentation page at http://nmap.org/docs.html.

Combining option switches can produce specific output on any given target. For example's sake, suppose you wanted to run a SYN port scan on a target as quietly as possible. The syntax would look something like this:

```
nmap 192.168.1.0/24 -sS -T0
```

If you wanted an aggressive XMAS scan, perhaps the following might be to your liking:

```
nmap 192.168.1.0/24 -sX -T Aggressive
```

nmap Switch	Description	nmap Switch	Description
-sA	ACK scan	-PI	ICMP ping
-sF	FIN scan	-Po	No ping
-sI	IDLE scan	-PS	SYN ping
-sL	DNS scan (a.k.a. List scan)	-PT	TCP ping
-sN	NULL scan	-oN	Normal output
-sO	Protocol scan	-oX	XML output
-sP	Ping scan	-T paranoid or -T0	Serial, slowest scan
-sR	RPC scan	-T sneaky or -T1	Serial, slow scan
-sS	SYN scan	-T polite or -T2	Serial, normal speed scan
-sT	TCP Connect scan	-T normal or -T3	Parallel, normal speed scan
-sW	Windows scan	-T aggressive or -T4	Parallel, fast scan
-sX	XMAS tree scan	-T Sneaky	Parallel, fastest scan

Table 4-3   nmap Switches

The combinations are literally endless and provide worlds of opportunity for your port-scanning efforts.

EXAM TIP   It is literally impossible for me to stress enough how well you need to know nmap. You will be asked tricky questions on syntax, scan types, and responses you'd expect from open and closed ports. The list goes on. Please do not rely solely on this writing, or any other, for your study. Download the tool. Play with it. Use it. It may very well mean the difference between passing and failing your exam.

Deciding which options to set really comes down to which type of scan you're wanting to run. A scan type will be defined by three things: what flags are set in the packets before delivery, what responses you expect from ports, and how stealthily the scan works. Generally speaking, there are seven generic scan types for port scanning:

- **TCP Connect**   Runs through a full connection (three-way handshake) on all ports. Easiest to detect, but possibly the most reliable. Open ports will respond with a SYN/ACK, closed ports with a RST/ACK.

- **SYN**   Known as a "half-open scan." Only SYN packets are sent to ports (no completion of the three-way handshake ever takes place). Responses from ports are the same as they are for a TCP Connect scan.

- **FIN**   Almost the reverse of the SYN scan. FIN scans run the communications setup in reverse, sending a packet with the FIN flag set. Closed ports will respond with RST, whereas open ports won't respond at all.

- **XMAS** A Christmas scan is so named because the packet is sent with multiple flags (FIN, URG, and PSH) set. Port responses are the same as with a FIN scan.

- **ACK** Used mainly for Unix/Linux-based systems. ACK scans make use of ICMP destination unreachable messages to determine what ports may be open on a firewall.

- **IDLE** Uses a spoofed IP address to elicit port responses during a scan. Designed for stealth, this scan uses a SYN flag and monitors responses as with a SYN scan.

- **NULL** Almost the opposite of the XMAS scan. The NULL scan sends packets with no flags set. Responses will vary, depending on the OS and version, but NULL scans are designed for Unix/Linux machines.

Table 4-4 will help greatly in your study efforts for the exam. You'll be asked repeatedly on the exam about a scan type and what response to expect from an open or closed port. A quick-and-easy tip to remember is that all scans return an RST on a closed port, with the exception of the ACK scan, which returns no response.

nmap handles all these scans, using the switches identified earlier, and more. In addition to those listed, nmap offers a "Windows" scan. It works much like the ACK scan but is intended for use on Windows networks, and provides all sorts of information on open ports. Many more switches and options are available for the tool. Again, although it's a good bet to study the information presented here, you absolutely need to download and play with the nmap tool to be successful on the exam and in your career.

Scan Type	Initial Flags Set	Open Port Response	Closed Port Response	Notes
Full (TCP Connect)	SYN	SYN/ACK	RST	Noisiest but most reliable
Half Open (Stealth or SYN Scan)	SYN	SYN/ACK	RST	No completion of three-way handshake. Designed for stealth but may be picked up on IDS sensors
XMAS	FIN/URG/PSH	No response	RST/ACK	Doesn't work on Windows machines
FIN	FIN	No response	RST/ACK	Doesn't work on Windows machines
NULL	No flags set	No response	RST/ACK	Doesn't work on Windows machines
ACK	ACK	RST	No response	Used in firewall filter tests

Table 4-4 Network Scan Types

A Fine Line

All our actions to this point have been beyond reproach—we know without a doubt they're legal because the information you gather in footprinting is open and available to anyone. Port scanning, though, is one of those gray areas in the virtual world. Is knocking on every port to see what's open and available the same thing as documenting everything I can find on the Internet about my target company? In 2000, a security consultant named Scott Moulton found himself in a very sticky situation involving a port scan, and wound up setting a precedent on the whole matter.

While testing security on the systems he was under contract for (the county's 911 call center), his port scan wound up touching a county-owned website and walking its firewall. His activities were quickly discovered and he was asked to stop scanning immediately—which he did. The county, however, filed a police report on the "suspicious activity" and on a web server owned by another business entity. His activities were reported as suspicious behavior, and the contractor lost his job and contract. Several weeks later, the Georgia Bureau of Investigation actually arrested him.

Mr. Moulton filed a countersuit, accusing the company of making false and defamatory criminal allegations against him. In deciding the case, the federal judge assigned to the case ruled, among other things, that this port scan did not constitute a crime: "The tests run by Plaintiff Moulton did not grant him access to Defendant's network. The public data stored on Defendant's network was never in jeopardy." In short, because the port scan itself did no damage and did not actually put the data at risk, there was no crime.

A benchmark case in the matter, this ruling generally established that port scanning is not a crime (with one *huge* caveat: The ruling was not given in a Circuit Court of Appeals and, therefore, is not a blanket precedent everywhere in the U.S.). However, use caution in your scanning. A denial-of-service attack *is* considered a crime, and depending on the effect of your scan on a particular network segment or device, you could be charged anyway. A good rule of thumb, especially because you're an ethical hacker, is simply to do your absolute best to avoid scanning anything you don't already have permission to touch. That way, you won't have to worry about crossing this very fine line.

NOTE Port sweeping and enumeration on a machine is also known as fingerprinting, although the term is normally associated with examining the OS itself. You can fingerprint operating systems with tools we've discussed already, along with goodies such as SolarWinds, Queso, and an old favorite, Cheops. Also, tools such as Netcraft and HTTrack are useful for fingerprinting web servers specifically.

Knowing how to read nmap output is just as important is learning the syntax of the command itself. The GUI version of the tool, Zenmap, makes reading this output very easy; however, the good news is the command-line output is just as simple. Additionally, the output is available via several methods. The default is called interactive, and it is sent to standard output (text sent to the terminal). Normal output displays less runtime information and warnings because it is expected to be analyzed after the scan completes rather than interactively. You can also send output as XML (which can be parsed by graphical user interfaces or imported into databases) or in a "greppable" format (for easy searching). A very brief example is displayed in Figure 4-9. Ports are displayed in output as open, closed, or filtered. Open is obvious, as is closed. Filtered means an FW or router is interfering with the scan.

Although nmap is the unquestioned leader of the port scanning pack, other tools are available that can also get the job done. SuperScan, available as a free download (evaluation) from McAfee, is another easy-to-use GUI-based program. It works well and provides several options from an intuitive front-end interface, providing for ping sweeps and port scans against individual systems or entire subnets. SuperScan's interface is shown in Figure 4-10.

hping is another very powerful tool for both ping sweeps and port scans (among other things). hping works on Windows and Linux versions, can act as a packet builder, and runs nearly any scan nmap can put out. The only real downside, for people like me who prefer pictures and clicking things, is that it's still a command-line-only tool. Just

```
Administrator: C:\Windows\system32\cmd.exe

C:\>nmap 192.168.1.101

Starting Nmap 5.21 ( http://nmap.org ) at 2011-01-26 20:41 Eastern Standard Time

Nmap scan report for 192.168.1.101
Host is up (0.026s latency).
Not shown: 991 closed ports
PORT        STATE SERVICE
135/tcp     open  msrpc
139/tcp     open  netbios-ssn
445/tcp     open  microsoft-ds
49152/tcp open  unknown
49153/tcp open  unknown
49154/tcp open  unknown
49155/tcp open  unknown
49156/tcp open  unknown
49157/tcp open  unknown
MAC Address: 1C:65:9D:18:E1:D4 (Unknown)

Nmap done: 1 IP address (1 host up) scanned in 2.36 seconds

C:\>_
```

Figure 4-9   nmap output

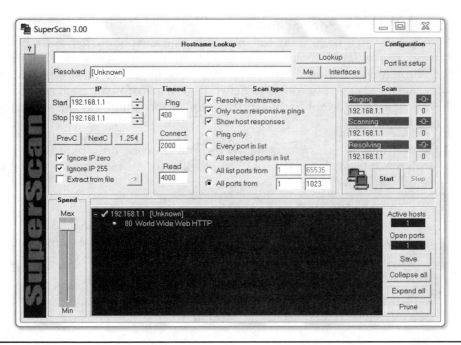

Figure 4-10 SuperScan

as with nmap, hping3 has specific syntax for what you're trying to accomplish, with tons of switches and options. For example, a simple ping sweep can be accomplished by typing in **hping3 -1 *IPaddress*.** Here are some other hping3 syntax examples of note:

- **Ping sweep**   hping3 –1 *IPaddress*
- **SYN scan**   hping3 –8 *IPaddress*
- **ACK scan**   hping3 –A *IPaddress*
- **XMAS scan**   hping3 –F –P -U *IPaddress*
- **UDP scan**   hping3 –2 *IPaddress*

NOTE   hping3 is much, much more than just a scanner. We cover it here because you may see it listed as such on the exam; however, hping3 is a serious packet manipulator as well.

Exercise 4-2: Using Port Scanning

For this exercise, you'll be running nmap against your own home network—however that network is set up. I'm using 192.168.1.0/24 as the subnet, because it is by far the most common private address range you'll find on home networks. You may need to adjust the range and targets to your own network—just adjust as you need and the steps will flow fine. Document your findings after each step and compare them—you may be surprised what you find!

1. To determine which systems are live on your network, run a ping sweep with nmap using the code here ("sP" provides for the ping, and "v" sets it to verbose mode):

   ```
   nmap -sP -v 192.168.1.0/24
   ```

2. To ensure we hit every device—because some may be blocking ICMP requests—try a TCP sweep. (Note: nmap uses port 80 on TCP scans by default. If you'd like to try a different protocol number, it follows the –PT switch.)

   ```
   nmap -PT 192.168.1.0/24
   ```

3. Port-scan one of your targets using a SYN scan. (Use any IP address you discover. "100" is used here as an example.)

   ```
   nmap -sS 192.168.1.100
   ```

   Note: A return of "filtered" indicates the system is protected by a firewall.

4. Attempt a UDP scan on the host ("port unreachable" indicates a closed port):

   ```
   nmap -sU 192.168.1.100
   ```

5. Try to fingerprint an operating system on the host:

   ```
   nmap -sS -O 192.168.1.100
   ```

6. Run a TCP full Connect scan on a host, outputting the results to a file called results.txt:

   ```
   nmap -sT -oN results.txt 192.168.1.100
   ```

Regardless whether your choice is running nmap on a Linux machine, harnessing command-line option power like a pro, or the simplicity of using SuperScan's GUI interface on a Windows machine, the goal is the same. Port scanning identifies which ports are open, and gives you more information in building your attack vectors. Each scan type you attempt will react differently and take different lengths of time to pull off (a UDP scan of Linux machines can take a *very* long time, for instance), and you'll definitely need to know the output to look for with each one. However, the tools are all designed to achieve the same overall end.

Other Scanning Tips and Tools

Scanning for ethical hacking isn't just using port scanners and identifying what's open on computer systems. A couple of other methods that may not immediately come to mind can help you build your ethical hacking case. (Unless, of course, you're an '80s movie buff and know exactly what I mean when I say, in a computerized voice, "Would you like to play a game?")

In 1983, a movie about a teenage hacker infiltrating the highest levels of our nation's defenses was released. *War Games* had the young (and very unethical, I might add) hacker break in to a system designed to control nuclear missile deployment. The system was covered by a multitude of security controls, but its designers had left one overlooked option open to the world, which the young man easily discovered—it was ready to answer the phone.

War dialing is a process by which an attacker dials a set of phone numbers specifically looking for an open modem. As you know, modems are designed to answer the call, and can easily provide back-door access to a system otherwise completely secured from attack. Although it's true there aren't as many modems in place anymore as there were in 1983, you'd be surprised how many are still in use as "emergency backup" for network administrators' remote access. A hacker finding one of these has to plan for a few minutes of gleeful dancing celebration before continuing with the attack.

 EXAM TIP   Tools for accomplishing war dialing are ToneLoc, THC-Scan, WarVOX (designed explicitly for VoIP systems), PAWS, and TeleSweep.

In addition to modems, another attack vector you can search for during scanning is wireless access points. *War driving* used to refer to, quite literally, driving around in a car looking for open access points. In the ethical hacking realm, it still indicates a search for open WAPs; however, the car may not be so necessary. With the proliferation of handheld devices making use of 802.11 wireless standards, finding access points is as easy as simply wandering around the facility. Additionally, several tools are available to help you not only in discovering wireless entry points, but in finding vulnerabilities in wireless networking. Silica, AirMagnet, and AirCheck (Fluke) are all tools on handheld devices that allow an attacker to walk around and gather—and sometimes even exploit—wireless access point vulnerabilities. We'll get into wireless hacking tools in Chapter 10.

One final thought on scanning—whether you're port scanning, war dialing, or searching for wireless openings, stealth is important. Hiding your activities from prying security-professional eyes is something you'll need to prepare for and master in each step of the hacking phases, and may be essential in scanning. Sometimes scanning can be interrupted by pesky firewalls or monitoring devices, and you'll be forced to disguise who you are and what you're up to. Options for accomplishing this include proxies, spoofing an IP address, tunneling, hiding files, and using source routing or an anonymizer.

A *proxy* is nothing more than a system you set up to act as an intermediary between you and your targets. In many instances, proxies are used by network administrators to control traffic and provide additional security for internal users. Hackers, though, can use that technology in reverse—sending commands and requests to the proxy, and letting the proxy relay them to the targets. Anyone monitoring the subnet sees the proxy trying all this naughtiness—not the hacker.

Proxying can be done from a single location or spread across multiple proxies, to further disguise the original source. Hundreds of free, public proxies are available to sign up for, and a simple Internet search will point you in the right direction. If you want to set up proxy chains, where multiple proxies further hide your activities, you can use tools such as ProxyChains (http://proxychains.sourceforge.net/), Soft-Cab's Proxy Chain Builder (www.softcab.com/proxychain/index.php), and Proxifier (www.proxifier.com).

Another great method for anonymity on the Web is The Onion Routing (Tor). Tor basically works by installing a small client on the machine, which then gets a list of other clients running Tor from a directory server. The client then bounces Internet requests across random Tor clients to the destination, with the destination end having very little means to trace the original request back. Communication between Tor clients is encrypted, with only the last leg in the journey—between the Tor "cloud" and the destination—sent unencrypted. One really important thing to keep in mind, though, is that *anyone* can be a Tor endpoint, so signing up to voluntarily have goodness-knows-what passing through your machine may not be in your best interests.

Spoofing an IP address is exactly what it sounds like—the hacker uses a packet-crafting tool of some sort to obscure the source IP address of packets sent from his machine. Many tools are available for this—hping, Scapy, or Komodia, for example. You can also find this functionality built into a variety of other scanning tools. Ettercap and Cain, usually thought of more for their sniffing capabilities, provide robust and powerful spoofing capabilities as well—heck, even nmap can spoof if you really want it to. Just be cautious in spoofing—sometimes you can spoof so well the information you're working so hard to obtain never finds its way back to you.

 EXAM TIP Remember, spoofing an IP address means any data coming back to the fake address will not be seen by the attacker. For example, if you spoof an IP address and then perform a TCP scan, the information won't make its way back to you.

Source routing provides yet another means to disguise your identity on a network. It was originally designed to allow applications to specify the route a packet takes to a destination, regardless of what the route tables between the two systems says. It's also beneficial to network managers in forcing traffic around areas of potential congestion. How is this useful to a hacker? The attacker can use an IP address of another machine on the subnet and have all the return traffic sent back, regardless of which routers are in transit. Protections against source-routing attacks are prevalent and effective, not to mention most firewalls and routers detect and block source-routed packets, so this may not be your best option.

Another ridiculously easy method for disguising your identity, at least for port 80 (HTTP) traffic, is to use an anonymizer. *Anonymizers* are services on the Internet that make use of a web proxy to hide your identity. Thousands of anonymizers are available—simply do a Google search and you'll see what I mean. Be careful in your choice, though—some of them aren't necessarily safe, and their owners are set up specifically to steal information and plant malware. I've personally used Anonymouse.org before and, other than annoying ads in the corner, have had no issues. Also, plenty of pay sites are available—just use common sense.

 EXAM TIP Ways to disguise your identity are built into a lot of tools and will be covered in more detail throughout the rest of this book. What you need to know about these methods for your exam are examples of tools that can accomplish the task and what each method means.

Whereas footprinting leads us to gather readily available information that provides a high-level view of the target, scanning is the next step along the path. In scanning, you're knocking on virtual doors to see who is home and what they're doing. We haven't gone inside yet, and we're certainly planning on doing so, but we still need to dig for some more information. Good hackers will spend 90 to 95 percent of their time gathering information for an attack. Let's continue on that path.

Enumeration

In its basic definition, to *enumerate* means to specify individually, to count off or name one by one. Enumeration in the ethical hacking world is just that—listing off the items we find within a specific target. If ports are doors and windows, and port scanning can be equated to knocking on them to see if they are open, enumerating is more akin to chatting with the neighbor at the door. When we enumerate a target, we're moving from passive information-gathering to a much more active state. No longer satisfied with just knowing which ports are open, we now want to find things like open shares and any easy-to-grab user account information. We can use a variety of tools and techniques, and a lot of it bleeds over from scanning. Before we get fully involved in enumerating, though, it's helpful to understand the security design of your target.

Windows Security Basics

Hands down the most popular operating system in the world is Microsoft Windows. Everything from old Windows 2000 to Windows 7 systems will constitute the vast majority of your targets out in the real world. Taking some time to learn some of the basics of its design and security features will pay dividends in the future.

Obviously enumeration can and should be performed on every system you find in your target network, regardless of operating system. However, because Windows machines will undoubtedly make up the majority of your targets, we need to spend a little more time on them. As a family of operating systems, Windows provides a wide range of targets, ranging from the ridiculously easy to the fairly hardened machines. Windows 2000 machines are still roaming around out there, and present an easy target, whereas Windows 2003 Server and Windows 7 up the ante quite a bit. Regardless of version, there are a few things that remain constant despite the passage of time. Some of this you may already know, and some of it you may not, but all of it is important to your future.

Everything in a Windows system runs within the context of an account. An account can be that of a user, running in something called user mode, or the system account, which runs in kernel mode. Actions and applications running in user mode are easy to detect and contain. Those running in kernel mode, though, can be hidden and run with absolute authority. Knowing this, a hacker must attempt to get code running in kernel mode as often as possible.

Only the Strong Survive

Almost every hacking course or lecture I've attended always winds up with a subset of the attendees asking, "Why did he spend all that time on *fill-in-the-old-operating-system* machines? Sure, we can hack those, but I thought he'd be showing us how to hack *fill-in-the-new-operating-system* machines." And I'm fairly sure there are a few of you out there thinking this already. Trust me, though, there's a method to the madness.

To illustrate this, imagine you're a bank thief casing your next victim. There are two banks right here in our little town, right across the street from each other. One has been around for a few decades, the other was just recently built. Without knowing anything else about the two banks, which one do you suppose might present more of an opportunity for you? Which one might have some complacency in its security staff? Which one is more likely to have older locks and vaults to deal with? Which one might have some routines you might be able to monitor and take advantage of? Unless you're trying to make a name for yourself as the greatest bank robber in the world, it's the older place every time.

When you're searching for information on a network to pen test, you're not looking for the latest and greatest. The idea is to find an opening that's worth trying. A machine, device, or setting that maybe got overlooked along the way is where I want to spend my time—not endlessly knocking at personal firewalls and trying to find a code break in some obscure Windows subroutine. No one in her right mind is going to try to steal gold out of Fort Knox—it's too well protected and a pointless site to spend time on. Gold that's stored under Mr. Johnson's mattress just down the road? Now we're talkin'.

Lions on the savannah don't choose prey with strong defenses. They go after targets they know they can take down with little effort and time. Be selective in your targets and don't worry so much about getting your name in the paper for breaking into the most recent OS release. Only the strong survive, so spend your time looking for the weak.

This is not to say that there are only two means of security control when it comes to accounts—quite the contrary, as I'm sure some of you were already running off to your MCSE books and pointing out the difference between rights and permissions and their effect on accounts. User rights are granted via an account's membership within a group and determine which system tasks an account is allowed to perform. Permissions are used to determine which resources an account has access to. The method by which Windows keeps track of which account holds what rights and permissions comes down to SIDs and RIDs.

A *Security Identifier* (SID) identifies user, group, and computer accounts and follows a specific format. A *Resource Identifier* (RID) is a portion of the overall SID identifying a specific user, computer, or domain. SIDs are composed of an 'S,' followed by a revision number, an authority value, a domain or computer indicator, and an RID. The RID portion of the identifier starts at 500 for the administrator account. The next account on the system, Guest, is RID 501. All users created for the system start at 1000 and increment from that point forward—even if their usernames are re-created later on. For example's sake, consider the following SID:

S-1-5-21-3874928736-367528774-1298337465-**500**

We know this is an administrator account because of the 500 at the end. An SID of S-1-5-22-3984762567-8273651772-8976228637-**1014** would be the account of the 14th person on the system (the 1014 tells us that).

 NOTE Linux uses a User ID (UID) and a Group ID (GID) in much the same way as Windows uses SIDs and RIDs. On a Linux machine, these can be found in the /etc/passwd file.

Another interesting facet of Windows security architecture you'll need to know as basic information involves passwords and accounts. As you know, a user ID and a password are typed in by users attempting to log in to Windows. These accounts are identified by their SIDs (and associated RIDs), of course, but the passwords for them must be stored somewhere, too. In Windows, that somewhere is C:\Windows\System 32\Config\SAM. The SAM database holds (in encrypted format, of course) all the local passwords for accounts on the machine. For those machines that are part of a domain, the passwords are stored and handled by the domain controller. We'll definitely get into cracking and using the SAM later on.

This section isn't necessarily a discussion of enumeration steps in and of itself, but it does cover some basics you'll definitely need to know moving forward. It doesn't do me any good to teach you enumeration steps if you don't really know what you're looking for. And now that we do have the basics down, let's get to work.

Enumeration Techniques

One enumeration/hacking technique that has been addressed with Windows XP and Windows 7 (and the couple of dozen Vista machines still running out there) is setting up a null session to take advantage of Windows underlying communication protocols. A null session occurs when you log in to a system with no user ID and password at all. In older Windows versions (2000), a null session could be set up using the net command, as follows:

```
net use \\<target>\IPC$ "" /u:""
```

Null sessions require TCP ports 135, 137, 139, and 445 to work, and have been virtually eliminated from the hacking arsenal since Windows XP was released.

Although many Windows XP and 7 machines have updated registry keys to prevent null sessions and the enumerations they provide, I guarantee you'll find more than a few vulnerable machines on the target network. Some tools that make use of the null session are SuperScan, User2SID, and SID2User. SuperScan is a great choice, due to its ease of use and the easy-to-read interface. After opening the tool, choose the Windows Enumeration tab, input the target name or IP address, and—voilà—one simple click and the users, shares, and other NetBIOS information on the target is on full display (see Figure 4-11).

User2SID and SID2User are also very valuable tools in your arsenal, allowing you to enumerate the SID given the user name, or the user name given the SID. For the sake of this discussion, if your target's security staff has changed the name of the administrator account on the machine, these two tools can save the day. From our discussion earlier regarding SIDs on Windows machines, we know the Administrator account on the machine ends in 500. Therefore, you can use User2SID to discover the SID for the usernames found in your enumeration.

Banner grabbing is one of the easiest enumerating methods. Basically the tactic involves sending an unsolicited request to an open port to see what, if any, default message (banner) is returned. Depending on what version of the application is running on the port, the returned banner (which could be an error message, HTTP header, or login message) can indicate a potential vulnerability for the hacker to exploit. A common method of performing banner grabbing is to use a simple tool already built into most operating systems—Telnet.

As we know already, Telnet runs on port 23. Therefore, if you simply type **telnet** **<IPaddress>** you'll send TCP packets to the recipient with the destination port set to 23. However, you can also point it at any other port number explicitly to test for connectivity. If the port is open, you'll generate some form of banner response. For exam-

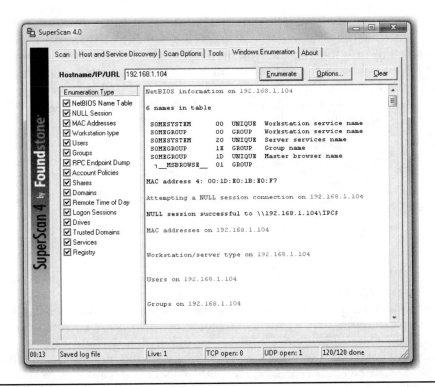

Figure 4-11   SuperScan enumeration screen

ple, suppose you sent a Telnet request to port 80 on a machine. The result may look something like this:

```
C:\telnet 192.168.1.15 80
HTTP/1.1 400 Bad Request
Server: Microsoft - IIS/5.0
Date: Sat, 29 Jan 2011  11:14:19 GMT
Content - Type: text/html
Content - Length: 87
<html><head><title>Error</title></head>
<body>The parameter is incorrect. <body><html>
Connection to host lost.
```

Just a harmless little error message, designed to show an administrator he may have made a mistake, right? It just happens to also tell an ethical hacker there's an old version of IIS on this machine (IIS/5.0). Other ports can also provide interesting nuggets. For example, if you're not sure if a machine is a mail server, try typing **telnet <ipaddress> 25**. If it is a mail server, you'll get an answer something like the following, which I received from a Microsoft Exchange Server:

```
220 mailserver.domain.com Microsoft ESMTP MAIL Service, Version: 5.0.2195.5329
ready at Sat, 29 Jan 2011 11:29:14 +0200
```

In addition to testing different ports, you can also use a variety of different tools and techniques for banner grabbing. One such tool is netcat (which we'll visit again later in this book). Known as the "Swiss army knife of hacking tools," netcat is a command-line networking utility that reads and writes data across network connections using TCP/IP. It's also a tunneling protocol, a scanner, and an advanced hacking tool. To try banner grabbing with this little jewel, simply type **nc <IPaddress or FQDN> <port number>**. Some sample netcat output for banner grabbing is shown here:

```
C:\ nc 192.168.1.20 80
HEAD / HTTP/1.0
HTTP/1.1 200 OK
Date: Mon, 28 Jan 2011 22:10:40 EST
Server: Apache/2.0.46 (Unix) (Red Hat/Linux)
Last-Modified: Tues, 18 Jan 2011 11:20:14 PST
ETag: "1986-69b-123a4bc6"
Accept-Ranges: bytes
Content-Length: 1110
Connection: close
Content-Type: text/html
```

As you can see, banner grabbing is a fairly valuable tool in gathering target information. Telnet and netcat can both perform it, but numerous other tools are available. As a matter of fact, most port scanners—including the ones we've covered already—are fully capable of banner grabbing and make use of it in preparing their output.

Another enumerating technique across the board is attempting to take advantage of SNMP. Simple Network Management Protocol was designed to manage IP-enabled devices across a network. As a result, if it is in use on the subnet, you can find out loads of information with properly formatted SNMP requests. Later versions of SNMP make this a little more difficult, but plenty of systems out there are still using the protocol in version 1.

SNMP works much like a dispatch center. A central management system set up on the network will make requests of SNMP agents on the devices. These agents respond to the requests by going to a big virtual filing cabinet on each device called the Management Information Base (MIB). The MIB holds all sorts of information, and it's arranged with numeric identifiers (called *Object Identifiers, or OIDs)* from general information to the very specific. The request points out exactly what information is requested from the MIB installed on that device, and the agent responds with only what is asked. MIB entries can identify what the device is, what operating system is installed, and even usage statistics. In addition, some MIB entries can be used to actually change configuration settings on a device. When the SNMP management station asks a device for information, the packet is known as an SNMP GET Request. When it asks the agent to make a configuration change, the request is an SNMP SET Request.

SNMP uses a community string as a form of password. The read-only version of the community string allows a requester to read virtually anything SNMP can drag out of the device, whereas the read-write version is used to control access for the SNMP SET requests. Two major downsides are involved in the use of both these community string passwords. First, the defaults, which are active on every SNMP-enabled device right out of the box—*all* of them—are ridiculously easy. The read-only default community string is *public*, whereas the read-write string is *private*. Assuming the network administrator left SNMP enabled and/or did not change the default strings, enumerating with SNMP is a snap.

NOTE   There are a couple of other quick notes worth bringing up with SNMP. First, SNMP enumeration doesn't work as well with later versions. SNMP version 3 encrypts the community strings, which makes enumeration harder. Second, although "public" and "private" are the default strings, some devices are configured to use other strings by default. It might be worthwhile researching them before you begin your efforts.

The second problem with the strings is that they are sent in clear text. So, even if the administrators took the time to change the default community strings on all devices (and chances are better than not they'll miss a few here and there), all you'll need to do to grab the new strings is watch the traffic—you'll eventually catch them flying across the wire. Tools you can use to enumerate with SNMP include SNMPUtil, OpUtils 5, and IP Network Browser (SolarWinds).

Chapter Review

Scanning and enumeration are important information-gathering steps for the ethical hacker. Scanning is the process of discovering systems on the network and taking a look at what open ports and applications they may be running. The steps for a generic scanning methodology are identifying live systems, discovering open ports, identifying the OS and services, and scanning for vulnerabilities.

A ping sweep is the easiest method for identifying active machines on the network. An ICMP Echo Request (Type 8) message is sent to each address on the subnet. Those that are up (and not filtering ICMP) reply with an ICMP Echo Reply (Type 0). Several tools can provide for ping sweeps—Angry IP Scanner, Pinger, WS_Ping, SuperScan, and Friendly Pinger are all examples.

Port scanning is the method by which systems on a network are queried to see which ports they are listening to. A port number, inside the transport layer protocol header (TCP or UDP), identifies which upper-layer protocol should receive the information contained within. Source numbers are set dynamically by the sender, using any port above 1023, whereas the destination port is usually one of the well-known ports—to identify what upper-layer application to talk to. The port numbers range from 0 to 65,535 and are split into three different groups: Well-known (0–1023), Registered (1024–49151), and Dynamic (49152–65535). Some of the more important well-known port numbers to remember are FTP (20/21), Telnet (23), SMTP (25), DNS (53), POP3 (110), NetBIOS (137–139) and SNMP (161/162).

At the transport layer, connectionless communication is accomplished with UDP (simple and very fast, but no reliability). TCP provides for connection-oriented communication (slower, but reliable). In TCP data exchange, a session must be established between the two systems first. To do this, the sender will forward a segment with the SYN flag set, indicating a desire to synchronize a communications session. This segment also contains a sequence number—a random number that helps maintain the legitimacy and uniqueness of this session.

When the recipient gets this segment, it responds with the SYN and ACK flags set, and acknowledges the sequence number by incrementing it by one. Additionally, the return segment will contain a sequence number generated by the recipient. When this segment is received by the original sender, it generates one more segment to finish off the synchronization. In this segment, the ACK flag is set, and the recipient's own sequence number is acknowledged. At the end of this three-way handshake, a communications channel is opened, sequence numbers are established on both ends, and data transfer can begin. In short, the abbreviated handshake reads "SYN, SYN/ACK, ACK."

One of the more important port-scanning tools available is nmap, which can perform many different types of scans (from simply identifying active machines to port scanning and enumeration) and can also be configured to control the speed at which the scan operates. In general, the slower the scan, the less likely you are to be discovered. It comes in both a command-line version and a GUI version (now known as Zenmap) and works on multiple OS platforms. nmap syntax is simple:

```
nmap <scan options> <target>
```

Dozens and dozens of scan options (or switches) are available, and combining them can produce several scan options. The "s" commands determine the type of scan to perform, the "P" commands set up ping sweep options, and the "o" commands deal with output. The "T" commands deal with speed and stealth, with the serial methods taking the longest amount of time. Parallel methods are much faster because they run multiple scans simultaneously. nmap switches you'll definitely see on the exam are –sS (SYN scan), - sA (ACK scan), -sO (protocol scan), -sX (XMAS scan), and all of the T commands.

There are seven generic scan types for port scanning. TCP Connect scans run through a full connection (three-way handshake) on all ports. They are the easiest to detect, but possibly the most reliable. Open ports will respond with a SYN/ACK, closed ports with an RST/ACK. SYN scans are known as half-open scans, with only SYN packets sent to ports (no completion of the three-way handshake ever takes place). Responses from ports are the same as they are for a TCP Connect scan. FIN scans run the communications setup in reverse, sending a packet with the FIN flag set. Closed ports respond with RST, whereas open ports won't respond at all. XMAS scans send multiple flags set (FIN, URG, and PSH). Port responses are the same as with a FIN scan. ACK scans are used mainly for Unix/Linux-based systems, and make use of ICMP destination unreachable messages to determine what ports may be open on a firewall. IDLE scans use a spoofed IP address to elicit port responses during a scan. Designed for stealth, this scan uses a SYN flag and monitors responses as with a SYN scan. Finally, NULL scans send packets with no flags set. Responses will vary, depending on the OS and version, but NULL scans are designed for Unix/Linux machines.

nmap output can be manipulated as well. The default is called "interactive," and it is sent to standard output. Normal output displays less runtime information and warnings because it is expected to be analyzed after the scan completes rather than interactively. You can also send output as XML (which can be parsed by graphical user interfaces or imported into databases) or in a "greppable" format (for easy searching). Other port-scanning tools include SuperScan, IPeye, THC-Amap, hping, and SNMP scanner.

War dialing is a process by which an attacker dials a set of phone numbers specifically looking for an open modem. As you know, modems are designed to answer the call, and they can easily provide back-door access to a system otherwise completely secured from attack. Tools for accomplishing war dialing are ToneLoc, THC-Scan, WarVOX (designed explicitly for VoIP systems), PAWS, and TeleSweep.

War driving used to refer to driving around in a car looking for open access points. In the ethical hacking realm, it still indicates a search for open WAPs; however, with the proliferation of handheld devices making use of 802.11 wireless standards, finding access points is as easy as simply wandering around the facility. Additionally, several tools are available to help you not only in discovering wireless entry points, but in finding vulnerabilities in wireless networking. Silica, AirMagnet, and AirCheck (Fluke) are all tools on handheld devices that allow an attacker to walk around and gather—and sometimes even exploit—wireless access point vulnerabilities.

Hiding your activities from prying security-professional eyes can be done using a proxy, spoofing an IP address, using source routing, or using an anonymizer. A proxy server is nothing more than a system you set up to act as an intermediary between you and your targets. The hacker sends commands and requests to the proxy, and the proxy relays them to the targets. Anyone monitoring the subnet sees the proxy trying all this naughtiness—not the hacker. Spoofing an IP address is exactly what it sounds like—the hacker uses a packet-crafting tool of some sort to obscure the source IP address of packets sent from his machine. There are many tools available for this, such as hping, Scapy, and Nemesis.

Source routing provides yet another means to disguise your identity on a network. It was originally designed to allow applications to specify the route a packet would take to a destination, regardless of what the route tables between the two systems said. The attacker can use an IP address of another machine on the subnet and have all the return traffic sent back regardless of which routers are in transit. Protections against source-routing attacks are prevalent and effective, so this may not be your best option. Another easy method for disguising your identity for port 80 (HTTP) traffic is to use an anonymizer. Anonymizers are services on the Internet that make use of a web proxy to hide your identity.

Good hackers will spend 90 to 95 percent of their time gathering information for an attack, and after scanning comes enumeration. Enumeration in the ethical hacking world is listing off the items we find within a specific target. When we enumerate a target, we're moving from passive information-gathering to a much more active state.

No longer satisfied with just knowing which ports are open, we now want to find things such as open shares and any easy-to-grab user account information.

Microsoft Windows machines—everything from old Windows 2000 to Windows 7 systems—will constitute the vast majority of your targets out in the real world, so it's important to know some security basics before enumerating them. Everything in a Windows system runs within the context of an account. An account can be that of a user, running in something called user mode, or the system account, which runs in kernel mode. Actions and applications running in user mode are easy to detect and contain. Those running in kernel mode, though, can be hidden and run with absolute authority.

User rights are granted via an account's membership within a group and determine which system tasks an account is allowed to perform. Permissions are used to determine which resources an account has access to. The method by which Windows keeps track of which account holds what rights and permissions comes down to SIDs and RIDs. A security identifier (SID) identifies user, group, and computer accounts and follows a specific format. A resource identifier (RID) is a portion of the overall SID identifying a specific user, computer, or domain.

SIDs are composed of an S, followed by a revision number, an authority value, a domain or computer indicator, and an RID. The RID portion of the identifier starts at 500 for the administrator account. The next account on the system, Guest, is RID 501. All users created for the system start at 1000 and increment from that point forward—even if their usernames are re-created later on.

Accounts are identified by their SID (and associated RID), of course, but the passwords for them must be stored somewhere, too. In Windows, passwords are stored in C:\Windows\System 32\Config\SAM. The SAM database holds encrypted versions of all the local passwords for accounts on the machine. For those machines that are part of a domain, the passwords are stored and handled by the domain controller.

A null session occurs when you log in to a system with no user ID and password at all. In older Windows versions (Windows 2000), a null session could be set up using the following command:

```
net use \\<target>\IPC$ "" /u:""
```

Null sessions require TCP ports 135, 137, 139, and 445 to work, and have been virtually eliminated from the hacking arsenal since Windows XP was released.

Linux systems use a User ID (UID) and a Group ID (GID) in much the same way as Windows uses SIDs and RIDs. On a Linux machine, these can be found in the /etc/passwd file.

Banner grabbing is one of the easiest enumerating methods and involves sending an unsolicited request to an open port to see what, if any, default error message (banner) is returned. Depending on what version of application is running on the port, the returned banner can indicate a potential vulnerability for the hacker to exploit. A common method of performing banner grabbing is to use Telnet aimed at a specific port. For example, to banner-grab from a suspected web server, telnet <IPAddress> 80 would attempt a connection over port 80.

Another tool for banner grabbing (and other uses) is netcat. Known as the "Swiss army knife of hacking tools," netcat is a command-line networking utility that reads and writes data across network connections using TCP/IP. It's also a tunneling protocol, a scanner, and an advanced hacking tool. To try banner grabbing with this little jewel, simply type **nc <IPaddress** or **FQDN> <port number>.**

SNMP enumeration may also prove useful. SNMP uses a community string as a form of password, with the read-only version of the community string allowing a requester to read virtually anything SNMP can drag out of the device. The read-write version is used to control access for SNMP SET requests, which can actually change settings on a device. The defaults for both of these strings are public (read-only) and private (read-write). Assuming the network administrator left SNMP enabled and/or did not change the default strings, enumerating with SNMP is relatively easy, and tools for accomplishing this are SNMPUtil and IP Network Browser (SolarWinds).

Questions

1. You are assigned to a pen test team and one of your peers tells you SNMP enumeration on the subnet today will be easy. You surmise this means SNMP is enabled and the defaults are still in place on many devices. When using a tool to craft your SNMP requests, what community string will you use for read-write?

    A. public

    B. private

    C. readwrite

    D. control

2. You want to perform banner grabbing against a machine (212.77.64.88) you suspect as being a web server. Assuming you have the correct tools installed, which of the following command-line entries will successfully perform a banner grab? (Choose all that apply.)

    A. Telnet 212.77.64.88 80

    B. Telnet 80 212.77.64.88

    C. nc –v –n 212.77.64.88 80

    D. nc –v –n 80 212.77.64.88

3. You are enumerating Windows machines and decide to attempt a null session. Which of the following statements is false regarding null sessions on Windows machines?

    A. Syntax for a null session is net use \\IPAddress \IPC$ "" /u: "".

    B. Null session attacks require SMB services and ports 135 and 137.

    C. Null session attacks work on all versions of Windows operating systems.

    D. Tools such as SID2User rely on a successful null session establishment to function.

4. You're using nmap to run port scans. What syntax will attempt a half-open scan as stealthily as possible?

   A. nmap –sT 192.168.1.0/24 –T0

   B. nmap –sX 192.168.1.0/24 –T0

   C. nmap –sO 192.168.1.0/24 –T0

   D. nmap –sS 192.168.1.0/24 –T0

5. What flag or flags are sent in the segment during the second step of the TCP three-way handshake?

   A. SYN

   B. ACK

   C. SYN-ACK

   D. ACK-FIN

6. What is the port number used by DNS?

   A. 161

   B. 445

   C. 53

   D. 67

7. A user on a computer wants to surf a web page on a server. The first segment leaving his machine has the SYN flag set, in order to set up a TCP communications channel over which he will receive the web page (HTML). When that segment leaves his machine, which of the following would be found in the port number in the Source Port field?

   A. 25

   B. 80

   C. 1022

   D. 49153

8. Which flag forces a termination of communications in both directions?

   A. RST

   B. FIN

   C. ACK

   D. PSH

9. You are examining the output of a recent SYN scan. You see a port from one machine has returned an RST-ACK. What is the state of the port?

   A. Open

   B. Closed

    C. Filtered

    D. Unknown

10. What is the term used to describe searching for open modems on a target?

    A. Port scanning

    B. Vulnerability scanning

    C. War driving

    D. War dialing

11. Which of the following methods of concealment involves a hacker spoofing an IP address to have packets returned directly to him regardless of the routers between sender and receiver?

    A. Proxy server

    B. Anonymizer

    C. Filtering

    D. Source routing

12. You are attempting to identify active machines on a subnet. What is the process of sending ICMP Echo requests to all IP addresses in the range known as?

    A. Ping sweep

    B. Ping crawl

    C. Port scan

    D. Enumeration

Answers

1. **B.** The default read-write community string for SNMP is private. Public is the default read-only string.

2. **A and C.** Both Telnet and netcat, among others, can be used for banner grabbing. The correct syntax for both have the port number last.

3. **C.** Null sessions are not a valid attack vector on Windows XP and newer machines. A null session is set up by typing **net use \\IPAddress \IPC$** "" /u: "" and requires SMB services and ports 135 and 137. Tools such as SID2User, DumpSec, and others rely on a successful null session establishment to function.

4. **D.** The syntax nmap –sS 192.168.1.0/24 –T0 runs a SYN (half-open) scan against the subnet 192.168.1.0 (.1 through .254) in "paranoid" mode.

5. **C.** A three-way TCP handshake has the originator forward a SYN. The recipient, in step 2, sends a SYN and an ACK. In step 3, the originator responds with an ACK. The steps are referred to as SYN, SYN-ACK, ACK.

6. **C.** DNS uses port 53 (both TCP and UDP).

7. **D.** Source port numbers are set by the originator, and come from the Dynamic port range (49152–65535). Well-known ports (0–1023) are used to identify the upper-layer application that will answer the request.

8. **A.** The RST flag forces both sides of the communications channel to stop. A FIN flag signifies an ordered close to the communications.

9. **B.** Closed ports during a SYN scan will return an RST-ACK. A SYN-ACK will be returned for open ports.

10. **D.** War dialing is the process of dialing all phone numbers in a given range to discover modems.

11. **D.** Source routing specifies the route a packet will take to a destination, regardless of what the route tables between the two systems say.

12. **A.** A simple means of identifying active machines on the network is to perform a ping sweep. It may not be the most reliable method, due to ICMP filtering, but it's still a good place to start.

Hacking Through the Network: Sniffers and Evasion

In this chapter you will learn about
- Sniffing and protocols that are susceptible to sniffing
- Describing active and passive sniffing
- Describing ethical hacking techniques for layer 2 traffic
- Sniffing tools and displays
- Describing sniffing countermeasures
- Intrusion detection system (IDS) types, use, and placement
- Describing signature analysis within Snort
- Listing IDS evasion techniques
- Firewall types, use, and placement
- Describing firewall hacking tools and techniques
- Use and placement of a honeypot

My office sits on the corner of two hallways, which dead-end just outside, with the door to the stairwell about five feet beyond. There's also a large window right at the end of the hallway looking out over the giant parking lot, with two big palm trees swaying in the eternal breeze just to the left. Oftentimes, people will walk down to the end of the hallway and look out the window for a while, longing for freedom during the middle of a harsh workday. And, oftentimes, they come down there to take or place personal calls on their cell phones. I know I was educated in Alabama, but I just assumed everyone knew that *sound travels*.

These people talk to their girlfriends, boyfriends, and, on a couple of occasions, the "other woman." They call up banks and talk about their accounts or loans. They call businesses they've applied to, trying to work out interview times and other assorted goodies. And all of this they do without any knowledge that someone is listening to all their conversations. Thankfully, for all these folks, I'm not an evil little guy. If I were, I could be drawing from several bank accounts. I could also set up and run a very successful dating agency—or a source for divorce proceedings.

In much the same way as in this example, people have conversations over a network all the time, without having any idea someone else could be listening in. In this chapter, we're going to discuss ways for you to sit in the cramped little corner office of the network wire, listening in on what people are saying over your target subnet. We'll also include a little discussion on efforts to stop your network intrusion and, hopefully, steps you can take around them.

Sniffing

Most people consider eavesdropping to be a little on the rude side. When it comes to your career as a pen tester, though, you're going to have to get over your societal norms and become an ace at it—well, an ace at *virtual* eavesdropping anyway. *Sniffing* is the art of capturing packets as they pass on a wire, or over the airwaves, to review for interesting information. This information could simply be addresses to go after, or information on another target. It can also be as high value as a password or other authentication code—believe it or not, some protocols send passwords and such in the clear, making things a heck of a lot easier for you. A sniffer is the tool you'll use to accomplish this, and a host of different ones are available.

Communications Basics

Before we get into sniffing and sniffers, per se, we should spend just a little more time discussing communications basics. In the last chapter, we broke down (at least, at a very high level) some of the salient information and activity that goes on with TCP and UDP. However, that's only one small step in the overall communications process. I know you're all groaning at yet another trip down the OSI reference model toll road, but it's a journey we'll just have to take together. Figure 5-1 shows the OSI model and

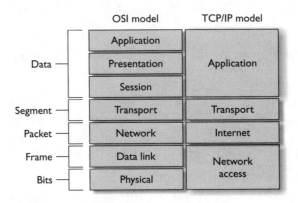

Figure 5-1 Communication model comparison

the actual TCP/IP stack, side by side, for comparison's sake. Because it's important to the remainder of the discussion (and because you'll see it on your exam), let's take a little stroll through the OSI reference model to see how the communication works between two systems.

OSI Model: A Quick Discussion

Starting at the top, the Application layer holds all the protocols that allow a user to access information on and across a network. For example, FTP allows users to transport files across networks, SMTP provides for e-mail traffic, and HTTP allows you to surf the Internet at work while you're supposed to be doing something else. The Presentation layer is designed to put the message into a format all systems can understand. For example, an e-mail crafted in Microsoft Outlook must be translated to pure ASCII code for delivery across a network. The Session layer is more of a theoretical entity, with no real manipulation of the data itself—its job is to open, maintain, and close a session. These three layers make up the "data layers" of the stack, and they map directly to the Application layer of the TCP/IP stack.

The next layer, Transport, is one of utmost importance to a hacker. This is where reliable end-to-end delivery of the message is ensured, along with segmentation, error correction (through retransmission of missing segments), and flow control. Protocols found here are TCP and UDP, among others. The Network layer then takes the segment from the Transport layer and addresses it. The address here is akin to a ZIP code—it's designed to get the packet to the network where the end station lives. Routed protocols, such as IP, can be found here.

The Data Link layer, next in line, then encapsulates the packet with a header and a trailer. The address found in this header is the physical address for the appropriate system on the subnet the frame is now traveling through (eventually it will be the address of the end station), known as the MAC address. For example's sake, consider the front of an envelope you put in the mailbox. The ZIP code is used to get it to the post office that knows where you, personally, live. Once it's in that post office, a mail carrier will read your physical address and deliver it to the correct house on the street. Network traffic is no different—much like the ZIP code gets your envelope to the post office, the IP address gets the packet to a router that knows which subnet your computer lives on. The physical address in the frame is intended to deliver it within the subnet it currently finds itself in, and is changed out as the frame header is stripped off and rebuilt along each subnet pathway. Figure 5-2 shows how the MAC address will change in the frame depending on where it's located.

Finally, at the Physical layer, everything is converted to electricity, light, radio waves, or whatever media is sending the message. Here, the frame is turned into bits for delivery. Timing and encoding occur here. From the hacking perspective, there's not a lot of action here, other than denial-of-service opportunities.

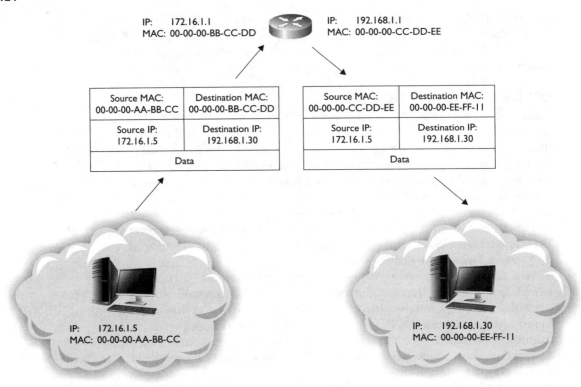

Figure 5-2 Frames during transit

Believe it or not, your understanding of this communications process is critical to your success in sniffing. If you don't know how addressing works, and what the protocols are doing at each layer, your time spent looking at a sniffer output will be nothing more than time wasted. Just how so, you may be asking? Well, let's take a look at the protocols and activities in each layer that will be of note to you in your sniffing.

Protocols of Interest

There are some important protocols in the upper layers for you to pay attention to as an ethical hacker—mainly because of their simplicity. When you think about an Application layer protocol, remember it normally relies on other protocols for almost everything else except its sole, primary purpose. For example, consider the Simple Mail Transport Protocol. SMTP was designed to do one thing—carry an e-mail message. It doesn't know anything about IP addressing, or encryption, or how big the network pipe is—its only concern is packaging ASCII characters together to be given to a recipient. Because it was written to carry nothing but ASCII, there is virtually no security built into the protocol at all. In other words, everything sent via SMTP, with no encryption added at another layer, is sent as clear text, meaning it can be easily read by someone sniffing the wire.

In another example, although FTP requires a user ID and password to access the server (usually), the information is passed in clear text over the wire. TFTP, SNMP, POP3, and HTTP are all Application layer protocols with information readily available to captured traffic—you just need to learn where to look for it. Sometimes data owners will use an insecure application protocol to transport information that should be kept secret. Sniffing the wire while these clear-text messages go across will display all that for you.

Protocols at the Transport and Network layers can also provide relevant data. TCP and UDP work in the Transport layer and provide the port numbers that both sides of a data exchange are using. TCP also adds sequence numbers, which will come into play later on during session hijacking. IP is the protocol working at the Network layer, and there is loads of information you can glean just from the packets themselves (see Figure 5-3). An IP packet header contains, of course, source and destination IP addresses. However, it also holds such goodies as the quality of service for the packet (Type of Service field) and information on fragmentation of packets along the way (Identification and Fragment Offset fields), which can prove useful in crafting your own fragmented packets later on.

The Data Link layer offers its own unique, and extremely interesting, information. As mentioned before, an IP packet provides the network address, which is needed to route the packet across several individual networks to its final destination. But inside each one of those individual networks, the frame needs a physical address (the MAC) to deliver it to a specific system. The MAC address of an intended recipient is actually the address burned onto the NIC itself. When the frame is being built inside the sending machine, the system uses a protocol called ARP (Address Resolution Protocol) to quite literally ask the subnet, "Does anyone have a physical address for the IP address I have here in this packet? If so, please let me know so I can build a frame and send it on."

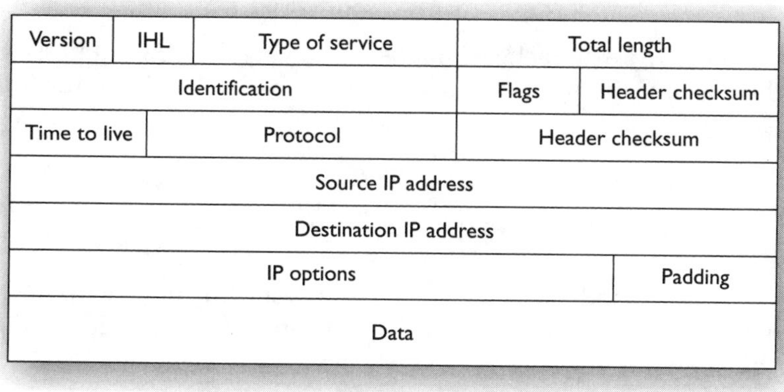

Version	IHL	Type of service	Total length	
Identification			Flags	Header checksum
Time to live		Protocol	Header checksum	
Source IP address				
Destination IP address				
IP options			Padding	
Data				

Figure 5-3 IP packet header

NOTE The MAC address (a.k.a. physical address) that is burned onto a NIC is actually made of two sections. The first half of the address, 3 bytes (24 bits), is known as the Organizational Unique Identifier, and is used to identify the card manufacturer. The second half is a unique number burned in at manufacturing, to ensure no two cards on any given subnet will have the same address.

Sometimes the message is not intended for someone in your network. Maybe it's a packet asking for a web page, or an e-mail being sent to a server somewhere up the Net. In any case, if the IP address of the packet being sent is not inside the same subnet, the router will usually respond with its MAC address. Why? Because the router knows it will be the one to forward the packet along the way. Once the packet is received, the router will open it up, look in the route table, and build a new frame for the next subnet along the route path. As that frame is being built, it will send another ARP request again: "Does anyone have a physical address for the IP address I have here in this packet? If so, please let me know so I can build a frame and send it on."

Want to know another interesting thing about ARP? The protocol retains a cache on machines as it works—at least, in many implementations it does. This really makes a lot of sense when you think about it—why continue to make ARP requests for machines you constantly talk to? To see this in action, you can use the ping, arp, and netsh commands on your Windows machine. By pinging a machine, you'll "arp" the MAC address of the system you're looking for. In Exercise 5-1, I use my machine (192.168.1.102) and ping my daughter's machine (192.168.1.101). As an aside, she's very excited to be part of "the hacking book."

Exercise 5-1: Viewing ARP Entries

This exercise is designed to demonstrate how MAC addresses are managed by ARP.

1. Ping a local machine. You can use any IP in your local subnet—for this exercise I pinged 192.168.1.101 from source 192.168.1.102.

2. Type **arp –a**. The ARP cache will appear, showing the MAC address ARP found for the machine. In the case of my test here, the display shows the following:

```
C:\arp -a
Interface 192.168.1.102 --- 0xd
Internet Address        Physical Address
192.168.1.1             00-13-10-fc-ce-6c
192.168.1.101           1c-65-9d-18-f1-d4
192.168.1.255           ff-ff-ff-ff-ff-ff
```

Notice the MAC address of my local router is shown, along with the MAC of my daughter's PC. The address ff-ff-ff-ff-ff-ff is the MAC address for the broadcast on our subnet.

3. Clear the ARP cache by typing **netsh interface ip delete arpcache**. To test its results, check the ARP cache again:

```
C:\ netsh interface ip delete arpcache
Ok.
C:\ arp -a
No ARP Entries Found
```

One final relevant note on ARP: The protocol works on a broadcast basis. In other words, requests ("Does anyone have the MAC for this IP address?") and replies ("I do. Here's my physical address—please add it to your cache.") are broadcast to every machine on the network. If they're not refreshed, the MAC addresses learned with ARP eventually fade away from the cache with time; not to mention new entries will wipe out old ones as soon as they're received.

All of this is interesting information, but just how does it help a hacker? Well, if you put on your logical thinking cap, you'll quickly see how it could be a veritable gold mine for your hacking efforts. A system on your subnet will build frames and send them out with physical address entries based on its ARP cache. If you were to, somehow, change the ARP cache on Machine A and alter the cached MAC address of Machine B to your system's MAC, *you* would receive all communication Machine A intended to send to Machine B. Suppose you went really nuts and changed the ARP entry for the *default gateway* on all systems in your subnet to your own machine? Now you're getting *all* messages everyone was trying to send out of the local network, often the Internet. Interested now?

The process of maliciously changing an ARP cache on a machine to inject faulty entries is known as *ARP poisoning* (a.k.a. *gratuitous ARP*)—and it's not really that difficult to achieve. As stated earlier, ARP is a *broadcast* protocol. So, if Machine A is sitting there minding its own business, and a broadcast comes across for Machine B that holds a different MAC address than what was already in the table, Machine A will instantly, and gladly, update its ARP cache—without even asking who sent the broadcast. To quote the characters from the movie *Dude, Where's My Car?*, "Sweet!"

 NOTE Tons of tools are available for ARP spoofing/poisoning; however, you have two big considerations when using them. First, the ARP entries need updating very frequently—to maintain your "control" you'll need to always have your fake entry update before any real update comes past. Second, remember ARP is a broadcast protocol, which means ARP poisoning attempts can trigger alerts pretty quickly.

Sniffing Techniques and Tools

So now that we know a little about the communications process and how sniffing a wire can be of great advantage to us, it must be time to discuss just how it's done. The process of sniffing comes down to a few items of great importance: what state the NIC is in, what wire you have access to, and what tool you're running. Because a sniffer is basically an application that pulls all frames off a medium for your perusal, and you already know the full communications process, I would imagine it's easy for you to understand why these three items are of utmost importance.

First, let's consider your NIC. This little piece of electronic genius works by listening to a medium (a wire most often, or the airwaves in the case of wireless). It reacts when electricity charges the wire, then begins reading the bits coming in. If the bits come in the form of a frame, it looks at the ones making up the destination address. If that address matches its own MAC address, the broadcast address for the subnet, or a multicast address it is aware of, it will pull the frame from the wire and begin working on it. In short, your NIC *normally* won't pull in or look at any frame not addressed to it. You have to tell it to.

A sniffer runs in something called *promiscuous mode.* This simply means that, regardless of address, if the frame is passing on the wire, the sniffer tells the NIC to grab it and pull it in. Most NICs have, or will accept, drivers that support promiscuous mode once a packet-capturing application has been installed. WinPcap is an example of a driver that allows the operating system to provide low-level network access and is used by a lot of sniffers on Windows machine NICs.

This brings up the second interesting point we brought up earlier—what wire, or medium, you have access to. Ethernet (because it's the most common, it's what we'll discuss) runs with multiple systems sharing a wire and negotiating time to talk based on CSMA/CD (Carrier Sense Multiple Access/Collision Detection). In short, anyone can talk anytime they want, so long as the wire is quiet. If two decide to talk at the same time, a collision occurs, they back off, and everyone goes at it again. As long as your system is within the same collision domain, you get every message intended for anyone else in the domain. You don't normally see them because your NIC usually forwards up the ones intended for you. So what constitutes a collision domain? Is the whole world in a collision domain? See Figure 5-4.

Collision domains are composed of all the machines *sharing* any given transport medium. In other words, if we're all connected to the same wire, and we use electricity to talk to one another, every time I send a message to one person on the wire, everyone

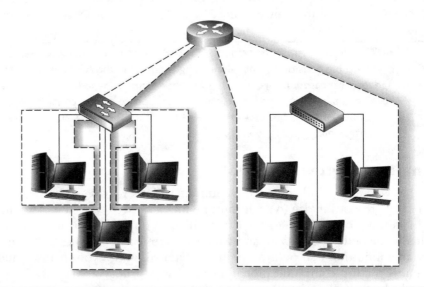

A switch splits the collision domain: 4 domains.
An attacker on A can only see traffic intended for A.

Shared media using a hub: 1 collision domain
An attacker on A can see all traffic for B and C.

Figure 5-4 Collision domains and sniffing

gets shocked. Therefore, only one of us can talk at a time—if two try it simultaneously, the voltage increases and the messages will get all garbled up.

In old 10Base2 networks, every machine was literally touching the same wire (using "T" connectors). In 10, 100, and 1000BaseT networks, which use twisted pair wiring and various connection devices, the media is segmented by several network devices. However, some of them split up that wire and some do not. Any systems connected to a hub all share the same collision domains. Those connected to a switch, however, are on their own collision domain—the switch only sends frames down that wire if they're intended for the recipient. This brings up a potential problem for the sniffing attacker. If we're connected to a switch, and we only receive messages intended for our own NIC, what good is it to sniff? Excellent question, and a good reminder that it's important to know what you actually have access to, media-wise (we'll answer the question a little later on in this chapter, so just keep reading).

Lastly, sniffing comes down to which tool you decide to use. There are literally tons of sniffers available. Some of them are passive sniffers, simply pulling in frames off the wire as they are received. Others are known as active sniffers, with built-in features to trick switches into sending all traffic their way. In the interest of time, page count, and your study (since this one will be on your exam), we're going to spend the next few moments discussing Wireshark. Ettercap, EtherPeek, and even Snort (better known as an IDS, though) are all examples of sniffers.

Packet Captures

Wireshark is probably the most popular sniffer available—mainly because it is free, stable, and works really well. Previously known as "Ethereal," Wireshark can capture packets from wired or wireless networks and provides a fairly easy-to-use interface. The top portion of the display is called the Packet List, and shows all the captured packets. The middle portion, Packet Detail, displays the sections within the frame and packet headers. The bottom portion displays the actual hex entries in the highlighted section. Once you get used to them, you'll be surprised what you can find in the hex entries— for one example, you can scroll through and pick up ASCII characters from a Telnet login session. Wireshark also offers an almost innumerable array of filters you can apply to any given sniffing session, which can fine-tune your results to exactly what you're looking for. Additionally, the good folks who created it have provided a multitude of sample captures for you to practice on. Let's try a short capture session to introduce the basics.

Exercise 5-2: Sniffing Network Traffic with Wireshark

I highly recommend you play with and use Wireshark on a continual basis. You'll be surprised what kind of unexpected information you can glean from your network. For test purposes on this exercise, be sure you're familiar with what it takes for the tool to be successful—and really get to know the filters. Here are the steps to follow:

1. Download and install Wireshark. Open the application. Figure 5-5 shows the home screen.

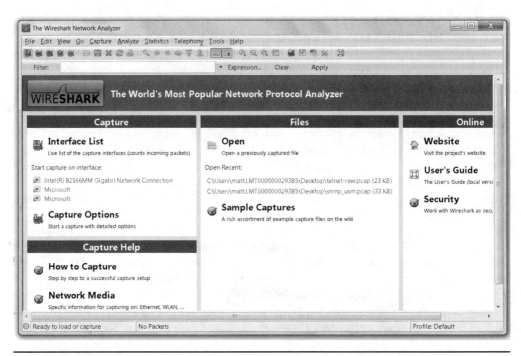

Figure 5-5 Wireshark home screen

2. Click your chosen interface in the Capture section, at the top left. (Hint: If you choose your wireless card, click Capture Options first, then turn off promiscuous mode—you'll catch more frames this way.) The Capture Review window appears.

3. Open a browser window and then go to www.yahoo.com. Close the browser window.

4. Click the Stop Capture button at the top of the screen (see Figure 5-6).

Figure 5-6
The Stop Capture
button

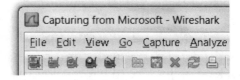

The packets will display in order, from first to last packet captured, in the top portion of the display. Notice the protocols are shown in different colors. Black generally indicates either an error or an encrypted packet.

5. Click the "Protocol" header. The protocols will align in alphabetical order. Click the first ARP packet and then expand the entries in the middle section. Scroll through some of the other packets and explore each one.

6. Scroll down to the first HTTP packet. Right-click and choose Follow TCP Stream. The pop-up window displays the entire surfing session—scroll through and see!

7. Clear the Expression window and type in the filter command to show only packets sent by your machine—for example, **ip.src == 192.168.1.100**.

8. Pick out a packet you received and note the IP address of the machine. Clear the Expression window and sort to display only packets to or from that machine—for example, **ip.addr == 192.168.1.150**.

NOTE   On some systems (I'm speaking specifically about Vista here, but this may apply to whichever OS you're running if you have it "locked down"), you may need to set the tool to run as administrator. Not doing so causes all sorts of headaches in trying to run in promiscuous mode.

Following a TCP stream is a great way to discover passwords in the clear. For instance, I downloaded one of the capture files from Wireshark (clicking Sample Captures in the Files section, in the center of the window, gives you plenty to download and play with) regarding a Telnet session. After opening the file, I sorted by protocol and selected the first Telnet packet I could find. A right-click, followed by selecting Follow TCP Stream, gave me the entire session—including the logon information, as shown in Figure 5-7.

Another great feature of Wireshark is its ability to filter a packet capture to your specifications. A filter can be created by typing in the correct stream in the filter window, by right-clicking a packet or protocol header and choosing Apply As Filter, or by clicking the Expression button beside the filter screen and checking off what you'd like. In any case, the filter will display only what you've chosen. For example, in Figure 5-8, only Telnet packets will be displayed. In Figure 5-9, all packets with the source address 192.168.0.2 will be shown.

Filters are of great use when you set up a packet capture for a long period of time. Instead of combing through millions of packets, apply a filter and only look at what you need. Other good examples of filters include host 192.168.1.102 (displays traffic to

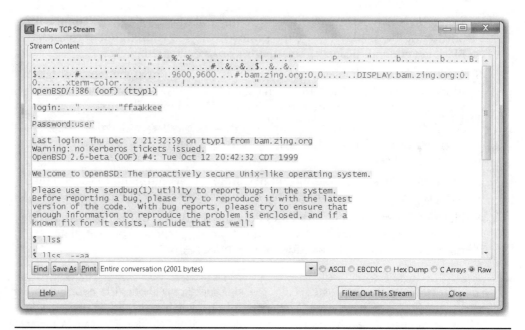

Figure 5-7   Telnet session in Wireshark

Figure 5-8
Telnet filter in
Wireshark

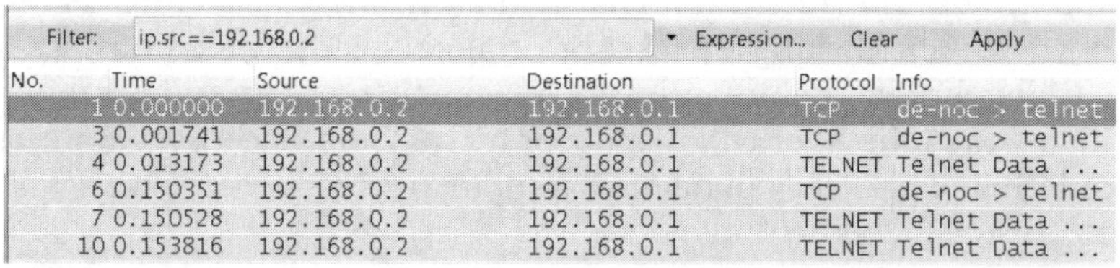

Figure 5-9
IP source address
filter

or from 192.168.1.102), net 192.168.1.0/24 (displays traffic to or from the subnet 192.168.1.1-255), and port 80 (displays all port 80 traffic). During a capture, you can also click the Capture Filters selection from the Capture menu item and choose all sorts of predefined goodies. For one example, No Broadcast and No Multicast is a good one to use if you want to cut down on the number of packets you'll have to comb through (only packets addressed explicitly to a system on the subnet will be shown). There are, literally, endless combinations of filters you can use. Take advantage of the sample captures provided by Wireshark and play with the Expression Builder—it's the only real way to learn.

EXAM TIP   Be very familiar with Wireshark filters and how to read output. Exam questions won't be too overly complicated if you apply a little logic and are aware of filter syntax and where to look on the output screen.

Another "old-school" tool you'll definitely see in use on your pen tests, and probably on your exam as well, is tcpdump. Although there is a Windows version (Win-Dump), tcpdump has been a Unix staple from way, way back, and many people just love the tool. There are no bells and whistles—this is a command line tool that simply prints out a description of the contents of packets on a network interface that match a given filter (Boolean expression). In short, you point tcpdump to an interface, tell it to grab all packets matching a Boolean expression you create, and voilà! These packets can be dumped to the screen, if you really like *Matrix*-y characters flying across the screen all the time, or you can dump them to a file for review later.

The syntax for this tool is fairly simple: tcpdump *flag(s) interface*. However, the sheer number of flags and the Boolean combinations you can create can make for some pretty elegant search strings. For a simple example, tcpdump -i eth1 puts the interface in listening mode, capturing pretty much anything that comes across eth1. If you were to add the -w flag, you could specify a file in which to save the data, for review later. If you get nuts with it, though, the Boolean expressions show tcpdump's power. The following command will show all data packets (no SYN, FIN, or ACK-only) to and from port 80:

```
tcpdump 'tcp port 80 and (((ip[2:2] - ((ip[0]&0xf)<<2)) - ((tcp[12]&0xf0)>>2))
!= 0)'
```

Take some time to review the tcpdump man page at www.tcpdump.org/tcpdump_man.html and you can see all sorts of great examples, as well as good write-ups on each of the flags available. But don't worry too much—no one is going to expect you to write a 35,000-character Boolean expression on the exam. You should, though, know basic flags for tcpdump—particularly how to put the interface in listening mode (-i) and how to write to a file (-w)—and how to use the tool.

Of course, you have plenty of other choices available in sniffers. Ettercap is a very powerful sniffer and man-in-the-middle suite of programs. It is available as a Windows tool, but works much better in its native Unix platform. Ettercap can be used as a passive sniffer, an active sniffer, and an ARP poisoning tool. Other great sniffers include Snort (most often discussed as an intrusion detection application), EtherPeek, WinDump, and WinSniffer.

 NOTE tcpdump is considered a built-in utility for all Unix systems, whereas Wireshark is typically considered a hacker tool and Ettercap is *always* considered a hacker tool. If you value your job, I'd highly suggest you don't install these on your work desktop.

Flooding and Spoofing

So you know the communications flow, which protocols are interesting, what functions and circumstances are important to sniffing, and even how to use a very popular sniffer. What's left? The answer is, of course, dealing with the problems you'll encounter along the way. Encryption, for the most part, isn't one you can normally work around—if it's in place you'll just have to work other angles. But collision domains and those pesky switches we talked about earlier? Those we may have some answers for.

One simple way around the limitations of a switch and your collision domain is to ARP poison your target. Because ARP works on a broadcast, the switch will merrily send any ARP packet out to all recipients—as an aside, the process of sending lots of broadcast traffic to a switch in order to force it out to all recipients is called *flooding*. Be careful, though, because most modern switches have built-in defenses for too many ARP broadcasts coming across the wire, and there are a wide variety of network monitoring tools administrators can put into use to watch for this. Additionally, some network administrators are smart enough to manually add the default gateway MAC permanently (arp -s) into the ARP cache on each device. A couple of tools that make ARP flooding as easy as pressing a button are Cain and Abel (a *great* Windows hacking tool) and dsniff (a collection of Linux tools holding a tool called ARPspoof).

Another method—although it doesn't work on many modern switches—is known as a *MAC flood*. A switch works by maintaining a table—known as the CAM (content addressable memory)—of all the MAC addresses that it learns about. Between ARPs and frames to and from the machine(s), switches learn pretty quickly which port to send messages down. However, when it's first turned on, and the CAM table is empty, the switch doesn't know which port to send any given message to. Therefore, when it receives that first message, it floods it to all ports, just like a hub would.

MAC flooding works by sending tons and tons of unsolicited MACs to the switch, filling up the CAM table. Because the CAM is finite in size, it fills up fairly quickly and entries begin rolling off the list. When a switch receives a message and there is no entry in the CAM table, it floods the message to all ports. Therefore, when the switch's CAM table is rolling out entries faster than it can look them up, the switch basically turns into a hub. This allows the attacker to see every packet on the switch—a fairly clever, and useful, trick. EtherFlood and Macof are examples of tools you can use to give this a try.

Most modern switches protect against MAC floods but may still be susceptible to MAC spoofing. We've already covered spoofing in general before, so this concept shouldn't be anything new to you. When a MAC address is spoofed, the switch winds up with multiple entries in the CAM table for a given MAC address. Unless port security is turned on, the latest entry in the table is the one that is used.

Port security refers to a security feature on switches that allows an administrator to manually assign MAC addresses to a specific port—if the machine connecting to the port does not use that particular MAC, it isn't allowed to connect. In truth, this type of implementation turns out to be a bit of a pain for the network staff, so most people don't use it that way. In most cases, port security simply restricts the number of MAC addresses connected to a given port. Say your Windows 7 machine runs six VMs for testing, each with its own MAC. As long as your port security allows for at least seven MACs on the port, you're in good shape. Anything less, the port will turn amber, SNMP messages will start firing, and you'll be left out in the cold—or have a network admin come pay you a visit.

EXAM TIP   You won't be asked exacting details on ARP spoofing or MAC flooding, but you do need to know the details of how both work.

For example, suppose "Good Machine," with MAC address 0A-0B-0C-AA-BB-CC, is on port 2. The switch has learned any frame addressed for that MAC should go to port 2, and no other. The attacker attaches "Bad Machine" to port 3 and wants to see all packets Good Machine is receiving. The attacker uses an application such as Packet Generator (from SourceForge) to create multiple frames with the source address of 0A-0B-0C-AA-BB-CC and sends them off (it doesn't really matter where). The switch will notice that the MAC address of Good Machine, formally on port 2, seems to have moved to port 3, and will update the CAM table accordingly. So long as this is kept up, the attacker will start receiving all the frames originally intended for Good Machine. Not a bad plan, huh?

Tools for spoofing a MAC address—or changing all sorts of info in the frame for that matter—are easy to find. Cain and Abel, a Windows tool, allows for some frame/packet manipulation, and does a great job of point-and-click ARP poisoning.

Scapy (native to Unix) allows for all sorts of packet/frame manipulation and can create streams of data for you. Packet Crafter is an older tool, but is still easy to use. SMAC is specifically designed for MAC spoofing.

Network Roadblocks

All this talk about sniffing and listening in on network conversations makes this whole sordid business sound pretty easy. However, our adversaries—those guys who manage and administer the network and systems we're trying to gain access to—aren't going to just sit by and let us take whatever we want without a fight. They are doing everything in their power to make it as difficult as possible for the aspiring ethical hacker—and that means taking advantage of a multitude of hardware and software tools. As stated before, as an ethical hacker, you certainly won't be expected to know how to crack the latest and greatest network roadblock efforts; however, you are expected to (and should) know what they are and what, if anything, you can do about them.

Intrusion Detection

Intrusion detection has come a long, long way in the past 15 years or so. What used to be a fringe effort, tacked on to someone's "real" job, now is a full-time career of its own. As the name implies, intrusion detection is all about identifying intrusion attempts on your network. Sometimes this is simply a passive effort—to notify others of what might be happening. Other times it becomes much more active in nature, letting one punch back, so to speak, at the bad guys. When it comes to ethical hacking, it's very useful to know how intrusion detection works and what, if anything, you can do to get around it.

IDSs (intrusion detection systems) are hardware and/or software devices that examine streams of packets for unusual or malicious behavior. Sometimes this is done via a signature list, where the IDS compares packets against a list of known traffic patterns that indicate an attack. When a match is made, the alarm sounds. Other IDSs may be anomaly- (or behavior-) based, and simply compare the traffic against what a normal day looks like. Anything unusual sounds the alarm.

 NOTE Anomaly- or behavior-based systems require a lot of thought and time in getting things properly set up. The IDS engine will need a significant amount of time to analyze traffic to determine what is "normal." In many cases, enterprise networks with good security staff will implement both anomaly- and signature-based systems to cover as many bases as possible.

They both have benefits and drawbacks. A signature-based system is only as good as the signature list itself—if you don't keep it up to date, newer intrusion methods may go undetected. A behavior-based system may be better at picking up the latest attacks, because they would definitely be out of the norm, but such systems are also known to drive administrators crazy with false positives—that is, an alarm showing an intrusion has occurred when, in reality, the traffic is fine and no intrusion attempt has occurred. Anomaly-based IDS is, by its nature, difficult because most network administrators simply can't know everything going on in their networks.

As an aside, although a false positive is easy enough to identify, you need to be familiar with another term in regard to IDS (and your exam). A *false negative* occurs when the IDS reports a particular stream of traffic is just fine, with no corresponding alarm or alert, when, in fact, an intrusion attempt did occur. False negatives are considered far worse than false positives, for obvious reasons. Unfortunately, many times these aren't discerned until well after an attack has occurred.

IDSs are also defined not only by what they use to make a decision, but also where they are located and their span of influence. A host-based IDS (also known as HIDS) is usually a software program that resides on the host itself. More often than not an HIDS is signature based, and its entire job is to watch that one host. It looks for traffic or events that would indicate a problem for the host itself. Some popular examples include Cybersafe, Tripwire, Norton Internet Security, and even firewalls and other features built into the operating system itself.

On the other hand, a network-based IDS sits, oddly enough, on the network perimeter. Its job, normally, is to watch traffic coming into, and leaving, the network. Whether signature- or anomaly- based, an NIDS will sit outside or inside the firewall, and will be configured to look for everything from port and vulnerability scans to active hacking attempts and malicious traffic. A large network may even employ multiple NIDSs at various locations in the network, for added security. An exterior NIDS outside the firewall would watch the outside world, whereas one placed just inside the firewall on the DMZ could watch your important server and file access. Dozens upon dozens of intrusion detection system and software options are available for you; however, the one used more often than any other, and the one you'll see on your exam more often than not, is Snort.

Tripwire

Several years ago, Tripwire was just a means to verify file integrity. The program did a great job monitoring files on a machine and notifying you if something was amiss. Somewhere along the way, though, Tripwire moved from being HIDS-focused to much more of a network-based IDS (NIDS) product. Today, Tripwire Enterprise 8.0 is one of the more respected IDS/IPS systems in the world. The "little tool that could" has broadened its horizons and now offers log aggregation, threat response, and even forensic analysis. However, its original roots, verifying file integrity, is still just as valid now as it ever was.

Snort

By far the most widely deployed IDS in the world, Snort is an open source IDS that, per its website, "combines the benefits of signature, protocol, and anomaly-based inspection." It has become the de facto standard for IDS and is in use on networks ranging from small businesses to U.S. government enterprise systems. It is a powerful sniffer, traffic logging, and protocol-analyzing tool that can detect buffer overflows, port scans, operating system fingerprinting, and almost every conceivable external attack or probe you can imagine. Its rule sets (signature files) are updated constantly, and support is easy to find.

Snort runs in three different modes. Sniffer mode is exactly what it sounds like, and lets you watch packets in real time as they come across your network tap. Packet Logger mode saves packets to disk for review at a later time. Network Intrusion Detection System mode analyzes network traffic against various rule sets you pick from, depending on your network's situation. NIDS mode can then perform a variety of actions based on what you've told it to do.

 NOTE A *network tap* is any kind of connection that allows you to see all traffic passing by. It can be as simple as a hub connected on the segment you'd like to watch or as complex as a network appliance created specifically for the task. Just keep two points in mind: First, where you place the tap determines exactly what, and how much, traffic you'll be able to see. Second, your tap should be capable of keeping up with the data flow (an old 486 running 10Mbps half-duplex connected to a fiber backbone running at 30MB on a slow day will definitely see some packet loss).

It's not completely intuitive to set up and use, but it isn't the hardest tool on the planet to master either. That said, as much as I know you'd probably love to learn all the nuances and command-line steps on how to set up and configure Snort completely, this book is about the ethical hacker and not the network security manager. We're charged with giving you the knowledge you'll need to pass the exam, and so we'll concentrate on the rules and the output. If you're really interested in all the configuration minutia, I'd suggest grabbing the user manual as a start. It's an easy read and goes into a lot of things we simply don't have the time or page count to do here.

The Snort "engine," the application that actually watches the traffic, relies on rule sets an administrator decides to turn on. For example, an administrator may want to be alerted on all FTP, Telnet, and CGI attack attempts, but could care less about denial-of-service attempts against the network. The engine running on that network, and the one running on the government enterprise down the street that's watching everything, are the same. The rule sets selected and put in place are what makes the difference.

The Snort configuration file resides in /etc/snort on Unix/Linux and c:\snort\etc\ on most Windows installations. The configuration file is used to launch Snort, and contains a list of which rule sets to engage at startup. To start Snort, a command like the following might be used:

```
snort -l c:\snort\log\ -c c:\snort\etc\snort.conf
```

Basically this says, "Snort application, I'd like you to start logging to the directory C:\
snort\log\. I'd also like you to go ahead and start monitoring traffic using the rule sets
I've defined in your configuration file located in C:\etc."

The configuration file isn't all that difficult to figure out either. It holds several variables that need to be set to define your own network situation. For example, the variable HOME_NET defines the subnet local to you. On my home network, I would define
the variable in the file to read as follows:

```
var HOME_NET 192.168.1.0/24
```

Other variables I could set are displayed in the overly simplified snort.conf file displayed next. In this instance, I want to watch out for SQL attacks but, because I'm not
hosting any web servers, I don't want to waste time watching out for HTTP attacks:

```
var HOME_NET 192.168.1.0/24
* Sets home network
var EXTERNAL_NET any
* Sets external network to any
var SQL_SERVERS $HOME_NET
* Tells Snort to watch out for SQL attacks on any device in the network defined as
* HOME.
var RULE_PATH c:\etc\snort\rules
* Tells Snort where to find the rule sets.
include $RULE_PATH/telnet.rules
* Tells Snort to compare packets to the rule set named telnet.rules and alert on
* anything it finds.
```

NOTE Some network security administrators aren't very concerned with
what's going on inside their networks and don't want to see any traffic at
all from them in their Snort logs. If you change the external variable to
EXTERNAL_NET !$HOME_NET, Snort will ignore packets generated by
your home network that find their way back inside.

If I were hosting websites, I'd turn that function on in the config file by using the
following entry:

```
var HTTP_SERVERS
```

SMTP_SERVERS, SQL_SERVERS, and DNS_SERVERS are also entries I could add,
for obvious reasons. To include a particular rule set, simply add the following line:

```
include $RULE_PATH/name_of_rule
```

Speaking of rule sets, there are scads of them. The rules for Snort can be downloaded from the Snort site at any time in a giant zip (tar) file. The rules are updated
constantly, so good administrators will pull down fresh copies often. Because the rules
are separate from the configuration, all you have to do to update your signature files is
to drop the new copy in the directory holding the old copy. One quick overwrite is all
that's needed!

A rule itself is fairly simple. It is composed of an action, a protocol, a source address/port, a destination address/port, and message parameters. For example, consider the following rule:

```
alert tcp !HOME_NET any -> $HOME_NET 31337 (msg :"BACKDOOR
ATTEMPT-Backorifice")
```

This rule tells Snort, "If you happen to come across a packet from any address that is not my home network, using any source port, intended for an address within my home network on port 31337, alert me with the message 'BACKDOOR ATTEMPT-Backorifice.'" Other options you can add to the message section include flags (indicating specific TCP flags to look for), content (indicating a specific string in the packet's data payload), and specialized handling features. For example, consider this rule:

```
alert tcp !$HOME_NET any -> $HOME_NET 23 (msg:"Telnet attempt..admin access";
content: "admin
```

The meaning: "Please alert on any packet from an address not in my home network and using any source port number, intended for any address that is within my home network on port 23, including the ASCII string 'admin.' Please write 'Telnet attempt.. admin access' to the log." As you can see, although it looks complicated, it's really not that hard to understand. And that's good news, because you'll definitely get asked about rules on the CEH exam.

 EXAM TIP You'll need to be intimately familiar with the basics of Snort rule syntax, as well as the raw output from the packet capture. Pay special attention in the output to port numbers—most questions can be answered just by knowing what port numbers go with which protocol, and where to find them in the output.

Lastly on Snort, you'll also need to know how to read the output. GUI overlays are ridiculously easy, so I'm not even going to bother here—you purchased this book, so I'm relatively certain you can read already. Command-line output, though, requires a little snooping around. A typical output is listed here (bold added for emphasis):

```
02/07-11:23:13.014491 0:10:2:AC:1D:C4 -> 0:2:B3:5B:57:A6 type:0x800 len:0x3C
200.225.1.56:1244 -> 129.156.22.15:443 TCP TTL:128 TOS:0x0 ID:17536 IpLen:20
DgmLen:48 DF
******S* Seq: 0xA153BD Ack: 0x0 Win: 0x2000 TcpLen: 28
TCP Options (4) => MSS: 1460 NOP NOP SackOK
0x0000: 00 02 B3 87 84 25 00 10 5A 01 0D 5B 08 00 45 00  .....%..Z..[..E.
0x0010: 00 30 98 43 40 00 80 06 DE EC C0 A8 01 04 C0 A8  .0.C@...........
0x0020: 01 43 04 DC 01 BB 00 A1 8B BD 00 00 00 00 70 02  .C............p.
0x0030: 20 00 4C 92 00 00 02 04 05 B4 01 01 04 02         .L..........
```

I know, it looks scary, but don't fret—this is simple enough. The first portion of the line indicates the date stamp at 11:23 on February 7. The next entry shows the source and destination MAC address of the frame (in this case, the source is 0:10:2:AC:1D:C4 and the destination is 0:2:B3:5B:57:A6). The Ethernet frame type and length are next, followed by the source and destination IPs, along with the associated port numbers. This frame, for example, was sent by 200.225.1.56, with source port 1244, destined for 129.156.22.15 on port 443 (can you say "SSL connection attempt"?). The portion reading "******S*" indicates the SYN flag was set in this packet, and the sequence and acknowledgment numbers follow. The payload is displayed in hex digits below everything.

Do you need to remember all this for your exam? Of course you do. The good news is, though, most of the time you can figure out what's going on by knowing where to find the port numbers and source/destination portions of the output. I bolded them in the preceding code listing for emphasis. I guarantee you'll see an output like this on your exam—be ready to answer questions about it.

IDS Evasion Tactics

Our brief exposure to IDSs here should give you pause as an ethical hacker—if these tools work so well, how can we ever break in without being noticed? It's a fair question, and the answer on some networks is, "You probably can't." Again, we're not looking to break into Fort Knox—we're looking for the easy target. If IDSs are set up correctly, located in the correct spot on the network, have the latest up-to-date signatures files, and have been on long enough to identify normal behavior, sure, your job is going to be tough. But just how many of those IDSs are perfectly located and maintained? How many are run by a security staff that is maybe a little on the complacent side? Think there may be some misconfigured ones out there, or maybe installations with outdated or corrupt signature files? Now we're talking!

So, how do we get around these things? First off, learn to slow down. Snort has a great signature file for tracking port scan attempts, but you do have to set it on a timer. I interviewed a perimeter security guy a little while back on this subject and asked him how long he thought, given enough patience, it would take me to port scan his entire network (he watches the perimeter of a huge enterprise network of more than 10,000 hosts). He sighed and told me if I kept everything under two minutes a pop, I can have the whole thing done in a matter of a couple of days. Slow down, scan smaller footprints, and take your time—it will eventually pay off.

Another method for trying to get past the watchful eyes of the security folks is to flood the network. The ethical hacker could set up some fake attacks, guaranteed to trigger a few alerts, along with tons and tons of traffic. The sheer volume of alerts might be more than the staff can deal with, and you may be able to slip by unnoticed.

Evasion through session splicing—a fancy term for *fragmentation*—is also a worthwhile tactic. The idea here is to put payload into packets the IDS usually ignores. SYN segments, for example, usually have nothing but padding in the data payload. Why not slide small fragments of your own code in there to reassemble later on? You can even try purposefully sending the segments out of order, or sending adjustments with the IP fragment field. The IDS might not pick up on this. Again, patience and time pay off.

NOTE Another extremely common IDS evasion technique in the web world (because it works against web and IDS filters well) is the use of Unicode characters. The idea is to use Unicode characters (U+0020 = a space, U+0036 = the number 6, and U+0041 = a capital A) instead of human-readable code to confuse the signature-based IDS. Sometimes this works and sometimes it doesn't—just keep in mind that many Unicode signature files are available to look for this very thing.

Some tools you may get asked about or see along the way for IDS evasion are Nessus (also a great vulnerability scanner), ADMmutate (able to create multiple scripts that won't be easily recognizable by signature files), NIDSbench (an older tool used for playing with fragment bits), and Inundator (a flooding tool). IDSInformer is another great tool that can use captured network traffic to craft, from start to finish, a test file to see what can make it through undetected. Additionally, many packet generating tools—such as Packet Generator and PackETH, shown in Figures 5-10 and 5-11—can do the job nicely.

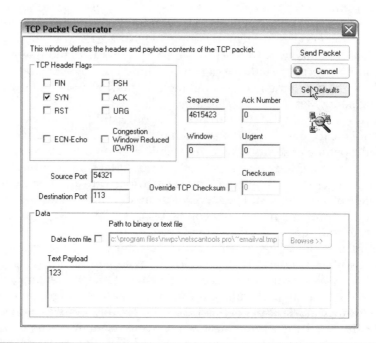

Figure 5-10 Packet Generator screenshot

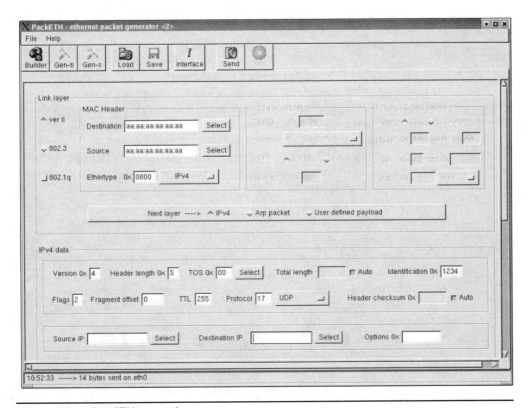

Figure 5-11 PackETH screenshot

Interview with the Hacker

Put down the sharp instruments and back away from the edge of the cliff—I'm not going to recite Anne Rice novel quotes to you. I am going to pay her the "sincerest form of flattery" by borrowing (stealing) her tagline from her book, though, and twisting it for my own use.

If you were to corner a pen tester, a *good* pen tester, and perform an interview on what they think about hacking—specifically dealing with IDS evasion—you'd probably hear the same couple of conclusions. I think we hit on them in this chapter already, but it's always helpful to see another perspective—to hear it laid out in a different way. To accomplish this, I chatted with our tech editor during the review of this chapter, and got some sound advice to pass along (credit goes to Mr. Horton for these gems):

- **The best nugget of wisdom we can give** If a business is an attacker's single target, *time is on the attacker's side.* There is so much noise on the Internet from random scans, probes, and so on, that a determined attacker can just take weeks and hide in it. As a pen tester, you rarely have that much time, and it is your greatest limitation. If you're expected to act as the bad guy and are given only seven days to perform, you *will* be detected. The trade-off between threat fidelity and unlimited time is difficult to balance.

- **Where real hackers thrive** Most true experts in the field don't spend time trying to *avoid* your signatures, they spend their time trying to make sure they *blend in.* The nemesis of all IDS is encryption: Your critical financial transaction sure looks like my remote agent traffic when they're both going through SSL. Although there are SSL termination points and other things you can use, the bottom line is that encryption makes IDS useless, barring some mechanism to decrypt before running it through.

- **"Cover fire" works in the virtual world too** If the attacker has a bunch of IP addresses to sacrifice to the giant network blocker in the sky, some nikto and nmap T5 scans might just do the trick to obfuscate the *real* attack. This is straight-up cover fire—and it *works*!

Remember, IDS is not foolproof—much like a firewall, it is simply one tool in your arsenal to defend against attacks. Encryption, stealth, and plain old cover fire can all work to your advantage as a pen tester.

Firewalls and Honeypots

While we're on the subject of network roadblocks, we can't ignore the one everyone has already heard of—the firewall. If you've watched a Hollywood movie having anything whatsoever to do with technology, you've heard mention of firewalls. And, if you're like me, you cringe every time they bring it up. Script writers must believe that a firewall is some kind of living, breathing entity that has the capability to automatically sense what the bad guys are doing, and anything that makes it past the firewall is free and clear. A firewall isn't the end-all of security, it's just one tool in the arsenal. Granted, it can be a very powerful tool, but it's just one piece of the puzzle, not the whole thing.

The Firewall

A *firewall* is an appliance within a network that is designed to protect internal resources from unauthorized external access. Firewalls work with a set of rules, *explicitly* stating what is allowed to pass from one side of the firewall to the other. Additionally, most firewalls work with an *implicit deny* principle, which means if there is not a rule defined to allow the packet to pass, it is blocked—there is no need to create a rule to deny packets. For example, there may be a rule saying port 80 is allowed to pass from external to internal, but if there is not a rule saying port 443 is allowed, SSL requests to internal resources will automatically be dropped.

Another interesting point on most firewalls is that the list of rules that determine traffic behavior is usually read in order, from top to bottom. As soon as a match is made, the decision on whether to pass the packet is made. For example, an ACL (Access Control List) that starts out with an entry of "allow ip any any" makes the firewall moot—every IP packet will be allowed to pass because the match is made on the first entry. Most firewalls are configured with rule sets to allow common traffic, such as port 80 if you're hosting web servers and port 53 for DNS lookups, and then rely on implicit deny to protect the rest of the network.

Many firewalls (just like routers) also implement Network Address Translation (NAT) at the border, and NAT can be implemented in many different ways. *Basic* NAT is a one-to-one mapping, where each internal private IP address is mapped to a unique public address. As the message leaves the network, the packet is changed to use the public IP, and when it is answered and routed back through the Internet to the firewall (or external router), NAT matches it back to the single corresponding internal address and sends it along its way. For example, a packet leaving 172.16.1.72 would be changed to 200.57.8.212 for its journey across the Internet. Although the rest of the world will see IP addresses in your public range, the true senders of the data packets are internal and use an address from any of the private network classes (192.168.0.0, 172.16–31.0.0, or 10.0.0.0).

In the real world, though, most organizations and individuals don't implement a one-to-one mapping—it's simply too expensive. A more common method of NAT is NAT overload, better known as Port Address Translation. This method takes advantage of the port numbers (and other goodies) unique to each web conversation to allow many internal addresses to use one external address. Although we could drop into an entire conversation here on how this works and what to watch for, I'm simply mentioning it so you won't be caught off guard by it—should you see it on the exam.

 NOTE If you didn't already know about NAT, I'd bet dollars to doughnuts you're a NAT "overloader" already. If you don't believe me, check your wireless router. How many devices do you have connected to it? Each one has its own *private* IP address assigned (probably in the 192.168.1.1–254 range), which we all know can't be routed to or from the Internet. And I'm absolutely certain you did not purchase a public IP address range from your provider, right? Open the configuration for your router and check the public-facing IP address—I'll bet you'll find you've been NAT-ing like a pro all along.

Much like IDSs, placement of firewalls is very important. In general, a firewall is placed on the edge of a network, with one port facing outward, at least one port facing inward, and another port facing towards a DMZ—an area of the network set aside for servers and other resources that the outside world would need access to. Some networks will apply additional firewalls throughout the enterprise to segment for all sorts of reasons.

A few quick definitions and terms need to be covered here as well. Most of us are already aware of the DMZ and how it is designed to separate internal hosts from Internet traffic dangers, creating a screened subnet between the internal network and the rest of the world. The *public zone* of your DMZ is connected to the Internet and hosts all the public-facing servers and services your organization provides. These *bastion hosts* sit outside your internal firewall and can withstand Internet traffic attacks. The *private zone* holds all the internal hosts that, other than responding to a request from inside that zone, no Internet host has any business dealing with. So, now that you know what the DMZ is and how it's arranged, we can discuss just what, exactly, a firewall is, how it works, and how we can get around it.

Originally, firewalls were all packet-filtering devices. They basically looked at the headers of packets coming through a port and made decisions on whether to allow them or not based on the ACLs configured. Although it does provide the ability to block specific protocols, the major drawback with packet filtering alone is twofold: It is incapable of examining the packet's payload, and it has no means to identify the state of the packet. This gave rise to stateful inspection firewalls.

Stateful inspection means the firewall has the means to track the entire status of a connection. For instance, if a packet arrives with the ACK flag set, but the firewall had no record of the original SYN packet, that would indicate a malicious attempt. A great example of the difference in firewalls is the virtual elimination of something called an *ACK tunnel*. The idea was a server on the outside could communicate with a client on the inside by sending only ACK segments. The packet-filtering firewall would ignore these packets, so long as they were destined for a "good" port. Stateful firewalls block these now, because no SYN packet was ever sent in the first place. In other words, a stateful firewall isn't just interested in the packets themselves, it's interested in communication streams.

 EXAM TIP HTTP tunneling is a firewall evasion technique you'll probably see at least mentioned on the exam. The short of it is, lots of things can be wrapped within an HTTP shell (Microsoft Office has been doing this for *years*). And, because port 80 is almost never filtered by a firewall, you can craft port 80 segments to carry payload for protocols the firewall may have otherwise blocked.

Knowing what a firewall is, where and how it's most likely to be used in the network, and how it works (via ACLs and/or stateful inspection) is only part of the battle. What we really need to know now is how we identify where the firewall is from the outside (in the middle of our footprinting and attack), and how we can get around it once we find it. Identifying a firewall location doesn't require rocket-scientist brainpower, because no one really even bothers to hide the presence of a firewall. As we covered earlier, a simple traceroute can show you where the firewall is (returning splats to let you know it has timed out). If you're using your sniffer and can look into the packets a little, an ICMP Type 3 Code 13 will show that the traffic is being stopped (filtered) by a firewall (or router). An ICMP Type 3 Code 3 will tell you the client *itself* has the port closed. A tool called Firewall Informer, and others like it, can help in figuring out where the firewall is. Lastly, banner grabbing—which we covered in the last chapter—also provides an easy firewall-identification method.

Once you find the firewall (easy), it's now time to find out ways to get through it or around it (not so easy). Your first step is to peck away at the firewall in such a manner as to identify which ports and protocols it is letting through and which ones it has blocked (filtered). This process of "walking" through every port against a firewall to determine what is open is known as *firewalking*. Tons of tools are available for this—from nmap and other footprinting tools, to a tool called Firewalk (for PacketStorm). Whether you set up an nmap scan and document the ports yourself, or use a program that does it for you, the idea is the same—find a port the firewall will allow through, and start your attack there. Just keep in mind this is generally a noisy attack and you will, most likely, get caught.

Of course, the best method available is to have a compromised machine on the inside initiate all communication for you. Usually firewalls—stateful or packet filtering—don't bother looking at packets with internal source addresses leaving the network. So, for example, suppose you e-mailed some code to a user and had them install it (go ahead, they will... trust me). The system on the inside could then initiate all communications for your hacking efforts from outside, and you've found your ticket to ride.

 NOTE Other firewall-hacking tools you may run across include, but are not limited to, CovertTCP, ICMP Shell, and 007 Shell. Remember, though, a compromised system inside the network is your best bet.

When it comes to the actual applications you can use for the task, packet-crafting and packet-generating tools are the ones you'll most likely come across in your career for evading firewalls and IDSs, although a couple of tools are specifically designed for the task. PackETH is a Linux tool from SourceForge that's designed to create Ethernet packets for "security testing." Another SourceForge product is Packet Generator, which allows you to create test runs of various packet streams to demonstrate a particular sequence of packets. Netscan also provides a packet generator in its tool conglomeration. All of these allow you to control the fields in frame and packet headers and, in some cases, interject payload information to test the entirety of the security platform. Not bad, huh?

The Honeypot

Our final network roadblock isn't really designed to stop you at all. Quite to the contrary, this one is designed to invite you in and make you comfortable. It provides you a feeling of peace and tranquility, consistently boosting your ego with little successes along the way—and, like a long lost relative, encourages you to stay for a while.

A *honeypot* is a system set up as a decoy to entice attackers. The idea is to load it up with all sorts of fake goodies, with not-*too*-easy vulnerabilities a hacker may exploit. An attacker, desperately looking for something to report as a success, would stumble upon the honeypot and spend all his time and effort there, leaving the real network, and resources, alone. Although it sounds like a great idea, a honeypot isn't without its own dangers.

By design, a honeypot will be hacked, so this brings up two very important points. First, anything and everything on a honeypot system is not to be trusted. Anything that has that many successful attacks against it could be riddled with loads of stuff you don't even know about yet. Don't put information or resources on the honeypot that can prove useful to an attacker, and don't trust anything you pull off it. Granted, the information and resources have to *look* legitimate; just make sure they're not.

Pooh's Paradise

Winnie the Pooh—that huggable little fluff-filled iconic yellow bear popularized by Walt Disney back in the 1960s—sure loved his honey. As much time as he spent with his face in real pots of honey, I have to imagine his favorite network appliance would have the same name. And I'm sure he'd find his way to some of the honeypot projects spanning the globe.

Honeypots aren't just to distract hackers, they're also great at tracking down all sorts of information. Combine this knowledge with the absolute loathing worldwide of unsolicited e-mail and those who forward spam, and it's not too difficult to see how groups of people might band their honeypots together in a coordinated effort to bring the spammers to a halt. Project Honey Pot is one such effort.

Project Honey Pot is a web-based network of honeypots using embedded software on various websites to collect information on spammers. The project collects IP addresses it catches harvesting e-mail addresses for spam purposes. This information is shared among various law-enforcement agencies to help combat private spammers worldwide. The information collected is also used in research and development of newer versions of the software to further improve the efforts of the group as a whole. Project Honey Pot was founded and is managed by Unspam Technologies, Inc (www.projecthoneypot.org).

Another collaboration of effort is The Honeypot Project, founded in 1999. An international, nonprofit (501c3) research organization dedicated to improving the security of the Internet at no cost to the public, The Honeypot Project raises awareness of threats and provides a "Know Your Enemy" series of papers. The project also provides security tools and techniques to help defeat cyber threats.

These collections, and others like them, demonstrate the good side of the Internet and networking altogether. Many open source projects like this are put together by well-meaning groups simply trying to make the world a better place. Pooh Bear, no doubt, would love them.

Second, the location of the honeypot is of utmost importance. You want this to be seen by the outside world, so you could place it outside the firewall. However, is that really going to fool anyone? Do you really think a seasoned attacker is just going to believe that an administrator protected everything on the network by putting everything behind a firewall, but just forgot this *really* important server on the outside? A better, more realistic placement is inside the DMZ. A hacker will discover pretty quickly where the firewall is, and placing a hard-to-find port backdoor to the honeypot is just the ticket to draw them in. Wherever the honeypot winds up being located, it needs to be walled off to prevent it becoming a launching pad for further attacks.

NOTE   Remember when we were discussing vulnerability scans a little while ago? Nessus does a good job, during a scan, of identifying where a honeypot is located. Another one of note is Send-Safe Honeypot Hunter.

KFSensor is one honeypot option available for network administrators, but bunches of them are available. Run a Google search for honeypot and you'll see what I mean. Source-Forge, NetSecurity, and many other vendors offer all sorts of honeypot versions. Honeyd is one option that even creates several virtual hosts for the hacker to lose himself in.

Chapter Review

Basic communication steps between two systems are defined by the OSI reference model and the TCP/IP protocol stack. Each layer holds specific protocols providing a unique function in the communication process. Application protocols oftentimes send information in the clear. Transport layer protocols handle sequencing and end-to-end session establishment, and are prime targets. Network and Data Link layer headers provide multiple sources for information.

The Physical layer (layer 2) address, also known as a MAC address, is burned onto the NIC itself. When the frame is being built inside the sending machine, the system uses a protocol called ARP (Address Resolution Protocol) to discover a machine on the current subnet that is capable of handling the frame. ARP also retains a cache on machines as it works. Commands used in monitoring and manipulating ARP are ping, arp, and netsh. The process of changing an ARP cache on a machine to interject faulty entries is known as ARP poisoning. Two tools for ARP flooding are Cain and Abel (a great Windows hacking tool) and dsniff (a collection of Linux tools holding a tool called ARPspoof).

Sniffing is the art of capturing packets as they pass on a wire or over the airwaves to review for interesting information. This information could be addresses to go after, information on another target, or even passwords sent in the clear. A sniffer runs in promiscuous mode, meaning regardless of address, if the frame is passing on the wire the NIC will pull it in and process it. Wireshark is probably the most popular sniffer available, and can capture packets from wired or wireless networks on a fairly easy-to-use interface.

In addition to ARP poisoning, another method for exploiting the limitations of a switch and your collision domain is known as MAC flooding. Filling the CAM with more MAC addresses than it can hold basically turns the switch into a hub, because it doesn't know which address to assign to which port and therefore simply floods every message from that point on. Most modern switches protect against this attack.

IDSs (intrusion detection systems) are hardware and/or software devices that examine streams of packets for unusual or malicious behavior. This is done via a signature list, where the IDS compares packets against a list of known traffic patterns that indicate an attack, or via a traffic comparison over time, where the anomaly-based system learns the normal traffic patterns of the subnet. A signature-based system is only as good as the signature list itself—if you don't keep it up to date, newer intrusion methods may go undetected. A behavior-based system may be better at picking up the latest attacks, because they would definitely be out of the norm. An anomaly-based system is more susceptible to false positives. A false negative occurs when traffic is deemed to be fine, with no alarm sounding when, in fact, an intrusion attempt did occur.

IDSs are either host based (HIDS) or network based (NIDS). HIDSs reside on the host itself, providing individual host protection. NIDSs provide monitoring of all network traffic, based on where the network tap is installed. Some popular HIDS examples include Cybersafe, Tripwire, Norton Internet Security, and even firewalls and other features built into the operating system itself.

Snort is an open source NIDS that combines the benefits of signature-, protocol-, and anomaly-based inspection. It has become the de facto standard for IDS and is in use on networks ranging from small businesses to U.S. government enterprise systems. It is a powerful sniffer, traffic logging, and protocol analyzing tool that can detect buffer overflows, port scans, operating system fingerprinting, and almost every conceivable external attack or probe you can imagine.

Snort rules are composed of an action, a protocol, a source address/port, a destination address/port, and message parameters. Here's an example:

```
alert tcp !HOME_NET any -> $HOME_NET 31337 (msg :"BACKDOOR ATTEMPT-Backorifice")
```

Raw Snort output provides all sorts of information, and the ports and addresses sections are of specific importance.

A firewall is an appliance within a network that is designed to protect internal resources from unauthorized external access. Firewalls work with a set of rules, explicitly stating what is allowed to pass from one side of the firewall to the other. Additionally, most firewalls work with an implicit deny principle. Firewalls can be discovered by traceroute, port-scanning tools, and a variety of other methods.

Firewalls are packet-filtering or stateful devices. Packet-filtering firewalls look at the headers of packets coming through a port and make a decision on whether or not to allow them based on the ACLs configured. Stateful firewalls have the means to track the entire status of a connection.

ACK tunneling and HTTP tunneling are examples of firewall evasion techniques, although stateful firewalls can help prevent ACK tunneling. Firewalking is the process of examining each port on the firewall to discover potential attack vectors. The best method of firewall evasion is to use a compromised machine on the inside to initiate all communication.

A honeypot is a system set up as a decoy to entice attackers. The honeypot location is very important, because the machine is designed to be attacked and needs to be walled off from the rest of your network.

Questions

1. Which of the following is *not* a defense against sniffing?

   A. Encrypting communication

   B. Implementing port security on all switches

   C. Moving to an all-switched network

   D. Using hubs within the network

2. A captured packet output from Snort shows the following:

```
02/07-11:23:13.014491 0:10:2:AC:1D:C4 -> 0:2:B3:5B:57:A6 type:0x800 len:0x3C
200.225.1.56:1244 -> 129.156.22.15:31337 TCP TTL:128 TOS:0x0 ID:17536 IpLen:20
DgmLen:48 DF
******S* Seq: 0xA153BD Ack: 0x0 Win: 0x2000 TcpLen: 28
TCP Options (4) => MSS: 1460 NOP NOP SackOK
0x0000: 00 02 B3 87 84 25 00 10 5A 01 0D 5B 08 00 45 00  .....%..Z..[..E.
0x0010: 00 30 98 43 40 00 80 06 DE EC C0 A8 01 04 C0 A8  .0.C@...........
0x0020: 01 43 04 DC 01 BB 00 A1 8B BD 00 00 00 00 70 02  .C............p.
0x0030: 20 00 4C 92 00 00 02 04 05 B4 01 01 04 02         .L...........
```

   Which of the following is correct regarding this output (choose all that apply)?

   A. The hacker is attempting an ACK tunnel attack against 200.225.1.56.

   B. The hacker is attempting to access a Backorifice install on 129.156.22.15.

   C. The attacker's IP address is 200.225.1.56.

   D. The attacker's IP address is 129.156.22.15.

3. Which layer of the TCP/IP protocol stack encapsulates data into frames?

   A. Data Link

   B. Application

   C. Network

   D. Network Access

4. You are reviewing a packet capture in Wireshark but only need to see packets from IP address 128.156.44.33. Which of the following filters will provide the output you wish to see?

   A. ip = = 128.156.44.33

   B. ip.address = = 128.156.44.33

   C. ip.src = = 128.156.44.33

   D. ip.source.address = = 128.156.44.33

5. During an out-brief from a pen test, you hear reference to an ACK tunnel attack failing against the firewall. From this fact alone, you can determine this is a ___ firewall.

   A. stateful

   B. stateless

   C. packet-filtering

   D. honeypot

6. You are configuring rules for your Snort installation and want to have an alert message of "Attempted FTP" on any FTP packet coming from an outside address intended for one of your internal hosts. Which of the following rules are correct for this situation?

   A. alert tcp $EXTERNAL_NET any -> $HOME_NET 23 (msg:"Attempted FTP")

   B. alert tcp $EXTERNAL_NET any -> $HOME_NET 25 (msg:"Attempted FTP")

   C. alert tcp $EXTERNAL_NET any -> $HOME_NET 21 (msg:"Attempted FTP")

   D. alert tcp $HOME_NET 21 -> $EXTERNAL_NET any (msg:"Attempted FTP").

7. In the Snort configuration file, which entry defines the location of the rules you will decide to implement?

   A. var RULES <*foldername*>

   B. var RULES_PATH <*foldername*>

   C. var RULES_<*foldername*>

   D. None of the above. The Snort conf file does not specify rule locations.

8. Machine A (with MAC address 00-01-02-AA-BB-CC) and Machine B (00-01-02-BB-CC-DD) are on the same subnet. Machine C, with address 00-01-02-CC-DD-EE, is on a different subnet. While sniffing on the fully switched network, Machine B sends a message to Machine C. If an attacker on Machine A wanted to receive a copy of this message, which of the following circumstances would be necessary?

   A. The ARP cache of the router would need to be poisoned, changing the entry for Machine A to 00-01-02-CC-DD-EE.

   B. The ARP cache of Machine B would need to be poisoned, changing the entry for the default gateway to 00-01-02-AA-BB-CC.

   C. The ARP cache of Machine C would need to be poisoned, changing the entry for the default gateway to 00-01-02-AA-BB-CC.

   D. The ARP cache of Machine A would need to be poisoned, changing the entry for Machine C to 00-01-02-BB-CC-DD.

9. An IDS installed on the network perimeter sees a spike in traffic during off-duty hours and begins logging and alerting. Which type of IDS is in place?

    A. Stateful

    B. Signature-based

    C. Anomaly-based

    D. Packet-filtering

10. In the Snort output listed here, which TCP flag (of flags) is set?

```
02/09-11:23:13.014491 0:10:A2:AD:EB:C5 -> 10:A2:B3:5C:57:AB type:0x800 len:0x3C
189.55.26.33:33541 -> 200.109.66.15:23 TCP TTL:128 TOS:0x0 ID:12365 IpLen:20
DgmLen:48 DF
***A**S* Seq: 0xA153BD Ack: 0xA01657 Win: 0x2000 TcpLen: 28
TCP Options (4) => MSS: 1460 NOP NOP SackOK
0x0000: 00 02 B3 87 84 25 00 10 5A 01 0D 5B 08 00 45 00  .....%..Z..[..E.
0x0010: 00 30 98 43 40 00 80 06 DE EC C0 A8 01 04 C0 A8  .0.C@...........
0x0020: 01 43 04 DC 01 BB 00 A1 8B BD 00 00 00 00 70 02  .C............p.
0x0030: 20 00 4C 92 00 00 02 04 05 B4 01 01 04 02        .L...........
```

    A. FIN

    B. ACK

    C. RST

    D. SYN

11. An attacker has successfully connected a laptop to a switch port and turned on a sniffer. The NIC is running in promiscuous mode, and the laptop is left alone for a few hours to capture traffic. Which of the following statements are true?

    A. The packet capture will provide the MAC addresses of other machines connected to the switch.

    B. The packet capture will only provide the MAC addresses of the laptop and the default gateway.

    C. The packet capture will display all traffic intended for the laptop.

    D. The packet capture will display all traffic intended for the default gateway.

Answers

1. **D.** Using a hub within a network actually makes life easier on the sniffer. A fully switched network and port security frustrate such efforts. Encryption is, by far, the best option.

2. **B and C.** In this output, the attacker (source IP listed first) has sent a SYN packet (S flag is set: " ******S*") to Backorifice (31337 is the destination port).

3. **D.** The Network Access layer includes the Data Link and Physical layers from the OSI reference model. Encapsulation into frames occurs at the Data Link layer in the OSI model, but in the Network Access layer of the TCP/IP stack.

4. **C**. ip.src = = *IPaddress* will display only those packets with the specified source IP address.

5. **A**. ACK tunneling doesn't work against stateful inspection firewalls. Stateful firewalls track the conversation, and a packet received without a SYN record would be dropped.

6. **C**. Snort rules follow the same syntax: *action protocol src address src port -> dest address port (options)*.

7. **B**. The RULES_PATH variable tells the config file where to find all Snort rules.

8. **B**. ARP poisoning is done on the machine creating the frame—the sender. Changing the default gateway entry on the sending machine results in all frames intended for an IP out of the subnet being delivered to the attacker. Changing the ARP cache on the other machine or the router is pointless.

9. **C**. IDSs can be signature- or anomaly-based. Anomaly-based systems build a baseline of normal traffic patterns over time—anything that appears outside of the baseline is flagged.

10. **B and D**. The output indicates the SYN and ACK flags are set (***A**S*).

11. **A and C**. Switches filter or flood traffic based on the address. Broadcast traffic—such as ARP requests and answers—are flooded to all ports. Unicast traffic—such as traffic intended for the default gateway—are sent only to the port on which the machine rests.

Attacking a System

6

In this chapter you will learn about
- Understanding passwords, password attacks, and password-cracking techniques
- Understanding Microsoft Authentication mechanisms
- Identifying various password-cracking tools, keyloggers, and spyware technologies
- Understanding privilege escalation
- Describing file-hiding methods, alternate data streams, and evidence erasure
- Identifying rootkits
- Understanding basic Linux file structure, directories, and commands
- Describing installation, configuration, and compilation of a Linux kernel, kernel patches, and LKMs
- Understanding GCC compilation commands
- Listing vulnerabilities and password-cracking techniques in Linux
- Understanding password cracking in Linux
- Understanding Linux hardening methods

Have you ever seen the movie *The Karate Kid*? Not that horrible remake from 2010, but the original one, from 1984. In the movie, Mr. Miyagi, an old martial arts master working as a local handyman, takes a young outcast who is being bullied by a local gang under his wing. He agrees to teach him karate to defend himself and, once "Daniel-san" agrees to do everything the master commands, he is told to show up the next morning. When Daniel-san shows up, Miyagi has him wax cars, repeating a circular motion to the left and right. The next day he has him paint a fence. The day after, Daniel-san sands the floors.

About the time Daniel has had enough and decides Miyagi isn't teaching him anything, he tells Miyagi he's quitting, and that he feels like all he's doing is chores for the old man. Miyagi stops him and demonstrates how all this repetitive motion, all this work he was doing, was actually training him for karate moves. The time he spent doing things that maybe didn't seem so important turned out to be the fundamentals he needed to be successful, and eventually made Daniel-san into a karate champion. Well, dear reader, "Wax on, wax off."

You've spent a lot of time reading about background information, and learning things that may not have seemed important up until now. All your learning thus far may not have seemed fun or sexy, but trust me, it was necessary. I know you've been chomping at the proverbial bit to start "real" hacking, and I applaud you for making your way thus far. This is the chapter where we start talking about actual system hacking—what to do once you're at the machine's front door. If you skipped ahead, go back and wax the cars in the first five chapters—you're going to need it moving forward.

Windows System Hacking

Not too long ago, I spent a lot of my professional life at the front of a classroom, teaching all sorts of goodies. In one class, on network security basics, a very nice lady in the back row started questioning my time usage. She couldn't figure out why I was spending so much time talking about Windows machines when she felt, almost religiously so, that Apple machines were so much better. I told her if I were teaching a class on portable music players, I'd spend my time on iPods, because they hold an incredible market share. If I were teaching on networking components, I'd surely spend my time on Cisco, whose market share at the time was ridiculous. But because I was teaching on computers and networks, I decide to stick with the operating system the overwhelming majority of users worldwide stick with—Windows. I didn't get a good student critique from her, but my point was and still is valid.

As of October 2009, Microsoft Windows computers made up an astonishing 91 percent of the market share for client operating systems in use on the Internet. So if we were going to…oh, I don't know…maybe write a chapter on password attacks, hacking into systems, and escalating privileges, I'd expect we'd spend the *vast* majority of our time on Microsoft Windows. You won't be able to simply read this chapter and then automatically hack into every machine you see, but I promise by the time you're done, you'll know a lot more about it. Before we get to anything else, though, we should spend a little time talking about the cornerstone of today's security—passwords.

Password Cracking

Security policy has always revolved around three things for the individual—something you are, something you have, and something you know. Some authentication measures use biometrics—fingerprints and such—to validate identity and grant access. Others use a token of some sort, such as a swipe badge or an ATM card, for authentication. But most security comes down to something you know, and that something is called a password. And before you get to cracking passwords, there are a few things you'll need to know.

Passwords 101

A password's strength is usually determined by two major functions—length and complexity. There's an argument to be made either one is better than the other, but there's no argument that both together—in one long and complex password—is the best. Password types basically are defined by what's in them, and can be made up of letters, numbers, special characters, or some combination of all. Passwords containing all numbers (for example, 12345678) or all letters (for example, AbcdEFGH) are less secure than those containing a combination of letters and numbers (for example, 1234AbcD). If you put all three together (for example, C3h!sgr8), you've got the best you can get.

Complexity aside, the length of the password is just as important—perhaps even more so. Without a long, overly complicated discussion, let's just apply a little deductive reasoning here: If a password cracker application has to only guess four characters, it's going to take exponentially less time than trying to guess five, six, or seven characters. Assuming you use nothing but alphabetic characters, upper- and lowercase, every character you add to the password raises the possible combinations by an exponent of 52. Therefore, the longer your password, and the more possible variables you have for each character in it, the longer it will take a password-cracking application and therefore the more secure you'll be.

NOTE It's a proven fact that most people on a given network will make their passwords the exact length of the minimum required. If the network administrator sets the minimum at eight characters, over 95 percent of the passwords will be only eight characters—very helpful to the password-cracking attacker. Of course, you're always welcome to use more than the minimum. As a matter of fact, Microsoft Windows systems will support passwords up to 127 characters in length.

Password Truth

Password complexity and length are important, don't get me wrong, but in and of themselves, they don't do much for real security. Yes, for your exam complexity is important, and length matters, but in reality, they can actually wind up making your network less secure if not implemented correctly. For example, suppose you require 17-character passwords that must contain lowercase letters, uppercase letters, numbers, and special characters, and must start with a number. How many of the users on your network are going to write that password down because they can't remember it? How many will carelessly leave those written notes around, or even carry those notes with them in their wallets or purses? And, of course, how many of them will be calling in for password resets frequently, opening up a whole world of social-engineering possibilities?

Want some real advice from someone who has seen both sides of the fence? Stick with simpler passwords, *but make the users change them more often.* I'll take a 12-character password made up of letters and numbers with a shelf life of only 20 days over a super-complex 12-character password good for 90 days *any time.* See, password cracking takes time. Even a simple password can take a long time to crack if it's long enough, and it's maddening to an attacker to finally crack one only to see the user has already updated to another password.

> This definitely may not be conventional thinking, but it works well and I will defend it from the mountaintop. Educate users to create simpler, but longer passwords by using a password phrase. "I'm writing a CEH book" makes one heck of a strong password. "ImWriting@CEHBook!" is 18 characters long, meets most complexity requirements, and I'd bet would take most hackers longer to crack than it's worth. Tell me I have to change it in 15 or 20 days and it's even more challenging. For that matter, a password of "LetmeinthisStupidComputer" is even better—25 characters and even easier to remember, making it a pretty good choice indeed. See what I mean?
>
> For the exam, stick with complexity and length, and stay away from using easy words in the password. In practice, make passwords easy to remember, but long, and change them very frequently.

EC-Council, in creating the CEH curriculum, has provided some essential tips on the creation of passwords. If you want to pass your exam, pay close attention to the following:

- The password must not contain any part of the user's name. For example, a password of "MattIsGr@8!" wouldn't work for the CEH exam, because you can clearly see my name there.

- The password must have a minimum of eight characters. Eight is okay. Nine is better. Seven? Not so good.

- The password must contain characters from at least three of the four major components of complexity—that is, special symbols (such as @&*#$), uppercase letters, lowercase letters, and numbers. U$e8Ch@rs contains all four, whereas use8chars uses only two.

Password Attacks

When it comes to actually attempting to crack passwords, four main attack types are defined within CEH. A *passive online* attack basically amounts to sniffing a wire in the hopes of either intercepting a password in clear text or attempting a replay or man-in-the-middle (MITM) attack. If a password is sent in clear text, such as in a Telnet session, the point is obvious. If it is sent hashed or encrypted, you can compare the value to a dictionary list or try a password cracker on the captured value. During the man-in-the-middle attack, the hacker will attempt to re-send the authentication request to the server for the client, effectively routing all traffic through the attacker's machine. In a replay attack, however, the entire authentication process is captured and replayed at a later time—the client isn't even part of the session.

In Plain Sight

We couldn't get through a discussion on passwords without mentioning encoding and the risks it entails. If you're a layer 1 (Physical layer) student like me, you know encoding as the method in which you convert a piece of information into another form or representation. For example, on a copper wire you might encode a slight tic upward in voltage as a "1," with a slight tic downward as a "0." On a fiber cable you may pick one light wavelength over another to play with bits. Well, step out of layer 1 for a second and apply this to encryption—or something that, at least, looks like it.

Base64 encoding is a method for taking binary code and representing it in an ASCII string. It's most commonly used when there is a need to encode binary data that needs be stored or transferred over media—particularly media that likes ASCII data. And it can be very helpful with identifying information in an HTTP environment. Like, say, a user ID or perhaps even a *password*.

It's great to have a good password policy, forcing your users to choose difficult, hard-to-crack passwords. It's even better for your web apps to implement all sorts of fancy encryption to protect data transfer. But if your user IDs and passwords are Base64 encoded and stored on the side (maybe as a parameter in an HTTP form, or even in a GET or a URL), you might as well forget the rest of it. Base64 isn't intended to be encryption, and there's no real decryption effort needed to read it—just plug it into any Base64 "decode" engine and voilà! Its sole purpose is to compress and compact the string for inclusion, and as a side effect it comes out in a somewhat unreadable manner. In short, it might dissuade a casual observer, but not an attacker looking for a way in.

Some passive online password hacking we've already done—just check back in Chapter 4, during the sniffing discussion. Other types of passive online password hacking can be done using specifically designed tools. One old-time favorite is Cain and Abel—a Windows-based sniffer/password cracker. You can set Cain up to sniff network traffic and leave it alone. Come back the next day and all the clear-text passwords, along with any hashes, will be stolen and ready for you. You can then use Cain for some offline brute-force or dictionary attacks on the password hashes you can't read. Let's take a look at an example via Exercise 6-1.

Exercise 6-1: Using Cain and Abel to Sniff Passwords

You can re-create this attack by following the steps outlined here—just change out the site(s) you're visiting. You can visit an FTP server (easy to download and install on a test system), websites, Telnet sessions on another machine, and more.

1. Download and install Cain and Abel, shown in Figure 6-1. Then open the program and click the Sniffer tab.

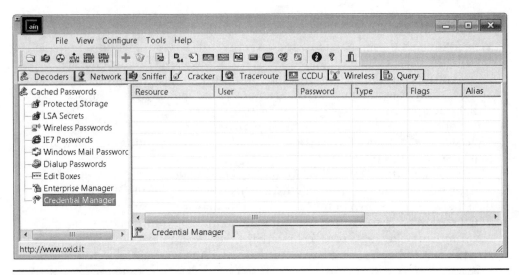

Figure 6-1 Cain

2. Click the Configure menu item and select the adapter you wish to sniff on, as shown in Figure 6-2. If you're using wireless, check the Don't Use Promiscuous Mode box at the bottom.

3. Click the Start Sniffing icon in the top left of the screen; then open a browser and head to a site requiring authentication, or start a Telnet, FTP, or MySQL login session. The more sites you hit and the more services you attempt to log on to, the more Cain will grab off the wire.

Figure 6-2
Configuration
window for Cain
sniffing

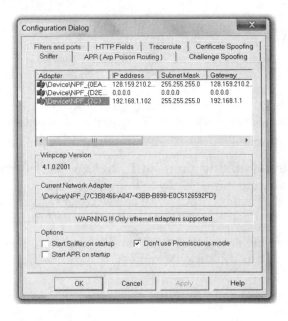

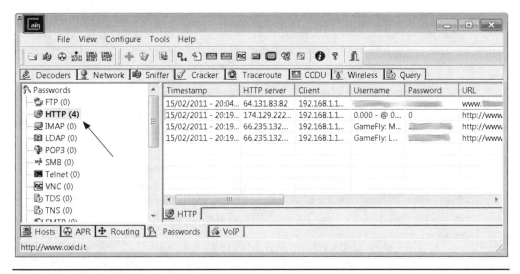

Figure 6-3 Passwords showing in Cain

4. After logging in to a few sites and services, close your browser and session(s) and then go back to Cain. Any passwords it picked up will show up on the left in bold. In Figure 6-3, you can see I grabbed an HTTP password in the clear (which I blurred out), along with a couple of other entries. Your display will most likely be different.

Any FTP, Telnet, or other password type Cain sees will be flagged and brought in for your perusal—even hashed or encrypted ones. Turn Cain on while you're surfing around for a day. I bet you'll be surprised what it picks up. And if you really want to see what a specific machine may be sending password-wise over the wire, try ARP poisoning with Cain (the button that looks like a radiation warning). The machine—or *all* of the machines if you spoof the default gateway MAC—will gladly send you everything!

Another technique you'll probably want to know about and try is called *sidejacking*. It's very helpful against those frustrating encrypted passwords and SSLs. The idea is to steal the cookies exchanged between two systems and ferret out which one to use as a replay-style attack. I suppose, technically, this isn't a password attack, but it's very apropos to our passive sniffing efforts. Two tools, Ferret and Hamster, are used to pull this off, and innumerable video tutorials on the Web show how easy these tools are to use.

Basically, you monitor the victim's traffic using a sniffer and packet-capture tool (Ferret), and a file called Hamster.txt is created. After the victim has logged in to a site or two, you fire up Hamster as a proxy, and the cookies and authentication streams from the captured TXT file will be displayed. You simply click through them until one works—it's that easy (of course, both machines must be on the same subnet). Installation of the tools can be a bit tricky, so be sure to check the help pages on the download site.

This can also be accomplished using a Firefox plug-in called Add N Edit Cookies (https://addons.mozilla.org/en-us/firefox/addon/add-n-edit-cookies/). If you have a couple of VMs to play with on your machine, try the following—you may be surprised at the results:

1. Clear your browser cache and then log in to just about any site you want.

2. Open Add N Edit Cookies. You'll notice several variables appear, such as PHPSESSID if it's PHP based, or three to four others if it's ASP or some other platform.

3. Go to your second VM (or machine), open Firefox, and open Add N Edit Cookies. Copy and paste (or just re-create) all the content from the first VM. Be sure to set the timeout to something interesting (such as the year 2020).

4. Open the site you had gone to from the original VM. Voilà!

A surprising majority of sites use this method of session identification, and are just as easily "hacked." For those that don't, a combination of URL variables, HTTP GETs, and all sorts of other things will frustrate your efforts and cause you to try other methods—if this is, indeed, your goal. In practice, getting the session IDs from a website through XSS or other means can be tricky (Internet Explorer, for example, has done a really good job of locking down access to session cookies), but I believe this validates our discussions on physical security: If an attacker has uninterrupted physical access to the machine, it's only a matter of time before the system is hacked, regardless of what security measures may already be in place. Internet Explorer plays with cookies differently, so there's some trickiness involved, but this is an easy way to sidejack.

A few other tools of note are Ettercap, ScoopLM, and KerbCrack. Ettercap we've already mentioned earlier, but it warrants another few minutes of fame here. As with Cain, you can ARP poison and sniff with Ettercap and steal just about anything the machine sends out. Ettercap can also help out against pesky SSL encryption (which prevents an easy password sniff). Because Ettercap is very customizable, you can set it up as an SSL proxy and simply park between your target and any SSL site the victim is trying to visit. I watched this happen on my own banking account in our lab where we worked. My co-worker simply put himself (virtually) between my system and the SSL site, stole the session, applied an Ettercap filter to pull out gzip compression, and the encoded strings were there for the taking. The only indication anything was out of sorts, on the user's side? A quick warning banner that the certificate needed looking at, which most people will click past without even thinking about it.

Speaking of SSL and its password-protecting madness, you should also check out sslsniff (www.thoughtcrime.org/software/sslsniff/). sslsniff was originally written to demonstrate and exploit IE's vulnerability to a specific "basicConstraints" man-in-the-middle attack, but has proven useful for many other SSL hacks (Microsoft has since fixed the original vulnerability). It is designed to man in the middle "all SSL connections on a LAN and dynamically generate certificates for the domains that are being accessed on the fly. The new certificates are constructed in a certificate chain that is signed by any certificate that you provide." Pretty good news for the budding pen tester, indeed.

NOTE Thoughtcrime has all sorts of other tools that warrant attention—maybe not in the password-cracking section here, but definitely worth your while. Take some time and explore their other offerings. Some are very cool hacking tools, and some, such as GoogleSharing and fakeroute, are just plain fun.

ScoopLM has a built-in password cracker and specifically looks for Windows authentication traffic on the wire to pull passwords from. KerbCrack also has a built-in sniffer and password cracker, specifically looking for port 88 Kerberos traffic.

NOTE In addition to the info here and all the notes and such accompanying this book, don't ignore the resources available to you on the Internet. Do a few searches for videos on "sniffing passwords" and any, or all, of the tools mentioned. And don't discount the websites providing these tools—you can usually find forums and all sorts of stories and help.

The second password attack type, active online, occurs when the attacker begins simply trying passwords—guessing them, for lack of a better word. Active online attacks take a much longer time than passive attacks, and are also much easier to detect. These attacks try to take advantage of bad passwords and security practices by individuals on a network. If you happen to have identified a dinosaur Windows NT or 2000 machine on your target network, you can bang away at the IPC$ share and guess all you want.

If you're facing Windows XP and Windows 7 machines, the old "administrator" C$ share is still usually valid and, as always, you can't lock out the true administrator account. You can try any variety of scripts available to run through usernames and passwords against this share—just keep in mind it's noisy and you're bound to get noticed. Decent network and systems administrators will change the local administrator account's name to something else (such as admin, sysadmin, or admin1), so don't be surprised if you wind up locking a few accounts out while trying to get to the real one.

Don't forget the old "net" commands. The use of null sessions isn't a lost art; you'll probably see a couple questions on this topic, and a lot of it is very beneficial in determining how you set up your password-sniffing and active online attacks. Here are a few to remember from your enumeration time:

- **net view /domain:***domainname* Shows all systems in the domain name provided
- **net view ***systemname* Provides a list of open shares on the system named
- **net use ***target***\ipc$ "" /u: "** Sets up a null session

Combined with tools such as the NetBIOS Auditing tool (NAT) and Legion, you can automate the testing of user IDs and passwords.

The other two attack types are offline and non-electronic. Offline attacks occur when the hacker steals a copy of the password file (remember our discussion on the SAM file earlier?) and works the cracking efforts on a separate system. These attacks usually require some form of physical access to the machine (not as hard as you'd like to believe in a lot of cases—trust me) where the attacker pulls the password file to removable media, then sneaks off to crack passwords at his leisure.

Password cracking offline can be done in one of three main ways—dictionary attack, hybrid attack, and brute-force attack. A *dictionary attack* is the easiest and by far the fastest attack available. This attack uses a list of passwords in a text file, which is then hashed by the same algorithm/process the original password was put through. The hashes are compared and, if a match is found, the password is cracked. Technically speaking, dictionary attacks are only supposed to work on words you'd find in a dictionary. They can work just as well on "complex" passwords too; however, the word list you use must have the exact match in it—you can't get close, it must be exact. You can create your own dictionary file or simply download any of the thousands available on the Internet.

A hybrid attack is a step above the dictionary attack. In the hybrid attack, the cracking tool is smart enough to take words from a list and substitute numbers and symbols for alpha characters—perhaps a zero for an *O*, an @ for an *a*. Hybrid attacks may also append numbers and symbols to the end of dictionary file passwords—bet you've never simply added a "1234" to the end of a password before, huh? By doing so, you stand a better chance of cracking passwords in a complex environment.

 NOTE Password cracking can also be sped up using "rainbow tables." The amount of time it takes a cracker to work is dramatically increased by having to generate all these hashes over and over again. A rainbow table does all this computation ahead of time, hashing every combination and creating huge files of hashes for comparison.

The last type is called a brute-force attack, and it's exactly what it sounds like. In a brute-force attack, every conceivable combination of letters, numbers, and special characters is compared against the hash to determine a match. Obviously, this is very time consuming, chewing up a lot of computation cycles and making this the longest of the three methods. However, it is your best option on complex passwords, and there is no arguing its effectiveness—given enough time, *every* password can be cracked using brute force. Granted, we could be talking about years here—maybe even hundreds of years—but it's always 100 percent effective over time.

If you cut down the number of characters the cracker has to work with, and reduce the number of variations available, you can dramatically reduce that time span. For example, if you're in a network and you know the minimum password length is eight characters, then there's no point in having your cracker go through all the variations of seven characters or less. Additionally, if you've got a pretty good idea the user doesn't like all special characters and prefers to stick with the "Fab Four" (!, @, #, and $), there's no sense in having your cracker try combinations that include characters such as &, *, and (.

For example—and to stick with a tool we've already been talking about—Cain is fairly good at cracking Windows passwords, given enough time and processing cycles. For this demonstration, I created a local account on my system and gave it a (purposefully) short, four character password: P@s5. Firing up Cain, I clicked the Cracker menu choice, clicked the LM&NTLM Hashes option on the left, then clicked the big blue plus sign (+) at the top. Once all my accounts and associated passwords were dumped (simulating a hacker who had snuck in and taken them without my knowledge), I clicked my new user, cut down the number of possible characters for Cain to try (instead of all alphanumeric and special characters, I cut it down to 10, simply to speed up the process), and started the cracking. Forty-six minutes later, almost on the button, the password was cracked.

Of course, multiple tools are available for password cracking. Cain, KerbCrack, and Legion have already been mentioned. Another is John the Ripper—one of the more "famous" tools available. John is a Linux tool that can crack Unix, Windows NT, and Kerberos passwords. You can also download some add-ons that allow John to crack other passwords types (MySQL, for instance). LC5, the next generation of the old L0phtcrack tool, does an excellent job on a variety of passwords. Regardless of the tool, remember that dictionary attacks are fastest, and brute force takes the longest.

EXAM TIP Passwords on Windows systems are found in the SAM file, located in c:\windows\system32\config (you might also be able to pull one from the c:\windows\repair folder). Passwords for Linux are found in /etc/shadow.

Finally, there is one other method of lifting passwords we need to cover. If implemented correctly, it works with 100 percent accuracy and always grabs passwords in clear text, thus requiring no time at all to crack them. It's also relatively easy to do and requires almost no technical knowledge at all.

Keylogging is the process of using a hardware device or software application to capture the keystrokes a user types. Using this method, it really doesn't matter what authentication method you're using, or whether you're salting a hash or not—the keystrokes are captured as they are typed, regardless of what they're being typed for. Keyloggers can be hardware devices—usually small devices connected between the keyboard cable and the computer—or software applications installed and running in the background. In either case, keyloggers are an exceptionally powerful and productive method for scoring big hits on your target. Most users have no means to even realize a software application is running in the background, and most people rarely, if ever, look behind their computers to check for a hardware device. When was the last time you checked yours?

EXAM TIP This should go without saying, but I'll say it anyway: Software keyloggers are easy to spot with antivirus and other scanning options, whereas hardware keyloggers are almost impossible to detect.

The last password attack type, non-electronic, is so powerful and so productive I'm going to devote an entire chapter to it later on. Social engineering takes on many different forms and is by far the best hacking method ever devised by humankind. When it comes to passwords, the absolute best way to get one is just to ask the user for it. Phrased the right way, when the user believes you to be someone from the IT department or a security agent, asking users flat out for their passwords will work about 50 percent of the time. Another productive method is *shoulder surfing*—that is, looking over the user's shoulder to watch the keystrokes. Refer to Chapter 7 for more information on this little jewel and other ridiculously easy social engineering efforts to discover passwords.

Windows Hashing

I can almost hear a few of you asking the question, "Why does he keep talking about cracking a *hash?* Aren't we supposed to be cracking passwords?" Well, yes and no. See, passwords aren't ever stored in their original state—they're encrypted, for obvious reasons. If a bad guy comes along and steals your password file, you don't want them sitting there in clear text. So, most operating system providers will only store the hash of a password locally.

With Windows machines, this hashing thing has a long history. Back in the days when people rewound movies after watching them (those of you who remember the VHS vs. Beta debate are nodding here at the reference), Windows 2000 and Windows NT–type machines used something called LAN Manager, and then NT LAN Manager, to hash passwords. LM hashing would first take the password and convert everything to uppercase. Then, if the password was less than 14 characters, it would add blank spaces to get it to 14. Then the new, all-uppercase, 14-character password would be split into two seven-character strings. These strings would be hashed separately, then both hashes would be combined for the output.

NOTE LM Authentication (DES) was used with Windows 95/98 machines. NTLM (DES and MD$) was used with Windows NT machines until SP3. NTLM v2 (MD5) was used after that. Kerberos came about with Windows 2000. All are still important to know and try, because many systems keep the authentication mechanisms around for backward-compatibility reasons.

Obviously, this makes things easier for a hacker. How so, you may be asking? Well, if a password is seven characters or less (or only uses one or two character spaces in the second portion), this significantly reduces the amount of time required to crack the rest of it—due to the fact that the LM hash value of seven blank characters will always be the same (AAD3B435B51404EE). For example, consider a password of M@tt123. The entire LM hash might look like this when we steal it: 9FAF6B755DC38E12AAD3B-435B51404EE. Because we know how the hash is created, we can split it in half to work on each side separately: 9FAF6B755DC38E12 is the first half, and AAD3B435B51404EE is the second. The first half we put through a cracker and get to work. The second, though, is easily recognizable as the hash value of seven blank characters! This tells us the password is seven characters or less, and greatly reduces the amount of time the cracking software will need to break the password.

 NOTE Steps an administrator can take to reduce the risk in regard to password theft and cracking are fairly common sense. Never leave default passwords in place after installs, follow naming rules with passwords (no personal names, pet names, birthdates, and so on), require longer passwords, and change them often. Additionally, constantly and consistently check every account with credentials higher than that of a normal user, and be very, very careful with accounts that have "permanent" passwords. If it's not going to be changed, it better be one heck of a good password. Lastly, remember that keeping an eye on event logs can be helpful in tracking down failed attempts at password guessing.

Of course, finding an easy-to-crack NTLM hash on your target system won't be easy. You'll first have to steal it, usually via physical access with a bootable CD or maybe even through a copy found on a backup tape. Even after it has been obtained, though, the addition of salting (discussed in Chapter 2 earlier) and the use of better methods for authentication (NTLMv2 and Kerberos, if you sniff the hash value) make life for a password cracker pretty tough. Most administrators are wising up and forcing users into longer passwords with shorter timeframes in which to keep them. Not to mention Windows has gotten *much* better at password security in the past decade or so. LM authentication has six different levels available now (0 is the Windows XP default, and 2 is the Windows 2003 default) and Kerberos transports the passwords much more securely than previously. Remember, though, you're not hunting the healthy—you're looking for the weak and overlooked.

Speaking of the healthy, we'll need a second or two here to discuss Kerberos authentication and passwords in "modern" Windows networking. Kerberos makes use of both symmetric and asymmetric encryption technologies to securely transmit passwords and keys across a network. The entire process is made up of a Key Distribution Center (KDC), an Authentication Service (AS), a Ticket Granting Service (TGS), and the Ticket Granting Ticket (TGT).

A basic Kerberos exchange follows a few easy, but very secure steps. The client first asks the KDC (which holds the AS and TGS) for a ticket, which will be used to authenticate throughout the network. This request is in clear text. The server will respond with a secret key, which is hashed by the password copy kept on the server (in Active Directory). This is known as the TGT. If the client can decrypt the message (and it should since it knows the password), the TGT is sent back to the server requesting a TGS service ticket. The server responds with the service ticket, and the client is allowed to log on and access network resources.

You'll note that, once again, the password itself is never sent. Instead, a hash value of the password, encrypted with a secret key known only by both parties and good only for that session, is all that's sent. This doesn't mean the password is unbreakable, it just means it's going to take a lot of time and effort. KerbSniff and KerbCrack are options, but be prepared—it's a long, grueling process.

Escalating Privileges and Maintaining Stealth

The only real problem with user IDs and password hacking is that, once you crack one, you're stuck with the privilege level of the user. Aside from that, assuming you do gain access, how can you continue to maintain that access while staying under cover? If the user account is not an administrator, or doesn't have access to interesting shares, then you're not much better off than you were before, and if you are so noisy in your attack, it won't do you much good anyway. Well, remember the five stages of hacking from way back in Chapter 1? During that discussion, there was a little Exam Tip for you about escalation of privileges—the bridge between gaining access and maintaining access. In this section, we'll go over some of the basics on escalating your current privilege level to something a little more fun, as well as some methods you can apply to keep your hacking efforts a little quieter.

Privilege Escalation

Unfortunately, escalating the privilege of an account you've hacked isn't a very easy thing to do—unless the system you're on isn't fully patched. Quite obviously, operating systems put in all sorts of roadblocks to prevent you from doing so. However, as you've no doubt noticed, operating systems aren't released with 100 percent of all security holes plugged. Rather, it's quite the opposite, and security patches are released with frequency to address holes, bugs, and flaws discovered "in the wild." In just one week during the writing of this chapter alone, Microsoft released 15 patches addressing a wide variety of issues—some of which involved the escalation of privileges.

Basically you have four real hopes for obtaining administrator (root) privileges on a machine. The first is to crack the password of an administrator or root account, which should be your primary aim (at least as far as the CEH exam is concerned) and makes the rest of this section moot. The second is to take advantage of a vulnerability found in the OS, or in an application, that will allow you access as a privileged user. Remember way back in Chapter 3 about the importance of paying attention to vulnerability websites? This is where that pays off. In addition to running vulnerability scanners (such as Nessus) to find holes, you should be well aware of what to already look for before the scanner gets the results back to you.

 NOTE Cracking a password in the real world of penetration testing isn't really the point at all. Getting access to the data or services, or achieving whatever generic goal you have, is the point. If this goal involves having administrative privileges, so be it. If not, don't sit there hammering away at an admin password because you believe it to be the "Holy Grail." Get what you came for and get out, as quickly and stealthily as you can.

For example, in December of 2009, both Java and Adobe had some very serious flaws in their applications that allowed attackers to run code at a privileged level. This information spread quickly and resulted in hacking and DoS attacks rising rather significantly until the fix actions came out. Once again, it's not something magic or overly technically complicated you're attempting to do here—you're just taking advantage of unpatched security flaws in the system. The goal is to run code—whatever code you choose—at whatever level is necessary to accomplish your intent. Sometimes this means running at an administrative level regardless of your current user level, which requires escalation and a little bit of noisiness, and sometimes it doesn't. Again, in the real world, don't lose sight of the end goal in an effort to accomplish something you read in a book.

The third method is to use a tool that will hopefully provide you the access you're looking for. One such tool, Metasploit, is an entire hacking suite in one and is a great exploit-testing tool (in other words, it's about a heck of a lot more than privilege escalation and will be discussed more as this book continues). You basically enter the IP address and port number of the target you're aiming at, choose an exploit, and add a payload—Metasploit does the rest. I find the web front end easier to use (see Figure 6-4) but some purists will tell you it's always command line or nothing.

Metasploit has a free version and a pay-for version, known as Metasploit Pro. The framework you can download for free works perfectly well, but the Pro version, although expensive, is simply unbelievable. To say Metasploit is an important player in the pen testing/hacking realm is akin to saying Mount Everest is "kind of" tall. It's a very powerful pen testing suite that warrants more attention than I have room for in this book. Visit the website (www.metasploit.com) and learn more about this opportunity for yourself. There are tons of help pages, communities, a blog board, and more, to provide assistance. Trust me—you'll need them.

Figure 6-4   Metasploit's main window

Sometimes Free Is Even Better!

Some of you—my tech editor included—are losing your collective minds because a $5,000 GUI front end for using Metasploit seems just a little on the ridiculous side. I agree, especially when there's a free alternative that may be just as good.

The happy folks at Armitage (http://fastandeasyhacking.com/) have done a great job putting together a GUI front end for Metasploit that is, in a word, awesome. There are manuals, videos, and screenshots aplenty to help you along, and the information is truly incredible. The developer states on the site that Armitage was developed because there are too many security professionals who don't know how to use Metasploit, and felt Metasploit could use a "non-commercial GUI organized around the hacking process." Again, from the site: "Armitage exists to help security professionals better understand the hacking process and appreciate what's possible with the powerful Metasploit framework. Security professionals who understand hacking will make better decisions to protect you and your information."

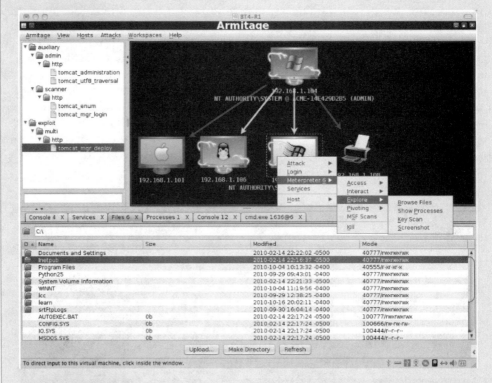

I highly recommend you go check it out. You won't see it mentioned on your exam—at least I don't think you will—but it's definitely worth checking out for your job. You won't be disappointed.

Other tools are definitely worth mentioning here. CANVAS and Core Impact are two other all-in-one packages (Core Impact is a *complete* pen testing toolset that is insanely expensive). Other tools used for privilege escalation (which, by the way, may or may not work depending on your OS and the level at which it is patched) are billybastard.c (useful on Windows 2003 and Windows XP machines) and GetAd (Windows XP). Older tools for "dinosaur" Windows 2000 and Windows NT devices you may find are GetAdmin and HK.exe.

Finally, the last method available may actually seem like cheating to you, because it's so ridiculously easy you might not have even thought about it. What if you just asked the current user to run an application for you? Then you don't need to bother with hacking and all that pesky technology at all. This type of social engineering will be discussed in greater detail in Chapter 7, but it's undeniably productive. You can simply put executable code in an e-mail and ask the user to click it—more often than not, they will! Craft a PDF file to take advantage of a known Adobe flaw on an unpatched system and send it to them—most of the time, they'll click and open it! This is by far the easiest method available and, probably, will wind up being your most effective over time. Stay tuned to learn more.

Stealth: Before, During, and After

So you've spent your time examining potential targets, mapping out open ports, scanning for vulnerabilities, and prepping for an attack. After a few tries you successfully steal a password and find yourself sitting on the machine, logged on and ready to go. Now that you're there, you have to be aware of all the attention that will be focused on your actions. Is the security administrator on the ball? Do they actively monitor the event logs on a regular basis? Is there a Host-based Intrusion Detection System (HIDS) on the machine? How can you get information from it quietly and unnoticed? Scary thoughts, huh?

Stealth in hacking truly comes down to patience—spend enough time, move slowly enough, and chances are better than not you'll go unnoticed. Lose patience and try to upload every groovy file you see on the machine and you'll quickly find yourself firewalled off and trapped. But there's also stealth involved in hiding files, covering your tracks, and maintaining access on the machine.

One really great way to hide files on Windows machines is through the use of alternate data streams (ADS) in the form of NTFS (New Technology File System) file streaming. ADS is a feature of the Windows-native NTFS to ensure compatibility with Apple file systems (called HFS). ADS has been around ever since the Windows NT days and has held on all the way through to current Windows releases: NTFS streaming still works on Windows 7 machines, believe it or not.

NTFS file steaming allows you to hide virtually any file behind any other file, rendering it invisible to directory searches. The file can be a text file, to remind you of steps to take when you return to the target, or even an executable file you can run at your leisure later on. To see this in action, let's run a little exercise.

NOTE It's noteworthy to point out here that *every* forensics kit on Earth checks for ADS at this point. Additionally, in modern versions of Windows, an executable that's run inside of a .txt file, for instance, will show up in the Task Manager as part of the parent. EC-Council writes this generically for the exam, and we've tried to stay true to that; however, there are some times when reality and the test collide so awkwardly we simply can't stay silent about it.

Exercise 6-2: NTFS File Streaming

In the first part of this exercise, you want to hide the contents of a file named want-tohide.txt. To do this, you're going to hide it behind a normal file that anyone browsing the directory would see. In the second part, you'll hide an *executable* behind a file. Here is the first set of steps to follow:

1. Create a folder called C:\FStream. Copy notepad.exe into the folder.

2. Create a text file (normal.txt) in the folder. Add some text to it—doesn't matter what—and then save the file. Create a second text file (wanttohide.txt), add text to it, and then save.

3. Open a command prompt and navigate to the C:\FStream folder. Type **dir** to show the contents. You should now have notepad.exe, normal.txt, and wanttohide.txt in the folder.

4. In the command prompt, enter **type wanttohide.txt > original.txt:hidden. txt**. This creates a copy of wanttohide.txt into a file called hidden.txt behind normal.txt.

5. Delete wanttohide.txt from the C:\FStream folder. Now anyone browsing will only see notepad.exe and normal.txt.

6. From the command prompt, enter start **c:\test\normla.txt:hidden.txt**. Voilà! Notepad opens and the contents of the text file are displayed.

Now let's try an executable file:

1. In the C:\FStream folder, create another text file named second.txt.

2. Open a command prompt and navigate to the folder. Enter the command **type notepad.exe > second.txt:notepad.exe**. This creates a hidden copy of notepad.exe behind the text file second.txt.

3. Delete notepad.exe from C:\test. Type **dir** at the command prompt and verify that no more executables are visible in the folder.

4. Enter start **c:\test\second.txt:notepad.exe** at the command prompt. Huzzah! You've just opened a hidden executable!

NOTE You can hide any file type behind any other file type using this method. Spreadsheets, slides, documents, and even image files will work too.

If you're a concerned security professional wondering how to protect against this insidious built-in Windows "feature," relax, all is not lost. Several applications, such as LNS and Sfind, are created specifically to hunt down ADS. Additionally, Windows Vista has a groovy little addition to the directory command (dir /r) that will display all file streams in the directory. Lastly, copying files to and from a FAT partition blows away any residual file streams in the directory.

Although it's not 100 percent certain to work, because most security professionals know to look for it, we can't neglect to bring up the attributes of the files themselves and how they can be used to disguise their location. One of these attributes—hidden— does not display the file during file searches of folder browsing (unless the admin changes the view to force all hidden files to show). In Windows, you can hide a file by right-clicking, choosing Properties, and checking the Hidden attribute check box. Of course, to satisfy you command-line junkies who hate the very thought of using anything GUI, you can also do this by issuing the attrib command:

```
attrib +h filename
```

Another file-hiding technique we've already hit on back in Chapter 2 is steganography. Sure, we could discuss encryption as a hiding technique here as well, but encrypting a file still leaves it visible—steganography hides it in plain sight. For example, if you've gained access to a machine and you want to ferret out sensitive data files, wouldn't it be a great idea to hide them in JPG files of the basketball game and e-mail them to your buddy? Anyone monitoring the line would see nothing but a friendly sports conversation. Tools for hiding files of all sorts in regular image or other files are ImageHide, Snow, Mp3Stego, Blindside, S-tools, wbStego, and Stealth. Refer back to Chapter 2 if you've forgotten most of our steganography discussion (and invest in some ginkgo biloba to address your short-term memory issues).

In addition to hiding files for further manipulation/use on the machine, covering your tracks while stomping around in someone else's virtual play yard is also a cornerstone of success. The first thing that normally comes to mind for any hacker is the ever-present event log, and when it comes to Windows systems there are a few details you should know up front. First, you'll need to comb over three main logs to cover your tracks—the application, system, and security logs.

The application log holds entries specifically related to the applications themselves, and only entries programmed by the developers get in. For example, if an application tries to access a file and the file has been corrupted or moved, the developer may have an error logged to mark that. The system log registers system events, such as drivers failing and startup/shutdown times. The security log records the juicy stuff—login attempts, access and activities regarding resources, and so on. To edit auditing (the security log won't record a thing unless you tell it to), you must have administrative privileges on the machine. Depending on what you're trying to do to the machine, one or all of these may need scrubbing. The security log, obviously, will be of primary concern, but don't neglect your tracks in the others.

Many times a new hacker will simply attempt to delete the log altogether. This, however, does little to cover your tracks. As a matter of fact, it usually sends a giant blaring signal to anyone monitoring log files that someone is messing around on the system. Why? Because anyone monitoring an event log will tell you it is *never* empty. If they're looking at it scrolling by the day before your attack, then come back the next day and see only 10 entries, someone's going into panic mode.

A far better plan is to take your time (a familiar refrain is building around this, can't you see?) and be selective in your event log editing. Some people will automatically go to the jugular and turn auditing off altogether, run their activities, then turn it back on. Sure, your efforts won't be logged in the first place, but isn't a giant hole in the log just as big an indicator as error events themselves? Why not go in, first, and just *edit* what is actually being audited. If possible, only turn off auditing on the things you'll be hitting—items such as failed resource access, failed logins, and so on. Then, go visit the log and get rid of those items noting your presence and activities. And don't forget to get rid of the security event log showing where you edited the audit log.

 NOTE Another tip for hiding tracks in regard to log files is to not even bother trying to hide your efforts, but rather simply corrupt the log file after you're done. Files corrupt all the time and, often, a security manager may not even bother to try to rebuild a corrupted version—assuming "stuff happens."

One last note on log files and, I promise, I'll stop talking about them: Did you know security administrators can move the default location of the log files? By default, everyone knows to look in %systemroot%\System32\Config to find the logs—each will have an .evt extension. However, updating the individual file entries in the appropriate registry key (HKEY_LOCAL_MACHINE\SYSTEM\CurrentControlSet\Services\EventLog) allows you to place them wherever you'd like. If you've gained access to a system and the logs aren't where they're supposed to be, you can bet you're in for a tough day—the security admin may already have eyes on you.

A few tools are available for taking care of event log issues. In Control Panel | Administrative Tools | Local Security Policy, you can set up and change the audit policy for the system. The top-level settings are found under Local Policies | Audit Policy. Other settings of note are found in the Advanced Audit Policy Configuration at the bottom of the listings under Security Settings. Other tools of note include, but are not limited to, elsave, WinZapper, and Evidence Eliminator. Lastly, Auditpol (shown in Figure 6-5) is a tool included in the old Windows NT Resource Kit that may be useful on older sys-

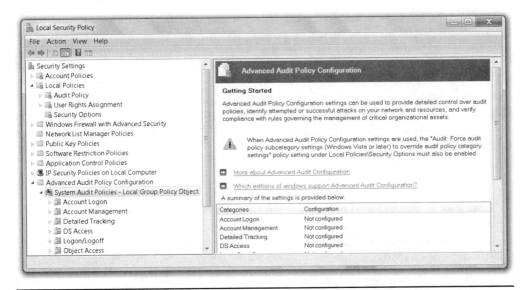

Figure 6-5   Windows Audit Policy

tems. You can use it to disable event logs on other machines. The following should do the trick:

```
c:\auditpol \\targetIPaddress /disable
```

Rootkits

Finally, no discussion on system hacking and maintaining stealth/access on the machine can be complete without bringing up rootkits. A *rootkit* is a collection of software put in place by an attacker that is designed to obscure system compromise. In other words, if a system has a properly introduced rootkit installed, the user and security monitors won't even know anything is wrong. Rootkits are designed to provide backdoors for the attacker to use later on and include measures to remove and hide evidence of any activity. Per the CEH objectives, there are three types of rootkits:

- **Application level**   As the name implies, these rootkits are directed to replace valid application files with Trojan binaries. These kits work inside an application and can use an assortment of means to change the application's behavior, user rights level, and actions.

- **Kernel level**   These rootkits attack the boot sectors and kernel level of the operating systems themselves, replacing kernel code with backdoor code. These are by far the most dangerous and are difficult to detect and remove.

- **Library level**   These rootkits basically make use of system-level calls to hide their existence.

Originally, rootkits started in the Linux realm and had two big flavors. In one setup, the rootkit replaced all sorts of actual binaries to hide processes. These were easily detectable, though, due to size—tools such as Tripwire could easily point out the existence of the rootkit. Later on, they evolved to being loaded as a drive or kernel extension—via something called a Loadable Kernel Module (LKM). Early rootkits in the Linux world included Adorm, Flea, and T0rm. Tools for helping discover rootkits already installed on a machine include chkrootkit and Rootkit Hunter.

When it comes to Windows system hacking, passwords are definitely the key, but obviously there are many other avenues to travel. In later chapters we'll cover looking

The Most Successful Rootkit You've Never Heard Of

If you've started implementing what has been written so far in this book, then you're already monitoring vulnerability and malware boards for news. And you already know about my topic here. Rootkits are hardly new—they've been around since LKMs reared their heads in the early Unix days—and it's not like they don't get media coverage: Sony's famous foray into rootkits in 2005 with their proprietary BMG CD software generated howls of protest worldwide and backfired quickly on them. But the rapid worldwide spread of the ubiquitous TDSS rootkit seems to be the best rootkit you've never heard of.

Starting in 2008, TDSS has become to malware promoters and writers what Linux was to the open source community. The rootkit has been "improved" and added to in multiple variations to make it the preeminent threat for casual, "drive-by" infection vectors. In 2009, an estimated 3 million systems were infected and effectively controlled by the TDSS rootkit. That number has since grown exponentially, and has spawned a worldwide effort at defeating and removing the rootkit.

TDSS has spread by peer-to-peer networks, by crack and keygen websites, and through various ad streams and social networking tie-ins that take advantage of any number of Java, Adobe, and other vulnerabilities users simply forget to patch. The kit initially needs administrator privileges to run; however, open vulnerabilities often allow that escalation and, in many cases, the user will simply voluntarily give permission, ignoring any pesky warning or error messages.

Once installed, this kit is virtually invisible. Sure, some antivirus programs will display a warning or two about it, and may even tell you flat out you're infected. However, most can't do a thing about it—once it's installed, you're cooked. Removal of the kit is possible using a few tools available on the Net, but be careful—many of the fixes are worse than the infection. Your best option is to simply reload the system.

This example just goes to show the threat is real, pervasive, and going on right now. Maybe word about TDSS has made it your way and maybe it hasn't. But if the machine you're on is beaconing to an ".ru" server about your clicks and links through Google and Yahoo!, you're probably a TDSS bot and don't even know it.

at some of them. For now, keep your eye on the SAM file, get some good practice in with online and offline attack tools, and practice covering your tracks.

NOTE Rootkits are exponentially more complicated than your typical malware application and reflect significant sophistication. If your company detects a customized rootkit and thinks they were targeted, it's time to get the FBI involved. And to truly scare the wits out of you, check out what a truly sophisticated rootkit can do: http://en.wikipedia.org/wiki/Blue_Pill_(malware).

Linux Hacking

The first section of this chapter started by letting you know the vast majority of machines you'll see in your testing will be Microsoft Windows boxes. However, no one cannot possibly write a book on computing—much less a book on hacking techniques, for goodness' sake—without including a discussion on the most popular, powerful operating system you may never have heard of. Not just because you may find a box or two you want to try to hack into, but also because the OS provides such a great platform for launching attacks. Linux comes in more flavors than your local ice cream shop can come up with and is largely available for free. People from around the world have openly and freely contributed to it and have developed many Windows-like offerings, as well as very powerful servers. In this section, we'll cover some of the basics you'll need to know with Linux and discuss just a few options you may have in hardening the box.

Linux Essentials

If you've spent any time in networking or computing over the past 20 years or so, I'm sure you've heard the Linux zealots screaming at you about how great and powerful their operating system is. Although I'd love to sit here and debunk them (mainly because it's just so much fun to rile them up), it actually *is* a great OS. Linux never had the ease of use Windows provided early on, and lost market share because of it. However, the OS has come a long way, and more than a few point-and-click Linux GUIs are available. Although we won't discuss all the versions here, I highly recommend you download a few ISOs and burn some bootable disks—you'll be amazed how easy to use some of the GUI versions have gotten.

NOTE Red Hat is one of the better known and most prevalent Linux "distros," but it's certainly not the only one. Ubuntu, Gentoo, SuSe, Fedora, and a thousand others are just as easy to use and just as powerful. Many have great GUI front ends, and some look surprisingly a lot like their Windows counterparts. A link to watch for all the crazy variants out there is http://distrowatch.com. You can get a good feel for which ones are most popular, which ones aren't, and what advantages they can offer you.

File System and Basic Commands

Any discussion on an OS has to start with the basics, and you can't get more basic than the file system. The Linux file system isn't that far removed from the NTFS layout you're already familiar with in Windows—it's just a little different. Linux starts with a root directory just as Windows does. The Windows root is (usually) C:\. The Linux root is just a slash (/). It also has folders holding specific information for specific purposes, just like Windows. The basic file structure for Linux is shown in Figure 6-6, and here's a list of the important folders you'll need to know:

- **/** A forward slash represents the root directory.

- **/bin** The bin directory holds all sorts of basic Linux commands (a lot like the C:\Windows\System32 folder in Windows).

- **/dev** This folder contains the pointer locations to the various storage and input/output systems you will need to mount if you want to use them—such as optical drives and additional hard drives or partitions. Note: *Everything* in Linux is a file. Everything.

- **/etc** The etc folder contains all the administration files and passwords. Both the password and shadow files are found here.

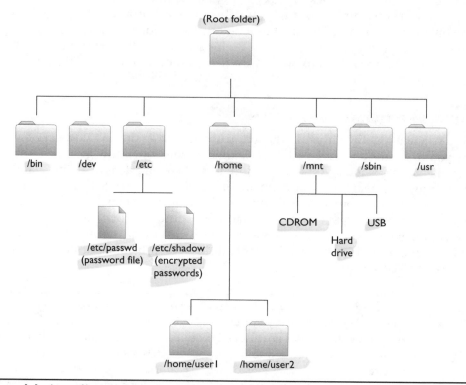

Figure 6-6 Linux file structure

- **/home** This folder holds the user home directories.

- **/mnt** This folder holds the access locations you've actually mounted.

- **/sbin** Another folder of great importance, the system binaries folder holds more administrative commands and is the repository for most of the routines Linux runs (known as *daemons*).

- **/usr** Amazingly enough, the usr folder holds almost all of the information, commands, and files unique to the users.

When you log in to the command line in a Linux environment, you will start in your assigned directory and can move around simply by using the cd (change directory) command. You'll need to, of course, define the path you wish to use, so it's very important to know where you are. Many terminal sessions display the path just to the left; however, if you're unsure, type **pwd** to see where you are and navigate from there. Other basic Linux commands of note can be found in Table 6-1.

 EXAM TIP When it comes to Linux essentials on the exam, know the important folder locations and the basic commands—especially the chmod command and how to equate the user rights to their numeric equivalents.

Command	Description
cat	Displays the contents of a file
cp	Copy
ifconfig	Much like ipconfig in Windows, this command is used to display network configuration information about your NIC.
kill	Kills a running process. (You must specify the process ID number.)
ls	Displays the contents of a folder. The -l option provides the most information about the folder contents.
man	Displays the "manual" page for a command (much like a help file)
passwd	Used to change your password
ps	Process status command. Using the -ef option will show all processes running on the system.
rm	Removes files. The command rm-r also recursively removes all directories and subdirectories on the path, and provides no wanring when deleting a write-protected file.
su	Allows you to perform functions as another user. The sudo command version allows you to run programs with "super user" (root) privileges.
adduser	Adds a user to the system

Table 6-1 Linux Commands

Security on files and folders is managed through your user account, your user's group membership, and three security options that can be assigned to each for any resource: read, write, and execute. These security rights can only be assigned by the owner of the object. Typing the command **ls -l** will display the current security settings for the contents of the directory you're in, which will appear like this:

```
drwxr-xr-x   2  user1    users  33654  Feb 18  10:23  direc1
-rw-r--r--   1  user1    users   4108  Feb 17  09:14  file1
```

The first column displays what the object is (the letter *d* indicates a folder, and blank indicates a file) along with the assigned permissions, which are listed as rwxr-wxrwx. The read, write, and execute options are displayed for user, group, and all others, respectively. For example, the file named "file1" has read and write assigned for the user, read-only for the group, and read-only for all others. The owner of the resources is also listed (user1), along with the assigned group (users).

These permissions are assigned via the chmod command and the use of the binary equivalent for each rwx group: Read is equivalent to 4, write is 2, and execute is 1. For example, the following command would set the permissions for file1 to "r--rw-r--":

```
chmod 464 file1
```

Opening things up for everyone, giving all permissions to everyone, would look like this:

```
chmod 777 file1
```

Obviously, knowing how to change permissions on a file or folder is an important little nugget for an ethical hacker.

Another important Linux fundamental deals with users, groups, and the management of each. Just as Windows has accounts created for specific purposes and with specific rights, Linux has built-in accounts for the management of the system. The most important of these user accounts is called root, and is the administrative control of the system. All users and groups are organized via a unique user ID (UID) and a group ID (GUID). Information for both can be found within the /etc/passwd file. Running a cat command on the file displays lines that look like this:

```
root:x:0:0:root:/root:/bin/bash
bin:x:1:1:bin:/bin:
…  ****** removed to save space ******
matt:x:500:500:Matt:/home/mat:/bin/csh
user2:x:501:501:User2:/home/us1:/bin/pop
```

Among other items in the file, you'll find the users are listed. Root—the administrative "god" account of the system, and the one you're trying to get to—is listed first, with its UID and GID set to 0. User "matt" is the first user created on this system (UID and GID are set to 500), and "user2" is the second (UID and GID set to 501). Immediately following the username is the password. Notice, in this case, the password is listed simply as "x," indicating the use of something called the shadow file.

Passwords in Linux

Passwords in Linux can be stored in one of two places. The first you've already met—the passwd file. If this is your chosen password storage location, all passwords will be displayed in clear text to anyone who has read privileges to the file. If you choose to use the shadow file, however, the passwords are stored, and displayed, encrypted. Lastly, and of special note to you, a budding ethical hacker: The shadow file is only accessible by root.

> **NOTE** Finding a non-shadowed system in the real world is just about impossible. The passwd file and the shadow file are covered here for purely academic purposes (in other words, they're on the test), and not because you'll get lucky out on the job. For the most part, every "nix" system you run into will be shadowed, just so you're aware.

Just as with Windows, pulling the passwords offline and working on them with a cracker is your best bet for system "owning." John the Ripper—a tool introduced earlier—works wonderfully well on Linux shadow files. The passwords contained within are actually hashes that, usually, have a salt assigned (also covered earlier). John will run through brute-force hashing and tackle the salt(s) for you. It may take a while, but trust me—John will get it eventually.

> **NOTE** More than a few Linux distributions are made explicitly for hacking. These distros normally have many hacking tools—such as John and Metasploit versions—built in. Backtrack, Phlack, and Auditor are just a few examples.

Exercise 6-3: Using John the Ripper

You can run this on virtually any installation of Linux you download. The instructions are purposefully generic so they'll work with nearly anything—whichever you like best. It's probably easier if you download a version with John already built in—such as Auditor or Backtrack—but you're welcome to run it on a test system with a full install. Here are the steps to follow:

1. Boot into your Linux installation and open a terminal window (command-line interface).

2. Create two users with the adduser command:

   ```
   adduser testusr1 -d /home/users/testusr1
   adduser testusr2 -d /home/users/testusr2
   ```

3. Set their passwords:

   ```
   passwd testusr1 pass
   passwd testusr2 P@ss
   ```

4. Start John the Ripper and point it to the shadow file. In this example, I'm changing to the directory and running the command directly. Depending on your version, some distros will have a direct link for John, or a tools directory for you to access it from. (Hint: You may want to copy the shadow and passwd files into the john directory. You can do this with the cp command: cp /etc/shadow /etc/john/shadow. If you do so, you won't need to specify a complete path to the shadow file in the following john command.)

```
cd /etc/john
./john /etc/shadow
```

5. As John gets to work, you can press the ENTER key to see how it's doing (the current password guess will be displayed). It probably won't take very long, but you'll soon see the passwords cracked and displayed. Obviously, the password containing the special character will (or should) take longer to guess.

Cracked passwords will also be stored in a file named john.pot. This file will append every time you run John and it finds a password, and can be viewed anytime using the cat command.

Linux Install Fundamentals

Now that you know a few of the fundamentals of using the Linux command structure and basic password hacking in the OS, it's also important for you to understand some Linux installation fundamentals. One of the reasons for the explosive growth of Windows as the OS of choice is the ease with which things can be added and removed from the OS. Linux isn't necessarily difficult to work with, but it's not nearly as easy either.

The simplest and easiest way to get a Linux installation is to simply download an ISO file and burn it to disk, or use an application (such as UNetbootin from www.sourceforge.net) to drop an image on a USB for you. With either the disk or the USB drive, you can boot into a Linux distribution with little problem. Figure 6-7 shows a few of the available distributions. Occasionally, though, whether you have a specific hardware need, a new piece of software to test, or you're simply masochistic in nature, you may want to compile a Linux kernel yourself. Assuming you are totally insane and want to do this on your own (I'm 20 years in the business and haven't seen the need to do so), you'll need to use a couple more commands and follow a lot more steps than this simple exposé on Linux has time for. What we'll do here is concentrate on what you'll need for the exam by looking at what you'll need to compile and configure an application within Linux.

First off, most install files will come in the form of a *tar* file—which is basically a zipped file (a tar file itself isn't compressed at all, it simply creates an index archive). gzip is the application most commonly used with a tar file to unzip to the raw files. After looking for the ubiquitous README file to learn what you'll need for the install, you'll need three commands to compile any program in Linux: ./configure, make, and make install.

Figure 6-7 Linux distributions

  EXAM TIP   You won't see a lot of questions on the exam regarding installation of Linux apps or kernel modules. You won't be asked specifics on how to compile code, but you will need to know the basic commands and the compiler name (GCC).

Lastly, if you happen to download an application in its raw form—maybe a C++ write-up or something like it—you'll need to compile it to a recognizable form for the OS. Linux comes with a built-in compiler called GNU Compiler Collection (GCC). GCC can compile and execute from several languages, such as C, C++, and Fortran. For example, if you had a C++ source file (sample.cpp) and wanted to compile it in Linux, the command might look something like this:

```
g++ sample.cpp newapp.exe
```

A source file in C could be compiled the same way—just change the initial command:

```
gcc sample.c newapp.exe
```

One final note on install necessities for your exam deals not with installing the OS, but with adding functionality. Linux kernel modules were invented early on to provide some modularity to the operating system. The thought was, "Why force the entire OS to be rewritten and reinstalled when we can simply add modules at the kernel level?" Admittedly, the idea was great and made the evolution and improvement of Linux skyrocket; however, it isn't without its problems.

NOTE The command to load a particular LKM is modprobe *LKM_name*.

As we discussed earlier, rootkits came about because of the LKM idea. Just as with many other seemingly great ideas in networking and computing, when put to the wrong use or in the wrong hands, it becomes deadly. Because of this, you'll need to be very, very careful when installing LKMs in your Linux load.

This section wasn't about making you a Linux expert; it was all about introducing you to the bare-bones basics you'll need to be successful on the exam, as well as for entering the career field. As with everything else we've discussed thus far, practice with a live system is your best option. Download a few distributions and practice—you won't regret it.

Hardening a Linux Machine

Now that you know a little about the fundamentals, we need to spend just a few paragraphs on what an administrator can do to harden the box—to protect it against hacking. Shockingly enough, most of this stuff will probably seem like common sense to you. However, we need to cover it here because you will definitely see some of this on your exam.

Ensuring the server is located in a physically secured location, with restricted access to the actual machine, should be a no-brainer. If you're struggling with that a little bit, consider how easy it is (on many Linux distributions) to change or delete the root password given physical access to the machine. For example, here's a new term you may not see on the exam, but you'd better come to grips with: single-user mode. Single-user mode was developed to allow multiuser operating systems to boot into a single "superuser" account, for emergency purposes: things such as maintenance tasks, network services, and—ahem—lost root passwords.

Entering single-user mode is reliant on being physically located at the machine, and is different from one operating system to another. Mac OS X, for example, allows single user by pressing CONTROL-S at power up, whereas Unix/Linux boxes may require the use of GRUB (Grand Unified Bootloader) to alter the boot. On some "nix" boxes, simply typing **linux single** at the lilo prompt at bootup is all you'll need. To figure it out for your own flavor, just use your friend and mine, Google, and do your own Internet search: There are more than a few tutorials and documents out there for you to take advantage of.

Also, be aware that physical access to a Linux machine may allow the attacker to use a Linux bootable disk, which of course starts you in root mode *without a password*. As root you can then do whatever you like, including altering passwords for the root account itself, or maybe creating an account for your own use or installing a backdoor. Or maybe you just open the shadow file and delete the root password altogether.

There are, of course, a few other obvious steps you can take, such as ensuring good password policy. Another obvious choice goes to your OS selection in the first place. None of the other steps and tools mentioned here will do you a lot of good if you install LKMs from anywhere, helter-skelter, or choose a bogus distribution in the first place. After you've installed a good, solid, trusted OS, be sure to follow that up with any security patching you find necessary.

Additionally, when it comes to your OS, be sure to turn off anything you're not using. Services such as FTP, TFTP, and Finger don't need to run unless you absolutely need them for a specific purpose. Remote access services such as rlogin, Telnet, and ssh definitely require careful thought for maintaining their access. Most remote access and services are kicked off in the /etc/inittab folder or from various boot scripts—if you don't absolutely need them, ditch them.

When it comes to user accounts and passwords, root is obviously the one you most want to protect. Although assigning a good password and changing it frequently is good practice, be sure to restrict the use of the su command as well. Remember that it is used to switch users (and sudo can be used to switch to root access), so restricting its use to a single group is always good policy. You can also restrict where root can log on from, and requiring that access locally will prevent remote users from hacking it. Passwords are best protected through use of the shadow file, as previously discussed. Just don't forget to change them frequently.

Another hardening step you can take on a Linux box is the same one you may have taken with any Windows box: Install an HIDS. In addition to many other issues we've already discussed, you can also use Tripwire, an application for performing integrity checks on important files. Tripwire may not protect against an attack, but it will certainly do a good job of letting you know of major changes to the box you may have otherwise missed.

Log file monitoring is also important on Linux boxes. Although a lot of the GUI versions of Linux have the same functionality as the Windows Event Viewer, you can also access the log files via the command line in /var/log. The last logged-on account has everything recorded in the /var/log/lastlog file—run a cat command on it and you'll see everything the user was up to.

NOTE   You can find a good list of available vulnerability scanners at http://sectools.org/vuln-scanners.html.

Finally, it's always good practice to run a vulnerability scanner against your machine—Linux, Windows, or any other. Tons of tools are set up for vulnerability and security scanning. Some are very specific to certain types of scans. For example, Stackguard and Libsafe are program code scanners, whereas N-Stealth, Nikto, and AppDetective look specifically at applications themselves. Others are made to look at the entirety of the system. Vulnerability scanners aren't foolproof: They rely on signatures just like anything else and, from time to time, miss something and allow a false positive as a result. Some tools available for vulnerability scanning are listed here:

- **Nessus** Nessus, shown in Figure 6-8, is very well known and has an excellent reputation. It used to be freely available as an open source product. An older version of Nessus is NeWT (Nessus Windows Technology). Nessus can be used to run a vulnerability scan across your entire subnet or can be aimed at a single machine.

- **Retina** A commercial vulnerability assessment scanner by eEye, Retina is used widely in DoD networks, mostly a GUI interface. Retina runs natively on a Windows machine and can scan subnets or individual systems.

- **Core Impact** Much more than a simple vulnerability scanner, Core Impact is a point-and-shoot comprehensive penetration testing product. It's very expensive, but is used widely within the federal government and by many commercial pen test teams.

- **SAINT** Much like Nessus, SAINT used to be open source but is now a commercial entity. SAINT runs natively on Unix.

Figure 6-8 Nessus vulnerability scanner

As stated before, you probably won't come across a whole bunch of Linux machines on your target subnet. Generally speaking, Linux will make up less than 5 percent of your targets. The good news, though, is that Linux machines are almost always really important, so hacking into them, or making use of them otherwise, is a high priority. Learn the basics, practice the installation of various tools and modules, and monitor the hardening techniques your adversaries will be using—it will pay off come pen test time.

Chapter Review

Authentication to any system can rely on three things: something you are (biometrics, such as fingerprints), something you have (a token or card of some sort), and something you know (a password). A password's strength is determined by two major functions—length and complexity. Password types are defined by what's in them, and can be made up of letters, numbers, special characters, or some combination of all three. In general, passwords must not contain any part of the user's name, must have a minimum of eight characters, and must contain characters from at least three of the four major components of complexity (special symbols, uppercase letters, lowercase letters, and numbers).

There are four types of password attacks. A passive online attack involves sniffing a wire in the hopes of intercepting a password in clear text or attempting a replay or man-in-the-middle attack. Sidejacking is another attack that's similar and is used against encrypted passwords and SSL by stealing cookies exchanged between two systems and replaying them. Cain, Ettercap, ScoopLM, and KerbCrack(KerbSniff) are examples of tools that accomplish this.

An active online attack occurs when the attacker begins simply guessing passwords. Active online attacks take much longer than passive attacks, and are also much easier to detect. These attacks try to take advantage of bad passwords and security practices by individuals on a network.

Offline attacks occur when the hacker steals a copy of the password file and works the cracking efforts on a separate system. These attacks usually require some form of physical access to the machine, where the attacker pulls the password file to removable media. Password cracking offline can be done in one of three major ways: dictionary attacks, hybrid attacks, and brute-force attacks.

A dictionary attack is the easiest and uses a list of passwords in a text file, which is then hashed by the same algorithm/process the original password was put through. This can also be sped up using "rainbow tables." A hybrid attack is a step above the dictionary attack. In a hybrid attack, the cracking tool takes words from a list and substitutes numbers and symbols for alphabetic characters. Hybrid attacks may also append numbers and symbols to the ends of dictionary file passwords. Brute-force attacks attempt every conceivable combination of letters, numbers, and special characters, comparing them against the hash to determine a match. This process is very time consuming, chewing up a lot of computation cycles and making this the longest of the three methods. Cain, KerbCrack, Legion, and John the Ripper are examples of brute-force password-cracking tools.

Keylogging is the process of using a hardware device or software application to capture the keystrokes a user types. With this method, keystrokes are captured as they are typed, regardless of what they're being typed for. Keyloggers can be hardware devices—usually small devices connected between the keyboard cable and the computer—or software applications installed and running in the background.

Non-electronic attacks involve social-engineering attempts, which can take on many different forms. This is perhaps the most effective and easiest method available. Productive methods include shoulder surfing and phishing.

Windows systems store passwords in hashed format. LM hashing, an older method, converts all password characters to uppercase, appends the remainder with blank spaces to reach 14 characters, and then splits the password and hashes both sides separately. The LM hash value of seven blank characters will always be the same (AAD3B-435B51404EE). LM authentication (DES) was used with Windows 95/98 machines. NTLM (DES and MD$) was used with Windows NT machines until SP3. NTLM v2 (MD5) was used after that. Kerberos came about with Windows 2000.

Escalation of privileges is the bridge between gaining access and maintaining access, and usually falls into four main options for obtaining administrator (root) privileges on a machine. The first is to crack the password of an administrator or root account. The second is to take advantage of a vulnerability found in the OS, or in an application, that will allow you access as a privileged user. The third method is to use a tool that, hopefully, provides you the results you're looking for. The last method involves more social engineering—such as putting executable code in an e-mail and asking the user to click it. This is the easiest method available and probably will wind up being your most effective over time.

Stealth in hacking truly comes down to patience—spend enough time, move slowly enough, and chances are better than not you'll go unnoticed. Hiding files in Windows (pre–Windows 7) can be done through the use of alternate data streams (ADS) in the form of NTFS file streaming. Editing a log file, not deleting it, is also a great method for hiding your tracks.

A rootkit is a collection of software put in place by an attacker that is designed to obscure system compromise. Rootkits are designed to provide backdoors for the attacker to use later on, and can be placed at the application level, kernel level, or library level.

Linux is a very powerful OS that can be used for several purposes. Red Hat is probably the best known and most prevalent Linux distribution—other examples are Ubuntu, Gentoo, SuSe, and Fedora. Hacking specific distributions include Backtrack and Auditor.

The Linux file system starts with a root directory just as Windows does. The Windows root is usually C:\, and the Linux root is just a slash (/). It also has folders holding specific information for specific purposes (/etc, for example). Security on files and folders is managed through your user account, your user's group membership, and three security options that can be assigned to each for any resource: read, write, and execute. These permissions are assigned via the chmod command and the use of the binary equivalent for each rwx group: Read is equivalent to 4, write is 2, and execute is 1. For example, the following command applies all permissions to everyone for the file:

```
chmod 777 file1
```

All users and groups are organized via a unique user ID (UID) and group ID (GUID). Information for both can be found within the /etc/passwd file. Passwords in Linux can be stored in the passwd file or in the shadow file, the latter of which encrypts the stored passwords. The passwords contained within are actually hashes that, usually, have a salt assigned. John the Ripper will run through brute-force hashing and tackle the salt(s).

Most install files will come in the form of a tar ball file—which is basically a zipped file. gzip is the application most commonly used with a tar ball to unzip to the raw files. The tar files themselves aren't compressed, they just provide indexing. A README file will show important information on the install. You need three commands to compile any program in Linux: ./configure, make, and make install. Compiling raw programs to a recognizable form for the OS can be done using the GNU Compiler Collection (GCC). GCC can compile and execute from several languages, such as C, C++, and Fortran.

Linux kernel modules (LKMs) were invented early on to provide some modularity to the operating system. LKMs allow functionality without forcing the entire OS to be rewritten and reinstalled. The command to load an LKM is

```
modprobe LKM_name
```

Hardening a Linux machine includes physical location, file, and user account security steps. Nessus, Retina, Core Impact, and SAINT are all examples of vulnerability scanners to assist in pointing out potential problems with a Linux install.

Questions

1 A security professional employs the tools LNS and Sfind during a monthly sweep. What is being searched for?

   A. Unauthorized LDAP access

   B. Linux kernel modules

   C. NFTS file streams

   D. Steganographic images

2. Which of the following would be considered an active online password attack?

   A. Guessing passwords against an IPC$ share

   B. Sniffing subnet traffic to intercept a password

   C. Running John the Ripper on a stolen copy of the SAM

   D. Sending a specially crafted PDF to a user for that user to open

3. Which of the following would be considered a passive online password attack?

   A. Guessing passwords against an IPC$ share

   B. Sniffing subnet traffic to intercept a password

   C. Running John the Ripper on a stolen copy of the SAM

   D. Sending a specially crafted PDF to a user for that user to open

4. You have successfully acquired a copy of the password hashes from a Windows XP box. In previous enumerations, you've discovered the network policy requires complex passwords of at least eight characters. Which of the following offline password attacks would be best suited to discovering the true passwords?

   A. Brute force

   B. Dictionary

   C. Hybrid

   D. Keylogging

5. You decide to hide a few files from casual browsing on a Windows XP box. Which command will successfully engage the hidden attribute on file.txt?

   A. attrib -hidden file.txt

   B. attrib file.txt +hidden

   C. attrib +h file.txt

   D. attrib file.txt -h

6. While pen testing a client, you discover that LM hashing, with no salting, is still engaged for backward compatibility on most systems. One stolen password hash reads 9FAF6B755DC38E12AAD3B435B51404EE. Is this user following good password procedures?

   A. Yes, the hash shows a 14-character, complex password.

   B. No, the hash shows a 14-character password; however, it is not complex.

   C. No, the hash reveals a seven-character-or-less password has been used.

   D. It is impossible to determine simply by looking at the hash.

7. You receive a tar file of installation code for an application. You unzip the file using gzip. Which commands will you need to use for the installation? (Choose all that apply.)

   A. ./configure

   B. make

   C. make install

   D. None of the above

8. Which Linux folder holds the password and shadow files?

   A. /bin

   B. /etc

   C. /sbin

   D. /sec

9. You suspect a rogue process is running in the background of your Linux installation. Which command will display all processes running on the system?

   A. ls -l

   B. ifconfig

   C. cp -all

   D. ps -ef

10. Which of the following is *not* a good option to follow in hardening a Linux system?

    A. Ensure the server is in an open and easily accessible location.

    B. Eliminate all unnecessary services and processes on the system.

    C. Periodically review the /var/log/lastlog file.

    D. Ensure all default passwords are changed and replaced with complex versions.

11. You have successfully acquired a passwd file. The entry for root is displayed here:

    `root:x:0:0:root:/root:/bin/bash`

    Which of the following is true regarding the root entry?

    A. The root account has no password set.

    B. The root account has a password set, but it is shadowed.

    C. It is impossible to tell from this entry whether or not the root account has a password.

    D. The root account password is root.

12. You wish to assign all privileges to the user, only read and write to the group, and only read access for all others for file1. Which command will accomplish this?

    A. chmod 421 file1

    B. chmod 124 file1

    C. chmod 764 file1

    D. chmod 467 file1

Answers

1. **C.** LNS and Sfind are both used to discover hidden files in ADS (NTFS file streaming).

2. **A.** Active online attacks revolve around guessing passwords. If you have an IPC$ share or the old C$ share, the Windows Administrator account cannot be locked out, so guessing passwords via brute force is sometimes beneficial.

3. **B.** Passive online attacks simply involve stealing passwords passed in clear text, or copying the entire password exchange in the hopes of pulling off a reply or man-in-the-middle attack.

4. **A.** A brute-force attack takes the longest amount of time, but because you know complex passwords are being used, this is your only option. A dictionary or hybrid attack may be worth running, if you know the users' propensities and habits in poor password choices, but brute force is the only way to try all combinations. Keylogging would have been a great choice *before* cracking things offline.

5. **C.** The proper syntax for assigning the hidden attribute to a file with the attrib command is attrib +h *filename*.

6. **C.** LM hashes pad a password with blank spaces to reach 14 characters, split it into two seven-character sections, and then hash both separately. Because the LM hash of seven blank characters is always AAD3B435B51404EE, you can tell from the hash that the user has only used seven or fewer characters in the password. Because CEH has recommended that a password be a minimum of eight characters, be complex, and expire after 30 days, the user is not following good policy.

7. **A, B, and C.** Many Linux applications come in the form of a tar file with README and CONFIGURE files to guide you through the installation. Most require the ./configure, make, and make install commands for the installation.

8. **B.** The "etc" folder holds administrative files as well as the password and shadow files.

9. **D.** The ps -ef command displays all processes running on the system.

10. **A.** Physical security is very important, regardless of operating system.

11. **B.** The second field in the entry, an *x*, indicates a shadowed password.

12. **C.** Read is equivalent to 4, write is 2, and execute is 1. To assign all privileges to the user, you use a 7. Read and write privileges to the group is a 6, and read-only to all others is a 4. Therefore, the syntax is as follows:

```
chmod 764 file1
```

Low Tech: Social Engineering and Physical Security

In this chapter you will learn about
- Defining social engineering
- Describing the different types of social-engineering attacks
- Describing insider attacks, reverse social engineering, dumpster diving, social networking, and URL obfuscation
- Describing phishing attacks and countermeasures
- Listing social-engineering countermeasures
- Describing physical security measures

When kids call home unexpectedly it usually means trouble; so when the phone rang that midsummer's day in Huntsville, Alabama, I just knew something was wrong. My daughter, 17 years old at the time, was nearly hysterical. Calling from the side of a fairly busy road, she frantically blurted out that the car had "blown up." Most people hearing this would instantly picture flames and a mushroom cloud, but I knew what she meant: It was simply kaput. So I calmed her down and drove out to check things out.

I tried to apply logic to the situation. She had been driving and the car just stopped, so my first thought was that the problem was electrical; I checked the battery and wiring. When those checked out I decided it may be a vacuum leak or other engine problem, so I looked over the engine. I checked for leaks, and even verified the pedal mechanisms were working. After about half an hour, I deduced this was beyond fixing on the side of the road, that it just *had* to be a computer problem, and called a tow.

The tow truck cost me $120, and took our van to a local shop about 10 minutes down the road from the house. The van actually made it to the shop before I got home, and as I walked through the front door the phone was already ringing. Donnie Anderson, a great repair man and a whiz of an auto mechanic, was laughing when I finally got to the phone. When I asked what was so funny, he said, "So, Matt, when was the last time you put gas in this thing?"

Sometimes we try to overcomplicate things, especially in this technology-charged career field we're in. We look for answers that make us feel more intelligent, to make us appear smarter to our peers. We seem to *want* the complicated way—to have to learn some vicious code listing that takes six servers churning away in our basement to break past our target's defenses. We look for the tough way to break in, when it's sometimes just as easy as asking someone for a key. Want to be a successful ethical hacker? Learn to take pride in, and master, the simple things. It's the gas in your tank that keeps your pen-test machine running.

This chapter is all about the nontechnical things you may not even think about as a "hacker." Checking the simple stuff first, targeting the human element and the physical attributes of a system, is not only a good idea, it's critical to your overall success.

Social Engineering

Every major study on technical vulnerabilities and hacking will say the same two things. First, the users themselves are the weakest security link. Whether on purpose or by mistake, users, and their actions, represent a giant security hole that simply can't ever be completely plugged. Second, an inside attacker poses the most serious threat to overall security. Although most people agree with both statements, they rarely take them in tandem to consider the most powerful—and scariest—flaw in security: What if the inside attacker *isn't even aware she is one?* Welcome to the nightmare that is social engineering.

Show of hands, class: How many of you have held the door open for someone racing up behind you, with his arms filled with bags? How many of you have slowed down to let someone out in traffic, allowed the guy with one item in line to cut in front of you, or carried something upstairs for the elderly lady in your building? I, of course, can't see the hands raised, but I'd bet most of you have performed these, or similar, acts on more than one occasion. This is because most of you see yourselves as good, solid, trustworthy people, and given the opportunity, most of us will come through to help our fellow man (or woman) in times of need.

For the most part, people *naturally* trust one another—especially when authority of some sort is injected into the mix—and they will generally perform good deeds for one another. It's part of what some might say is human nature, however that may be defined. It's what separates us from the animal kingdom, and the knowledge that most people are good at heart is one of the things that makes life a joy for a lot of folks. Unfortunately it also represents a glaring weakness in security that attackers gleefully, and very successfully, take advantage of.

 EXAM TIP Most of this section and chapter deal with insider attacks—whether the user is a willing participant or not. It's important to remember, though, that the disgruntled employee (whether still an insider to the organization or recently fired, still with the knowledge to cause serious harm) represents the single biggest threat to a network.

Social engineering is the art of manipulating a person, or a group of people, into providing information or a service they otherwise would never have given. Social engineers prey on people's natural desire to help one another, their tendency to listen to authority, and their trust of offices and entities. For example, I'd bet 90 percent or more of users will say, if asked directly, that they should never share their password with anyone. However, I'd bet out of that same group, 30 percent or more of them will gladly hand over their password—or provide an easy means of getting it—if they're asked nicely by someone posing as a help desk employee or network administrator. Put that request in a very official looking e-mail, and the success rate will go up even higher.

NOTE From the truly ridiculous files regarding social engineering, Infosecurity Europe did a study where they found 45 percent of women and 10 percent of men were willing to give up their password during the study...for a *chocolate bar*. (www.geek.com/articles/news/women-are-more-likely-to-give-up-passwords-for-chocolate-20080417/)

Social engineering is a nontechnical method of attacking systems, which means it's not limited to people with technical know-how. Whereas technically minded people might attack firewalls, servers, and desktops, social engineers attack the help desk, the receptionist, and the problem user down the hall everyone is tired of working with. It's simple, easy, effective, and darn near impossible to contain.

Human-Based Attacks

All social-engineering attacks fall into one of two categories: human-based or computer-based. Human-based social engineering uses interaction in conversation or other circumstances between people to gather useful information. This can be as blatant as simply asking someone for their password, or as elegantly wicked as getting the target to call you with the information—after a carefully crafted setup, of course. The art of human interaction for information-gathering has many faces, and there are simply more attack vectors than we could possibly cover in this or any other book. However, here are just a few:

- **Dumpster diving** Exactly what it sounds like, dumpster diving requires you to get down and dirty, digging through the trash for useful information. Rifling through the dumpsters, paper-recycling bins, and office trashcans can provide a wealth of information. Things such as written-down passwords (to make them "easier to remember") and network design documents are obvious, but don't discount employee phone lists and other information. Knowing the employee names, titles, and upcoming events makes it much easier for a social engineer to craft an attack later on. Although technically a physical security issue, dumpster diving is covered as a social engineering topic per EC-Council.

- **Impersonation** In this attack, a social engineer pretends to be an employee, a valid user, or even an executive (or other VIP). Whether by faking an identification card or simply by convincing employees of his "position" in the company, an attacker can gain physical access to restricted areas, thus providing further opportunities for attacks. Pretending to be a person of authority, the attacker might also use intimidation on lower-level employees, convincing them to assist in gaining access to a system. Of course, as an attacker, if you're going to impersonate someone, why not impersonate a tech support person? Calling a user as a technical support person and warning him of an attack on his account almost always results in good information.

- **Technical support** A form of impersonation, this attack is aimed at the technical support staff themselves. Tech support professionals are trained to be helpful to customers—it's their goal to solve problems and get users back online as quickly as possible. Knowing this, an attacker can call up posing as a user and request a password reset. The help desk person, believing they're helping a stranded customer, unwittingly resets a password to something the attacker knows, thus granting him access the easy way.

- **Shoulder surfing** If you've got physical access, it's amazing how much information you can gather just by keeping your eyes open. An attacker taking part in shoulder surfing simply looks over the shoulder of a user and watches them log in, access sensitive data, or provide valuable steps in authentication. Believe it or not, shoulder surfing can also be done "long distance," using telescopes and binoculars (referred to as "surveillance" in the real world). And don't discount eavesdropping as a side benefit too—while standing around waiting for an opportunity, an attacker may be able to discern valuable information by simply overhearing conversations.

- **Tailgating and piggybacking** Although many of us use the terms interchangeably, there is a semantic difference between them—trust me on this. *Tailgating* occurs when an attacker has a fake badge and simply follows an authorized person through the opened security door—smoker's docks are great for this. *Piggybacking* is a little different in that the attacker doesn't have a badge but asks for someone to let her in anyway. She may say she's left her badge on her desk or at home. In either case, an authorized user holds the door open for her even though she has no badge visible.

NOTE In hacker lingo, potential targets for social engineering are known as "Rebecca" or "Jessica." When communicating with other attackers, the terms can provide information on whom to target—for example, "Rebecca, the receptionist, was very pleasant and easy to work with."

Lastly, a really devious social-engineering impersonation attack involves getting the *target* to call *you* with the information, known as *reverse social engineering*. The attacker will pose as some form of authority or technical support and set up a scenario whereby the user feels he must dial in for support. And, like seemingly everything involved in this certification exam, specific steps are taken in the attack—advertisement, sabotage, and support. First, the attacker advertises or markets his position as "technical support" of some kind. In the second step, the attacker performs some sort of sabotage—whether a sophisticated DoS attack or simply pulling cables. In any case, the damage is such that the user feels they need to call technical support—which leads to the third step: The attacker attempts to "help" by asking for login credentials, thus completing the third step and gaining access to the system.

NOTE This actually points out a general truth in the pen-testing world: Inside-to-outside communication is always more trusted than outside-to-inside communication. Having someone internal call you, instead of the other way around, is akin to starting a drive on the opponent's one-yard line; you've got a much greater chance of success this way.

For example, suppose a social engineer has sent an e-mail to a group of users warning them of "network issues tomorrow," and has provided a phone number for the "help desk" if they are affected. The next day, the attacker performs a simple DoS on the machine, and the user dials up, complaining of a problem. The attacker then simply says, "Certainly I can help you—just give me your ID and password and we'll get you on your way...."

Regardless of the "human-based" attack you choose, remember presentation is everything. The "halo effect" is a well-known and studied phenomenon of human nature, whereby a single trait influences the perception of other traits. If, for example, a person is attractive, studies show people will assume they are more intelligent and will also be more apt to provide them with assistance. Humor, great personality, and a "smile while you talk" voice can take you far in social engineering. Remember, people want to help and assist you (most of us are hard-wired that way), especially if you're pleasant.

Computer-Based Attacks

Computer-based attacks are those attacks carried out with the use of a computer or other data-processing device. These attacks can include specially crafted pop-up windows, tricking the user into clicking through to a fake website, and SMS texts, which provide false technical support messages and dial-in information to a user. These can get very sophisticated once you inject the world of social networking into the picture. A quick jaunt around Facebook, Twitter, and LinkedIn can provide all the information an attacker needs to profile, and eventually attack, a target. Lastly, spoofing entire websites, wireless access points, and a host of other entry points is often a goldmine for hackers.

Social networking has provided one of the best means for people to communicate with one another, and to build relationships to help further personal and professional goals. Unfortunately, this also provides hackers with plenty of information on which to build an attack profile. For example, consider a basic Facebook profile: Date of birth, address, education information, employment background, and relationships with other people are all laid out for the picking (see Figure 7-1). LinkedIn provides that and more—showing exactly what specialties and skills the person holds, as well as peers they know and work with. A potential attacker might use this information to call up as a "friend of a friend" or to drop a name in order to get the person's guard lowered and then to mine for information.

The simplest, and by far most common method of computer-based social engineering is known as *phishing*. A phishing attack involves crafting an e-mail that appears legitimate, but in fact contains links to fake websites or to download malicious content. The e-mail can appear to come from a bank, credit card company, utility company, or any number of legitimate business interests a person might work with. The links contained within the e-mail lead the user to a fake web form in which information entered is saved for the hacker's use.

Phishing e-mails can be very deceiving, and even a seasoned user can fall prey to them. Although some phishing e-mails can be prevented with good perimeter e-mail filters, it's impossible to prevent them all. The best way to defend against phishing is to educate users on methods to spot a bad e-mail. Figure 7-2 shows an actual e-mail I received some time ago, with some highlights pointed out for you. Although a pretty good effort, it still screamed "Don't call them!" to me.

Figure 7-1   A Facebook profile

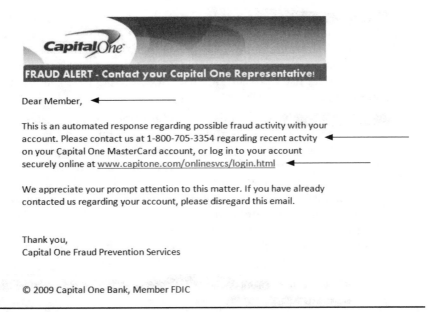

Figure 7-2 Phishing example

The following list contains items that may indicate a phishing e-mail—items that can be checked to verify legitimacy:

- *Beware unknown, unexpected, or suspicious originators.* As a general rule, if you don't know the person or entity sending the e-mail, it should probably raise your antenna. Even if the e-mail is from someone you know, but the content seems out of place or unsolicited, it's still something to be cautious about. In the case of Figure 7-2, not only was this an unsolicited e-mail from a known business, but the address in the "From" line was cap1fraud@prodigy.net—a far cry from the *real* Capital One, and a big indicator this was destined for the trash bin.

- *Beware whom the e-mail is addressed to.* We're all cautioned to watch where an e-mail's from, but an indicator of phishing can also be the "To" line itself, along with the opening e-mail greeting. Companies just don't send messages out to *all* users asking for information. They'll generally address you, personally, in the greeting instead of providing a blanket description: "Dear Mr. Walker" vs. "Dear Member." This isn't necessarily an "Aha!" moment, but if you receive an e-mail from a legitimate business that doesn't address you by name, you may want to show caution. Besides, it's just rude.

- *Verify phone numbers.* Just because an official-looking 800 number is provided does not mean it is legitimate. There are hundreds of sites on the Internet to validate the 800 number provided. Be safe, check it out, and know the friendly person on the other end actually works for the company you're doing business with.

- *Beware bad spelling or grammar.* Granted, a lot of us can't spell very well, and I'm sure e-mails you receive from your friends and family have had some "creative" grammar in them. However, e-mails from MasterCard, Visa, and American Express aren't going to have misspelled words in them, and they will almost never use verbs out of tense. Note in Figure 7-3 that the word *activity* is misspelled.

- *Always check links.* Many phishing e-mails point to bogus sites. Simply changing a letter or two in the link, adding or removing a letter, changing the letter *o* to a zero, or changing a letter *l* to a one completely changes the DNS lookup for the click. For example, www.capitalone.com will take you to Capital One's website for your online banking and credit cards. However, www.capita1one.com will take you to a fake website that looks a lot like it, but won't do anything other than give your user ID and password to the bad guys. Additionally, even if the text reads www.capitalone.com, hovering the mouse pointer over it will show where the link really intends to send you.

 NOTE Using a *sign-in seal* is an e-mail protection method in use at a variety of business locations. The practice is to use a secret message or image that can be referenced on any official communication with the site. If you receive an e-mail purportedly from the business that does not include the image or message, you should suspect it's probably a phishing attempt. This sign-in seal is kept locally on your computer, so the theory is no one can copy or spoof it.

Although phishing is probably the most prevalent computer-based attack you'll see, there are plenty of others. Many attackers make use of code to create pop-up windows users will unknowingly click, as shown in Figure 7-3. These pop-ups take the user to malicious websites where all sorts of badness is downloaded to their machines, or users are prompted for credentials at a realistic-looking web front. By far the most common modern implementation of this is the prevalence of fake antivirus (AV) programs taking advantage of outdated Java installations on systems. Usually hidden in ad streams on legitimate sites, JavaScript is downloaded that, in effect, takes over the entire system, preventing the user from starting any new executables.

Figure 7-3
Fake AV pop-up

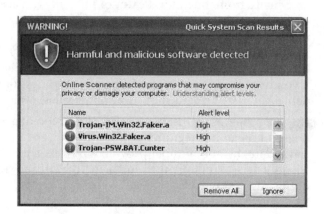

Another very successful computer-based social-engineering attack involves the use of chat or messenger channels. Attackers not only use chat channels to find out personal information to employ in future attacks, but they make use of the channels to spread malicious code and install software. In fact, IRC is one of the primary ways zombies (computers that have been compromised by malicious code and are part of a "botnet") are manipulated by their malicious code masters.

And, finally, we couldn't have a discussion on social-engineering attacks without at least a cursory mention of how to prevent them. Setting up multiple layers of defense, including change-management procedures and strong authentication measures, is a good start, and promoting policies and procedures is also a good idea. Other physical and technical controls can also be set up, but the only real defense against social engineering is user education. Training users—especially those in technical-support positions—how to recognize and prevent social engineering is the best countermeasure available.

The Science of Close Enough

So you're a business owner, and you've read enough so far to know it's important to create, maintain, and enforce a good overall security policy in an effort to keep everyone educated and to protect your systems. The problem is, it's simply impossible to do. Well, nearly impossible anyway.

Most businesses just don't have a "culture of security," and most don't necessarily care to develop one. This isn't because they don't believe in security or don't see the value in it, but rather because it goes against everything our mothers tried to teach us as kids. The "security culture" is insensitive, and goes against the principle of "our employees are our most valuable asset." Not to mention it generally requires people to be suspicious, prying, and intolerant; as we've talked about already in this chapter, that's just not how Mom raised us. We *want* to be helpful, good-natured, trusting people, and the owners and managers of the company want to believe their people are just that. A policy telling us to question everything and everyone, and challenge strangers in the hallway for their badges (requiring a—gasp!—*physical* confrontation and *speaking* to another human being), seems like it's in bad form and, let's be honest, will wind up hurting people's sensibilities and feelings.

In the real world, it seems the only companies that *do* adopt a true security culture are government contractors, banks, hospitals, and casinos, better known as frequent targets of sophisticated adversaries. This isn't because government employees, bank tellers, or casino associates are heartless, emotionless automatons immune to your petty sensibilities. It's usually because these entities simply *have* to be this way. Whether by government regulation and requirement, or by the simple fact of survival, these groups know what it takes to make it in the security world, and they don't really have a choice.

But what about your company or business? Is there really a Catch-22 where security policy and education are concerned? Well, consider just a few examples. You can start with IT training for your employees, but as we've all seen so often before, it's not always the most useful thing on the planet. Your productive employees complain it's a waste of their valuable work time and, although it does provide knowledge to your employees, some would say reading the phone book provides knowledge in a similar fashion (in other words, not very well). Additionally, IT training rarely presents real-world examples where simply being nice results in millions of dollars in losses—or the potential for it. How about an incentive program, then, where people are rewarded for calling out badgeless wanderers or other security violators? Usually this results in vigilante "Barney Fifes" running around the business, making things worse rather than better. So what about enforcing a punitive policy, wherein someone with a password under their keyboard gets fired? Now you've got huge morale problems to deal with.

The hopeless situation security personnel and managers find themselves in doesn't have an easy solution. It requires patience, effort, and time. A good friend of mine once said that IT security engineering is "the science of getting close enough." That may sound weird, because "close enough" isn't good enough when an open vulnerability winds up losing business or personal assets, but when you pause the knee-jerk reaction for a moment and think about it, he's right. Balance your efforts, risk-analyze what you're protecting and what efforts you might take to do so, and only apply measures where needed. Security for a 10-person company that builds $1 widgets will, and should, look different from security for a bank with $1 billion in holdings.

Physical Security

Physical security is perhaps one of the most overlooked areas in an overall security program. For the most part, all the NIDS, HIDS, firewalls, honeypots, and security policies you put into place are pointless if you give an attacker physical access to the machine(s). And you can kiss your job goodbye if that access reaches into the network closet, where the routers and switches sit.

From a penetration test perspective, it's no joyride either. Generally speaking, physical security penetration is much more of a "high-risk" activity for the penetration tester than many of the virtual methods we're discussing. Think about it: If you're sitting in a basement somewhere firing binary bullets at a target, it's much harder for them to actually figure out where you are, much less to lay hands on you. Pass through a held-open door and wander around the campus without a badge, and someone, eventually, will catch you. When strong IT security measures are in place, though, determined attackers will move to the physical attacks to accomplish the goal. This section covers the elements of physical security you'll need to be familiar with for the exam.

Physical Security 101

Physical security includes the plans, procedures, and steps taken to protect your assets from deliberate or accidental events that could cause damage or loss. Normally people in our particular subset of IT tend to think of locks and gates in physical security, but it also encompasses a whole lot more. You can't simply install good locks on your doors and ensure the wiring closet is sealed off to claim victory in physical security; you're also called to think about those events and circumstances that may not be so obvious. These physical circumstances you need to protect against can be natural, such as earthquakes and floods, or manmade, ranging from vandalism and theft to outright terrorism. The entire physical security system needs to take it all into account and provide measures to reduce or eliminate the risks involved.

Furthermore, physical security measures come down to three major components: physical, technical, and operational. *Physical measures* include all the things you can touch, taste, smell, or get shocked by. For example, lighting, locks, fences, and guards with Tasers are all physical measures. *Technical measures* are a little more complicated. These are measures taken with technology in mind, to protect explicitly at the physical level. For example, authentication and permissions may not come across as physical measures, but if you think about them within the context of smart cards and biometrics, it's easy to see how they should become technical measures for physical security. *Operational measures* are the policies and procedures you set up to enforce a security-minded operation. For example, background checks on employees, risk assessments on devices, and policies regarding key management and storage would all be considered operational measures.

EXAM TIP Know the three major categories of physical security measures and be able to identify examples of each.

To get you thinking about a physical security system and the measures you'll need to take to implement it, it's probably helpful to start from the inside out and draw up ideas along the way. For example, inside the server room or the wiring closet, there are any number of physical measures we'll need to control. Power concerns, the temperature of the room, and the air quality itself (dust can be a killer, believe me) are examples of just a few things to consider. Along that line of thinking, maybe the ducts carrying air in and out need special attention. For that matter, someone knocking out your AC system could affect an easy denial of service on your entire network, couldn't it? What if they attack and trip the water sensors for the cooling systems under the raised floor in your computer lab? Always something to think about....

How about some technical measures to consider? What about the authentication of the server and network devices themselves—if you allow remote access to them, what kind of authentication measures are in place? Are passwords used appropriately? Is there virtual separation—that is, a DMZ they reside in—to protect against unauthorized access? Granted, these aren't physical measures by their own means (authentication might cut the mustard, but location on a subnet sure doesn't), but they're included here simply to continue the thought process of examining the physical room.

Continuing our example here, let's move around the room together and look at other physical security concerns. What about the entryway itself: Is the door locked? If so, what is needed to gain access to the room—perhaps a key? In demonstrating a new physical security measure to consider—an operational one, this time—who controls the keys, where are they located, and how are they managed? We're already covering enough information to employ at least two government bureaucrats and we're *not even outside the room yet.* You can see here, though, how the three categories work together within an overall system.

NOTE You'll often hear that security is "everyone's responsibility." Although this is undoubtedly true, some people hold the responsibility a little more tightly than others. The physical security officer (if one is employed), information security employees, and the CIO are all accountable for the system's security.

Another term you'll need to be aware of is *access controls*. Access controls are physical measures designed to prevent access to controlled areas. They include biometric controls, identification/entry cards, door locks, and man traps. Each of these is interesting in its own right.

Biometrics includes the measures taken for authentication that come from the "something you are" concept. Biometrics can include fingerprint readers, face scanners, retina scanners, and voice recognition (see Figure 7-4). The great thing behind using biometrics to control access—whether physically or virtually—is that it's very difficult to fake a biometric signature (such as a fingerprint). The bad side, though, is a related concept: Because the nature of biometrics is so specific, it's very easy for the system to read false negatives and reject a legitimate user's access request.

Can I Offer You a Hand?

Brad Horton and I were chatting about biometric security measures, and this little story was so good I couldn't help but add it to the chapter.

It seems that several years ago Brad had permission to access one of the largest raised floors in the commercial world. Obviously, physical security measures were of utmost importance to protect this virtual cornucopia of computerized wonderment and power from unauthorized access. When queried about their access control, the security team pointed to a hand scanner as a biometric access control device. During the discussion, one of the team members asked, "Well, couldn't they just chop your hand off and get through?" After some chuckling and snickering, the security lead answered, "Of course, the device manufacturer thought about that, and it checks for an adequate temperature of the hand." Brad replied, pointing to a Dominos heat wrap pizza box, "So, if I make sure to keep the severed limb at a nice 98.6 degrees, or close to it, I'm good to go?"

Sure, this is funny—in a strange, George Romero way—but it illustrates a couple of valid points. First, reliance on a security measure simply because it is in place is a path to disaster. And, second, even the most outlandish of plans and actions, no matter how silly or unbelievable to you, may still prove to be your security undoing. Don't discount an idea just because you don't think it's possible. It may not be *probable*, but it's still *possible*.

Figure 7-4
Biometrics

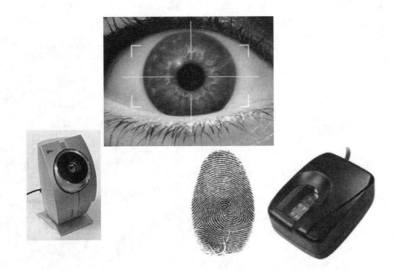

In fact, most biometric systems are measured by two main factors. The first, false rejection rate (FRR), is the percentage of time a biometric reader will deny access to a legitimate user. The percentage of time that an *unauthorized* user is granted access by the system, known as false acceptance rate (FAR), is the second major factor. These are usually graphed on a chart, and the intercepting mark, known as crossover error rate (CER), becomes a ranking method to determine how well the system functions overall. For example, if one fingerprint scanner had a CER of 4 and a second one had a CER of 2, the second scanner would be a better, more accurate solution.

From the "something you have" authentication factor, identification and entry cards can be anything from a simple photo ID to smart cards and magnetic swipe cards. Also, tokens can be used to provide access remotely. Smart cards have a chip inside that can hold tons of information, including identification certificates from a PKI system, to identify the user. Additionally, they may also have RFID features to "broadcast" portions of the information for "near swipe" readers. Tokens generally ensure at least a two-factor authentication method, as you need the token itself and a PIN you memorize to go along with it.

The man trap, designed as a pure physical access control, provides additional control and screening at the door or access hallway to the controlled area. In the man trap, two doors are used to create a small space to hold a person until appropriate authentication has occurred. The user enters through the first door, which must shut and lock before the second door can be cleared. Once inside the enclosed room, which normally has clear walls, the user must authenticate through some means—biometric, token with pin, password, and so on—to open the second door (Figure 7-5 shows one example from Hirsch electronics). If authentication fails, the person is trapped in the holding area until security can arrive and come to a conclusion. Usually man traps are monitored with video surveillance or guards.

Figure 7-5
Man trap

So far we've covered some of the more common physical security measures—some of which you probably either already knew or had thought about. But there are still a few things left to consider in the overall program. For example, the problem of laptop and USB drive theft and loss is a growing physical security concern. Controlling physical access to devices designed to be mobile is out of the question, and educating your laptop users doesn't stop them from being victims of a crime.

The best way to deal with the data loss is to implement some form of encryption (a.k.a. data-at-rest controls). As mentioned earlier in this book, this will encrypt the drive (or drives), rendering a stolen or lost laptop a paperweight. If you're going to allow the use of USBs, investing in encrypted versions is well worth the cost. Iron Key and Kingston drives are two examples. For the laptop, you can use any of a number of encryption software systems designed to secure the device. Some, such as McAfee's Endpoint Protection, encrypt the entire drive at the sector level and force a pre-boot login known only by the owner of the machine. Systems like this may even take advantage of smart cards or tokens at the pre-boot login to force two-factor authentication.

Other tools can encrypt the entire drive or portions of the drive. TrueCrypt is a free, open-source example of this that can be used to encrypt single volumes (treated like a folder) on a drive, a non-system partition (such as a USB drive), or the entire drive itself (thus forcing a pre-boot login). Suppose, for example, you wanted to protect sensitive data on a laptop, like the one I'm using right now, in the event of a theft or loss. You could create an encrypted TrueCrypt volume in which to store the files by following the steps shown in Exercise 7-1.

Exercise 7-1: Using TrueCrypt to Secure Data at Rest

In this exercise, we'll demonstrate how simple using TrueCrypt to create a secured, encrypted storage volume truly is.

1. After installing TrueCrypt, open the application by double-clicking the shortcut.

2. At the TrueCrypt home screen, shown in Figure 7-6, click Create Volume. The Volume Creation Wizard screen will appear, providing three options (the descriptions under each title describe what they are). Leave the Encrypted File Container option checked and click Next.

3. The Volume Type window allows you to choose between a standard encrypted volume and a "hidden" one. The hidden volume option is there to protect you, should you be forced to reveal a password. The idea being that an encrypted volume, with a separate access password, is hidden inside a standard volume. If you are forced to reveal the password for the encrypted volume, no one will be able to tell whether or not any of the remaining space is a hidden volume. In this case, we'll create a standard volume, so just click Next.

Figure 7-6 TrueCrypt home screen

4. In the Volume Location window, click Select File. Browse to C:\ and create the file tcfile (no extension needed). Click Next.

NOTE In this step you are creating the "file" that will serve as your encrypted *volume*. To any outsider it will appear as a single file. You will need to mount it as a volume, using TrueCrypt later to manipulate files.

5. Accept the defaults in the Encryption Options screen. Click Next. Then choose a volume size (for this example 10MB should do). Click Next.

6. Choose a password at the Volume Password screen, shown in Figure 7-7. This will be used to access the encrypted volume later.

NOTE Underneath the password box is a check box labeled "Use keyfiles." If this option is checked, TrueCrypt prompts you to choose any file on your system as a key, along with your password, to access the volume. This can be *any* file (so long as you don't change it) from music to text to graphics. In this exercise we won't use one, but just know that this option can provide extra security, should you want it.

Figure 7-7
TrueCrypt Volume
Password screen

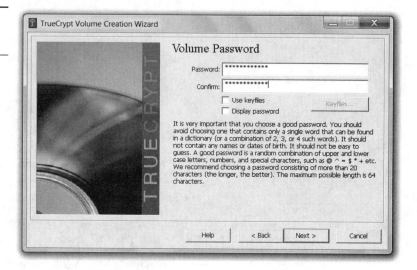

7. At the Volume Format screen, read the information about the random pool and click Format. After formatting, the screen will display Volume Created. Click Next and then Cancel at the Creation Wizard screen.

8. To mount your drive, at the TrueCrypt main window, click Select File and navigate to tcfile (created earlier). Select any drive letter appearing at the top of the screen (in Figure 7-8, I selected "F:") and then click Mount.

9. Type in your password and click OK. You'll see the drive mounted at the top of the window.

10. To test and use your newly encrypted drive, open an Explorer window—you'll see "F:" mounted as a drive just like your other partitions, as shown in Figure 7-9. You can drag and drop files into and out of it all you'd like. Once it is dismounted, it will remain encrypted with the encryption formats you chose earlier. (To dismount the drive, select the drive letter in the TrueCrypt window and click Dismount.)

Figure 7-8   Mounting a volume in TrueCrypt

Figure 7-9
Mounted TrueCrypt
volume

As a technical measure within physical security, TrueCrypt is hard to beat. It's easy to use, very effective, and provides a lot of options for a variety of uses—not to mention it's free, which should make the boss happy. The only cautionary note to offer here is that the use of the key itself provides real security, not just a password. If your USB drive plugs in and requires a password to decrypt, you're protected only by that password. Unless, of course, you *remove the keyfile and store it separately*. Most users, because of convenience or ignorance, just keep the keyfile (if they bother generating one at all) on the same computer. Worse, they sometimes conveniently label it something such as "keyfile." If the goal is to add something to a password-protected system, you must do it effectively, and this requires keyfile management at the user level.

NOTE A lot of software is made freely available, but its creators still seek funds, through voluntary donations, to make their offering better. Just as many, many others do, TrueCrypt has a donations link on their front page. Whether you donate to this, or any other freeware development tool you use, is your own choice.

A few final thoughts on setting up a physical security program are warranted here. The first is a concept I believe anyone who has opened a book on security in the past 20 years is already familiar with—layered defense. The "defense in depth" or layered security thought process involves not relying on any single method of defense, but rather stacking several layers between the asset and the attacker. In the physical security realm, these are fairly easy to see: If your data and servers are inside a building, stack layers to prevent the bad guys from getting in. Guards at an exterior gate checking badges and a swipe card entry for the front door are two protections in place before the bad guys are even in the building. Providing access control at each door with a swipe card, or biometric measures, adds an additional layer. Once an attacker is inside the room, technical controls can be used to prevent local logon. In short, layer your physical security defenses just as you would your virtual ones—you may get some angry users along the way, huffing and puffing about all they have to do just to get to work, but it'll pay off in the long run.

I'm an Excellent Driver...and Not a Bad Pen Tester Either

Have you ever seen the movie *Rain Man*? In it, a guy finds he has an autistic brother who happens to be a genius with numbers. He, of course, takes his brother to Las Vegas and makes a killing on the casino floor. In an iconic pop-culture favorite scene from the movie, early on in their relationship, the autistic brother says, "I'm an excellent driver." He would've made an excellent pen tester too.

Suppose you're surrounded by true math nerds on your pen test team. Also, suppose you have a goal of gaining access to a server room. Someone in the group is going to start estimating success rates for each layer of security you'll have to go through (a.k.a. Mr. Spock on *Star Trek*). Let's say there's an estimated 10 percent chance of getting past guards, a 30 percent chance of getting past a secretary, a 25 percent chance of getting into the server room physically, and a 35 percent chance of breaking into a server after gaining physical access. So what, you may ask, is the overall probability of someone doing *all* of these and successfully gaining server access? Why, that happens to be 0.26 percent, or a 1-in-385 chance.

I know you're probably thinking, "So what? Why should I care about crazy math problems and probabilities multiplying? What's all this got to do with pen testing?" Have you ever heard the term *defense in depth*? How about *layered security*? These concepts work because of probability. Sure, you might talk your way past a secretary—heck, you might even find a way to charm your way past a guard or two. But getting past all the layers of physical security to get to the target? You've got a better chance of beating *Rain Man* at blackjack.

Another thought to consider, as mentioned earlier, is that physical security should also be concerned with those things you can't really do much to prevent. No matter what protections and defenses are in place, an F5 tornado doesn't need an access card to get past the gate. Hurricanes, floods, fires, and earthquakes are all natural events that could bring your system to its knees. Protection against these types of events usually comes down to good planning and operational controls. You can certainly build a strong building and install fire-suppression systems; however, they're not going to prevent anything. In the event something catastrophic does happen, you'll be better off with solid disaster-recovery and contingency plans.

From a hacker's perspective, the steps taken to defend against natural disasters aren't necessarily anything that will prevent or enhance a penetration test, but they are helpful to know. For example, a fire-suppression system turning on or off isn't necessarily going to assist in your attack. However, knowing the systems are backed up daily and offline storage is at a poorly secured warehouse across town could become very useful.

Finally, there's one more thought we should cover (more for your real-world career than for your exam) that applies whether we're discussing physical security or trying to educate a client manager on prevention of social engineering. There are few truisms in life, but one is absolute: Hackers *do not care* that your company has a policy. Many a pen tester has stood there listening to the client say, "That scenario simply won't (or shouldn't, or couldn't) happen because we have a policy against it." Two minutes later, after a server with a six-character password left on a utility account has been hacked, it is evident the policy requiring 10-character passwords didn't scare off the attacker at all, and the client is left to wonder what happened to the *policy*. Policy is great, and policy should be in place. Just don't count on it to actually prevent anything on its own. After all, the attacker doesn't work for you and couldn't care less what you think.

Physical Security Hacks

Believe it or not, hacking is not restricted just to computers, networking, and the virtual world—there are physical security hacks you can learn, too. For example, most elevators have an express mode that lets you override the selections of all the previous passengers, allowing you to go straight to the floor you're going to. By pressing the Door Close button and the button for your destination floor at the same time, you'll rocket right to your floor while all the other passengers wonder what happened.

Others are more practical for the ethical hacker. Ever hear of the bump key, for instance? A specially crafted bump key will work for all locks of the same type by providing a split second of time to turn the cylinder. See, when the proper key is inserted into the lock, all of the key pins and driver pins align along the "shear line," allowing the cylinder to turn. When a lock is "bumped," a slight impact forces all of the bottom pins in the lock, which keeps the key pins in place. This separation only lasts a split second, but if you keep a slight force applied, the cylinder will turn during the short separation time of the key and driver pins, and the lock can be opened.

Other examples are easy to find. Some Master brand locks can be picked using a simple bobby pin and an electronic flosser, believe it or not. Combination locks can be easily picked by looking for "sticking points" (apply a little pressure and turn the dial slowly—you'll find them) and mapping them out on charts you can find on the Internet. I could go on and on here, but you get the point. Don't overlook physical security—no matter which side you're employed by.

Chapter Review

Social engineering is the art of manipulating a person, or a group of people, into providing information or a service they otherwise would never have given. Social engineers prey on people's natural desire to help one another, to listen to authority, and to trust offices and entities. Social engineering is a nontechnical method of attacking systems.

All social-engineering attacks fall into one of two categories: human-based or computer-based. Human-based social engineering uses interaction in conversation or other circumstances between people to gather useful information.

Dumpster diving is an attack where the hacker digs through the trash for useful information. Rifling through dumpsters, paper-recycling bins, and office trashcans can provide a wealth of information, such as passwords (written down to make them "easier to remember"), network design documents, employee phone lists, and other information.

Impersonation is an attack where a social engineer pretends to be an employee, a valid user, or even an executive (or other VIP). Whether by faking an identification card or simply convincing the employees of his "position" in the company, an attacker can gain physical access to restricted areas, providing further opportunities for attacks. Pretending to be a person of authority, the attacker might also use intimidation on lower-level employees, convincing them to assist in gaining access to a system.

A technical support attack is a form of impersonation aimed at the technical support staff themselves. An attacker can call up posing as a user and request a password reset. The help desk person, believing they're helping a stranded customer, unwittingly resets a password to something the attacker knows, thus granting him access the easy way.

Shoulder surfing is a basic attack whereby the hacker simply looks over the shoulder of an authorized user. If you've got physical access, you can watch users log in, access sensitive data, or provide valuable steps in authentication.

Tailgating and piggybacking are two closely related attacks on physical security. Tailgating occurs when an attacker has a fake badge and simply follows an authorized person through the opened security door—smoker's docks are great for this. *Piggybacking* is a little different in that the attacker doesn't have a badge but asks for someone to let him in anyway. Attackers may say they've left their badge on the desk, or forgot it at home. In either case, an authorized user holds the door open for them despite the fact they have no badge visible.

In reverse social engineering, the attacker will pose as someone in a position of some form of authority or technical support and then set up a scenario whereby the user feels they must dial in for support. Specific steps are taken in this attack—advertisement, sabotage, and support. First, the attacker will advertise or market their position as "technical support" of some kind. Second, the attacker will perform some sort of sabotage—whether a sophisticated DoS attack or simply pulling cables. In any case, the damage is such that the user feels they need to call technical support—which leads to the third step, where the attacker attempts to "help" by asking for login credentials and thus gains access to the system.

Computer-based attacks are those attacks carried out with the use of a computer or other data-processing device. The most common method of computer-based social engineering is known as phishing. A phishing attack involves crafting an e-mail that appears legitimate, but in fact contains links to fake websites or downloads malicious content. The links contained within the e-mail lead the user to a fake web form in which the information entered is saved for the hacker's use.

Another very successful computer-based social-engineering attack is through the use of chat or messenger channels. Attackers not only use chat channels to find out personal information to employ in future attacks, but they make use of the channels to spread malicious code and install software. In fact, IRC (Internet Relay Chat) is the primary way zombies (computers that have been compromised by malicious code and are part of a "bot-net") are manipulated by their malicious code masters.

Setting up multiple layers of defense—including change management procedures and strong authentication measures—is a good start in mitigating social engineering. Also, promoting policies and procedures is a good idea as well. Other physical and technical controls can be set up, but the only real defense against social engineering is user education. Training users—especially those in technical support positions—how to recognize and prevent social engineering is the best countermeasure available.

Physical security measures come down to three major components: physical, technical, and operational. Physical measures include all the things you can touch, taste, smell, or get shocked by. For example, lighting, locks, fences, and guards with Tasers are all physical measures. Technical measures are implemented as authentication or permissions. For example, firewalls, IDS, and passwords are all technical measures designed to assist with physical security. Operational measures are the policies and procedures you set up to enforce a security-minded operation.

Biometrics includes the measures taken for authentication that come from the "something you are" category. Biometric systems are measured by two main factors. The first, false rejection rate (FRR), is the percentage of time a biometric reader will deny access to a legitimate user. The percentage of time that an unauthorized user is granted access by the system, known as false acceptance rate (FAR), is the second major factor. These are usually graphed on a chart, and the intersecting mark, known as crossover error rate (CER), becomes a ranking method to determine how well the system functions overall.

The man trap, designed as a pure physical access control, provides additional control and screening at the door or access hallway to the controlled area. In the man trap, two doors are used to create a small space to hold a person until appropriate authentication has occurred. The user enters through the first door, which must shut and lock before the second door can be cleared. Once inside the enclosed room, which normally has clear walls, the user must authenticate through some means—biometric, token with pin, password, and so on—to open the second door.

Questions

1. Jim, part of a pen test team, has attained a fake ID badge and waits next to an entry door to a secured facility. An authorized user swipes a key card and opens the door. Jim follows the user inside. Which social engineering attack is in play here?

    A. Piggybacking

    B. Tailgating

    C. Phishing

    D. None of the above

2. John socially engineers physical access to a building and wants to attain access credentials to the network using nontechnical means. Which of the following social-engineering attacks would prove beneficial?

    A. Tailgating

    B. Piggybacking

    C. Shoulder surfing

    D. Sniffing

3. Bob decides to employ social engineering during part of his pen test. He sends an unsolicited e-mail to several users on the network advising them of potential network problems, and provides a phone number to call. Later on that day, Bob performs a DoS on a network segment and then receives phone calls from users asking for assistance. Which social-engineering practice is in play here?

    A. Phishing

    B. Impersonation

    C. Technical support

    D. Reverse social engineering

4. Phishing, pop-ups, and IRC channel use are all examples of which type of social-engineering attacks?

    A. Human-based

    B. Computer-based

    C. Technical

    D. Physical

5. As part of a pen test team, Jenny decides to search for information as quietly as possible. After watching the building and activities for a couple of days, Jenny notices the paper-recycling bins sit on an outside dock. After hours, she rifles through some papers and discovers old password files and employee call lists. Which social-engineering attack did Jenny employ?

    A. Paper pilfering

    B. Dumpster diving

    C. Physical security

    D. Dock dipping

6. Which threat presents the highest risk to a target network or resource?

   A. Script kiddies

   B. Phishing

   C. A disgruntled employee

   D. A white hat attacker

7. Jerry is performing a pen test with his team and decides to attack the wireless networks. After observing the building for a few days, Jerry parks in the parking lot and walks up to the loading dock. After a few minutes, he plants a wireless access point configured to steal information just inside the dock. Which security feature is Jerry exploiting?

   A. War driving

   B. Physical security

   C. Dock security

   D. War dialing

8. Phishing e-mail attacks have caused severe harm to Bob's company. He decides to provide training to all users in phishing prevention. Which of the following are true statements regarding identification of phishing attempts? (Choose all that apply.)

   A. Ensure e-mail is from a trusted, legitimate e-mail address source.

   B. Verify spelling and grammar is correct.

   C. Verify all links before clicking them.

   D. Ensure the last line includes a known salutation and copyright entry (if required).

9. Lighting, locks, fences, and guards are all examples of _____ measures within physical security.

   A. Physical

   B. Technical

   C. Operational

   D. Exterior

10. Background checks on employees, risk assessments on devices, and policies regarding key management and storage are examples of ____ measures within physical security.

    A. Physical

    B. Technical

    C. Operational

    D. None of the above

Answers

1. **B**. In tailgating, the attacker holds a fake entry badge of some sort and follows an authorized user inside.

2. **C**. Because he is already inside (thus rendering tailgating and piggybacking pointless), John could employ shoulder surfing to gain the access credentials of a user.

3. **D**. Reverse engineering occurs when the attacker uses marketing, sabotage, and support to gain access credentials and other information.

4. **B**. Computer-based social-engineering attacks include any measures using computers and technology.

5. **B**. Dumpster diving—that is, rifling through waste containers, paper recycling, and other trash bins—is an effective way of building information for other attacks.

6. **C**. Everyone recognizes insider threats as the worst type of threat, and a disgruntled employee on the inside is the single biggest threat for security professionals to plan for and deal with.

7. **B**. Although Jerry is using a wireless access point, physical security breakdowns allowed him to perform his attack.

8. **A, B, and C**. Phishing e-mails can be spotted by who they are from, who they are addressed to, spelling and grammar errors, and unknown or malicious embedded links.

9. **A**. Physical security controls fall into three categories: physical, technical, and operational. Physical measures include lighting, fences, and guards.

10. **C**. Operational measures are the policies and procedures you set up to enforce a security-minded operation.

Web-Based Hacking: Servers and Applications

In this chapter you will learn about
- Identifying features of common web server architecture
- Describing web server and web application attacks
- Identifying web server and application vulnerabilities
- Identifying web application hacking tools

Have you ever heard of Alexander the Great? A king of Macedonia (in Northern Greece), he created one of the largest empires in history by the ripe old age of 30. Tutored by Aristotle, he was one of the most intelligent military strategists in all of history. As a matter of fact, he was *undefeated* in battle and is considered one of the most successful commanders of all time, with his tactics and exploits still being taught in military circles today.

Along the way to creating his empire, Alexander conquered the great Persian Empire, crushing Xerxes in a series of battles across many years. In his march across the empire, Alexander was faced with a conundrum in the city of Persepolis. Considered impenetrable to attack, the city was surrounded by strong, thick walls, and was nearly self-sufficient, able to simply wait out most attackers and their armies. After some time thinking on the subject—dare I say "footprinting" his target?—he noticed one potential weakness: The people of Persepolis liked their commerce, and traded openly just outside the walls of the city.

Alexander maneuvered and manipulated trading until he could finally slip something into one of the carts headed back into the city, which just happened to be headed to the eastern part of the city—the seat of government. The resulting fire, started from inside the walls and causing all sorts of havoc, distracted the city's defenses enough that Alexander simply pushed through the front door and sacked the once proud enclave.

I know you're wondering what this story, as interesting as it may be, has to do with hacking. If you think about it, though, it is a microcosm of where you should be focusing a large portion of your pen test hacking attention. Businesses and corporations are like those ancient cities, with so many defenses arrayed against you they seem impenetrable. But most of them—heck, *all* of them—have some sort of a website facing the exterior world; in short, a way in is always there. It may take some time to figure out how to use that public-facing web server or application to get a fire started inside the gate, but trust me, it's worth it. This chapter is all about web servers and applications and how you can exploit them. After all, if the target is going to trust them, why not have a look?

Attacking Web Servers

Regardless what your potential target offers to the world—whether it's an e-commerce site, a suite of applications for employees and business partners to use, or just a means to inform the public—that offering must reside on a server designed to provide things to the world. And let's just face it: Web servers are unique entities in the virtual world we play in. Think about it—we spend loads of time and effort trying to hide everything else we own. We lock servers, routers, and switches away in super-secure rooms and disguise entire network segments behind NAT and DMZs. Web servers, though, are thrown to the proverbial wolves. We stick them right out front and open access to them. Sure, we try our best to secure that access, but the point still remains: Web servers are open targets the entire world can see. And you can rest assured those open targets will get a strong look from attackers.

Web Services Architecture

At its most basic, a web server acts like any other server you already know about—it responds to requests from clients and provides a file or service in answer. In this case, a request first comes from a client to open a TCP connection on (usually) port 80 (443). After agreeing to the handshake, the server waits for an HTTP GET request from the client. This request asks for specific HTML code representing a website page. The server then looks through a storage area and finds the code that matches the request, and provides it to the client.

This all sounds simple enough, but there's really a multitude of issues to think about just in that exchange. How does the server validate what the client is asking for? Does the server respond only to specific verbiage in the request, or can it get confused and respond with other actions? Where are the actual files of HTML (and other) code stored, and how are the permissions assigned to them? I could go on and on, but I think you can understand my point.

When it comes to web servers, there are two major players on the block. Yes, I realize that many, many more server products are available to host sites from, and I'm sure they have benefits and drawbacks that make them better choices for specific applications in any unique situation. However, just as we spent most of our time covering Windows hacking, we're going to concentrate on Internet Information Services (IIS) and Apache servers (see Figure 8-1) for a couple of reasons. First, they simply make up the vast majority of servers out there. Second, they're the only two mentioned in the CEH objectives. But don't get too concerned—you won't be saddled with a lot of minutia on the exam concerning these two web servers. Most of this information is delivered here because I think it's important for you to know as a hacker. No, we're not going to dive so far down into scripting that you'll be bored, but we are going to at least brush the strokes wide enough so you're familiar with the terminology and the very basics of the servers.

Apache servers (www.apache.org) make up the majority of web hosts on the Internet. Apache is an open source, very powerful, and very fast web server that typically runs on a Unix or Linux platform, although you can load and use it on a wide variety of operating systems. By and large, Apache servers haven't seemed to display as many, or as serious, vulnerabilities as their Microsoft IIS peers, but this isn't to say they are foolproof. Several critical vulnerabilities on Apache servers have come to light in the past (check any of the vulnerabilities sites we referenced in previous chapters), making them as easy a target as anything else.

IIS servers are easy-to-manage, Windows-based options for the web provider. Originally, IIS was riddled with security concerns, and finding an IIS 5 or earlier server at your target is cause for wild celebration on the pen test team. However, the later versions have done a much better job of tightening down the security screws. From Microsoft's own description, "IIS 7.0 includes a new modular design that allows for a lessened attack surface and increased performance. IIS 7.0 introduces a hierarchical configuration system allowing for simpler site deploys, a new Windows Forms–based management application, new command-line management options, and increased support for the .NET framework."

Figure 8-1
IIS and Apache

IIS: Death by a Thousand Cuts

IIS has a long, sad history of exploit vulnerability. Since version 6.0 it has become a lot more secure; however, the initial versions were fraught with all sorts of weaknesses. For example, back in 2001, buffer overflows were a huge issue in IIS. Both ISAPI (Internet Server Application Programming Interface) and IPP printer overflow attacks were easily exploitable. The exploit code for the attacks came in many different forms (which can easily be found on the Internet for your perusal) and always showed the same type of display buried in the code. It's included here because you simply need to be able to identify what a buffer overflow looks like, both on an exam and in real life:

```
int main ( int argc, char *argv[]) {
"\x47\x45\x54\x20\x2f\x4e\x55\x4c\x4c\x2e\x70\x72\x69\x6e\x74\x65\x72\x20"
"\x48\x54\x54\x50\x2f\x31\x2e\x30\x0d\x0a\x42\x65\x61\x76\x75\x68\x3a\x20"
"\x90\x90\x90\x90\x90\x90\x90\x90\x90\x90\x90\x90\x90\x90\x90\x90\x90"
"\x90\x90\xeb\x03\x5d\xeb\x05\xe8\xf8\xff\xff\xff\x83\xc5\x15\x90\x90\x90"
"\x8b\xc5\x33\xc9\x66\xb9\xd7\x02\x50\x80\x30\x95\x40\xe2\xfa\x2d\x95\x95"
"\x64\xe2\x14\xad\xd8\xcf\x05\x95\xe1\x96\xdd\x73\x60\x7d\x95\x95\x95\x95"
"\xc8\x1e\x40\x14\x7f\x9a\x6b\x6a\x6a\x1e\x4d\x1e\xe6\xa9\x96\x66\x1e\xe3"
"\xed\x96\x66\x1e\xeb\xb5\x96\x6e\x1e\xdb\x81\xa6\x78\xc3\xc2\xc4\x1e\xaa"
```

Even more disconcerting were the source disclosure attacks. From Microsoft's tech write-up on the vulnerability (MS01-004 on TechNet), this attack could reveal site design (including hidden areas) and even passwords. An attacker simply appended "+.htr" to the global.asa file (easily done through netcat) and could then ask the server virtually anything.

IIS was also notorious for Unicode directory traversal attacks. A URL similar to

```
http://any_Server//scripts/..%c0%af.. %c0%af.. %c0%af.. %c0%af../winnt/
system32/cmd.exe
```

would launch a command shell on the server, offering quick and easy access to the attacker. In a famous example of this, the "Nimda" worm (so named because it's "admin" spelled backward) took advantage of this weakness on IIS 4.0 and 5.0 in 2001 and wreaked havoc across millions of servers on the Internet.

IIS saw a complete rewrite in version 7.0, which addressed the security issues that had plagued it in the past. The current version of IIS is 7.5 and is included with Windows 7 and Windows Server 2008 R2.

NOTE If you really want to learn about web server architecture and how it all works, why not play with it yourself? Apache web servers are relatively easy to install and run, and there's plenty of assistance and help on the Internet to get you started. Download the server and host a website or two inside your home network—it's really the best way to learn.

Whether it's an Apache or an IIS server, scripting is always a concern. CGI (Common Gateway Interface) is a standard method for web servers to pass a user's request to an application program and receive data back to forward to the user. In the case of a simple web page, the user clicks a link and the server provides the HTML for the page. However, if the user enters data into a form, that data generally needs to be passed to an application of some sort. This back and forth is known as CGI, and any number of scripts can be written to handle all sorts of data exchanges between the server, the application, and the user.

Exercise 8-1: Determine the Web Server Type

In this exercise you'll use some banner-grabbing techniques we covered earlier in the book to see which web server your site is being delivered from. I've left the actual web address as "anywhere.com," so you can simply replace it with the website(s) of your choice.

Using Telnet, follow these steps:

1. Open a command prompt.

2. Type **telnet www.anywhere.com 80**.

If the administrator hasn't adjusted the banners to protect himself, the results should show which type of server you're looking at. For example, it may look like this:

```
HTTP/1.1 400 Bad Request
Server: Microsoft-IIS/5.0
Date: THU, 5 May 2011 20:36:17 GMT
Content-Type: text/html
Content-Length: 87
<html><head><title>Error</title></head><body>
The parameter is incorrect. </body></html>
Connection to host lost.
```

Using netcat, follow these steps:

1. Create a txt file called testfile.txt that reads this way:

```
GET HEAD / 1.0
CR
CR
```

2. Run netcat by typing the following command from the appropriate directory (where it is installed):

```
nc -vv webserver 80 < testfile.txt
```

Again, if available, the banner for the site server will display.

For example, you may have a web page allowing a client to enter data into a form. Suppose you need some work done on the data, and depending on the result, a specific message is sent back to the user. You could create a CGI "application" to accomplish this, call it into action on the form, and give it control. If the code, for example, were to read

```
<form method="POST" action="http://www.anywhere.com/cgi-bin/anyapplication.pl">
```

you'd basically be telling the web server for "anywhere.com" to pass the information, and control, over to a CGI application named "anyapplication.pl."

Because CGI scripts can run essentially arbitrary commands on your system with the permissions of the web server user, they can be extremely dangerous if not carefully checked. Additionally, all CGI scripts on the server will run as the same user, so they have the potential to conflict (accidentally or deliberately) with other scripts (an attacker could, for example, write a CGI script to destroy all other CGI databases).

SSI (Server Side Includes), another scripting-type security concern, involves directives placed in HTML pages that are evaluated on the server while the pages are being served. They let you add dynamically generated content to an existing HTML page, without having to serve the entire page via a CGI program or some other dynamic technology. SSIs are useful for including a common piece of code throughout a site, such as a page header, a page footer, or a navigation menu. However, SSIs can increase the load on the server itself and, probably even more important, they can execute any CGI script or program under the permissions of the user. The httpd.conf file in Apache controls this access.

SSI is very simple, and recognizes only text commands falling into the same basic syntax:

```
<!--#directive parameter=value parameter=value -->
```

The most common SSI command is "include," and to use this in a page, you would use the #include statement. This command tells the server to include another file (one that you can update once and change the content on all pages in your site, for example) and tells it the file name that should be included. For example, you might find the command

```
<!--#include FILE="somefile.doc"-->
```

inside the HTML for a page, where somefile.doc would be displayed as part of the page.

SSI commands can include anything from basic documents and formatting instructions (for date and time, for instance) to results of other scripts (CGI). The config parameter allows you set formatting options, whereas the exec parameter will run the script you define in the command. SSI also provides for many conditional directives (such as an if-then) that can be used for a large variety of tasks.

The Right Player for the Right Position

If you're putting together a football team, you don't put the small, skinny, fast kid on the line—you put him at wide out, or maybe in a slot or scatback position. The big guys don't go out there to run passing routes; they're for the interior line, to provide protection and push the opposing players out of the running lanes. And if you put the guy with the single facemask bar and the soccer-style kicking leg in as a linebacker, your team is in for a long day.

The point is, you have to know where to put each person based on their ability, skills, mindset, interests, and desires. The same is true for a pen test team. To put together a truly successful team, you'll have members that have strengths in some areas and weaknesses in others. Some of your guys will just have a knack for picking out vulnerable ports on just the right machine in your thousand-plus-seat nmap scan. Some will just be so good at social engineering *you'll* be afraid to answer any of their questions. And some—usually the nerds among the nerds of your little group—will have an almost uncanny talent for cracking web servers. They'll just *see* scripting weaknesses and vulnerabilities, and won't mind sitting there scratching at web interfaces to find a way in.

Put your people in the right positions, and let them run with the ball of their choice. Your team will be more successful if they're working on what they're good at.

Web Attacks

So we know a little about web server architecture and have a little background information on the terminology, but the question remains: How do we hack them? A good question, and one we'll tackle in this section. As with many other attack vectors we've discussed in this book so far, web server attacks are broad, multiple, and varied. We'll hit the highlights here, both for your career and for your exam.

Directory traversal is one form of attack that's very common and very successful—at least on older servers. To explore this attack, think about the web server architecture. When you get down to it, it's basically a big set of files in folders, just like any other server you have on your network. The server software is designed to accept requests and answer by providing files from specific locations on the server. It follows, then, that there are other folders on the server, maybe *outside* the website delivery world, that hold important commands and information.

For a *very* broad example, suppose all of a website's HTML files, images, and other goodies are located in a single folder (FOLDER_A) off the root of the machine, while all the administrative files for the server itself are located in a separate folder (FOLDER_B) off the root. Usually HTML requests come to the web server software asking for a web page, and by default the server goes to FOLDER_A to retrieve them. However, what if you could somehow send a request to the web server software that instead says, "Mr. Server, I know you normally go to FOLDER_A for HTML requests. But this time, would you please just jump up and over to FOLDER_B and execute this command?" Figure 8-2 shows this in action.

Welcome to directory traversal. In this attack, the hacker attempts to access restricted directories and execute commands outside intended web server directories. Also known as the dot-dot-slash attack, directory climbing, and backtracking, this attack basically sends HTTP requests asking the server to drop back to the root directory and give access to other folders. An example of just such a command might look like this:

```
http://www.example.com/../../../../directory_of_choice\command.exe
```

The dot-dot-slashes are intended to take the shell back to the root and then to execute command.exe in the directory of choice. This may take a little trial and error, and it isn't effective on servers that take steps to protect input validation, but it's definitely worth your time.

A major problem with directory traversal is that it's sometimes fairly noisy. Signature-based IDSs have all sorts of rules in place to look for dot-dot-slash strings and the like. One method for getting around this is to use Unicode in the string to represent the

HTTP://../../../../../Windows\system32\cmd.exe

Server directs the request away from wwwroot, up to the root folder, then down to system32, where a command shell is opened on the web server.

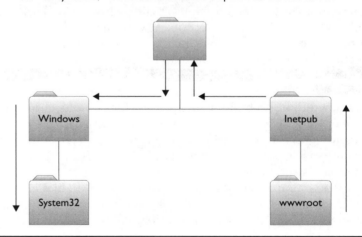

Figure 8-2   Directory traversal

dots and slashes. As you're probably already aware, several Unicode strings can be used to represent characters and codes. In general, the "%2e" code can represent a dot, whereas "%sf" can represent a slash. Putting them together, your Unicode string would look like this:

```
%2e%2e%2f
```

Additionally, don't be afraid to mix up your Unicode in different variations: %2e%2e/ and ..%2f are examples.

 EXAM TIP This dot-dot-slash attack is also known as a variant of "Unicode" or unvalidated input attack. Unicode is a standard for ensuring consistent encoding and text representation, and can be accepted by servers for malicious purposes. *Unvalidated input* means the server has not been configured to accept only specific input during an HTTP GET, so an attacker can craft the request to ask for command prompts, to try administrative access passwords, and so on.

Another attack that sometimes involves a lot of trial and error is called parameter tampering (a.k.a. URL tampering). In this attack, the hacker simply manipulates parameters within the URL string in hopes of modifying data—such as permissions and elevation of privileges, prices and quantities of goods, and credentials. The trick is to simply look at the URL and find parameters you can adjust and re-send.

Suppose, for example, you're surfing on a weak banking site, transferring money from one account to another, and the URL appears like this:

```
http://weakbank.com/sample?Toacct=1234&Fromacct=5678&credAmnt=50
```

Some interesting parameters in this URL might be the "From" and "To" accounts, as well as (what appears to be, anyway) the credit amount of the transfer. Suppose you changed the "Fromacct=5678" parameter to another account number at the bank (one that's not yours) and sent that to the server? For that matter, if you're going to change the URL, aim high and change the "Amnt=50" parameter to something really worthwhile—say 5000 or so?

For another example, suppose you're tracking orders on a website for a target business, and your order shows like this in the URL:

```
http://example.com/orderdetail.asp?orderID=101
```

The page displays your name, address, phone number, and the order details. Well, what if you changed the orderID field to 102? Perhaps you could gain information on other orders and build some solid intelligence to aid your attacks.

You could even use this to affect pricing on poorly built shopping cart sites. For example, consider this URL:

```
http://example.com/add.asp?ItemID=513&Qty=1&Price=15
```

Maybe you consider it offensive to pay $15 for the volleyball you're adding to the cart. So why not change the "Price" parameter to something a little more palatable—such as 5? Again, these parameter manipulations are innumerable and don't necessarily work on everything—in fact, even the most basic of security on sites should prevent most of this—but they're definitely worth a shot.

NOTE Despite the ease with which these parameter-manipulation attacks can be carried out, and the full knowledge of administrators of their existence, you'd be surprised how many sites are vulnerable to this very thing. These types of attacks are extremely common—even on "secure" sites.

Finally, URL obfuscation can be used to bypass basic ACLs. Very often, ACLs block on IP addresses (and occasionally on the text string itself). To get around this, change the IP address of the site you're attempting to attack to an encoded binary equivalent. In other words, don't send a text URL (http://www.badsite.com) or an IP address (http://200.58.77.66). Instead, change the IP to its equivalent and try that. Here are the steps involved:

1. Convert each number of the IP address to its octet binary (200=11001000, 58=00111010, 77=01001101, and 66=01000010).

2. Combine the binaries together to form one long, 32-bit string (11001000001110100100110101000010).

3. Convert the 32-bit binary back to a decimal number (11001000001110100100110101000010 = 3359264066).

4. Enter this number in the URL and give it a shot—it should convert to the proper IP address and take you to the site: http://3359264066.

EXAM TIP You will definitely see, somewhere on your exam, a question or two involving binary equivalents. My advice to you is to save those for the end of the exam. For me, math is easy but takes a while to do. Don't bog yourself down trying to figure out what 3359264066 equates to in binary so you can convert it back to the IP address. After you're done with the other questions, come back and take a look. Sometimes a shortcut (such as noticing that an even number always ends with the last bit set to 0, whereas an odd number ends with the last bit set to 1) is the key to solving it quickly.

Another version of parameter tampering (trust me) involves manipulating the hidden field *on the source code itself.* See, back in the day, web developers simply didn't think users would bother looking at the source code (assuming they were too stupid) and they relied on poor coding practices. The thought was that if the users didn't see it displayed in their browsers, they wouldn't know it was there. To take advantage of this, developers used an HTML code attribute called "hidden." Despite the fact that it's a very well-known vulnerability, especially on shopping sites, and it's a generally accepted fact that the web page itself shouldn't be holding this information, the use of the hidden attribute for pricing and other options is still pretty prevalent. To see how it works, check out the following code I took from a website I found today:

```
<INPUT TYPE=HIDDEN NAME="item_id" VALUE="SurfBoard_81345"
<INPUT TYPE=HIDDEN NAME="price" VALUE="659.99"
<INPUT TYPE=HIDDEN NAME="add" VALUE="1"
...
```

Suppose I *really* wanted a surfboard, but *really* didn't want to pay $659.99 for it. I could simply save the code from this page to my desktop (be sure to check for Unicode encoding if prompted to), change the "price" value to something more reasonable, such as 9.99, save the code, and then open it in a browser. The same web page would appear, and when I clicked the "Add to Cart" button, the surfboard would be added to my cart, with a cost to me of $9.99. Obviously, this amounts to theft, and you could get into a world of trouble trying this, so please don't be ridiculous and get yourself in trouble. The idea here isn't to show you how to steal things, it's to show you how poor coding can cost a business. Not to mention that the hidden field can carry all sorts of other things too. For example, might the following line, which I found on another forum website earlier, be of interest to you?

```
<INPUT TYPE=HIDDEN NAME="Password" VALUE="Xyc756r"
```

Another web server attack vector we just can't pass on talking about deals with passwords themselves. After all, somebody has login credentials to this big machine to affect configuration changes, don't they? So doesn't it follow that, were we to somehow steal this password, we would be able to effect changes to the server? You can use a tool such as Brutus (www.hoobie.net) to try brute-forcing web passwords over HTTP, or THC-Hydra, which is a pretty fast network logon cracker. Of course, any of the other password-cracking options we've already discussed in Chapter 6 may be applicable here as well.

Finally, don't overlook the all-in-one attack frameworks, such as Metasploit (shown in Figure 8-3), that can make short work of web servers. Metasploit will cover lots of options for you, including exploitation of known vulnerabilities and attacking passwords over Telnet, SSH, and HTTP. A basic Metasploit exploit module consists of five actions: Select the exploit you wish to use, configure the various options within the

Figure 8-3   Metasploit

exploit, select a target, select the payload (that is, what you want to execute on the target machine), and then launch the exploit. Simply find a web server within your target subnet, and fire away!

Web Applications

Web applications are another issue altogether, although many of the same attacks and lines of reasoning will bleed over here from the web server side. A web application, in terms of your CEH exam, fills an important gap between the website front end and the actual database performing the work. Users interact with the website to affect database or other dynamic content instances, but it's the web app that's actually performing the magic. Web applications are increasingly becoming an attack vector of choice, due in large part to their sheer numbers and the lack of standardization across the board. Many web apps are created "in house" by the business and, as a result, usually have vulnerabilities built in, due to a lack of security oversight during their creation. This section is all about the attacks you might see and use in hacking web applications.

Application Attacks

Web applications are most often hacked due to inherent weaknesses built into the program at inception. Developers might overlook known vulnerabilities, forget to patch security flaws, or leave default passwords and accounts open for exploitation. A patient hacker can scratch away at the application looking for these vulnerabilities, eventually finding their way in. It's obviously impossible to cover every single one of these vulnerabilities and the attacks that work on them, because each is dependent on the circumstances and the individual application. Just know, for now, that this is probably how a lot of successful web hacks are eventually going to work.

One very successful web application attack deals with injecting malicious commands into the input string. The objective is much like that of the URL-tampering methods discussed earlier in this chapter: to pass exploit code to the server through poorly designed input validation in the application. This can occur using a variety of different methods, including *file injection* (where the attacker injects a pointer in the web form input to an exploit hosted on a remote site), *command injection* (where the attacker injects commands into the form fields instead of the expected test entry), and *shell injection* (where the attacker attempts to gain shell access using Java or other functions). The most common of these, though, and the one you'll definitely see on your exam, is a very specialized form of injection attack involving the database language itself.

SQL Injection

Because this is such an important topic in the world of hacking and web security, we need to set some ground rules and expectations first. SQL injection is, by far, the most common and most successful injection attack technique in the world. This attack leads to credit card theft, identity theft, and destruction of data across the Internet. It pops up nearly everywhere—the next big credit card theft story you read will, most likely, be due to an SQL injection attack of some sort. All of this should lead you to believe, then, that learning and mastering SQL is a skill you will want to hone as a successful ethical hacker. And although that is true, it's not what we're going to do here.

Becoming an SQL master is not what this book is about, nor do we have the space or time to cover every facet of it—or even most of them, for that matter. Our job here is twofold. Primarily it's to help you pass the test, and secondarily it's to assist you in becoming a true ethical hacker. You're going to get the basics here—both for your exam and your career—but it's going to be just enough to whet your appetite. If you really want to become a seasoned master at this, study SQL and learn all you can about how it works. For now, though, let's cover the basics and what you need to know.

Structured Query Language (SQL) is a computer "language" designed for managing data in a relational database system. The relational database itself is simply a collection of tables (consisting of rows, which hold individual fields containing data) tied together using some common field (key) that you can update and query. Each table has a name given to it that is referenced when you perform queries or updates. SQL comes into play when you are adding, deleting, moving, updating, or viewing the data in those tables and fields. It's not too overwhelmingly complicated to do the simple stuff, but the SQL queries can, eventually, get pretty complex.

For example, let's consider the SELECT command. SELECT is used to choose the data you'd like to perform an action on. The statement starts, amazingly enough, with the word "SELECT," followed by innumerable options and elements to define what you wish to act upon and what that action will be. A command of

```
SELECT * FROM Orders
```

says, "Database, I'd like you to pull all records from the table named Orders." Tweaked a little, you can get more granular. For example,

```
SELECT OrderID, FirstName, LastName FROM Orders
```

will pull everything in the OrderID, first name, and last name columns from the table named "Orders." When you start adding other command options such as WHERE (setting up a conditional statement), LIKE (defining a condition where something is similar to a given variable), AND, and OR (self-explanatory), you can get even crazier. For example,

```
SELECT OrderID, FirstName, LastName FROM Orders WHERE LastName = 'Walker'
```

will pull all orders made by some dude with the last name of Walker.

In addition to SELECT, there are a bunch of other options and commands of great interest to a hacker. For example, can you—with no other SQL experience or knowledge—probably figure out what the command "DROP TABLE *tablename*" does? Any of you that didn't respond with "Delete the table *tablename* from the database," should immediately start taking Ginkoba to improve your cognitive and deductive skills. How about the commands INSERT or UPDATE? As you can see, SQL in and of itself isn't rocket science. It is, though, very powerful and commands a lot of respect. Researching command language syntax for everything SQL can offer will pay off dividends in your career—trust me on this.

So, we know a little about SQL databases, and have a basic understanding of how to craft query commands, but the big question is, "So what? Why is this so important?" In answer, pause for just a moment and consider where a database might reside in a web server/application arena you're trying to hack, and what it's there to do. The front end takes input from the user through the web server and passes it through an application or form to the database to actually adjust the data. And what, pray tell, is on this database? Maybe items such as credit card account numbers, personally identifiable information, and account numbers and passwords don't interest you, but I promise you can find all of that and more in a web-serviced database.

SQL injection occurs when the attacker injects SQL queries directly into the input form. Properly constructed, the SQL command bypasses the intent of the front end and executes directly on the SQL database. For example, consider Figure 8-4 and the sample SQL shown there. The form is constructed to accept a user ID and password from the

Figure 8-4
SQL injection

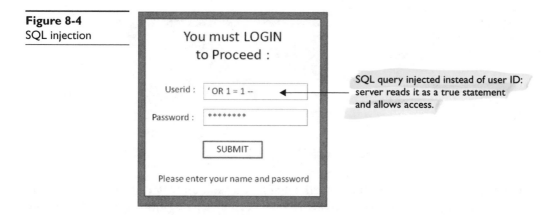

You must LOGIN
to Proceed :

Userid : 'OR 1 = 1 --

SQL query injected instead of user ID:
server reads it as a true statement
and allows access.

Password : ********

SUBMIT

Please enter your name and password

user. These entries are placed into an SQL query that says, "Please compare the user-name given to the password in its associated field. If this username matches this pass-word, allow access." What we injected changed the original query to say, "You can compare whatever you'd like, but 1=1 is a true statement, so allow access please."

NOTE   You can also try SQL injection up in the URL itself. For example, you can try to pass authentication credentials by changing the URL to read something like this: http://www.example.com/?login='OR 1=1- -.

Of course, knowing this isn't any good to you if you can't figure out whether the target site is vulnerable to SQL injection in the first place. To find out, check your target for a web login page, and instead of entering what's asked at the web form, simply try a single quote (') and see what kind of error message, if any, you receive. If that doesn't work, try entering *anything*' **or 1=1- -** and see what you get. If you receive an error message like the one shown in Figure 8-5, you're more than likely looking at a site vulnerable to SQL injection.

Most developers are familiar with this little SQL "test," and *lots* of things have been done to prevent its use. Many C++ and .NET applications now simply explode with errors when they are sent a single quote (or some variant thereof) and other special characters, and this input never even gets processed by the application. Another effort involves the so-called "Magic Quotes" in Apache, which filters out (escapes) the characters before the application ever sees them. Of course, use of "fuzzing attack" tools such as Burp can make use of the error messaging *itself* to point out the underlying potential vulnerabilities on the system.

To see SQL in action, consider a website that has a "Forgot your password? Click here and we'll send it to you" message. After clicking the button, you get a pop-up window asking you to insert your e-mail address. You type it in, hit ENTER, and your password is

Figure 8-5
SQL error message

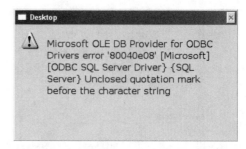

e-mailed to your account on file. Well, what if you send an SQL command in the form instead and ask the database to create (INSERT) a new record in the user and password table just for you? The command

```
anything' ; INSERT INTO cust ('cust_Email', 'cust_Password', 'cust_Userid',
'cust_FirstName', 'cust_LastName') VALUES ( 'attacker_emailAddress@badplace.com',
'P@ssw0rd', 'Matt' , 'Matthew', 'Walker') ; - -
```

says to the database, "Database, you have a table there named *cust*. I think that probably stands for customers. So if you would, please enter into the fields labeled Email, Password, Userid, FirstName, and LastName these new values I'm supplying for you. Thank you, and hack ya later."

For that matter, if you're at a site requiring login, why not just try bypassing the authentication altogether? Try logging in using SQL statements. For example,

```
admin ' - - or admin ' /*
```

might be beneficial. You can also try the old standby

```
' or 1=1 - -
```

or some variation thereof, such as

```
')
```

or

```
('1'='1- -
```

In any case, you can find bunches of these types of SQL strings to try on the Internet. One cautionary note, though: Brute forcing SQL this way isn't the quietest means of gaining access. If you're banging away with 10,000 variations of a single open quote, you're going to get noticed.

There are tons and tons of SQL injection examples, and just as many names given for the attacks. We can't cover them all here, but I will be kind enough to provide you a couple of attack names and definitions for your study (please keep in mind that anything other than basic SQL will have some significant semantic differences, so always Google the database version you're trying):

- **Union query**   The thought here is to make use of the UNION command to return the union of your target database with one you've crafted to steal data from it.

- **Tautology**   An overly complex term used to describe the behavior of a database system when deciding whether or not a statement is true. Because user IDs and passwords are often compared, and the "true" measure allows access, if you trick the database by providing something that is already true (1 does, indeed, equal 1), then you can sneak by.

- **Blind SQL injection**   This occurs when the attacker knows the database is susceptible to injection, but the error messages and screen returns don't come back to the attacker. Because there's a lot of guesswork and trial and error, this attack takes a long while to pull off.

- **Error-based SQL injection**   This isn't necessarily an attack so much as an enumeration technique. The objective is to purposely enter poorly constructed statements in an effort to get the database to respond with table names and other information in its error messages.

As always, you can peck around with this stuff and learn it manually, or you can take advantage of tools already created to make your job easier. sqlmap and sqlninja are both automated scanners designed to look specifically for injection vulnerabilities. Another one I've seen in play is called Havij, which allows all enumeration, code execution on the target, file system manipulation, and all sorts of madness over SQL connections. SQLBrute is a tool that, amazingly enough, allows you to blast through predefined SQL injection queries against a target. Others include, but are not limited to, Pangolin, SQLEXEC, Absinthe, and BobCat.

 NOTE   Protection against SQL injection usually comes down to security-minded web and database design in the first place. However, you can make use of tools and signatures to at least monitor for attempts; for one example, you can check the Snort signatures for pre-built SQL rules and then block or monitor for attempts using the signatures.

Cross-Site Scripting

Second in our romp through web applications and server attacks are *cross-site scripting* (XSS) attacks. This can get a little confusing, but the basics of these attacks come down to website design and dynamic content. Usually when a web form pops up, the user inputs something and then some script dynamically changes the appearance or behavior of the website based on what has been entered. XSS occurs when the bad guys take advantage of that scripting (Java, for instance) and have it perform something other than the intended response.

For example, suppose a pen-test member discovers a website at the target that appears to be vulnerable to XSS. He puts together an e-mail message that, of course, looks official and sends it to internal users. The link embedded in the e-mail contains naughty code written to take advantage of the website. The user, unknowingly, clicks the link while logged on and sends the bad code to the web server. The server then does what it's supposed to—it processes the code sent from an authorized user. Wham! Hack city.

 EXAM TIP You'll need to know what XSS is and what you can do with it. Also, be able to recognize that a URL such as the following is an indicator of an XSS attempt: http://IPADDRESS/";!- -"<XSS>=&{()}.

XSS can be used to perform all sorts of badness on a target server. In addition to simply bringing it down in a good old DoS attack, XSS can also be used to steal users' cookies, to upload malicious code to users connected to the server, and to send pop-up messages to users. One of the classic attacks of XSS involves getting access to "document.cookie" and sending it to a remote host. That variable typically contains all the session information stored on a user's browser. So what about that PHP session ID that identifies the user to the website? Well, the attacker has it now and can masquerade as the user all day, plugged into a session. XSS attacks can vary by application and by browser, and can range from nuisance to severe impact depending on what the attacker chooses to do. They represent the second largest attack vector online today (SQL still being #1).

 NOTE RSnake and http://ha.ckers.org/xss.html are authoritative sources for XSS attacks.

Buffer Overflows

A buffer overflow attack is one that should never be successful in modern technology, but still remains a great weapon in your arsenal, due to poorly designed applications. To truly use this attack, you're probably going to have to become a good computer programmer, which I'm sure just excites you to no end. The good news on this, though, is twofold. First, many Metasploit-like tools make this much easier for you to attempt. Second, you only need to know the basic mechanics of the attack for your CEH exam.

The most basic definition of a *buffer overflow* is an attempt to write more data into an application's pre-built buffer area in order to overwrite adjacent memory, execute code, or crash a system (application). In short, you input more data than the buffer is allocated to hold. The result can be anything from crashing the application or machine to altering the application's data pointers, allowing you to run different executable code.

The buffer overflow attack categories are as follows:

- **Stack** This idea comes from the basic premise that all program calls are kept in a stack and executed in order. If you affect the stack with a buffer overflow, you can perhaps change a function pointer or variable to allow code execution.

- **Heap** Also referred to as heap overflow, this attack takes advantage of the memory "on top of" the application, which is allocated dynamically at runtime. Because this memory usually contains program data, you can cause the application to overwrite function pointers.

- **NOP Sled** A NOP sled makes use of a machine instruction called "no-op." In the attack, a hacker sends a large number of NOP instructions into the buffer, appending command code instruction at the end. Because this attack is so common, most IDSs protect against it. For example, check out the code capture shown in Figure 8-6; the NOP sled should be easy to spot!

In addition to good coding techniques, to avoid allowing the overflow in the first place, sometimes developers can make use of "canaries" or "canary words." The idea comes from the old mining days, when canaries were kept in cages in various places in a mine. The canary was more susceptible to poison air and would, therefore, act as a warning to the miners. In buffer overflow and programming parlance, *canary words* are known values placed between the buffer and control data. If a buffer overflow occurs, the canary word will be altered first, triggering a halt to the system. Tools such as StackGuard make use of this for stack protection.

Figure 8-6
NOP sled code
example

```
33 00 20 ac 27 1e 24 20 32 60 69 92 e3 18 92 68 9b 18 99   A..ï(...1@2..Ñ:...
40 40 22 e4 ee df 21 f7 ff  22 b5 23 bf ff  58 58 bb 20 22  .6...oTOO@pxP.)..
80 31 c7 89 54 4f 43 66 89 5d ce 66 67 75 ee 27 89 4d f0   4u%300$n%.314u%201$n
6e 24 90 90 90 90 90 90 90 90 90 90 90 90 90 90 90 90 90   $n.................
90 90 90 90 90 90 90 90 90 90 90 90 90 90 90 90 90 90 90   ..................
90 90 90 90 90 90 90 90 90 90 90 90 90 90 90 90 90 90 90   ..................
90 90 90 90 90 90 90 90 90 90 90 90 90 90 90 90 90 90 90   ..................
90 90 90 90 90 90 90 90 90 90 90 90 90 90 90 90 90 90 90   ..................
90 90 90 90 90 90 90 90 90 90 90 90 90 90 90 90 90 90 90   ..................
90 90 90 90 90 90 90 90 90 90 90 90 90 90 90 90 90 90 90   ..................
90 90 90 90 90 90 90 90 90 90 90 90 90 90 90 90 90 90 90   ..................
90 90 90 90 90 90 90 90 90 90 90 90 90 90 90 90 90 90 90   ..................
90 90 90 90 cd 80 89 e5 d2 51 66 89 67 e5 31 db 31 54 53   ...1Û1E1À..FÎ..á10%f
f3 8d 4d 08 8d 0c 55 cd 80 ff  ff  2f 69 62 63 77 73 2f 46  seïc..%302ÿ.192u%303Ć1
0c 5c 44 65 66 23 2d a3 43 44 e3 89 c3 31 c0 88 46 07 89   EôCf.]ifCEï.'..MBD.ô
e5 31 db 31 89 c3 d0 43 cd 31 c0 88 46 07 89 45 0c b0 24   .EïEªÜF.E..ŁDC Ïẓ..Ã
41 cd 80 eb 08 31 c3 c3146 55 cd 80 ff  34 2c b3 25 12 1b  CÍ..DC¿.À1FêÐ1..1%u
32 31 f7 ff  22 b5 23 24 8a 45 0c b0 0b 89 7f 35 1d 87 99  AÍ.ê.^..u.1.F..DfôMu¿
34 75 25 33 30 30 24 6e!25 2e 32 31 33 75 25 66 b4 3a 6e   ô.M..U..Áéÿÿ
```

Cookies

A *cookie* is a very small, text-based file that is stored on your system for use by the web server the next time you log in. It can contain all sorts of information, including authentication details, site preferences, shopping cart contents, and session details. Cookies are sent in the header of an HTTP response from a web server and may or may not have an expiration date. The original intent was to provide a continuous, stable web view for customers, and to make things easier for return surfers.

The problem, of course, is that seemingly everything designed to make our technological life easier can be co-opted for evil. Cookies can definitely prove very valuable to the hacker, and a tool such as the Cookie Editor add-on for Firefox opens up all sorts of parameter-tampering opportunities. Cookies themselves aren't executable—they're just text files, after all—however, they can be manipulated to use as spyware (cookies can be used to track computer activity), change pricing options, and even to authenticate to a server. For example, an entry in a cookie reading "ADMIN=no" can be changed to read "ADMIN=yes," thus providing administrative access to site controls.

Passwords can sometimes also be stored in cookies, and although it's a horrible practice, it's still fairly prevalent. Access to a target's physical machine and the use of a tool to view the cookies stored on it (such as Karen's Cookie Viewer) might give you access to passwords the user has for various websites. And, if they are like most people, it's nearly a guarantee that the password you just lifted is being reused on another site or account. Additionally, don't be thrown off by cookies with long, seemingly senseless text strings beside the user ID sections. On a few, you may be able to run them through a Unicode (or Base64) decoder to reveal the user's password for that site.

Undead Cookies

An interesting vocabulary term you may not be aware of is *zombie cookie*, which is a cookie that's re-created after deletion from backups stored outside your browser's normal cookie storage area. Just like the undead from a George Romero film, zombie cookies are difficult to remove—you can kill them all you want, but they *keep coming back* (cue ridiculous horror music here). They may even install on a browser that does not receive cookies, making them truly sneaky little undead text files.

These may sound like completely evil little beings, but they're actually pretty common. Sites such as Google, ESPN, and Yahoo! all make use of zombie cookies. Why, you might ask? Two major reasons: These cookies allow tracking of personal browsing habits, which provides obvious benefits to the site owners, and (probably on the more ethical side of things) it helps the site appear consistent and professional to the user.

Exercise 8-2: Cookie Editing

Editing parameters on a cookie can lead to substantive gains for an attacker. This exercise introduces you to the Cookie Editor add-on (you'll see it again, trust me). You'll have to experiment more on your own to see the true results. Here are the steps to follow:

1. Download and install the Cookie Editor for Firefox (https://addons.mozilla.org/en-us/firefox/addon/edit-cookies/) and then restart Firefox.

2. Open the cookie editor by selecting Tools | Cookie Editor. All the cookies stored by Firefox on your machine are displayed (see Figure 8-7).

3. Scroll through and select a cookie and then click the Edit button. The resultant Add/Edit Cookie dialog box is shown in Figure 8-8.

Note the fields you can alter. Try several cookies on the machine to see unique differences. Over time, you may find some interesting tidbits (such as the "ADMIN=no" example) to play with.

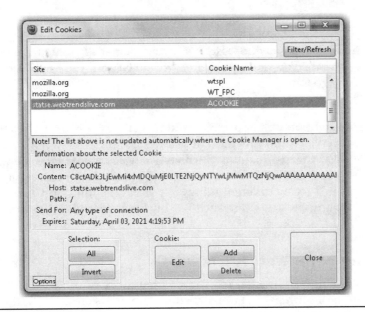

Figure 8-7 Firefox cookie editor

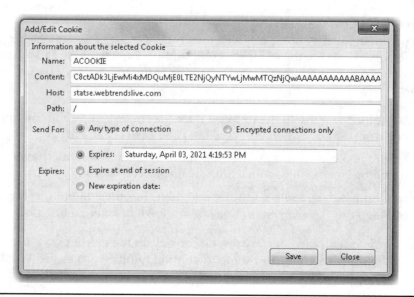

Figure 8-8 Editing a cookie

NOTE A few web application scanning tools are Whisker (an older tool), N-Stealth, WebInspect, AppDetective, and Nikto. If you have the means to use them, go for it.

One final thought on web application testing isn't actually a hack at all, but it sure is productive. A very common method of security testing (hacking) a web application is to simply try using it in a manner in which it wasn't intended to be used. This isn't applying some groovy hacker tool or scripting code to inject through some James Bond type of ploy, it's just trying different things out with an application—sometimes even by accident. As many a tester will say, with a chuckle in his voice, "It's not a hack, it's a *feature.*"

Protecting Your Web Resources

Web servers are successfully attacked for a variety of reasons. Bugs in the software, misconfiguration of settings, and unpatched security flaws are some of the more common reasons, but securing an Apache or an IIS server really comes down to the same things you'd check on with any server. Keep it up to date with the latest versions and patches, and ensure permissions are set appropriately (especially anything "default" that could be exploited by an attacker). As always, you should control administrative access as much as possible, and keep a sharp eye on your logs, to monitor against bad-guy influence. Lastly, keep a sharp eye on vulnerability research and trends, and never run the web server as a user with any elevated privileges. If you're having problems with Apache and just run everything in root because it's easier, or your IIS permissions are all amok so you run it as admin, all your apps are also running with root/admin privileges. As a friend of mine said a few days ago, "We in IT security have to be right 100 percent of the time—the hackers only have to be right *once*." Don't make it easy for them.

Identifying Web Server Vulnerabilities

We've already covered some of the "10,000-foot view" footprinting efforts that will help you identify the web servers themselves. The use of whois and, more intimately, banner grabbing can help with valuable information you'll need along the way. To get a little bit closer in, use some tools and actions that are more specialized for web servers themselves. For example, Netcraft can provide some great high-level information. httprecon and ID Serve work really well in identifying, reliably, the web server architecture and OS, and httprint provides lots of really cool information. Other tools such as Burp Suite can give you insight into content on the site the owner probably didn't want disclosed. And don't discount a method already mentioned earlier in this book—tools such as BlackWidow and HTTrack can make a copy of the website on your system for your review.

In addition, if you have a means to get it running against the web server, a vulnerability scanner will practically give you everything you need to gain access. Nessus is probably the most common vulnerability scanner available, but it's certainly not the only option. Nikto is a vulnerability scanner more suited specifically for web servers (see Figure 8-9). An open source tool, Nikto scans for virtually everything you can think of, including file problems, script errors, and server configuration errors. It can even be configured within Nessus to kick off a scan automatically when a web server is discovered! Plug-ins and signatures are numerous and varied, and update automatically for you. The only drawback is that it's a relatively noisy tool, so you won't be running it stealthily.

In any case, a good vulnerability scan against a web server is about as close to a guarantee as anything we've talked about thus far. By their very design they're open to the world, and many—not all, but many—will have something overlooked. Take your time and be patient; eventually your efforts will pay off.

Figure 8-9
Nikto web banner

Countermeasures and Hardening

Hardening a machine, as we've already discussed, involves applying all the appropriate and practical security measures to secure it against known vulnerabilities and attacks. And as stated earlier, most of this should be common sense and will apply whether we're talking about a web server or a file server inside the organization. However, hardening is an explicit objective within CEH, so we'll definitely take the time here to cover the highlights:

- Keep up to date with patching and hot fixes. Of course, you should test and verify everything before patching a production server, just don't fall too far behind. Remember, by the time the patch has been released, the vulnerability has already been known for quite some time.

- Remove everything that is not absolutely necessary for the machine to function. Some items to look at deleting include, but are not limited to, unnecessary services, files (header files, archives, old text documents), directories, ISAPI filters, user accounts, and protocols. Not just some of them, *all* of them; anything not directly supporting your server's mission needs to go.

- Use common sense and extreme caution in allowing remote access. SSH is better than Telnet any day. Using an encrypted tunnel (IPSec) is even better.

- Try to keep your web applications and scripts on a separate partition from your operating system, for obvious reasons.

- Ensure your programmers use secure coding techniques; no unvalidated input, protection against buffer overflow, and so on.

- Restrict the information shown in banner and error messages.

- Always keep a sharp eye on your user accounts. Disable or remove all the known "default" accounts, use good authentication measures and passwords, and apply least privilege (only what they need and no more) to all accounts. Lastly, don't forget there's more to this than just your server—all of this applies to *database* user accounts too!

- Apply due diligence in managing passwords. No default passwords for anything should remain on your server, and even though most modern systems won't allow it, you should *never* have an account with a *blank* password.

There are also a few steps you can take specific to the web server type you choose. Apache, for example, requires someone with a nice Linux/Unix touch to truly secure. A couple of basics include, but aren't limited to:

- Protect files and folders created by root. Apache normally starts as root, then switches to a user (defined by a directive) to serve web requests. If non-root users can then modify files that root either executes or writes, then the system is open to root compromises.

- Control SSI. In addition to the extra performance demands on the server, SSI can also run into security issues by executing CGI at elevated user levels. In mitigation, an administrator can enable "suexec." Normally, SSI (or CGI) runs at the user level on the server user. Suexec lets Apache users run these scripts under different user IDs. This can considerably reduce the risk of allowing users to develop and run private scripts.

- Control CGI. Don't allow users to execute CGI scripts from just any directory. Limit them to special directories you can control. And while you're at it, make sure the scripts are clean to begin with.

- Watch your .htaccess. After you configure security, some crafty user might come behind you and set up an .htaccess file to overwrite your security settings. Remove the override potential in the server configuration file up front.

Finally, more than a few tools are available to help you in hardening your machine. A quick Internet search will show you exactly what I mean. A couple of note include IIS Lockdown and MBSA. IIS Lockdown is a tool designed to secure an IIS server based on the parameters you provide; the steps to secure a file server are different than for a web server, for instance. A quick note of caution here: Be really careful with this tool, because you may wind up securing yourself out of the machine!

Microsoft Baseline Security Analyzer (MBSA) is a good tool to see your patching levels on Microsoft machines (see Figure 8-10). It's easy to use and provides a pretty easy-to-understand report on the security of your machine. Of course, most vulnerability scanners (Nessus, Core Impact, GFI LANguard, and others) will also tell you what's missing on the machine, but MBSA is easy to use, free, and designed specifically for Windows systems.

Figure 8-10
MBSA

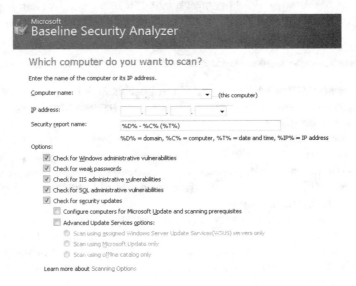

Chapter Review

A web server acts like any other server you already know about, but it responds to TCP connection requests on port 80 or 443. The server waits for an HTTP GET request from the client and responds with specific HTML code representing a website page. The server then looks through a storage area and finds the code that matches the request, and provides it to the client.

Apache servers (www.apache.org) make up the majority of web hosts on the Internet. Apache is an open source, very powerful, and very fast web server that typically runs on a Unix or Linux platform. Internet Information Services (IIS) servers are easy-to-manage Windows-based options for the web provider.

Common Gateway Interface (CGI) provides a standard method for web servers to pass a user's request to an application program and receive data back to forward to the user. Because CGI scripts can run essentially arbitrary commands on your system with the permissions of the web server user, they can be extremely dangerous if not carefully checked. Additionally, all CGI scripts on the server will run as the same user, so they have potential to conflict with other scripts (an attacker could, for example, write a CGI script to destroy all other CGI databases).

Server Side Includes (SSIs) are directives placed in HTML pages, and they are evaluated on the server while the pages are being served. They let you add dynamically generated content to an existing HTML page without having to serve the entire page via a CGI program, or other dynamic technology. SSIs are useful for including a common piece of code throughout a site, such as a page header, a page footer, or a navigation menu. The httpd.conf file in Apache controls this access.

Directory traversal is a web attack whereby the attacker manipulates the URL parameters to navigate the directory structure on the server itself. This can lead to file access and even command shell operation. This is also known as the dot-dot-slash attack, directory climbing, and backtracking. Attackers basically send HTTP requests asking the server to drop back to the root directory and give access to other folders. An example of just such a command might look like this:

```
http://www.example.com/../../../../directory_of_choice/command.exe
```

The dot-dot-slashes are intended to take the shell back to the root and then to execute command.exe in the directory of choice. A Unicode version of this attack might appear as %2e%2e%2f.

Parameter tampering (a.k.a. URL tampering) occurs when the hacker manipulates parameters within the URL string in hopes of modifying data—such as permissions and elevation of privilege, prices and quantities of goods, and credentials.

Brutus (www.hoobie.net), THC-Hydra, and Metasploit are all useful tools in attacking web servers and applications.

A web application fills an important gap between the website front end and the actual database performing the work. Users interact with the website to affect database or other dynamic content instances, but the web application actually performs the work. Web applications are most often hacked due to inherent weaknesses built into the program at inception. Developers might overlook known vulnerabilities, forget to patch security flaws, or leave default passwords and accounts open for exploitation.

One very successful web application attack deals with injecting malicious commands into the input string. The objective is much like the URL-tampering methods discussed in this chapter: to pass exploit code to the server through poorly designed input validation in the application. This can occur using a variety of different methods, including file injection (where the attacker injects a pointer in the web form input to an exploit hosted on a remote site), command injection (where the attacker injects commands into the form fields instead of the expected test entry), and shell injection (where the attacker attempts to gain shell access using Java or other functions).

SQL injection is, by far, the most common and most successful injection attack technique in the world. Structured Query Language (SQL) is a computer "language" designed for managing data in a relational database system. The relational database itself is simply a collection of tables (consisting of rows, which hold individual fields containing data) tied together using some common field (key) that you can update and query. Each table has a name given to it that is referenced when you perform queries or updates. SQL comes into play when you are adding, deleting, moving, updating, or viewing the data in those tables and fields.

SQL queries generally begin with the SELECT command. SELECT is used to choose the data you'd like to perform an action on. In addition to SELECT, there are several additional options and commands of great interest to a hacker. For example, "DROP TABLE *tablename*" will delete the table *tablename* from the database. INSERT and UPDATE are also easy to understand.

SQL injection occurs when the attacker injects SQL queries directly into the input form. Properly constructed, the SQL command bypasses the intent of the front end and executes directly on the SQL database. To find out if a site is susceptible to SQL injection, check your target for a web login page, and instead of entering what's asked for on the web form, simply try a single quote (') and see what kind of error message, if any, you receive. If that doesn't work, try entering **anything' or 1=1- -** and see what you get. The attack names and definitions for SQL are union query, tautology, blind SQL injection, and error-based SQL injection.

sqlmap, Havij, and sqlninja are all automated scanners designed to look specifically for injection vulnerabilities. SQLBrute is a tool that allows you to blast through predefined SQL injection queries against a target. Others include, but are not limited to, Pangolin, SQLEXEC, Absinthe, and BobCat.

Cross-site scripting (XSS) attacks take advantage of dynamic content on sites. XSS occurs when hackers take advantage of that scripting (Java, for instance) on the server and have it perform something other than the intended response. An example might look like

```
http://IPADDRESS/";!- -"<XSS>=&{()}
```

or using a

```
'<script>something</script>'
```

entry in a web form. In addition to a DoS attack, XSS can be used to steal users' cookies, to upload malicious code to users connected to the server, and to send pop-up messages to users. XSS attacks represent the second largest attack vector online today.

A buffer overflow attack is an attempt to write more data into an application's prebuilt buffer area in order to overwrite adjacent memory, execute code, or crash a system (application). The result can be anything from crashing the application or machine to altering the application's data pointers, allowing you to run different executable code. Buffer overflow attack categories include stack, heap, and NOP sled.

In addition to good coding techniques, sometimes developers can make use of "canaries" or "canary words." In buffer overflow and programming parlance, canary words are known values placed between the buffer and control data. If a buffer overflow occurs, the canary word will be altered first, triggering a halt to the system. Tools such as StackGuard make use of this for stack protection.

A cookie is a very small, text-based file that is stored on your system for use by the web server the next time you log in. It can contain all sorts of information, including authentication details, site preferences, shopping cart contents, and session details. Cookies can definitely prove very valuable to the hacker, and a tool such as the Cookie Editor add-on for Firefox opens up all sorts of parameter-tampering opportunities. Cookies themselves aren't executable; however, they can be manipulated to use as spyware (cookies can be used to track computer activity), change pricing options, and even to authenticate to a server.

Web servers are successfully attacked for a variety of reasons. Bugs in the software, misconfiguration of settings, and unpatched security flaws are some of the more common reasons, but securing an Apache server or an IIS server really comes down to the same things you'd check on with any server. Keep it up to date with the latest versions and patches, and ensure permissions are set appropriately (especially anything "default" that could be exploited by an attacker). As always, you should control administrative access as best you can, and keep a watch on your logs, to monitor against bad-guy influence. Lastly, keep a sharp eye on vulnerability research and trends. As a friend of mine said a few days ago, "We in IT security have to be right 100 percent of the time—the hackers only have to be right *once*."

A vulnerability scanner will attempt to provide the necessary hardening, and hacking, information on a web server. Nessus is probably the most common vulnerability scanner available, but it's certainly not the only option. Nikto is an open source vulnerability scanner suited specifically for web servers. It can even be configured within Nessus to kick off a scan automatically when a web server is discovered.

Questions

1. You are examining log files and notice several connection attempts to a hosted web server. Several attempts appear as such:

```
http://www.example.com/%2e%2e/%2e%2e/%2e%2e/%2e%2e/%2e%2e/windows\system32\cmd.exe
```

What type of attack is in use?

A. SQL injection

B. Unicode parameter tampering

C. Directory traversal

D. Cross-site scripting

2. The accounting department of a business notices several orders that seem to have been made erroneously. In researching the concern, you discover it appears the price of items on several web orders do not match the listed price on the public site. You verify the web server and the ordering database do not seem to have been compromised. Additionally, no alerts have displayed in the Snort logs concerning a possible attack on the web application. Which of the following might explain the attack in play?

A. The attacker has copied the source code to his machine and altered hidden fields to modify the purchase price of the items.

B. The attacker has used SQL injection to update the database to reflect new prices for the items.

C. The attacker has taken advantage of a Server Side Include that altered the price.

D. The attacker used Metasploit to take control of the web application.

3. Which of the following would best represent a parameter-tampering attack?

A. http://example.com/add.asp?ItemID=513&Qty=1&Price=15

B. http://www.example.com/search.asp?lname=walker%27%update%20 usertable%20%20set%3d%23hAxor%27

C. http://www.example.com/../../../../../../windows\system32\cmd.exe

D. http://www.example.com/?login='OR 1=1-

4. You are examining IDS logs and come across the following entry:

```
Mar 30 10:31:07 [1123]: IDS1661/NOPS-x86: 64.118.55.64:1146-> 192.168.119.56:53
```

What can you infer from this log entry?

A. The attacker, using address 192.168.119.56, is attempting to connect to 64.118.55.64 using a DNS port.

B. The attacker, using address 64.118.55.64, is attempting a directory traversal attack.

C. The attacker is attempting a known SQL attack against 192.168.119.56.

D. The attacker is attempting a buffer overflow against 192.168.119.56.

5. A junior security employee tells you a web application has halted. An examination of the syslog shows an entry from the web application, indicating the canary word has been altered. What does this message indicate?

   A. The NIDS has blocked an attempted attack.

   B. The firewall has failed in protecting the subnet.

   C. A buffer overflow attack has been successful.

   D. A buffer overflow was attempted, but failed.

6. A pen-test member is experimenting with a web form on a target website and receives the following error message:

   Microsoft OLE DB Provider for ODBC Drivers error '80040e08' [Microsoft] {OBDC SQL Server Driver}

   What might this error indicate?

   A. The application may be vulnerable to directory traversal.

   B. The application may be vulnerable to SQL injection.

   C. The application may be vulnerable to buffer overflow.

   D. None of the above.

7. Which character is the best choice to start an SQL injection attempt?

   A. Colon

   B. Semicolon

   C. Double quote

   D. Single quote

8. Jim has been hired to manage a web server. He wants to examine the server for vulnerabilities as a first step to plan his hardening efforts. Which of the following tools would be the best choice for this situation?

   A. BlackWidow

   B. HTTrack

   C. Burp Suite

   D. Nessus

9. A member of the pen test team examines a cookie he received from a live session on the target's web server. Here's a portion of the cookie text:

   lang=en-us; ADMIN=no; y=1; time=13:27GMT;

   Which of the following should he infer regarding this information?

   A. The site is most likely vulnerable to SQL injection.

   B. The site is not likely to be vulnerable to SQL injection.

   C. The site is vulnerable to parameter tampering.

   D. None of the above.

10. An attacker inputs the following into the Search text box on an entry form: <script>'It Worked'</script>. The attacker then clicks the Search button and a pop-up appears stating "It Worked." What can you infer from this?

    A. The site is vulnerable to buffer overflow.

    B. The site is vulnerable to SQL injection.

    C. The site is vulnerable to parameter tampering.

    D. The site is vulnerable to XSS.

Answers

1. **C.** This connection is attempting to traverse the directory from the Inetpub folders to a command shell for the attacker. Unicode is used in this example to bypass potential IDS signatures.

2. **A.** In this case, because the logs and IDSs show no direct attack, it's most likely the attacker has copied the source code directly to his machine and altered the hidden "price" fields on the order form. All other types of attack would have, in some form or fashion, shown themselves easily.

3. **A.** Parameter tampering is fairly easy to identify when the URL contains a price, access permissions, or account information identified by an integer. Answers B and D are obviously SQL injection attempts, and answer C is directory traversal.

4. **D.** The log file shows that the NOP sled signature is being used against 192.168.119.56. There is no indication in the log file about SQL or directory traversal.

5. **D.** A canary word is created specifically to look for and indicate buffer overflow attacks. The fact that the application stopped processing immediately indicates the attack was logged but was not successful.

6. **B.** The error message blatantly states a Microsoft SQL Server instance is answering the bogus request, thus indicating a possible SQL injection target.

7. **D.** The single quote should begin SQL injection attempts.

8. **D.** Nessus is a vulnerability scanner that can be used against a variety of systems, including web servers.

9. **C.** The text of the cookie reading "ADMIN=no" is of special significance. An attacker using a tool such as Cookie Editor might change it to read "ADMIN=yes" to elevate privileges for further attacks.

10. **D.** This indicates a cross-site scripting vulnerability.

Wireless Network Hacking

In this chapter you will learn about
- Identifying wireless network architecture and terminology
- Identifying wireless network types and forms of authentication
- Describing WEP and WPA wireless encryption
- Identifying wireless hacking methods and tools
- Defining Bluetooth hacking methods

When I was a youngster, I remember one of my favorite places to run to in the local Wal-Mart was the automotive aisles. In addition to all the great stuff I could dream about saddling a car down with, they also had "police" scanners out in the open, for anyone to play with. I would scan the waves listening for police chases and picking up all sorts of great information. One day, I was flipping through the channels and heard someone say "Wal-Mart." I flipped back and discovered I was on the same channel the Wal-Mart folks were using for in-store communication. I locked it, turned the speakers up loud, and listened from afar as the store clerks wandered around, laughing at all the fun as they tried to figure out what they were hearing.

Maybe it's not the wireless hack of my life, but it was my first—and I didn't even realize that's what it was called. See, back in the early 80's, that's all wireless hacking *could* be—telephone, CB, and other voice items. Today, though, we've got worlds of wireless to discover and play with.

Admit it—you're hooked on wireless. I can say that with some degree of certainty because statistics tell me the chances are better than not that you're communicating wirelessly *right now*, as you're reading this chapter. Maybe you've got your laptop right there, tied in to your home network, or you're sitting at some coffee shop (trying to look *really* smart). Maybe you've even got one of those blinking things stuck in your ear, communicating over Bluetooth with your cell phone. And if you're doing neither right now, I'd bet your network at home is still chirping away, even though you're not there to use it, right? Surely you didn't shut it all down before you left for the day.

Look at virtually any study on wireless usage statistics in the United States and you'll find we simply can't live without wireless anymore. We use it at home, with wireless routers and access points becoming just as ubiquitous as refrigerators and toasters. We expect it when we travel, using hotspot access at airports, hotels, and coffee shops. We use wireless keyboards, mice, and virtually anything else we can point at and click (ceiling fan remote controls are all the rage now, don't you know). We have our vehicles tied to cell phones, our cell phones tied to Bluetooth ear receivers, and satellite beaming television to our homes. Heck, we're sometimes even beaming GPS information from our *dogs*.

Wireless is here to stay, and what a benefit it is to the world. The freedom and ease of use with this medium is wonderful and, truly, is changing our society day by day. However, along with that we have to use a little caution. If data is sent over the airwaves, it can be received over the airwaves—by anyone. Maybe not in clear text, and maybe not easily discernable, but it can be received. Therefore, we need to explore the means of securing our data and preventing accidental spillage. And that, dear reader, is what this chapter is all about.

Wireless 101

Although it's important to remember that any discussion on wireless should include all wireless mediums (phones, keyboards, and so on), this section is going to focus primarily on wireless data networking. I'm not saying you should forget the rest of the wireless world—far from it. In the real world you'll find as many, if not more, hacking opportunities outside the actual wireless world network. What we do want to spend the vast majority of our time on, however, are those that are *testable* issues. And, because EC-Council has defined the objectives this way, we will follow suit.

Network Architecture and Standards

A wireless network is built with the same concerns as any other media you decide to use. You have to figure out the physical makeup of the transmitter and receiver (NIC), and how they talk to one another. There has to be some order imposed on how clients communicate, to avoid collisions and useless chatter. There also must be rules for authentication, data transfer, size of packets, and so on. In the wireless data world, these are all defined with standards, known as the *802.11 series*. Although you probably won't get more than a couple of questions on your exam referencing the standards themselves, you still need to know what they are and basic details about them. These standards are summarized in the following table:

Wireless Standard	Operating Speed (Mbps)	Frequency (GHz)
802.11a	54	5
802.11b	11	2.4
802.11g	54	2.4
802.11n	100 +	2.4–5

NOTE A couple of other standards you may see referenced are 802.11i and 802.16. 802.11i is an amendment to the original 802.11 series standard and specifies security mechanisms for use on the WLAN (wireless LAN). 802.16 was written for the global development of broadband wireless metropolitan area networks. Referred to as "WiMax," it provides speeds up to 40Mbps, and is moving toward gigabit speed.

Lastly, I have to at least mention the terms 3G, 4G, and Bluetooth. 3G and 4G refer to third- and fourth-generation mobile telecommunications, respectively, and offer broadband-type speeds for data usage on mobile devices (cell phones and such). The actual technology behind these transmission standards is tweaked from mobile carrier to mobile carrier—so unlike a wireless NIC complying with 802.11g working with any manufacturer's access point with the same standard, one company's devices may not work with another's on 3G or 4G. Bluetooth refers to a very open wireless technology for data exchange over a relatively short range (10 meters or less). It was designed originally as a means to reduce cabling, but has become a veritable necessity for cell phones and other mobile devices. We'll delve more into Bluetooth, and all the standards, as we move through the chapter.

As for a basic wireless network setup, you're probably already well aware of how it's done. There are two main modes a wireless network can operate in. The first is "ad hoc," which is much like the old point-to-point networks in the good old days. In ad hoc mode, your system connects directly to another system, as if a cable were strung between the two. Generally speaking, you shouldn't see ad hoc networks appearing very often, but park yourself in any open arena (such as an airport or bus station) and see how many pop up.

Infrastructure mode is the one most networks are set up as and the one you'll most likely be hacking. Whereas ad hoc connects each system one to another, infrastructure makes use of an access point (AP) to funnel all wireless connections through. A wireless access point is set up to connect with a link to the outside world (usually some kind of broadband router). This is an important consideration when you think about it—wireless devices are usually on completely different subnets than their wired cousins. If you remember our discussion on broadcast and collision domains, you'll see quickly why this is important to know up front.

Clients connect to the access point using wireless NICs—if the access point is within range and the device understands what it takes to connect, it is allowed access to the network. Wireless networks can consist of a single access point or multiple ones, thus creating overlapping "cells" and allowing a user to roam freely without losing connectivity. This is also a very important consideration when we get to generating wireless packets later on in this chapter. The client needs to "associate" with an access point first, then "disassociate" when it moves to the next one. This dropping and reconnecting will prove vital later on, trust me.

We should probably pause here for a brief introduction to a couple of terms. Keep in mind these may not necessarily be testable items as far as EC-Council is concerned, but I think they're important nonetheless. When you have a single access point, its "footprint" is called a *BSA (basic service area)*. Communications between this *single* AP and its clients is known as a *BSS (basic service set)*. Suppose, though, you want to extend the range of your network by adding multiple access points. You'll need to make sure the channels are set right, and after it's set up, you will have created an *ESS (extended service set)*. As a client moves from one AP in your subnet to another, so long as you've configured everything correctly, they'll disassociate from one AP and (re)associate with another seamlessly. This movement across multiple APs within a single ESS is known as *roaming*. Okay, enough vocabulary. Time to move on.

Another consideration to bring up here deals with the access points and the antennas they use. It may seem like a weird (and crazy) thing to discuss physical security concerns with wireless networks, because by design they're accessible from anywhere in the coverage area. However, that's exactly the point: Many people don't consider it and it winds up costing them dearly. Most standard APs use an omnidirectional antenna, which means the signal emanates from the antenna in equal strength 360 degrees from the source. If you were to, say, install your AP in the corner of a building, three-quarters of your signal strength is lost to the parking lot. And the guy sitting out in the car hacking your network will be very pleased by this.

Hide and Seek

One of the greatest benefits to wireless technologies is always a huge problem for incident responders in IT security—mobility. Wireless laptops in an enterprise network are great—you can move from presentation room to presentation room, from building to building, and never lose connectivity. It's fantastic from a productivity standpoint, and here at Kennedy Space Center, it's not just a nice convenience, it's darn-near a requirement for some folks. But imagine the poor incident response staff (me) trying to track down a malware-infected laptop on the move across multiple buildings in a campus.

Thankfully, we have some eyes to help us on this. Much like other enterprise networks, inside and outside of government, our IT security staff watches all sorts of traffic and behaviors on the network. One nice little feature we have is a "heat signature" for our mobile clients. It's not overly long or technically complicated, and it's probably done 100 ways on 100 different networks, but the short of it is we can track a machine's location on the network using its association and IP logs (that is, its "heat" signature). Much like the *Predator* aliens in Arnold Schwarzenegger's movie, when I get the word on a malware-infected client, I can watch where he is and where he's going, thus helping me to zoom in on my target.

A better option may be to use a directional antenna, also sometimes known as a "Yagi" antenna. Directional antennas allow you to focus the signal in a specific direction, which greatly increases signal strength and distance. The benefit is obvious in protecting against the guy out in the parking lot. However, keep in mind this signal is now greatly increased in strength and distance—so you may find that the guy will simply drive from his corner parking spot close to the AP to the other side of the building, where you're blasting wireless out the windows. The point is, wireless network design needs to take into account not only the type of antenna used, but where it is placed and what is set up to contain or corral the signal. The last thing you want is for some kid with a Pringles can a block away tapping into your network. The so-called "cantenna" is very real, and can boost signals amazingly. Check out Figure 9-1 for some antenna examples.

NOTE A Yagi antenna is merely one type of directional antenna. However, its name is used as a euphemism for all directional antennas—almost like the brand Coke is used a lot in the South to indicate soda. I'm not sure why that is, but I suspect it's because people just like saying "Yagi."

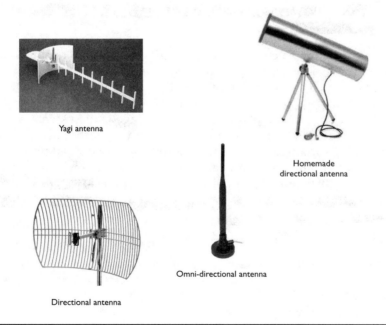

Yagi antenna

Homemade
directional antenna

Omni-directional antenna

Directional antenna

Figure 9-1 Wireless antennas

Other antennas you can use are dipole and parabolic grid. Dipole antennas have, quite obviously, two signal "towers" and work omnidirectionally. Parabolic grid antennas are one type of directional antenna and work a lot like satellite dishes. They can have phenomenal range (up to 10 miles), but aren't in use much. Another directional antenna type is the loop antenna, which looks like a circle. And, in case you were wondering, a Pringles can *will* work as a directional antenna. Google it and you'll see what I mean.

So you've installed a wireless access point and created a network for clients to connect to. To identify this network to clients who may be interested in joining, you'll need to assign an *SSID, or Service Set Identifier*. The SSID is not a password, and provides *no security* at all for your network. It is simply a text word (32 characters or less) that *identifies* your wireless network. SSIDs are broadcast by default and are easily obtainable even if you try to turn off the broadcast (in an effort dubbed "SSID cloaking"). The SSID is part of the header on every packet, so its discovery by a determined attacker is a given and securing it is virtually a moot point.

EXAM TIP If you see a question on wireless security, you can ignore any answer with SSID in it. Remember that SSIDs do nothing for security, other than identify which network you're on. Encryption standards, such as WEP and WPA, and physical concerns (placement of APs and antennas used) are your security features.

Once the AP is up and a client comes wandering by, it's time to authenticate so an IP address can be pulled. Wireless authentication can happen in more than a few ways, from the simplistic to the very complicated. A client can simply send an 802.11 authentication frame with the appropriate SSID to an AP, and have it answer with a verification frame. Or, the client might participate in a challenge/request scenario, with the AP verifying a decrypted "key" for authentication. Or, in yet another twist, you may even tie the whole thing together with an authentication server (Radius), forcing the client into an even more complicated authentication scenario. The key here is to remember there is a difference between association and authentication. *Association* is the action of a client connecting to an AP, whereas *authentication* actually identifies the client before it can access anything on the network.

Lastly, after everything is set up and engineered appropriately, you'll want to take some steps toward security. This may seem a laughable concept, because the media is open and accessible to anyone within range of the AP, but there *are* some alternatives available for security. Some are better than others, but as the old saying goes, some security is better than none at all.

There are a host of wireless encryption topics and definitions to cover. I briefly toyed with an exhaustive romp through all of them, but decided against it after thinking about what you really *need* to know for the exam. Therefore, I'll leave some of the "in-the-weeds" stuff for another discussion, and many of the definitions to the glossary, and just stick with the big three here: WEP, WPA, and WPA-2.

WEP stands for Wired Equivalent Privacy and, in effect, doesn't really encrypt anything. Now I know you purists are jumping up and down screaming about WEP's 40- to 232-bit keys, yelling that RC4 is an encryption algorithm, and questioning whether a guy from Alabama should even be writing a book at all. But trust me, it's not what WEP was intended for. Yes, "encryption" is part of the deal, but WEP was never intended to fully protect your data. It was designed to give people using a wireless network the same level of protection someone surfing over an Ethernet wired hub would expect: If I were on a hub, I wouldn't expect that the guy in the parking lot could read what I send and receive because he wouldn't have physical access to the wire.

Now think about that for a moment—*wired equivalent privacy*. Do you consider a hub secure? Granted, it's harder than sitting out in the hallway with an antenna and picking up signals without even entering the room, but does it really provide anything other than a discouragement to casual browsers? Of course not, and so long as it's implemented that way, no one can be upset about it.

WEP uses something called an initialization vector (IV) and, per its definition, provides for confidentiality and integrity. It calculates a 32-bit integrity check value (ICV) and appends it to the end of the data payload and then provides a 24-bit IV, which is combined with a key to be input into an RC4 algorithm. The "keystream" created by the algorithm is encrypted by an XOR operation and combined with the ICV to produce "encrypted" data. Although this all sounds well and good, it has one giant glaring flaw: It's ridiculously easy to crack.

Enough to Do the Job

So let's get this out of the way first: Per EC-Council and every other organization providing hacking guidelines and information, WEP is not a secure protocol. When it comes to your exam and when you're advising business clients on the job, WEP is never a good choice. But what about at home—is it good enough for your personal wireless network?

For 99 percent of the populace out there, WEP makes a good choice. Worried about random people driving by and picking up packets? WEP is good enough. Worried about stopping your creepy neighbor next door from using your network? WEP is good enough. In fact, outside of stopping the 15-year-old script-kiddie hacker who is bored and has nothing better to do, you're secure. And, if you're really that worried about it, why not just change the keys out every so often? Combine this with turning off DHCP as well as stopping SSID broadcast and/or MAC filtering, and you're in good shape. Unless, of course, your neighborhood is filled with elite, state-funded hackers with an active interest in your Facebook login.

Once again, this is written with reality and your home network in mind. Turning off broadcast SSID, using MAC filtering, and implementing WEP are *not* the best choices by themselves on your exam. For your test, remember WPA-2 is best, SSID is sent in every packet anyway, and MAC filtering can be overcome by spoofing.

WEP's initialization vectors are relatively small and, for the most part, get reused pretty frequently. Additionally, they're sent in clear text as part of the header. When you add this to the fact that we all know the cipher used (RC4) and that it wasn't ever really designed for more than one-time usage, cracking becomes a matter of time and patience. An attacker simply needs to generate enough packets in order to analyze the IVs and come up with the key used. This allows him to decrypt the WEP shared key on the fly, in real time, and renders the encryption useless.

 EXAM TIP Attackers can get APs to generate bunches of packets by sending disassociate messages. These aren't authenticated by any means, so the resulting barrage of "Please associate with me" packets are more than enough for the attack. Another option would be to use ARP to generate packets.

A better choice in encryption technology is WPA (Wi-Fi Protected Access) or WPA-2. WPA makes use of something called TKIP (Temporal Key Integrity Protocol), a 128-bit key, and the client's MAC address to accomplish much stronger encryption. The short of it is, WPA changes the key out (hence the "temporal" part of the name) every 10,000 packets or so, instead of sticking with one and reusing it, as WEP does. Additionally, the keys are transferred back and forth during an EAP (Extensible Authentication Protocol) authentication session, which makes use of a four-step handshake process to prove the client belongs to the AP, and vice versa.

Weird Science

I'm sure you've seen your share of mathematical tomfoolery that appears to be "magic" or some Jedi mind trick. These usually start out with something like "Pick a number between 1 and 10. Add 13. Divide by 2," and so on, until the number you picked is arrived at. Magic, right? Well, I've got one here for you that is actually relevant to our discussion on WEP cracking.

In the world of probability, there is a principle known as the "birthday problem." The idea is that if you have a group of at least 23 random people, the odds are that two of them will share the same birthday. There's a lot of math here, but the short of it is if you have 366 people, the probability is 100 percent. However, drop the number of people down to just 57 and the probability only drops one percentage point. Therefore, next time you're in a big group of people, you can probably win a bet that at least two of them share the same day as a birthday.

So just how is this relevant to hacking? Well, the mathematics for this little anomaly led to a cryptographic attack called the *birthday attack*. The same principles of probability that'll win you a drink at the bar applies to cracking hash functions. Or, in this case, WEP keys.

WPA-2 is much the same process; however, it was designed with the government and the enterprise in mind. You can tie EAP or a Radius server into the authentication side of WPA-2, allowing you to make use of Kerberos tickets and all sorts of additional goodies. Additionally, WPA-2 uses AES for encryption, ensuring FIPS 140-2 compliance—not to mention AES is just plain *better*.

Finding and Identifying Wireless Networks

Now that we've covered some of the more mundane, definition-style high-level things you'll need to know, we need to spend a little time discussing how you might actually find a wireless network to hack. I realize, given the sheer numbers of wireless networks out there, that telling you we're going to discuss how to find them sounds about as ridiculous as me saying we're going to spend the rest of this chapter talking about how to find *air*, but trust me—I'm going somewhere with this.

We're not talking about finding *any* wireless network—that's too easy. If you don't believe me, purchase a wireless router from your local store and plug it in next to a window in your upstairs room—I'd bet solid cash you're going to see at least one of your neighbors' networks broadcasting an SSID, and probably a bunch more. If that's not enough for you, go buy a cup of coffee, take a flight somewhere, go to the mall, or buy a burger at the local fast-food joint. Chances are better than not they're going to have a wireless network set up for your use.

 NOTE Another easy way of finding wireless networks is to make use of a service such as WIGLE (http://wigle.net). WIGLE users register with the site and use NetStumbler in their cars, with an antenna and a GPS device, to drive around and mark where wireless networks can be found.

So, we're obviously not talking about finding a wireless network for you to use. What we are hoping to cover here is how you can find *the* wireless network you're looking for—the one that's going to get your team inside the target and provide you access to all the goodies. Some of the methods and techniques we cover here may seem to be a waste of your time and, in a couple of cases, a bit on the silly side. Just keep in mind we're talking about them because you'll be tested on them, but also because you may need to employ them to find *the* one you're looking for.

First up in our discussion of wireless network discovery are the "war" options. No matter which technique we're talking about, the overall action is the same: An attacker travels around with a Wi-Fi–enabled laptop looking for open wireless access points/ networks. In war driving, the attacker is in a car. War walking has the attacker on foot. War flying? I'm betting you could guess it involves airplanes.

One other "war" definition of note you'll definitely see hit on in the exam is "war chalking." A *war chalk* is a symbol drawn somewhere in a public place indicating the presence of a wireless network. These can indicate free networks, hidden

SSIDs, pay-for-use hotspots, and which encryption technique is in use. The basic war chalk involves two parentheses back to back. Added to this can be a key through the middle (indicating restricted Wi-Fi), a lock (indicating MAC filtering), and all sorts of extra entries. Some examples are shown in Figure 9-2.

Generally speaking, these aren't much use to you in the real world; however, there are some things about them you might be *very* interested in. Usually the double parentheses will also have a word written above or below, which indicates the SSID or even the administrative password for the access point. Various other information (such as bandwidth) can be found written down as well—this depends totally on the chalk "artist" and what he feels like leaving. Additionally, as you can tell from our examples here, you may also find workarounds for pay sites, MAC addresses to clone, and all sorts of stuff you can use in hacking.

EXAM TIP You will definitely need to know war chalking and its symbols for the exam.

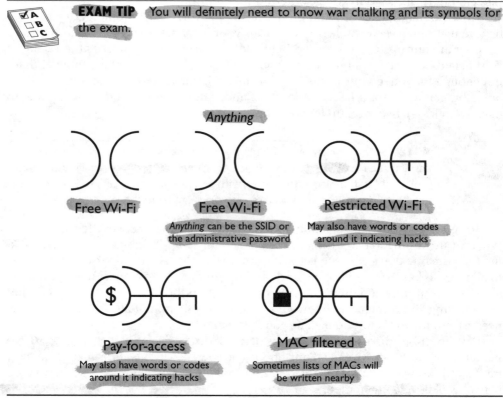

Figure 9-2 War chalking symbols

The Coolness Factor

Sometimes things catch on and sometimes they don't, but every once in a while a fad finds its way into even the nerdiest of circles. War chalking as a fad amongst people who really needed or used it didn't really last all that long, and probably hit its heyday sometime back when wireless hotspots were hard to come by. In 2002, it might have taken some driving around to find a wireless network to connect to and, if memory serves, *everyone* was trying to jack into the Internet for free.

War chalking, in a sort of weird ironic twist, actually turned into something more suited for marketers than a true hacking breakthrough. Sure, it was fun to think about secret messages, encoded "hobo-language" style that only the true nerds understood. But, alas, it didn't continue in the same rush and fashion in which it started. That said, Mr. Paul Boutin, in an article on the subject some years ago, probably put it best: "War chalking, it seems, is so cool it doesn't even matter if anyone is really doing it or not."

Give me some big Crayola chalk. I'm headed out front right now.

(If you're interested, the referenced article dealt with a store in San Francisco that actually benefitted from displaying their war chalk right in the front window: "Wi-Fi Users: Chalk This Way," Paul Boutin, www.wired.com/gadgets/wireless/news/2002/07/53638.)

Another option in wireless network discovery is the use of a wide array of tools created for that very purpose. However, before we explore the tools you'll see mentioned on your exam, it's relevant at this point to talk about the wireless adapter itself. No matter how great the tool is, if the wireless adapter can't pull the frames out of the air in the correct manner, all is lost. Some tools are built this way, and only work with certain chipset adapters—which can be very frustrating at times.

The answer for many in wireless hacking is to invest in an AirPcap dongle (www.cacetech.com)—a USB wireless adapter that offers all sorts of advantages and software support (see Figure 9-3). Sure it's expensive, but it's worth it. Barring this, you may need to research and download new and different drivers for your particular card. The madwifi project may be an answer for you (http://madwifi-project.org). At any rate, just keep in mind that, much like the ability of our wired adapters to use promiscuous mode for our sniffing efforts, discussed earlier in this book, not all wireless adapters are created equal, and not all will work with your favorite tool. Be sure to check the user guides and man pages for lists and tips on correctly configuring your adapters for use.

Figure 9-3
AirPcap USB

 NOTE Although people often expect any wireless card to do the trick, it simply won't, and frustration begins before you ever get to sniffing traffic, much less hacking. I have it on very good authority that, in addition to those mentioned, Ubiquiti cards (www.ubnt.com/) may be the top-tier card in this realm.

I've already made mention of WIGLE (http://wigle.net), and how teams of miscreant hackers have mapped out wireless network locations using GPS and a tool called NetStumbler (see Figure 9-4). NetStumbler (www.netstumbler.com), the tool employed in this endeavor, can be used for identifying poor coverage locations within an ESS, detecting interference causes, and finding any rogue access points in the network (we'll talk about these later). It's Windows-based, easy to use, and compatible with 802.11a, b, and g.

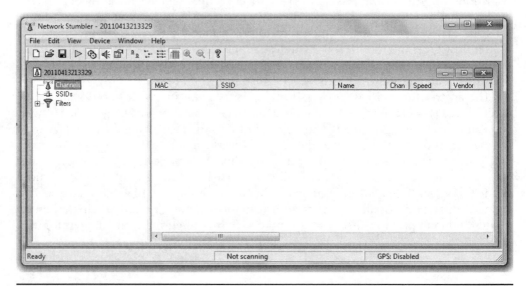

Figure 9-4 NetStumbler

Although it's usually more of a wireless packet analyzer/sniffer, Kismet is another wireless discovery option. It works on Linux-based systems and, unlike NetStumbler, works passively, meaning it detects access points and clients without actually sending any packets. It can detect access points that have not been configured (and would then be susceptible to the default out-of-the-box admin password) and will determine which type of encryption you might be up against. You might also see two other interesting notables about Kismet on your exam: First, it works by "channel hopping," to discover as many networks as possible and, second, it has the ability to sniff packets and save them to a log file, readable by Wireshark or tcpdump.

Another great network discovery tool is NetSurveyor (see Figure 9-5). This free, Windows-based tool provides many of the same features as NetStumbler and Kismet. Additionally, it supports almost all wireless adapters without any significant additional configuration—which is of great benefit to hackers who can't afford, or don't have, an AirPcap card. NetSurveyor acts as a great tool for troubleshooting and verifying proper installation of wireless networks. To try it out, simply download and install the tool, then run it. It will automatically find your wireless adapter and begin scanning. Click through the different menu options and check out all the information it finds without you needing to configure a thing!

Figure 9-5　NetSurveyor

Wireless Sniffing

Finally, although it technically has nothing to do with actually *locating* a network, we do need to cover some basics on wireless sniffing—and what better place to do it than right here, just after we've discovered a network or two to watch. Much about sniffing a wireless network is exactly the same as sniffing its wired counterpart. The same protocols and authentication standard weaknesses you looked for with Wireshark off that switch port are just as weak and vulnerable on wireless. Authentication information, passwords, and all sorts of information can be gleaned just from watching the air and, although you are certainly welcome to use Wireshark, a couple of tools can help you get the job done.

Just a few of the tools specifically made for wireless sniffing include some we've already talked about—NetStumbler and Kismet—and some that we haven't seen yet, including OmniPeek, AirMagnet WiFi Analyzer Pro, and WiFi Pilot. Assuming you have a wireless adapter that is compatible and can watch things in promiscuous mode, OmniPeek is a fairly well-known and respected wireless sniffer. In addition to the same type of traffic analysis you would see in Wireshark, OmniPeek provides network activity status and monitoring in a nice dashboard for up-to-the-minute viewing.

AirMagnet WiFi Analyzer, from Fluke Networks, is an incredibly powerful sniffer, traffic analyzer, and all-around wireless network-auditing software suite. It can be used to resolve performance problems and automatically detect security threats and vulnerabilities. Per the company website (www.airmagnet.com/products/wifi_analyzer/), AirMagnet includes the "only suite of active WLAN diagnostic tools, enabling network managers to easily test and diagnose dozens of common wireless network performance issues including throughput issues, connectivity issues, device conflicts and signal multipath problems." And for you compliance paperwork junkies out there, AirMagnet also includes a compliance reporting engine that maps network information to requirements for compliance with policy and industry regulations.

NOTE   Although it's not just a packet capture suite, don't discount Cain and Abel. In addition to WEP cracking and other hacks, Cain can pull clear text passwords out of packet captures in real time, on wired or wireless networks. Just a thought.

The point here isn't to rehash everything we've already talked about regarding sniffing. What you need to get out of this is the knowledge that sniffing is beneficial to wired and wireless network attacks, and the ability to recognize the tools we've mentioned here. I toyed with the idea of including exercises for you to run through, but they would be totally dependent on your wireless adapter (and its compatibility with the tools), as well as the network(s) available for you to watch. Instead, I'm going to recommend you go out and download these tools. Most, if not all, are either free or have a great trial version for your use. Read the usage guides and determine your adapter compatibility, then fire them up and see what you can capture. You won't necessarily gain much, exam-wise, by running them, but you will gain valuable experience for your "real" work.

Wireless Hacking

When it comes to hacking wireless networks, the truly great news is you probably won't have much of it to do. The majority of networks have no security configured at all, and even those that do have security enabled don't have it configured correctly. According to studies recently published by the likes of the International Telecommunications Union (ITU) and other equally impressive organizations, over half of all wireless networks don't have any security configured at all, and of the remainder, nearly half could be hacked within a matter of seconds. If you think that's good news for hackers, the follow-up news is even more exciting: Wireless communication is expected to grow *tenfold* within the next few years. Gentlemen, and ladies, start your engines.

Wireless Attacks

First things first: Wireless hacking does not need to be a complicated matter. Some very easy and simple attacks can be carried out with a minimum of technical knowledge and ability. Sure, there are some really groovy and, dare I say, elegant wireless hacks to be had, but don't discount the easy ones. They will probably pay as many dividends as the ones that take hours to set up.

For example, take the concept of a rogue access point. The idea here is to place an access point of your own somewhere—heck, you can even put it outside in the bushes—and have legitimate users connect to your network instead of the original. Just consider the possibilities! If someone were to look at his wireless networks and connect to yours, because the signal strength is better or yours is free whereas the others are not, they basically sign over control to you. You could configure completely new DNS servers and have your AP configure them with the DHCP address offering. That would then route users to fake websites you create, providing opportunities to steal authentication information. Not to mention you could funnel everything through a packet capture.

Sometimes referred to as "evil twin," an attack like this is incredibly easy to pull off. The only drawback is they're sometime really easy to see, and you run a pretty substantial risk of discovery. You'll just have to watch out for true security-minded professionals, because they'll be on the lookout for rogue APs on a continual basis and (should) have plenty of tools available to help them do the job.

NOTE   Cisco is among the leaders in rogue access point detection technologies. Many of their access points can be configured to look for other access points in the same area. If they find one, they send SNMP or other messages back to administrators for action, if needed. The link here provides more information, in case you're interested: http://www.cisco.com/en/US/tech/tk722/tk809/ technologies_white_paper09186a0080722d8c.shtml. (Credit goes to our tech editor, Mr. Brad Horton, for this addition.)

Don't Try This at Home

Before I start this example, I must caution you, dear reader, not to attempt a setup like this unless a client has hired you explicitly to do so. This episode is here simply to demonstrate how it can be done, not as a blueprint for you to become a criminal. If you try something like this and wind up in court, which you will, don't come crying to me saying this book was your reason for doing it. I've warned you. Okay, on with the show.

I saw, firsthand, how easy rogue access point attacks can be on a trip long, long ago. The team I was traveling with was composed of seasoned professionals who, if they weren't the good guys, would be a scary group to have arrayed against you in the virtual world. We were staying in a well-known hotel chain that offered wireless, at a cost, to guests in the room. If you went downstairs, though, their business network was free. The SSIDs for the networks serving the guests were "hotel," whereas the business network downstairs—the free one—was named "hotel_conf." (I, of course, have changed the SSIDs here to protect the innocent, although if you've stayed in this particular chain, you'll recognize them.)

I was chatting about wireless with one of our team members and he mentioned how easy rogue access points were. I, a novice to the game, asked for more knowledge and he showed me a setup that blew my mind. He had a wireless router you could purchase from any electronics store, and configured an SSID on it to read "hotel_conf." Within a matter of a minute or so, literally, a dozen guests tried to connect to it, thinking they had somehow tapped into the free network downstairs and hoping to save a few bucks on Internet access. The DHCP service running on the AP not only gave out Internet access via the NAT working behind the scenes, but gave us—the attackers—a leg up: We knew the IP addresses and MACs already, and could've attacked them with anything in the arsenal. *Anything.* If this had been anything other than a five-minute lesson to a newbie in the field, those people may have had all sorts of information stolen from them.

 EXAM TIP Rogue APs (evil twins) may also be referenced as a "misassociation" attack.

Another truly ridiculous attack is called the "ad hoc connection attack." To be honest, it shouldn't ever be successful, but after years in the security management business, I've seen users do some pretty wild things, so almost nothing surprises me anymore. An ad hoc connection attack occurs when an attacker simply sits down with a laptop somewhere in your building and advertises an ad hoc network from his laptop. Believe it or not, people will, eventually, connect to it. Yes, I know it's tantamount to walking up to a user with a crossover cable in hand and asking, "Excuse me, would you please plug this in to your system's NIC? The other end is in my computer and I'd like easy access to you." But what can you do?

Another attack on the relatively easy side of the spectrum is the denial-of-service effort. This can be done in a couple of ways, neither of which is particularly difficult. First, you can use any number of tools to craft and send de-authenticate (disassociate) packets to clients of an AP, which will force them to drop their connections. Granted, they may try to immediately climb back aboard, but there's nothing stopping you from performing the same action again.

The other easy DoS wireless attack is to jam the wireless signal altogether, using some type of jamming device and, usually, a high-gain antenna/amplifier. All wireless devices are susceptible to some form of jamming and/or interference—it's simply a matter of placing enough signal out in the airwaves that the NICs can't keep up. Tons of jammer options are available (a quick Google search on wireless jammers will show you around 450,000 pages on the subject), ranging from 802.11 networks to Bluetooth and other wireless networking technologies. No, the giant jar of jam used in the movie *Spaceballs* won't work, but anything generating enough signals in a 2.4GHz range would definitely put a crimp in an 802.11b network.

 NOTE A cautionary note here: According to FCC rules and the Communication Act of 1934, marketing, selling, and/or using a jammer is a federal offense and can result in seriously nasty punishment. Want further proof? Check almost any electronic device in your house right now: There will be an FCC warning saying that it will not create interference and that it will accept all interference.

MAC Spoofing

One defense wireless network administrators attempt to use is to enforce a MAC filter. Basically it's a list of MAC addresses that are allowed to associate to the AP—if your wireless NIC's address isn't on the list, you're denied access. The easy way around this is to monitor the network to figure out which MAC addresses are in use on the AP and simply spoof one of them. On a Unix/Linux machine, all you need do is log in as root, disable the interface, enter a new MAC, and re-enable the device:

```
ifconfig wlan0 down
ifconfig wlan0 hw ether 0A:15:BD:1A:1B:1C
ifconfig wlan0 up
```

Tons of tools are also available for MAC spoofing. A couple of the more easy-to-use ones are SMAC and TMAC. Both allow you to change the MAC address with just a couple of clicks and, once you're done, to return things to normal with a click of the mouse. Check out both of these tools in Exercise 9-1.

Exercise 9-1: MAC Spoofing

MAC spoofing is a skill that's relatively easy to learn and is applicable in several hacking applications across the spectrum. In this exercise, we'll just stick with two tools—TMAC and SMAC. Here are the steps to follow:

1. Download and install SMAC (www.klcconsulting.net/smac/) and TMAC (www.technitium.com/tmac/index.html).

2. Open SMAC (see Figure 9-6). You may need to click Proceed if you have a trial or free version.

3. Click the Ipconfig button and scroll through to find your current MAC address. You could also open a command prompt and enter the **ipconfig /all** command to do the same thing.

4. Select an adapter from the list, then click the Random button just to the right of the New Spoofed MAC Address boxes. Note the new MAC generated here. You could also have typed in a MAC you know would work in a given network.

5. Click the Update MAC button. Note your adapter MAC address change in the window.

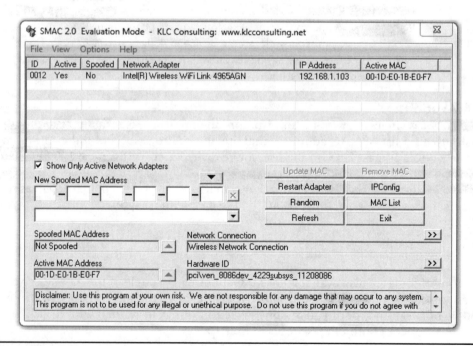

Figure 9-6 SMAC open screen

Figure 9-7
SMAC Screenshot

NOTE Your adapter normally must be stopped and started again to make these types of changes. If you go to the Options menu in SMAC, you can set this to run automatically for you (see Figure 9-7).

6. Click the Remove MAC button and close SMAC.

7. Open the TMAC tool (see Figure 9-8).

8. Click the Change MAC button at the bottom and type in a MAC address of your choosing (see Figure 9-9). Alternatively, you can use the Random MAC Address button.

Figure 9-8 TMAC open screen

Figure 9-9
TMAC screenshot

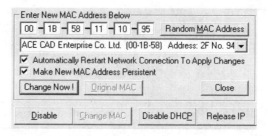

9. Ensure the Automatically Restart Network Connections check box is marked, and click the Change Now! button. Once again, verify the MAC address change with an **ipconfig /all** command.

10. Click the Original MAC button, then close the tool.

WEP Attacks

Cracking WEP is ridiculously easy and can be done with any number of tools. The idea revolves around generating enough packets to effectively guess the encryption key. The weak initialization vectors we discussed already are the key—specifically, the fact that they're reused and sent in clear text. Regardless of the tool, the standard WEP attack follows the same basic series of steps:

1. Start a compatible wireless adapter on your attack machine and ensure it can both inject and sniff packets.

2. Start a sniffer to capture packets.

3. Use some method to force the creation of thousands and thousands of packets (generally by using "de-auth" packets).

4. Analyze these captured packets (either in real time or on the side) with a cracking tool.

We'll go through a couple of different WEP attacks to give you an idea how this works. Obviously these will be different for your network and situation, so I'll have to keep these examples generalized. If you get lost along the way, or something doesn't seem to make sense, just check out any of the online videos you can find on WEP cracking.

Our first example uses Cain and Abel. In this example, we take a very easy pathway using a tool that makes the process almost too easy. One note of caution: Cain and Abel will not crack the codes as quickly as some other methods, and is somewhat picky about the adapter you use. I highly recommend using an AirPcap dongle if you want to try this out for yourself. Here are the steps to follow:

1. Fire up a compatible wireless adapter. For example, you could use an AirPcap card (which will also give you options in its configuration to set specifically for WEP cracking).

2. Open Cain and Abel, click on the wireless menu option, and select the AirPcap card.

3. Select the Hopping on BG Channel option from the Lock on Channel section, ensure the Capture WEP IVs box is checked (see Figure 9-10), and then click the Passive Scan button.

4. Wait until the tool has collected at least one million packets, then click Stop (you can speed this up using a variety of tools or simply another adapter injecting anything you can think of).

5. Click on the Analyze button on the left.

6. Select the SSID you wish to crack and then click on the Korek's Attack button. It will take some time—in most cases, a seriously long time—but eventually Cain will display the WEP key.

Figure 9-10
Cain and Abel

Our second example uses Aircrack-ng. In this case, we're using a BackTrack installation, where wlan0 is your adapter. Your adapter may show up with a completely different name—simply replace it in the commands shown in the following steps.

1. Open the Konsole and change the MAC address of your adapter before starting:

```
airmon-ng stop wlan0               //Disable Airmon monitoring mode.
ifconfig wlan0 down                //Disable the wireless interface.
macchanger --mac 00:11:22:33:44:55 wlan0 //Changes the MAC address. Not
                                          completely necessary, but makes
                                          things easier later.
ifconfig wlan0 up                  //Enable the adapter again.
airmon-ng start wlan0              //Enable Airmon monitoring again.
```

2. Capture wireless network information by typing **airodump –ng wlan0**. Save the information (BSSID and so on) for later. For use in this example, we'll say your target network is named WNET, on channel 3, with a BSSID of 00:22:29:BC:75:4C.

3. Type **airodump-ng –c 3 –w WNET - - bssid 00:22:29:BC:75:4C**. This begins the capture of WEP cracking packets from the target network. Don't close this shell—it must stay up and running (all packets are being captured to a ".cap" file).

4. Inject fake authentication packets to generate the packets you'll need to crack WEP. To do this, type **aireplay –ng -1 0 –a 00:22:29:BC:75:4C –h 00:11:22:33:44:55 wlan0**. You can also accomplish this by sending ARP replays (by typing **aireplay-ng -3 0 –b 00:22:29:BC:75:4C –h 00:11:22:33:44:55 wlan0**). In either case, or if you want go ahead and use both, wait until you've captured at least 35,000 packets to continue (50,000 is better; 100,000 is best).

5. Launch another Konsole window. Navigate to your home directory and find the name of the packet capture file there (it will end in .cap). For this example, we'll use filename.cap.

6. Type **aircrack-ng –b 00:22:29:BC:75:4C filename.cap**. The WEP key, once cracked, will display next to the "KEY FOUND!" line (see Figure 9-11).

Figure 9-11 WEP key cracked using aircrack	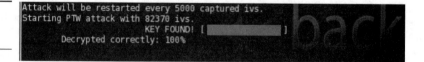

EXAM TIP Both Cain and Aircrack both make use of the Korek implementation. However, Aircrack is *much faster* at cracking WEP.

We could go on, but you can see the point I'm making here. WEP is easy to crack, and more than a few tools are available for doing so. KisMAC, WEPCrack, chopchop, and Elcomsoft's Wireless Security Auditor tool are just a few of the other options available.

Bluetooth Attacks

Lastly, we can't finish any wireless attack section without visiting, at least on a cursory level, our friendly little Bluetooth devices. After all, think about what Bluetooth is for: connecting devices, usually mobile (phones), wirelessly over a short distance. And what do we keep on mobile devices nowadays? The answer is everything. E-mail, calendar appointments, documents, and just about everything else you might find on a business computer is now held in the palm of your hand. It should seem fairly obvious, then, that hacking that signal could pay huge dividends.

Bluetooth definitely falls into the wireless category and has just a few things you'll need to consider for your exam and for your career. Although hundreds of tools and options are available for Bluetooth hacking, the good news is their coverage on the exam is fairly light, and most of it comes in the form of identifying terms and definitions. With that in mind, we'll cover some basics on Bluetooth and the four major Bluetooth attacks, and then follow up with a very brief discussion on some tools to help you pull them off.

Part of what makes Bluetooth so susceptible to hacking is the very thing that makes it so ubiquitous—its ease of use. Bluetooth devices are easy to connect one to another and can even be set to look for other devices for you automatically. Bluetooth devices have two modes: a discovery mode and a pairing mode. *Discovery mode* determines how the device reacts to inquiries from other devices looking to connect, and it has three actions. The *discoverable* action obviously has the device answer to all inquiries, *limited discoverable* restricts that action, and *non-discoverable* tells the device to ignore all inquiries.

Whereas discovery mode details how the device lets others know it's available, *pairing mode* details how the device will react when another Bluetooth system asks to pair with it. There are basically only two versions: Yes, I will pair with you, or no, I will not. *Non-pairable* rejects every connection request, whereas *pairable* accepts all of them. Between discovery and pairing modes, you can see how Bluetooth was designed to make connection easy.

Bluetooth attacks, taking advantage of this ease of use, fall into four general categories. *Bluesmacking* is simply a denial-of-service attack against a device. *Bluejacking* consists of sending unsolicited messages to, and from, mobile devices. *Bluesniffing* is exactly what it sounds like, and, finally, *Bluescarfing* is the actual theft of data from a mobile device.

EXAM TIP Know the "blue" attacks and definitions in Bluetooth. You won't be asked in-depth technical questions on them, but you will need to determine which attack is being used in a given scenario.

Although they're not covered in depth on your exam, you should know some of the more common Bluetooth tools available. Of course, your first action should be to find the Bluetooth devices. BlueScanner (from SourceForge) does a great job of finding devices around you, but it will also try to extract and display as much information as possible. BT Browser is another great, and well-known, tool for finding and enumerating nearby devices. Bluesniff and btCrawler are other options, providing nice GUI formats for your use.

In a step up from that, you can start taking advantage of and hacking the devices nearby. Super Bluetooth Hack is an all-in-one software package that allows you to do almost anything you want to a device you're lucky enough to connect to. If the device is a smartphone, you could read all messages and contacts, change profiles, restart the device, and even make calls as if they're coming from the phone itself. Other attack options include bluebugger and Bluediving (a full penetration suite for Bluetooth). Check Appendix A in the back of the book for more Bluetooth hacking tools.

Chapter Review

A wireless network is built with the same concerns as any other media you decide to use, and these are all defined with standards, known as the 802.11 series. 802.11a can attain speeds up to 54Mbps and uses the 5GHz range. 802.11b has speeds of 11Mbps at 2.4GHz, and 802.11g is 54Mbps at 2.4GHz. 802.11n has speeds over 100Mbps and uses a variety of ranges in a MIMO format between 2.4GHz and 5GHz.

Two other standards of note are 802.11i and 802.16. 802.11i is an amendment to the original 802.11 series standard and specifies security mechanisms for use on the WLAN (wireless LAN). 802.16 was written for the global development of broadband wireless metropolitan area networks. Referred to as "WiMax," it provides speeds up to 40Mbps and is moving toward gigabit speed.

There are two main modes a wireless network can operate in. The first is "ad hoc," where your system connects directly to another system, as if a cable were strung between the two. Infrastructure mode makes use of an access point (AP) to funnel all wireless connections through. A wireless access point is set up to connect with a link to the outside world (usually some kind of broadband router) and clients associate and authenticate to it. Clients connect to the access point using wireless NICs—if the access point is within range and the device understands what it takes to connect, it is allowed access to the network. Wireless networks can consist of a single access point or multiple ones, thus creating overlapping "cells" and allowing a user to roam freely without losing connectivity. The client needs to "associate" with an access point first, then "disassociate" when it moves to the next one.

When there is a single access point, its "footprint" is called a BSA (basic service area). Communication between this single AP and its clients is known as a BSS (basic service set). If you extend the range of your network by adding multiple access points, the setup is known as an ESS (extended service set). As a client moves from one AP in your subnet to another, so long as everything is configured correctly, it'll disassociate from one AP and (re)associate with another seamlessly. This movement across multiple APs within a single ESS is known as roaming.

Wireless network design needs to take into account not only the type of antenna used, but where it is placed and what is set up to contain or corral the signal. Physical installation of access points is a major concern, because you will want to avoid spillage of the signal and loss of power. Most standard APs use an omni-directional antenna, which means the signal emanates from the antenna in equal strength 360 degrees from the source. Directional antennas allow you to focus the signal in a specific direction, which greatly increases signal strength and distance. Other antennas you can use are dipole and parabolic grid. Dipole antennas have, quite obviously, two signal "towers" and work omnidirectionally. Parabolic grid antennas work a lot like satellite dishes and can have phenomenal range (up to 10 miles), but aren't in use much.

To identify a wireless network to clients who may be interested in joining, an SSID (service set identifier) must be assigned. The SSID is not a password, and provides no security at all for your network. It is a text word (32 characters or less) that only distinguishes your wireless network from others. SSIDs are broadcast by default and are easily obtainable even if you try to turn off the broadcast (in an effort dubbed SSID cloaking). The SSID is part of the header on every packet, so its discovery by a determined attacker is a given and securing it is virtually a moot point.

Wireless authentication can happen in more than a few ways, from the simplistic to the very complicated. A client can simply send an 802.11 authentication frame with the appropriate SSID to an AP, and have it answer with a verification frame. Or, the client might participate in a challenge/request scenario, with the AP verifying a decrypted "key" for authentication. Or, in yet another twist, you may even tie the whole thing together with an authentication server (Radius), forcing the client into an even more complicated authentication scenario. The key here is to remember there is a difference between association and authentication. Association is the action of a client connecting to an AP, whereas authentication actually identifies the client before it can access anything on the network.

WEP stands for Wired Equivalent Privacy and provides very weak security for the wireless network. Using 40-bit to 232-bit keys in an RC4 encryption algorithm, WEP's primary weakness lies in its reuse of initialization vectors (IVs)—an attacker can simply collect enough packets to decode the WEP shared key. WEP was never intended to fully protect your data—it was designed to give people using a wireless network the same level of protection someone surfing over an Ethernet wired hub would expect.

WEP's initialization vectors are relatively small and, for the most part, get reused pretty frequently. Additionally, they're sent in clear text as part of the header. An attacker simply needs to generate enough packets in order to analyze the IVs and come up with the key used. This allows the attacker to decrypt the WEP shared key on the fly, in real time, and renders the encryption useless. Attackers can get APs to generate packets by sending disassociate messages. These aren't authenticated by any means, so the resulting barrage of "Please associate with me" packets is more than enough for the attack.

A better choice in encryption technology is WPA (Wi-Fi Protected Access) or WPA-2. WPA makes use of TKIP (Temporal Key Integrity Protocol), a 128-bit key, and the client's MAC address to accomplish much stronger encryption. The short of it is, WPA changes the key out (hence the "temporal" part of the name) every 10,000 packets or so, instead of sticking with one and reusing it. Additionally, the keys are transferred back and forth during an EAP (Extensible Authentication Protocol) authentication session, which makes use of a four-step handshake process in proving the client belongs to the AP, and vice versa.

WPA-2 is much the same process; however, it was designed with the government and the enterprise in mind. You can tie EAP or a Radius server into the authentication side of WPA-2, allowing you to make use of Kerberos tickets and all sorts of additional goodies. Additionally, WPA-2 uses AES for encryption, ensuring FIPS 140-2 compliance.

The "war" options are discussed in reference to wireless network discovery. No matter which technique is being discussed, the overall action is the same: An attacker travels around with a Wi-Fi–enabled laptop looking for open wireless access points/networks. In war driving, the attacker is in a car. War walking has the attacker on foot. War flying has the attacker in an airplane.

Another "war" definition of note is *war chalking*. A war chalk is a symbol drawn somewhere in a public place indicating the presence of a wireless network. These can indicate free networks, hidden SSIDs, pay-for-use hotspots, and which encryption technique is in use. The basic war chalk involves two parentheses back to back. Added to this can be a key through the middle (indicating restricted Wi-Fi), a lock (indicating MAC filtering), and all sorts of extra entries. Usually the double parentheses will also have a word written above or below, which indicates the SSID or the administrative password for the access point.

Another option in wireless network discovery is the use of a wide array of tools created for that very purpose. However, no matter how great the tools are, if the wireless adapter can't pull the frames out of the air in the correct manner, all is lost. Some tools are built this way, and only work with certain chipset adapters—which can be very frustrating at times.

An AirPcap dongle is a USB wireless adapter that offers all sorts of advantages and software support. If you don't have one, you may need to research and download new and different drivers for your particular card. The Madwifi project may be an answer. Just keep in mind that, much like the ability of our wired adapters to use promiscuous mode for our sniffing efforts (discussed earlier in this book), not all wireless adapters are created equal, and not all will work with your favorite tool. Be sure to check the user guides and man pages for lists and tips on correctly configuring your adapters for use.

WIGLE (http://wigle.net) helps in identifying geographic locations of wireless networks; teams of hackers have mapped out wireless network locations using GPS and a tool called NetStumbler. NetStumbler (http://www.netstumbler.com) can be used for identifying poor coverage locations within an ESS, detecting interference causes, and finding any rogue access points in the network. It's Windows-based, easy to use, and compatible with 802.11a, b, and g.

Kismet is another wireless discovery option. It works on Linux-based systems and, unlike NetStumbler, works passively, meaning it detects access points and clients without actually sending any packets. It can detect access points that have not been configured (and would then be susceptible to the default out-of-the-box admin password) and will determine which type of encryption you might be up against. It works by "channel hopping" to discover as many networks as possible and has the ability to sniff packets and save them to a log file, readable by Wireshark or tcpdump.

Another great network discovery tool is NetSurveyor. This free, Windows-based tool provides many of the same features as NetStumbler and Kismet. Additionally, it supports almost all wireless adapters without any significant additional configuration—which is of great benefit to hackers who can't afford, or don't have, an AirPcap card. NetSurveyor acts as a great tool for troubleshooting and verifying optimal installation of wireless networks.

Wireless sniffing is the next important step in hacking wireless networks. Much about sniffing a wireless network is exactly the same as sniffing its wired counterpart. The same protocols and authentication standard weaknesses you looked for with Wireshark off that switch port are just as weak and vulnerable on wireless. Authentication information, passwords, and all sorts of information can be gleaned just from watching the air.

Just a few of the tools specifically made for wireless sniffing—in addition to NetStumbler and Kismet—include OmniPeek, AirMagnet WiFi Analyzer Pro, and WiFi Pilot. Assuming you have a wireless adapter that is compatible and can watch things in promiscuous mode, OmniPeek is a fairly well-known and respected wireless sniffer. In addition to the same type of traffic analysis you would see in Wireshark, OmniPeek provides network activity status and monitoring in a nice dashboard for up-to-the-minute viewing. AirMagnet WiFi Analyzer, from Fluke Networks, is an incredibly powerful sniffer, traffic analyzer, and all-around wireless network auditing software suite. It can be used to resolve performance problems and automatically detect security threats and vulnerabilities.

The rogue access point is an easy attack on a wireless network whereby an attacker sets up an access point near legitimate APs and tricks users into associating and authenticating with it. Sometimes referred to as an "evil twin," an attack like this is easy to attempt. The only drawback is this attack is sometime really easy to see, and you run a pretty substantial risk of discovery. You'll just have to watch out for true security-minded professionals, because they'll be on the lookout for rogue APs on a continual basis and (should) have plenty of tools available to help them out.

An ad hoc connection attack takes advantage of the ad hoc mode of wireless networking. An ad hoc connection attack occurs when an attacker simply sits down with a laptop somewhere in your building and advertises an ad hoc network from his laptop, and people eventually begin connecting to it.

Denial-of-service efforts are also easy attacks to attempt. This can be done in a couple ways, neither of which is particularly difficult. First, you can use any number of tools to craft and send de-authenticate (disassociate) packets to clients of an AP, which will force them to drop their connections. Granted, they may try to immediately climb back aboard, but there's nothing stopping you from performing the same action again. The other easy DoS wireless attack is to jam the wireless signal altogether, using some type of jamming device and, usually, a high-gain antenna/amplifier. All wireless devices are susceptible to some form of jamming and/or interference—it's simply a matter of placing enough signal out in the airwaves that the NICs can't keep up. Tons of jammer options are available (a quick Google search on wireless jammers will show you around 450,000 pages on the subject), ranging from 802.11 networks to Bluetooth and other wireless networking technologies.

One defense wireless network administrators attempt to use is to enforce a MAC filter. Basically it's a list of MAC addresses that are allowed to associate to the AP—if your wireless NIC's address isn't on the list, you're denied access. The easy way around this is to monitor the network to figure out which MAC addresses are in use on the AP and simply spoof one of them.

Cracking WEP is ridiculously easy and can be done with any number of tools. The idea revolves around generating enough packets to effectively guess the encryption key. The weak initialization vectors we discussed already are the key—that is, they're reused and sent in clear text. Regardless of the tool, the standard WEP attack follows the same basic series of steps:

1. Start a compatible wireless adapter on your attack machine and ensure it can both inject and sniff packets.

2. Start a sniffer to capture packets.

3. Use some method to force the creation of thousands and thousands of packets (generally by using "de-auth" packets).

4. Analyze these captured packets (either in real time or on the side) with a cracking tool.

Tools for cracking WEP include Cain and Able and Aircrack (both use Korek, but Aircrack is faster) as well as KisMAC, WEPCrack, chopchop, and Elcomsoft's Wireless Security Auditor tool.

Bluetooth refers to a very open wireless technology for data exchange over relatively short range (10 meters or less). It was designed originally as a means to reduce cabling, but has become a veritable necessity for cell phones and other mobile devices. Although hundreds of tools and options are available for Bluetooth hacking, the good news is their coverage on the exam is fairly light, and most of it comes in the form of identifying terms and definitions.

Bluetooth devices have two modes—a discovery mode and a pairing mode. Discovery mode determines how the device reacts to inquiries from other devices looking to connect, and has three actions. The discoverable action obviously has the device answer to all inquiries, limited discoverable restricts that action, and non-discoverable tells the device to ignore all inquiries.

Pairing mode details how the device will react when another Bluetooth system asks to pair with it. There are basically only two versions: Yes, I will pair with you, or no, I will not. Non-pairable rejects every connection request, whereas pairable accepts all of them.

Bluetooth attacks, taking advantage of this ease of use, fall into four general categories. Bluesmacking is simply a denial-of-service attack against a device. Bluejacking consists of sending unsolicited messages to, and from, mobile devices. Bluesniffing is exactly what it sounds like, and, finally, Bluescarfing is the actual theft of data from a mobile device.

Some of the more common Bluetooth tools available for hacking include BlueScanner (from SourceForge), BT Browser, Bluesniff, and btCrawler. After identifying nearby devices, Super Bluetooth Hack is an all-in-one software package that allows you to do almost anything you want to a device you're lucky enough to connect to. Other attack options include bluebugger and Bluediving (a full penetration suite for Bluetooth).

Questions

1. An access point is discovered using WEP. The ciphertext sent by the AP is encrypted with the same key and cipher used by its stations. What authentication method is being used?

   A. Shared key

   B. Asynchronous

   C. Open

   D. None

2. You are discussing wireless security with your client. He tells you he feels safe with his network because he has turned off SSID broadcasting. Which of the following is a true statement regarding his attempt at security?

   A. Unauthorized users will not be able to associate because they must know the SSID in order to connect.

   B. Unauthorized users will not be able to connect because DHCP is tied to SSID broadcast.

   C. Unauthorized users will still be able to connect because non-broadcast SSID puts the AP in ad hoc mode.

   D. Unauthorized users will still be able to connect because the SSID is still sent in all packets, and a sniffer can easily discern the string.

3. You are discussing wireless security with your client. He tells you he feels safe with his network as he has implemented MAC filtering on all access points, allowing only MAC addresses from clients he personally configures in each list. You explain this step will not prevent a determined attacker from connecting to his network. Which of the following explains why the APs are still vulnerable?

   A. WEP keys are easier to crack when MAC filtering is in place.

   B. MAC addresses are dynamic and can be sent via DHCP.

   C. An attacker could sniff an existing MAC address and spoof it.

   D. An attacker could send a MAC flood, effectively turning the AP into a hub.

4. A new member of the pen test team has discovered a WAP that is using WEP for encryption. He wants a fast tool that can crack the encryption. Which of the following is his best choice?

   A. AirSnort

   B. Aircrack, using Korek implementation

   C. NetStumbler

   D. Kismet

5. You are advising a client on wireless security. The NetSurveyor tool can be valuable in locating which potential threat to the network's security?

   A. Identifying clients who are MAC spoofing

   B. Identifying clients who haven't yet associated

   C. Identifying access points using SSIDs with less than eight characters

   D. Identifying rogue access points

6. A pen test team member is attempting to crack WEP. He needs to generate packets for use in Aircrack later. Which of the following is the best choice?

   A. Use aireplay to send fake authentication packets to the AP.

   B. Use Kismet to sniff traffic, which forces more packet transmittal.

   C. Use NetStumbler to discover more packets.

   D. There is no means to generate additional wireless packets—he must simply wait long enough to capture the packets he needs.

7. You set up an access point near your target's wireless network. It is configured with an exact copy of the network's SSID. After some time, clients associate and authenticate to the AP you've set up, allowing you to steal information. What kind of attack is this?

A. Social engineering

B. WEP attack

C. MAC spoofing

D. Rogue access point

8. Your client is confident in her wireless network security. In addition to turning off SSID broadcast and encrypting with WEP, she has also opted for the use of directional antennas instead of omnidirectional. These are set up along the east side of the building, pointing west, to provide coverage. In this case, does the placement provide adequate security for the network?

A. Yes, directional antennas do a better job than omnidirectional.

B. Yes, directional antennas force mutual authentication for clients.

C. No, attackers can simply place themselves on the west side of the building, and the signals may travel for miles.

D. No, the placement of antennas in a wireless network is irrelevant.

9. Which of the following is a true statement?

A. Configuring a strong SSID is a vital step in securing your network.

B. An SSID should always be more than eight characters in length.

C. An SSID should never be a dictionary word or anything easily guessed.

D. SSIDs are important for identifying networks, but do little to nothing for security.

10. Which wireless encryption technology makes use of temporal keys?

A. WAP

B. WPA

C. WEP

D. EAP

11. You are walking through your target's campus and notice a symbol on the bottom corner of a building. The symbol shows two backwards parentheses with the word *tsunami* across the top. What does this mean?

A. Nothing. The symbol is most likely graffiti.

B. The war chalking symbol indicates the direction of the Yagi antenna inside the building.

C. The war chalking symbol indicates a wireless flood area.

D. The war chalking symbol indicates a wireless hotspot with a default password of *tsunami*.

Answers

1. **A.** WEP uses shared key encryption, which is part of the reason it is so susceptible to cracking.

2. **D.** Turning off the broadcast of an SSID is a good step, but SSIDs do nothing in regard to security. The SSID is included in every packet, regardless of whether it's broadcast from the AP.

3. **C.** MAC filtering is easily hacked by sniffing the network for a valid MAC, then spoofing it, using any number of options available.

4. **B.** Aircrack, using the Korek implementation, is a very fast tool for cracking WEP, assuming you've collected at least 50,000 packets.

5. **D.** NetSurveyor, and a lot of other tools, can display all sorts of information about the network. Of the choices listed, a rogue access point is the only true security threat to the wireless network.

6. **A.** Aireplay can send fake authentication packets into the network, causing storms of packets for use in WEP cracking. It can also be used to generate ARP messages for the same purpose.

7. **D.** Setting up a rogue access point is one of the easiest methods to attack a wireless network. If the network administrator is careless, it can pay huge dividends.

8. **C.** Wireless signals can travel for miles—especially when the signal strength and power is focused in one direction, instead of being beaconed out 360 degrees.

9. **D.** An SSID is used for nothing more than identifying the network. It is not designed as a security measure.

10. **B.** WPA uses temporal keys, making it a much stronger encryption choice than WEP.

11. **D.** Any time there is a word written above or beside a war chalk symbol (two backward parentheses), it indicates either the SSID or, more commonly, the administrative password to the AP itself.

CHAPTER 10

Trojans and Other Attacks

In this chapter you will learn about
- Defining Trojans and their purpose
- Identifying common Trojan ports
- Identifying Trojan deployment methods
- Identifying Trojan countermeasures
- Defining viruses and worms
- Identifying virus countermeasures
- Describing DoS attacks
- Defining common DoS attack types
- Describing session hijacking and sequence prediction

I love deep sea fishing. I always have. There's just something about the waves, the blue water, and never knowing what's on the end of the line until you see it up by the boat. I started fishing as a very young child and grew up around the water. By the time I was 15, I thought I'd seen everything the fishing world could throw at me. But, like most people at 15, I was sorely mistaken.

One day we were out on a long trip where I was attempting (rather poorly, I might add) to act as a deck hand—baiting lines, cleaning up, and making sure everyone was having a good time. On the way back in, after all the bait was gone, we spotted a nice line of sargassum weed floating in the rip current—usually a good sign of temperature breaks in the water, and a good place to fish. The captain slowed the boat and I set up several rods with lures for trolling behind the boat. After a quick run to ensure the lines were good, we circled back and pulled the lures right beside the sargassum, just to see what we might pick up before heading all the way in. After just a second or two, one of the reels started screaming. Then a second one went. Then the third kicked in. We all knew right then what it was—mahi.

The school of mahi that came flying out from under that weed line was nothing short of epic. Fish were everywhere, and the gold and green of their bodies flashing through the blue water was a sight to behold. Pandemonium broke out on the boat, and everyone grabbed a line; everyone, of course, except me. I didn't have a line rigged and was a little too slow in grabbing one. Alan, the captain, looked over at me between yells to the guys on where to go and said, "You gonna fish?" I shrugged my shoulders and pointed to the only rod left on the boat—an old spinning reel with nothing tied on it but a snap swivel. With no bait and all the lures tied up already, I figured all I could do was watch and maybe help gaff one or two of the bigger ones into the boat.

Alan grabbed a hook—*a bare hook*—and stuck it on the swivel. Then he ripped off a piece of the aluminum foil from his sandwich wrapper and stuck it right on the hook. Not even with flair or purpose—he just rammed it on there and handed me the rod. "Chuck this in," he said. I scoffed, literally, and thought he was just having fun with the new kid. Nevertheless, I let out some line and dropped the hook into the water. Within seconds I had a fish on. I caught three fish from the school that day—on a piece of aluminum foil.

Alan taught me many, many more lessons on fishing, but the central concept of that day is relevant to our discussion in this chapter—you can often catch more than you expect by using tools and circumstances in unexpected ways. A lot of the terms and issues we discuss here may not necessarily seem like a hacker's paradise, but I can promise you it's all relevant. And we'll cover these terms and issues for two very important reasons: You'll be a better pen test member by taking advantage of everything at your disposal, and it's all on your test!

The "Malware" Attacks

Malware is generally defined as software designed to harm or secretly access a computer system without the owner's informed consent. And, more often than not, people in our profession think of it as hostile, intrusive, or annoying, and definitely something to be avoided. From the perspective of a hacker, though, some of this may actually be useable—provided it's done within the confines of an agreed-upon contract in a pen test. Let me be absolutely clear here: I am *not* encouraging you to write, promote, or forward viruses or malware of any kind. I'm simply providing you what you need to be successful on your exam.

Trojans, Backdoors, Viruses, and Worms

I read somewhere that software is considered to be malware based on the perceived *intent* of the creator rather than any particular features. That's actually a very good way to think of it from the ethical hacking perspective. Whereas most people think of viruses, worms, and Trojans as a means to spread destruction, and a huge inconvenience to computing life, to an ethical hacker the Trojan might actually look like a good means to retain access to a machine—simply one of many tools in the arsenal. Additionally, there are a ton of "legitimate" applications, add-ons, toolbars, and the like that aren't intended to be malware—but they may as well be. In some cases, that's what they actually turn out to be because they steal data for advertising purposes. Although we'll avoid the in-depth minutia that's sure to bore you into dropping this undertaking altogether and taking up wedding planning, we will spend a little time on the highlights of Trojans and viruses.

 NOTE Want another ridiculous term to add to your arsenal? Some states now define malware as "computer contaminant." Until I researched details for this chapter, I would have assumed that to be the crumbs in my keyboard.

Trojans (a.k.a. Backdoors)

A *Trojan* is software that appears to perform a desirable function for the user prior to running or installing it, but instead performs a function, usually without the user's knowledge, that steals information or otherwise harms the system (or data). Ask most people what they think of Trojans and they'll talk about the famous wooden horse of Troy, Symantec AntiVirus signatures, a thousand tales of woe involving computer crashes, and sometimes certain, shall I say, "hygiene" items not intended for discourse in this particular book. To us ethical hackers, though, the word *Trojan* really means a method to gain, and maintain, access on a machine we've been paid to target.

The idea of a Trojan is pretty simple. First, send an innocent-looking file to your target, inviting them to open it. They open it and, unaware, install software that makes your job easier. This software might be designed to steal specific types of information to send back, act as a keylogger, or perform 1,000 other equally naughty tasks. Some of them can even provide remote control–type access to a hacker any time he feels like it. For the ethical hacker, the ultimate goal is to provide something we can go back to later—a means to maintain our access. Although a backdoor isn't a Trojan, and a Trojan isn't a backdoor, they're tied together in this discussion and on your exam: The Trojan is the means to deliver it, and the backdoor provides the open access.

Most *malware* Trojans are downloaded from the Internet (usually via some weird Java drive-by vulnerability, peer-to-peer application, or web application "feature"), grabbed via an IRC channel, or clicked on as an attachment in an e-mail. The absolute easiest way you can get a target to provide you access to their machine, short of asking them for it (see social engineering), is to send a Trojan. More often than not, they'll open it and happily install whatever you want. The question becomes, then, how do you make it look like a legitimate application? The answer is to use a wrapper.

 EXAM TIP Overt channels are legitimate communication channels used by programs across a system or a network, while covert channels are used to transport data in unintended ways.

Wrappers are programs that allow you to bind an executable of your choice (Trojan) to an innocent file your target won't mind opening. For example, you might use a program such as EliteWrap to embed a backdoor application with a game file (.EXE). Your target opens the latest version of Elf Bowling and starts rolling strikes. Meanwhile your backdoor is installing and sits there waiting for your use later. If you'd like to see how easy it is, check out Exercise 10-1.

Exercise 10-1: Using EliteWrap

In this exercise we'll use EliteWrap to put an executable (calc.exe) into an innocent TXT file for our target to install. Obviously calculator isn't going to harm anything, but the point will be made—you can wrap any executable into a TXT file, or any file for that matter. Here are the steps to follow:

1. Download EliteWrap and then open a command prompt and navigate to the elitewrap folder. Enter the command **elitewrap**.

2. The following code listing shows the entries (in bold):

```
Enter name of output file: install.exe
Perform CRC-32 checking? [y/n]: y
Operations: 1 - Pack only
            2 - Pack and execute, visible, asynchronously
            3 - Pack and execute,  hidden, asynchronously
            4 - Pack and execute, visible,  synchronously
            5 - Pack and execute,  hidden,  synchronously
            6 - Execute only,      visible, asynchronously
            7 - Execute only,       hidden, asynchronously
            8 - Execute only,      visible,  synchronously
            9 - Execute only,       hidden,  synchronously

Enter package file #1: stuff.txt
Enter operation: 1
Enter package file #2: c:\windows\system32\calc.exe
Enter operation: 8
Enter command line: stuff.txt
Enter package file #3: <ENTER>
```

3. Close the command prompt and navigate back to the EliteWrap folder in Windows Explorer.

4. Double-click the stuff.txt file in the folder. The empty text file will open, as will calculator.

 NOTE There are plenty of options in this tool, and you can wrap several applications into one package. Additionally, this is not the only, or even the best, wrapper available. Also, these programs will almost always trigger your antivirus program—they have their own signatures and don't provide much cover.

There are innumerable Trojans, and uses for them, in the computing world today. In CEH parlance, they've been categorized into different groups, each fairly easy to understand without much comment or explanation on my part. For example, I'm fairly certain you could understand that a Trojan that changes the title bar of an Excel spreadsheet to read "YOU'VE BEEN HACKED!" would fall into the "Defacement Trojan" category, as opposed to the Proxy Server, FTP, or VNC Trojan category. One we will spend a little time on, though, is the command shell Trojan, because that's one you'll definitely be tested on.

A *command shell Trojan* is intended to provide a backdoor to the system that you connect to via command-line access. A great, shining example of this is Netcat—and although all the purists out there are screaming "NETCAT IS NOT A TROJAN!", just bear with me. It's talked about in this section for a reason, and it does illustrate the point well. Known as the *Swiss army knife* of TCP/IP hacking, Netcat provides all sorts of control over a remote shell on a target (see Figure 10-1). It can be used for all sorts of naughtiness. For example, to establish command-line access to the machine, use **nc –e IPaddress Port#**. Tired of Telnet? Just try the **–t** option. And for the main point of this section (backdoor access to a machine), when installed and executed on a remote machine, Netcat opens a listening port of your choice. From your attack machine, you connect using the open port—and voilà! For example's sake, **nc –l –p 5555** opens port 5555 in a listening state on the target machine. You can then type **nc IPAddress –p 5555** and connect to the target machine—a raw "Telnet-like" connection. And, just for fun, do you think the following command might provide something interesting (assuming we're connecting to a Linux box)?

```
nc -l -p 5555 < /etc/passwd
```

```
C:\>nc.exe -h
[v1.11 NT www.vulnwatch.org/netcat/]
connect to somewhere:   nc [-options] hostname port[s] [ports] ...
listen for inbound:     nc -l -p port [options] [hostname] [port]
options:
        -d              detach from console, background mode

        -e prog         inbound program to exec [dangerous!!]
        -g gateway      source-routing hop point[s], up to 8
        -G num          source-routing pointer: 4, 8, 12, ...
        -h              this cruft
        -i secs         delay interval for lines sent, ports scanned
        -l              listen mode, for inbound connects
        -L              listen harder, re-listen on socket close
        -n              numeric-only IP addresses, no DNS
        -o file         hex dump of traffic
        -p port         local port number
        -r              randomize local and remote ports
        -s addr         local source address
        -t              answer TELNET negotiation
        -u              UDP mode
        -v              verbose [use twice to be more verbose]
        -w secs         timeout for connects and final net reads
        -z              zero-I/O mode [used for scanning]
port numbers can be individual or ranges: m-n [inclusive]

C:\>
```

Figure 10-1   Netcat Help

NOTE Netcat can be used for outbound or inbound connections, over TCP or UDP, to or from any port on the machine. It offers DNS forwarding, port mapping and forwarding, and proxying. You can even use it as a port scanner, if you're really in a bind.

In covering Trojans, we're also duty bound to at least take a cursory glance at how to defend against them. First off, you should probably know some of the more common port numbers used by various Trojans (see Table 10-1). To be completely honest, these may or may not be of value to you in the real world—a real hacker won't bother with protocols you're going to be watching for—but you'll definitely see them on your exam.

So how would you spot these ports in use on your system? By looking for them, of course. Several programs are available to you to keep an eye on the port numbers you have in use on your system. An old stand-by built into your Windows system command line is netstat. Entering the command **netstat –an** will show you all the connections and listening ports in numerical form, as shown in Figure 10-2.

netstat will show all connections in one of several states—everything from SYN_SEND (indicating active open) to CLOSED (server has received an ACK from the client and closed the connection). In Figure 10-2, you'll see several port numbers in a listening state—waiting for something to come along and ask for them to open. Another useful netstat command is netstat -b. This displays all active connections and the processes or applications that are using them—pretty valuable information in ferreting out spyware and malware.

Table 10-1	Trojan Name	Port
Trojan Port Numbers	TCP Wrappers	421
	Doom	666
	Snipernet	667
	Tini	7777
	WinHole	1080–81
	RAT	1095, 1097–8
	SpySender	1807
	Deep Throat	2140, 3150
	NetBus	12345, 12346
	Whack a Mole	12362, 12363
	Back Orifice	31337, 31338

Figure 10-2

netstat

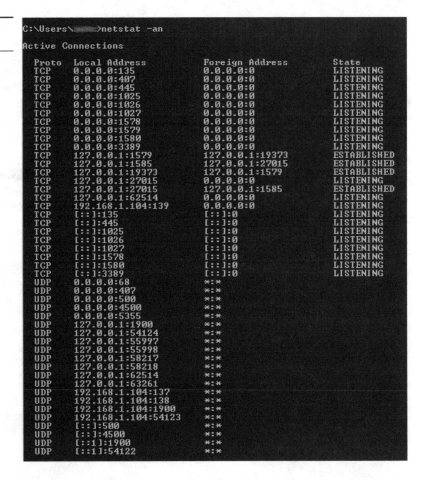

```
C:\Users\        >netstat -an

Active Connections

  Proto  Local Address           Foreign Address         State
  TCP    0.0.0.0:135             0.0.0.0:0               LISTENING
  TCP    0.0.0.0:407             0.0.0.0:0               LISTENING
  TCP    0.0.0.0:445             0.0.0.0:0               LISTENING
  TCP    0.0.0.0:1025            0.0.0.0:0               LISTENING
  TCP    0.0.0.0:1026            0.0.0.0:0               LISTENING
  TCP    0.0.0.0:1027            0.0.0.0:0               LISTENING
  TCP    0.0.0.0:1578            0.0.0.0:0               LISTENING
  TCP    0.0.0.0:1579            0.0.0.0:0               LISTENING
  TCP    0.0.0.0:1580            0.0.0.0:0               LISTENING
  TCP    0.0.0.0:3389            0.0.0.0:0               LISTENING
  TCP    127.0.0.1:1579          127.0.0.1:19373         ESTABLISHED
  TCP    127.0.0.1:1585          127.0.0.1:27015         ESTABLISHED
  TCP    127.0.0.1:19373         127.0.0.1:1579          ESTABLISHED
  TCP    127.0.0.1:27015         0.0.0.0:0               LISTENING
  TCP    127.0.0.1:27015         127.0.0.1:1585          ESTABLISHED
  TCP    127.0.0.1:62514         0.0.0.0:0               LISTENING
  TCP    192.168.1.104:139       0.0.0.0:0               LISTENING
  TCP    [::]:135                [::]:0                  LISTENING
  TCP    [::]:445                [::]:0                  LISTENING
  TCP    [::]:1025               [::]:0                  LISTENING
  TCP    [::]:1026               [::]:0                  LISTENING
  TCP    [::]:1027               [::]:0                  LISTENING
  TCP    [::]:1578               [::]:0                  LISTENING
  TCP    [::]:1580               [::]:0                  LISTENING
  TCP    [::]:3389               [::]:0                  LISTENING
  UDP    0.0.0.0:68              *:*
  UDP    0.0.0.0:407             *:*
  UDP    0.0.0.0:500             *:*
  UDP    0.0.0.0:4500            *:*
  UDP    0.0.0.0:5355            *:*
  UDP    127.0.0.1:1900          *:*
  UDP    127.0.0.1:54124         *:*
  UDP    127.0.0.1:55997         *:*
  UDP    127.0.0.1:55998         *:*
  UDP    127.0.0.1:58217         *:*
  UDP    127.0.0.1:58218         *:*
  UDP    127.0.0.1:62514         *:*
  UDP    127.0.0.1:63261         *:*
  UDP    192.168.1.104:137       *:*
  UDP    192.168.1.104:138       *:*
  UDP    192.168.1.104:1900      *:*
  UDP    192.168.1.104:54123     *:*
  UDP    [::]:500                *:*
  UDP    [::]:4500               *:*
  UDP    [::1]:1900              *:*
  UDP    [::1]:54122             *:*
```

Also, port-scanning tools can make this easier for you. Fport is a free tool from McAfee that reports all open TCP/IP and UDP ports and maps them to the owning applications. Per the McAfee site, "this is the same information you would see using the 'netstat -an' command, but it also maps those ports to running processes with the PID, process name, and path." What's Running, TCPView, and IceSword are also nice port-monitoring tools you can download and try out.

 NOTE   Process Explorer is a free tool from Microsoft (formerly from SysInternals) that comes highly recommended. It can tell you almost anything you'd want to know about a running process. Another free Microsoft offering formerly from SysInternals is AutoRuns. It is without question one of the better tools for figuring out what runs at startup on your system.

If you're on a Windows machine, you'll also want to keep an eye on the Registry, drivers, and services being used, and your startup routines. When it comes to the Registry, you can try to monitor it manually, but I'd bet within a day you'd be reduced to a blubbering fool curled into the fetal position in the corner. It's far easier to use monitoring tools designed for just that purpose. Options include, but are not limited to, SysAnalyzer, Tiny Watcher, Active Registry Monitor, and RegShot. Additionally, many antivirus and malware scanners will watch out for Registry errors. Malwarebytes will display all questionable Registry settings it finds on a scan, for one example.

EXAM TIP Windows will automatically run everything located in Run, RunServices, RunOnce, and RunServicesOnce, and you'll find that most questions on the exam are centered around or show you settings from HKEY_LOCAL_MACHINE.

Services and processes are all big indicators of Trojan activity on a machine. Aside from old, reliable Task Manager, processes and services can be monitored using gobs of different tools. Just a few mentioned for your perusal are Windows Service Manager, Service Manager Plus, and Smart Utility. And don't forget to check the startup routines, where most of these will be present—it won't do you much good to identify a bad service or process and kill it, only to have it pop up again at the next start. On a Windows machine, a simple msconfig command will open a configuration window showing you all sorts of startup (and other) settings you can work with (see Figure 10-3).

Figure 10-3
MSConfig

Lastly, I think the EC-Council folks would probably revoke my CEH certification if I neglected to mention Tripwire and SIGVERIF here. See, verifying the integrity of critical files is considered one of those bedrock-type actions you need to take in protecting against/detecting Trojans. Tripwire has been mentioned before in this book and bears repeating here. It is a very well-respected integrity verifier that can act as a HIDS in protection against Trojans. SIGVERIF is built into Windows machines to help verify the integrity of critical files on the system. To see how it works, just follow the instructions you can find right there on your own Windows Help file (see Exercise 10-2).

Exercise 10-2: Using SIGVERIF to Verify Integrity on a Windows 7 System

Windows XP instructions are very similar (check out http://support.microsoft.com/kb/308514 for XP Windows instructions). Here are the steps to follow to use SIGVERIF to verify integrity on a Windows 7 system:

1. Click the Start button and type **sigverif** in the run line. Press ENTER.

2. At the File System Verification window, click Start (see Figure 10-4).

3. When the run has completed, a pop-up will notify you. Click OK.

4. Click the Advanced button on the File System Verification window.

5. Click the View Log button to view information on critical files and their last modified dates and so on (see Figure 10-5).

Figure 10-4
SIGVERIF start page

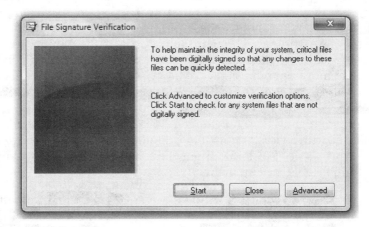

```
SIGVERIF - Notepad                                                    ─ □ X
File  Edit  Format  View  Help
*********************************

Microsoft Signature Verification

Log file generated on 4/24/2011 at 8:14 PM
OS Platform: Windows (x64), Version: 6.1, Build: 7600, CSDVersion:
Scan Results: Total Files: 162, Signed: 162, Unsigned: 0, Not Scanned: 0

File                     Modified      Version      Status        Catalog              Signed By
─────────────────        ──────────    ─────────    ──────────    ──────────           ──────────────────
[c:\program files\nvidia corporation\uninstall]
nvdisp.nvu               11/20/2009    2:5.00       Signed        nv_disp.cat          Microsoft Windows Hard
nvudisp.exe              11/20/2009    2:5.00       Signed        nv_disp.cat          Microsoft Windows Hard
[c:\windows\system32]
batt.dll                 7/13/2009     2:6.1        Signed        nt5.cat              Microsoft Windows
clfs.sys                 7/13/2009     2:6.1        Signed        nt5.cat              Microsoft Windows
ctapo64.dll              3/5/2007      2:5.00       Signed        stwrt64.cat          Microsoft Windows Hard
ctppld.dll               3/5/2007      2:5.00       Signed        stwrt64.cat          Microsoft Windows Hard
dpinst.exe               11/20/2009    2:5.00       Signed        nv_disp.cat          Microsoft Windows Hard
fsquirt.exe              7/13/2009     2:5.1        Signed        Microsoft-windows-C1 Microsoft Windows
```

Figure 10-5 SIGVERIF output

 NOTE The log file for SIGVERIF is called sigverif.txt and can be found in the Windows folder. The log is, by default, overwritten each time the tool is run. Third-party drivers that are not signed are displayed as "Not Signed," and indicate a good spot to begin your search.

Viruses and Worms

The good news regarding viruses and worms is there's not a whole lot here for you to remember for your exam—and what you do need to know are simple definitions. The bad news is I'm not sure how helpful they'll be to you in your real career. I mean, we *have* to cover them because CEH has them listed as an objective and you will see a couple of questions, but I doubt they're something you'll be whipping out as part of a pen test in measuring a client's security. Then again, maybe that's what they want you to look at. For me, though, these represent the bottom of the barrel in networking and computing. The guys who write and propagate these things tend to do nothing more than cause havoc and muck things up for a while. OK, enough on that. To borrow some geek humor from our technical editor here, "rant over," or better put, "</rant>."

A virus is defined as a self-replicating program that reproduces its code by attaching copies into other executable codes. In other words, viruses create copies of themselves in other programs. I'm not going to bore you with how to determine if your system is infected with a virus or not—I'm assuming you're smart enough to know that already. What we *do* need to know about these, though, are a few of the virus types and the definitions that go with them:

- **Boot sector virus** Also known as a system virus, this virus type actually moves the boot sector to another location on the hard drive, forcing the virus code to be executed first. They're almost impossible to get rid of once you get infected. You *can* re-create the boot record—old-school fdisk or mbr could do the trick for you—but it's not necessarily a walk in the park.

- **Shell virus**   Working just like the boot sector virus, this virus type wraps itself around an application's code, inserting its own code before the application's. Every time the application is run, the virus code is run first.

- **Multipartite virus**   Attempts to infect both files and the boot sector at the same time. This generally refers to a virus with multiple infection vectors. This link describes one such DOS-type virus: http://www.f-secure.com/v-descs/ neuroqui.shtml. It was multipartite, polymorphic, retroviral, boot sector, and generally a pretty wild bit of code.

- **Macro virus**   Usually written with VBA (Visual Basic for Applications), this virus type infects template files created by Microsoft Office—normally Word and Excel. The Melissa virus was a prime example of this.

- **Polymorphic code virus**   This virus mutates its code using a built-in polymorphic engine. These viruses are very difficult to find and remove because their signatures constantly change.

- **Metamorphic virus**   This virus type rewrites itself every time it infects a new file.

Another malware definition you'll need to know is the worm. A *worm* is a self-replicating malware computer program that uses a computer network to send copies of itself to other systems without human intervention. Usually it doesn't alter files, but it resides in active memory and duplicates itself, eating up resources and wreaking havoc along the way. The most common use for a worm in the hacking world is the creation of bot-nets, which we've already discussed. This army of robot systems can then be used to accomplish all sorts of bad things.

The most common example of a worm, and the one you'll get asked about on the exam, is the Conficker worm. This worm disables services, denies access to administrator shared drives, locks users out of directories, and restricts access to security-related sites. Symptoms include an "Open folder to view files—Publisher not specified" message in the AutoPlay dialog box, as shown in Figure 10-6. (The original, and legitimate, Windows option reads "Open Folder to view files using Windows Explorer.") Conficker spreads as soon as it is opened (by clicking the first option) to open shares, unpatched systems on the network, and systems with weak passwords. Systems with up-to-date patches and even decent passwords are usually safe.

 EXAM TIP   We've already mentioned them before, but anyone who has performed incident response understands that keyloggers are considered malware just like everything else. Just remember an antivirus (AV) program is not going to help with those hardware keyloggers. They can catch software all day long, but the dongle plugged in between the keyboard and system is immune and nearly untraceable.

Figure 10-6
File Open
Autoplay—Conficker
infection symptom

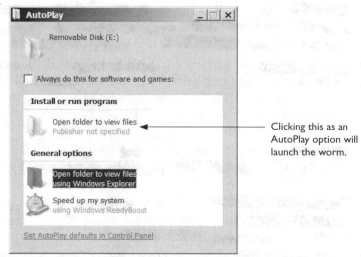

Clicking this as an
AutoPlay option will
launch the worm.

Finally, the last thing we're required to cover here is countermeasures and mitigation: just how you're supposed to protect against viruses and worms. Obviously a good antivirus program is a must (unless you're loading hacking tools to play with—then they become horrendously annoying), and you can find good ones that are free or you can pay for one from one of the more well-known providers. The only real key to an effective AV application is keeping it up to date. Your system is only as good as your signature files, and if you're asleep at the wheel in keeping them updated, you're opening yourself up to infection.

Another good option, at least in an enterprise scenario set up for testing and analysis, is the sheepdip computer. A *sheepdip* system is set up to check physical media, device drivers, and other files for malware before they are introduced to the network. Typically, this computer is used for nothing else and is isolated from the other computers—meaning it is not connected to the network at all. Sheepdip computers are usually configured with a couple of different AV programs, port monitors, Registry monitors, and file integrity verifiers.

NOTE Time for a little insight and vocabulary lesson in the real world versus your exam. Terms such as "netizen" (a.k.a. cybercitizen: a person actively involved in online communities) and "technorati" (not only a blog search engine, but a term of endearment for the technically astute among us) are perfectly acceptable to the techno-geeks you'll be working with, on and off pen test teams. Groovy discussions about "podcasting on a Web 2.0 site while creating mashups of tweets" are probably just fine. But to borrow a line from the great American cinematic classic *Office Space*, regarding the term "sheepdip" in the real world: "I believe you'd get your rear kicked saying something like that, man."

Remaining Attacks

Have you ever been on a really long road trip? You know the ones I'm talking about, right? When you leave you're really excited, and the miles just seem to pass along happily. Then, somewhere along the way, things change. The excitement dies down, and before you know it the miles become a burden instead of a joy. Everything seems like it takes forever, and the road becomes the enemy, with each road sign mocking your progress instead of marking it. Then, just as things are near their worst, you see the sign with your destination listed on it. It might read 200 miles, it might read 500, but instantly your spirits are lifted.

Have you noticed that at that point you start driving faster? Do you know why? Because you can see the end from there. Once the destination is within reach, once you can see that proverbial light at the end of the tunnel, your natural instinct is to sprint. There's no need for bathroom breaks—no need to stop and look at the world's largest ball of twine—because you are so close to the end you just want to get there and rest. It's perfectly natural, and the way our minds work.

Well, dear reader, we both find ourselves at an interesting juncture here. You and I have been on a long journey so far. It started out exciting, and there was a lot to look at and pass the time with. Now we're close to the end (you've no doubt looked at the table of contents and know where we are) and you're tired of reading. Heck, *I'm tired of writing,* and the temptation for both of us is to sprint; to blast through the rest and just *finish,* for goodness' sake. Trust me, though, we've just got two big points to get through here. I'll keep them short and to the point, but I'll need to know you're willing to do your part and stick with me. Come on, we're almost there.

 NOTE   Arctic safety briefings will tell you many people who were found frozen to death were found on the edge of visual contact with a destination that could provide safety. The theory goes that people were so distressed from hypothermia that the sight of safety caused them to either collapse or stop to rest for a moment, resulting in an inability to go further. Not a testable item, but it fits with the allegory here. As an aside, many were found without coats: It turns out severe hypothermia is known to make you feel warm before you freeze. And you thought this book would be boring.

Denial of Service

We've already defined a denial-of-service attack and a distributed denial-of-service attack, but this section is here to go into a little more detail (namely because there are CEH objectives yet to cover on the subject). For example, you may or may not be aware that a DoS is generally thought of as a last-resort attack. This isn't always true—there are plenty of examples where DoS was the whole point. In some cases the attacker just wants to embarrass the target, or maybe prevent the spread of information. But, sometimes, when a hacker is tired of trying to break through your defenses, she may simply resort to "blowing it up" out of frustration.

Obviously, this is completely different for the ethical hacker. We're not going to perform DoS attacks *purposely,* unless our client wants or allows us to. Sure, there may be some unintended DoS symptoms against a particular system or subnet, but we're generally not going after DoS as an end result. As an aside, you'll need to make sure your client understands the risks involved with testing—sometimes knocking on doors causes the security system to lock them all, and you don't want your client coming back at you unaware this could have happened.

The standard DoS attack seeks to accomplish nothing more than taking down a system, or simply denying access to it by authorized users. From this standpoint, the DoS might prove useful to an ethical hacker. For example, what if you removed the security personnel's rights to watch the network? This could allow you a few minutes to hack at will, without worry of getting caught. *Until they notice* they have no rights, of course—it won't take long.

The distributed denial of service (DDoS) attack, obviously, comes not from one system, but many—and they're usually part of a bot-net. The *bot-net* is a network of zombie computers the hacker can use to start a distributed attack from (examples of bot-net software/Trojans are Shark and Poison Ivy). These systems can sit idly by, doing other work for, literally, months before being called into action. That action may be as simple as sending a ping or performing some other task relevant to the attack at hand. Normally the preferred communications channel used to signal the bots is IRC or ICQ (Internet Chat Query).

 EXAM TIP In addition to knowing the basics given here in this section regarding DoS, you should familiarize yourself with the term *phlashing,* which refers to a DoS attack that causes permanent damage to a system. Usually this includes damage to the hardware itself and can also be known as "bricking" a system.

The DoS and DDoS attacks themselves are as numerous and varied as the items in the buffet lines in Las Vegas. They can range from the very simple to the fairly complex, and can require a system or many to pull it off. For a simple example, just try someone's login credentials incorrectly three times in a row on a government network. Voilà! You've successfully DoS'd their account. Other relatively simple methods could be sending corrupt SMB messages on Windows machines to "blue screen" the device. Or maybe you simply "arp" the machine to death, leaving it too confused to actually send a message anywhere. The methods are, literally, innumerable.

There are a few, though, you'll need for your exam, and I've thankfully provided a short list for you here—with all the salient information you'll need:

- **SYN attack** The hacker will send thousands upon thousands of SYN packets to the machine with a false source IP address. The machine will attempt to respond with a SYN/ACK but will be unsuccessful (because the address is false). Eventually, all the machine's resources are engaged and it becomes a giant paperweight.

- **SYN flood**   In this attack, the hacker sends thousands of SYN packets to the target, but never responds to any of the return SYN/ACK packets. Because there is a certain amount of time the target must wait to receive an answer to the SYN/ACK, it will eventually bog down and run out of available connections.

- **ICMP flood**   Here, the attacker sends ICMP Echo packets to the target with a spoofed (fake) source address. The target continues to respond to an address that doesn't exist and eventually reaches a limit of packets per second sent.

- **Application level**   A simple attack whereby the hacker simply sends more "legitimate" traffic to a web application than it can handle, causing the system to crash.

- **Smurf**   The attacker sends a large number of pings to the broadcast address of the subnet, with the source IP spoofed to that of the target. The entire subnet will then begin sending ping responses to the target, exhausting the resources there. A *fraggle* attack is similar, but uses UDP for the same purpose.

- **Ping of death**   (This isn't a valid attack with modern systems, but is still a definition you may need.) In the ping of death, an attacker fragments an ICMP message to send to a target. When the fragments are reassembled, the resultant ICMP packet is larger than the maximum size and crashes the system.

More than a few tools are dedicated to performing DoS on systems. LOIC (Low Orbit Ion Cannon) is a simple-to-use DDoS tool that floods a target with TCP, UDP, or HTTP requests (see Figure 10-7). Originally written open source to attack various Scientology websites, the tool has many people voluntarily joining a bot-net to support all sorts of attacks. As recently as this year, LOIC was used in a coordinated attack against Sony's PlayStation network, and the tool has a track record of other successful hits: the Recording Industry Association of America, PayPal, MasterCard, and several other companies have all fallen victim to LOIC.

Others include Trinity, Tribe Flood Network, and R-U-Dead-Yet. Trinity is a Linux-based DDoS tool much like LOIC. Tribe Flood Network is much the same, using voluntary bot-net systems to launch massive flood attacks on targets. R-U-Dead-Yet (known by its acronym RUDY) performs DoS with HTTP POST via long form field submissions. We could go on here, but I think you get the point. Do a quick Google search for "DoS Tool" or "DDos Tool"—you'll find more than you need to know.

 NOTE   Another really groovy DoS tool worth mentioning here (even though I don't think it's part of your exam) is Slowloris. Slowloris is a really cool TCP DoS tool that basically ties up open sockets and causes services to hang. It's useful against web servers and doesn't consume large amounts of bandwidth (http://www-ng.cert-ist.com/eng/ressources/Publications_ArticlesBulletins/Environnementreseau/200906_slowloris/_print/).

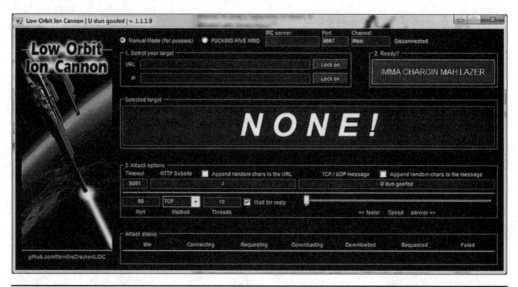

Figure 10-7 LOIC

Finally, when it comes to countermeasures against DoS attacks, you've probably heard all this before, so we don't need to spend large amounts of time on the subject. Actions such as disabling unnecessary services, using a good firewall policy, and keeping security patches and upgrades up to date are pretty standard fare. Additionally, the use of a good NIDS can help against attacks from across the network. Strong, security-conscious code should be an absolute for your applications, and the use of tools such as Skydance can help detect and prevent DoS attacks. You might also look into network ingress filtering as well as some network auditing tools to help along the way.

Session Hijacking

Unlike DoS attacks, session hijacking attempts aren't trying to break anything or shut off access, necessarily. The idea is fairly simple: The attacker waits for a session to begin and, after all the pesky authentication gets done, jumps in to steal the session for himself. This differs a little from the spoofing attacks we've talked about to this point. In spoofing you're pretending to be someone else's address with the intent of sniffing their traffic while they work. *Hijacking* refers to the active attempt to steal the entire session from the client: The server isn't even aware of what happened and the client simply connects again in a different session.

From a high-level view, TCP session hijacking sounds relatively easy. First, the hacker tracks the session, watching the sequence numbers and the flow of packet headers. Next, the hacker "desynchronizes" the connection by sending a TCP reset or FIN to the client, causing it to close its side of the session. Lastly (at the same time), using the info gathered during the first step, the hacker begins sending packets to the server with the predicted (guessed) session ID—which is generated by an algorithm using the sequence numbers. If the hacker gets it right, he has taken over the session because the server thinks it's the original client's next packet in the series. The following more completely describes the session hijack steps (per EC-Council):

1. Sniff the traffic between the client and the server.
2. Monitor the traffic and predict the sequence numbering.
3. Desynchronize the session with the client.
4. Predict the session token and take over the session.
5. Inject packets to the target server.

NOTE Session hijacking can be done via brute force, calculation, or stealing. Additionally, you can always send a preconfigured session ID to the target— when the target clicks to open it, simply wait for authentication and jump in.

TCP session hijacking is possible because of the way TCP works. As a session-oriented protocol, it provides unique numbers to each packet, which allows the receiving machine to reassemble them in the correct, original order, even if they are received out of order. The synchronized packets we've talked about throughout the book set these sequence numbers (SNs) up. With over four billion combinations available, the idea is to have the process begin as randomly as possible. However, it is statistically possible to repeat sequence numbers and, even easier, to guess what the next one in line will be.

NOTE It is fair to note that sequence attacks are *exceptionally rare* in cases where you're not in the middle. A definitive paper on the subject, despite its age, can be found here: http://lcamtuf.coredump.cx/newtcp/. It provides images of sequence numbers from various operating system implementations and gives an idea of how statistically successful (or unsuccessful) you'll be in messing with them.

So, just for clarity's sake, let's go back to our earlier discussion on TCP packets flying through the ether. The initial sequence number (ISN) is sent by the initiator of the session in the first step (SYN). This is acknowledged in the second handshake (SYN/ACK) by incrementing that ISN by one, and another ISN is generated by the recipient. This second number is acknowledged by the initiator in the third step (ACK), and from there on out communication can occur. The window size field will tell the recipient how much he can send before expecting a return acknowledgment. Combine all of them together and, over time, you can watch the whole thing in action. For example, consider Figure 10-8.

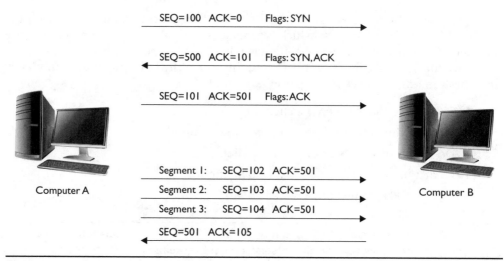

SEQ=100 ACK=0   Flags: SYN

SEQ=500 ACK=101   Flags: SYN, ACK

SEQ=101 ACK=501   Flags: ACK

Segment 1:   SEQ=102 ACK=501
Segment 2:   SEQ=103 ACK=501
Segment 3:   SEQ=104 ACK=501

SEQ=501 ACK=105

Computer A

Computer B

Figure 10-8 TCP communication

NOTE There are also windowing attacks for TCP that shrink the data size window.

After the handshake, for every data payload transmitted the sequence number is incremented. In the first two steps of the three-way handshake, the ISNs are exchanged (in this case, 100 and 500) and then are incremented based on the delivery of data. In our example here, Computer A sends 3 bytes with an initial sequence number of 102, so each packet sequence number will increment accordingly—102, 103, and 104, respectively. The receiver then sends an acknowledgment of 105 because that is the next byte it expects to receive in the next packet.

Seems easy enough, but once you add in window size and take into account the fact that the numbers aren't simple (like the 100 and 500 in our example), it can get hairy pretty quickly. The window size, you may recall, tells the sender how many outstanding bytes it can have on the network without expecting a response. The idea is to improve performance by allowing more than one byte at a time before requiring the "Hey, I got it" acknowledgment. This sometimes complicates things because the sender may cut back within the window size based on what's going on network-wise and what it's trying to send.

EXAM TIP You'll need to remember that the sequence numbers increment on acknowledgment. Additionally, you'll almost certainly get asked a scenario version of sequence numbering (if I were writing the test, I'd give you one). You'll need to know, given an acknowledgment number and a window size, what sequence number would be acceptable to the system. For example, an acknowledgment of 105 with a window size of 200 means you could expect sequence numbering from 105 through 305.

Thankfully, a multitude of tools are available to assist in session hijacking. We've mentioned Ettercap before—a packet sniffer on steroids—but not in the context of actively hijacking sessions. It's an excellent man-in-the-middle tool and can be run from a variety of platforms (although it is Linux native). Hunt and T-sight are probably the two best known session hijacking tools. Hunt can sniff, hijack, and reset connections at will, whereas T-sight (commercially available) can easily hijack sessions as well as monitor additional network connections. Other tools include, but are not limited to, Paros (more known as a proxy), Burp Suite, Juggernaut (a well-known Linux based tool), Hamster, and Ferret.

NOTE You've heard of session hijacking and man-in-the-middle, but what about man-in-the-*browser*? An MIB attack occurs when the hacker sends a Trojan to intercept browser calls. The Trojan basically sits between the browser and libraries, allowing a hacker to watch, and interact within, a browser session.

Countermeasures for session hijacking are, again, usually common-sense issues. For one thing, using unpredictable session IDs in the first place protects against hijacking (remember this one). Other options include using encryption to protect the channel, limiting incoming connections, minimizing remote access, and regenerating the session key after authentication is complete. And lastly, of course, user education is key. Oftentimes an uneducated user won't think twice about clicking past the security certificate warning, or reconnecting after being suddenly shut down. Education can help with this, even if it's only one or two instances, here and there.

Chapter Review

Malware is generally defined as software designed to harm or secretly access a computer system without the owner's informed consent. Software is considered to be malware based on the perceived *intent* of the creator rather than any particular features. Malware can also be defined as a "computer contaminant."

A Trojan is software that appears to perform a desirable function for the user prior to running or installing it, but instead performs a function, usually without the user's knowledge, that steals information or otherwise harms the system (or data). To us ethical hackers, the word Trojan really means a method to gain, and maintain, access on a target we've been paid to target.

Trojans are installed by sending the target an innocent-looking file, inviting him to open it. Once opened, it installs the Trojan, which is designed to steal specific types of information to send back, act as a keylogger, or perform other tasks—including providing a backdoor to the system for future access. Overt channels are legitimate communication channels used by programs across a system or a network, whereas covert channels are used to transport data in unintended ways. Most malware Trojans are downloaded from the Internet, grabbed via an IRC channel, or clicked on as an attachment in an e-mail.

To make a Trojan appear as a legitimate application, the use of a wrapper is required. Wrappers are programs that allow you to bind an executable of your choice (Trojan) to an innocent file your target won't mind opening. For example, you might use a program like EliteWrap to embed a backdoor application with a game file (.EXE).

In CEH parlance, Trojans are categorized into different groups, each fairly easy to understand. These categories include Defacement, Proxy, FTP, VNC, and command shell. A command shell Trojan is intended to provide a backdoor to the system that you connect to via command-line access. An example of this is Netcat. Known as the Swiss army knife of TCP/IP hacking, Netcat provides all sorts of control over a remote shell on a target. When installed and executed on a remote machine, it opens a listening port of your choice. Entering the command **nc –l –p 5555** opens port 5555 in a listening state on the target machine. You can then type **nc IPAddress –p 5555** and connect to the target machine with a raw "Telnet-like" connection. Netcat can be used for outbound or inbound connections, over TCP or UDP, to or from any port on the machine. It offers DNS forwarding, port mapping and forwarding, and proxying. You can even use it as a port scanner.

Some of the more common port numbers used by various Trojans are found in the following table (you'll need to memorize them for your exam):

Trojan Name	Port
TCP Wrappers	421
Doom	666
Snipernet	667
Tini	7777
WinHole	1080–81
RAT	1095, 1097–8
SpySender	1807
Deep Throat	2140, 3150
NetBus	12345, 12346
Whack a Mole	12362, 12363
Back Orifice	31337, 31338

Several programs are available to you to keep an eye on the port numbers you have in use on your system. A Windows system command-line option is netstat. Entering the command **netstat –an** will show all connections and listening ports in numerical form. There are also port-scanning tools to make this easier for you. What's Running, Fport, TCPView, and IceSword are all examples.

Prevention also requires keeping an eye on the Registry, drivers and services being used, and your startup routines. Options include, but are not limited to, SysAnalyzer, Tiny Watcher, Active Registry Monitor, and RegShot. Additionally, many antivirus and malware scanners will watch out for Registry errors. Malwarebytes will display all questionable Registry settings it finds on a scan, for one example. As an aside, Windows will automatically run everything located in Run, RunServices, RunOnce, and RunServicesOnce, and you'll find that most questions on your exam are centered around or show you settings from HKEY_LOCAL_MACHINE.

Services and processes are all big indicators of Trojan activity on a machine. Task Manager is a built-in option; however, processes and services can be monitored using many different tools. Windows Service Manager, Service Manager Plus, and Smart Utility are a few examples. And don't forget to check the startup routines, where most of these will be present—it won't do you much good to identify a bad service or process and then kill it, only to have it pop up again at the next startup.

Tripwire and SIGVERIF are used to verify the integrity of critical files, which is considered one of those bedrock actions you need to take in protecting against/detecting Trojans. Tripwire is a very well-respected integrity verifier that can act as a HIDS in protection against Trojans, providing a warning when critical files are altered. SIGVERIF is built into Windows machines to help verify the integrity of critical files on the system.

A virus is defined as a self-replicating program that reproduces its code by attaching copies into other executable codes. In other words, viruses create copies of themselves in other programs. A few of the virus types and the definitions that go with them include the following:

- **Boot sector virus** Also known as a system virus, this virus type actually moves the boot sector to another location on the hard drive, forcing the virus code to be executed first. They're almost impossible to get rid of once you get infected. You *can* re-create the boot record—old-school fdisk or mbr could do the trick for you—but it's not necessarily a walk in the park.

- **Shell virus** Working just like the boot sector virus, this virus type wraps itself around an application's code, inserting its own code before the application's. Every time the application is run, the virus code is run first.

- **Multipartite virus** Attempts to infect both files and the boot sector at the same time. This generally refers to a virus with multiple infection vectors. This link describes one such DoS-type virus: http://www.f-secure.com/v-descs/ neuroqui.shtml. It was multipartite, polymorphic, retroviral, boot sector, and generally a pretty wild bit of code.

- **Macro virus**   Usually written with VBA (Visual Basic for Applications), this virus type infects template files created by Microsoft Office—normally Word and Excel. The Melissa virus was a prime example of this.

- **Polymorphic code virus**   This virus mutates its code using a built-in polymorphic engine. These viruses are very difficult to find and remove because their signatures constantly change.

- **Metamorphic virus**   This virus type rewrites itself every time it infects a new file.

A worm is a self-replicating malware computer program that uses a computer network to send copies of itself to other systems without human intervention. Usually it doesn't alter files, but it resides in active memory and duplicates itself, eating up resources and wreaking havoc along the way. The most common use for a worm in the hacking world is the creation of bot-nets.

The most common example of a worm is the Conficker worm, which disables services, denies access to administrator shared drives, locks users out of directories, and restricts access to security-related sites. Symptoms include an "Open folder to view files—Publisher not specified" message in the AutoPlay dialog box. (The original, and legitimate, Windows option reads "Open Folder to view files using Windows Explorer.") Conficker spreads as soon as it is opened (by clicking the first option) to open shares, unpatched systems on the network, and systems with weak passwords. Systems with up-to-date patches and even decent passwords are usually safe.

To protect against viruses and Trojans, a good antivirus program is a must, and you can find good ones that are free or you can pay for one from one of the more well-known providers. The key to an effective AV application is keeping it up to date. Your system is only as good as your signature files. Another good option is the sheepdip computer. A sheepdip system is set up to check physical media, device drivers, and other files for malware before they are introduced to the network. Typically, this computer is used for nothing else and is isolated from the other computers—meaning it is not connected to the network at all. Sheepdip computers are usually configured with a couple of different AV programs, port monitors, Registry monitors, and file integrity verifiers.

A denial-of-service attack is generally thought of as a last-resort attack, and is designed to prevent legitimate users from accessing resources. The standard DoS attack seeks to accomplish nothing more than taking down a system, or simply denying access to it by authorized users. The distributed denial-of-service (DDoS) attack comes not from one system, but many.

A bot-net is a network of zombie computers the hacker can use to start a distributed attack from (examples of bot-net software/Trojans are Shark and Poison Ivy). These systems can sit idly by, doing other work for, literally, months before being called into action. That action may be as simple as sending a ping or performing some other task relevant to the attack at hand. Normally the preferred communications channel used to signal the bots is IRC or ICQ. Another DoS term is phlashing, which refers to a DoS attack that causes permanent damage to a system—usually damage to the hardware itself.

Here's a sampling of DoS and DDoS attacks:

- **SYN attack**   The hacker will send thousands upon thousands of SYN packets to the machine with a false source IP address. The machine will attempt to respond with a SYN/ACK but will be unsuccessful (because the address is false). Eventually, all the machine's resources are engaged and it becomes a giant paperweight.

- **SYN flood**   In this attack, the hacker sends thousands of SYN packets to the target, but never responds to any of the return SYN/ACK packets. Because there is a certain amount of time the target must wait to receive an answer to the SYN/ACK, it will eventually bog down and run out of available connections.

- **ICMP flood**   Here, the attacker sends ICMP Echo packets to the target with a spoofed (fake) source address. The target continues to respond to an address that doesn't exist and eventually reaches a limit of packets per second sent.

- **Application level**   A simple attack whereby the hacker simply sends more "legitimate" traffic to a web application than it can handle, causing the system to crash.

- **Smurf**   The attacker sends a large number of pings to the broadcast address of the subnet, with the source IP spoofed to that of the target. The entire subnet will then begin sending ping responses to the target, exhausting the resources there. A fraggle attack is similar, but uses UDP for the same purpose.

- **Ping of death**   (This isn't a valid attack with modern systems, but is still a definition you may need.) In the ping of death, an attacker fragments an ICMP message to send to a target. When the fragments are reassembled, the resultant ICMP packet is larger than the maximum size and crashes the system.

Also, more than a few tools are dedicated to performing DoS on systems. LOIC (Low Orbit Ion Cannon) is a simple-to-use DDoS tool that floods a target with TCP, UDP, or HTTP requests. Others include Trinity, Tribe Flood Network, and R-U-Dead-Yet.

Countermeasures against DoS attacks include disabling unnecessary services, using a good firewall policy, and keeping security patches and upgrades up to date. All these are pretty standard fare. Additionally, the use of a good NIDS can help against attacks from across the network. Strong, security-conscious code should be an absolute for your applications, and the use of tools such as Skydance can help detect and prevent DoS attacks. You might also look into network ingress filtering as well as some network auditing tools to help along the way.

Unlike DoS attacks, session hijacking attempts aren't trying to break anything or shut off access. A session hijack takes advantage of a connection that is already active and authenticated. This differs a little from spoofing in that spoofing is pretending to be a different address with the intent of sniffing traffic while the client works. Hijacking refers to the active attempt to steal the entire session from the client: The server isn't even aware of what happened and the client simply connects again in a different session. Session hijack steps include the following:

1. Sniff the traffic between the client and the server.
2. Monitor the traffic and predict the sequence numbering.
3. Desynchronize the session with the client.
4. Predict the session token and take over the session.
5. Inject packets to the target server.

TCP session hijacking is possible because of the way TCP works. As a session-oriented protocol, it provides unique numbers to each packet, which allows the receiving machine to reassemble them in the correct, original order, even if they are received out of order. Sequence numbers increment on acknowledgment and are an absolute must in stealing the session token.

A multitude of tools are available to assist in session hijacking. Ettercap is an excellent man-in-the-middle tool and can be run from a variety of platforms (although it is Linux native). Hunt and T-sight are probably the two best-known session-hijacking tools. Hunt can sniff, hijack, and reset connections at will, whereas T-sight (commercially available) can easily hijack sessions as well as monitor additional network connections. Other tools include, but are not limited to, Paros (more known as a proxy), BurpSuite, Juggernaut (a well-known Linux-based tool), Hamster, and Ferret.

A man-in-the-browser attack occurs when the hacker sends a Trojan to intercept browser calls. The Trojan basically sits between the browser and libraries, allowing a hacker to watch, and interact within, a browser session.

Countermeasures for session hijacking are using unpredictable session IDs, using encryption to protect the channel, limiting incoming connections, minimizing remote access, and regenerating the session key after authentication is complete. Additionally, user education is a valuable mitigation.

Questions

1. You are monitoring network traffic and notice a lot of ICMP packets headed to one server in the subnet. The MAC address listed in each packet reads FF:FF:FF:FF:FF:FF. What attack is underway?

   A. SQL injection

   B. MAC spoofing

   C. Session hijacking

   D. Smurf

2. Your client is confident that his enterprise antivirus protection software will eliminate and prevent malware in his system. Will this signature-based antivirus system protect against polymorphic viruses?

    A. Yes. No matter the virus, the generic signatures will catch it.

    B. Yes. All signature-based systems also use a heuristics engine to catch these.

    C. No. Because the system compares a signature to the executable, polymorphic viruses are not identified and quarantined.

    D. No, because the system compares file sizes to potential viruses and would catch the polymorphic that way.

3. The Melissa virus exploited security problems in Microsoft Excel and Word. What type of virus was it?

    A. Macro

    B. Named

    C. Stealth

    D. Multipartite

4. What is the default port (or ports) used by Back Orifice? (Choose all that apply.)

    A. 666

    B. 777

    C. 31337

    D. 31338

5. Which of the following would be a good choice for session hijack attempts? (Choose all that apply.)

    A. Ettercap

    B. Tini

    C. Hunt

    D. Nessus

6. Which of the following is the best way to protect against session hijacking?

    A. Use only nonroutable protocols.

    B. Use unpredictable sequence numbers.

    C. Use a file verification application, such as Tripwire.

    D. Use good password policy.

7. Which of the following attacks an already-authenticated connection?

    A. Smurf

    B. Denial of service

    C. Session hijacking

    D. Phishing

8. How does Tripwire (and programs like it) help against Trojan attacks?

   A. Tripwire is an AV application that quarantines and removes Trojans immediately.

   B. Tripwire is an AV application that quarantines and removes Trojans after a scan.

   C. Tripwire is a file-integrity-checking application that rejects Trojan packets intended for the kernel.

   D. Tripwire is a file-integrity-checking application that notifies you when a system file has been altered, thus indicating a Trojan.

9. What is a wrapper, in the context of a discussion on Trojans?

   A. A program used to bind the Trojan to a legitimate file

   B. A program used to encrypt the Trojan

   C. A program used to alter the executable portion of the Trojan to avoid detection

   D. None of the above

10. During a TCP data exchange, the client has offered a sequence number of 100, and the server has offered 500. During acknowledgments, the packet shows 101 and 501, respectively, as the agreed-upon sequence numbers. With a window size of 5, which sequence numbers would the server willingly accept as part of this session?

    A. 102 through 104

    B. 102 through 501

    C. 102 through 502

    D. Anything above 501

Answers

1. **D.** In a Smurf attack, the attacker attempts to DoS a box by sending ping requests to the subnet's broadcast address, with the target's source address spoofed in the packets. This results in a flood of ICMP packets to the server. The MAC address in these packets indicates broadcast.

2. **C.** Polymorphic viruses constantly change their code in order to defeat the signature-based comparison of the executable.

3. **A.** Macro viruses, like Melissa, take advantage of macro functionality in files.

4. **C and D.** Back Orifice uses 31337 and 31338 by default.

5. **A and C.** Ettercap, Hunt, T-sight, Juggernaut, and others are good session-hijacking tools.

6. **B**. Unpredictable sequence numbers make session hijacking nearly impossible.

7. **C**. Session hijacking takes advantage of connections already in place, and already authenticated.

8. **D**. Tripwire is one of the better-known file integrity verifiers, and it can help prevent Trojans by notifying you immediately when an important file is altered.

9. **A**. A wrapper, such as EliteWrap, is used to bind the Trojan to a legitimate file, in hopes the user executes and installs it.

10. **A**. Starting with the acknowledged sequence number of 101, the server will accept packets between 102 and 106 before sending an acknowledgment.

CHAPTER 11

The Pen Test: Putting It All Together

In this chapter you will learn about
- Describing penetration testing, security assessments, and risk management
- Defining automatic and manual testing
- Listing the pen test methodology and deliverables

Maybe it hasn't been Amelia Earhart's solo trip across the Atlantic, or Columbus sailing the ocean blue, but you have to admit, it has been a long journey. We've covered everything that should be relevant for your upcoming exam, and even a few things that might make you a better hacker. And some of the stuff we covered is just plain cool. So now we find ourselves here at the last chapter, where everything comes together for the ethical hacker.

Note I didn't say "for the *hacker,*" because you're not going to be *just* a hacker. You're going to be a different breed, working to improve security and safeguard data and resources—not the other way around. You'll be doing good work for the betterment of your society. Sure, that may sound corny to some of you, but I truly believe it. And I know, if you believe your profession is making the world a better place, the pride you have in it will result in you becoming better and better at it each and every day. Before too long, you'll look back on this little book like one of those English 101 books from college, and wonder at how far you've come.

So let's take just a few paragraphs here and discuss the penetration test, where you'll put into practice what you've read in a book. I promise this won't take long—it's a short chapter, and I'm pretty sure you deserve a break.

Methodology and Steps

Much has been made so far in this book about steps and taking a logical approach to hacking. I can honestly say that most of that is purely for your exam—for your "book knowledge," if you will. Hackers will take advantage of any opportunity as it presents itself, and they'll always look for the easy way in. Why bother running through all the steps of a hacking attack on a machine that's either too secured to allow a breach (easily and within a decent timeframe) or doesn't present a pot of gold at the end of the attack rainbow? However, all that said, we're going to run through steps, phases, and definitions in this chapter—just so you have what you need for your exam. Buckle up, let's ride.

The Security Assessments

Every organization on the planet that has any concern whatsoever for the security of its resources must perform various security assessments—and some don't have a choice, if they need to comply with FISMA or other various government standards (see Figure 11-1). In CEH parlance, a *security assessment* is any test that is performed in order to assess the level of security on a network or system. The security assessment can belong to one of two categories: a security audit (otherwise known as a vulnerability assessment) or a penetration test.

A security audit scans and tests a system or network for existing vulnerabilities, *but does not intentionally exploit any of them*. This vulnerability assessment is designed to uncover potential security holes in the system and report them to the client for their action. This assessment does not fix or patch vulnerabilities, nor does it exploit them—it simply points them out for the client's benefit.

 NOTE It's a good idea to keep in mind the difficulty of the "find but don't test" theory of vulnerability assessments. For instance, say you believe there might be an SQL injection vulnerability in a website. But to determine if it's vulnerable, you have to attempt to insert SQL—which *is* pen testing. Very often, the only way to verify the existence of a vulnerability *must be* to test for it.

Figure 11-1
NIST and FISMA
logos

A penetration test, on the other hand, not only looks for vulnerabilities in the system but actively seeks to exploit them. The idea is to show the potential consequences of a hacker breaking in through unpatched vulnerabilities. Pen tests are carried out by highly skilled individuals pursuant to an agreement signed before testing begins. This agreement spells out the limitations, constraints, and liabilities between the organization and the penetration test team. This agreement is designed to maximize the effectiveness of the test itself while minimizing operational impact.

Start Right, Finish Safe

I think too many people have the idea that ethical hacking/pen testing is a cookie-cutter, one-size-fits-all operation. In reality, each situation, and each client, is different. What works for one client may not work for another, and tests and deliverables that make one client happy might result in a lawsuit from another. That's why the initial agreement, signed long before any testing begins, is so important.

Although most people automatically think of this as a "get out of jail free" card, it's much more than that. You'll need to cover everything you can think of, and a lot of things you haven't. For example, you might agree up front that no denial-of-service attacks are to be performed during the test, but what happens if your port scanner accidentally brings down a server? Will you be liable for damages? In many cases, a separate indemnity form releasing you from financial liability is also necessary.

Definition of project scope will help to determine if the test is a comprehensive examination of the organization's security posture, or a targeted test of a single subnet/system. You may also find a need to outsource various efforts and services. In that case, your service level agreements (SLAs) need to be iron-clad in defining your responsibility in regard to your consultant's actions. In the event of something catastrophic or some serious, unplanned disruption of services, the SLA spells out who is responsible for taking action to correct the situation. And don't forget the nondisclosure terms: Most clients don't want their dirty laundry aired and are taking a very large risk in agreeing to the test in the first place.

If you'd like to see a few examples of pen test agreement paperwork, just do some Google searching. SANS has some great information available, and many pen test providers have basics about their agreements available. Keep in mind you won't find any single agreement that addresses everything—you'll have to figure that out on your own. Just be sure to do everything up front, before you start testing.

Speaking of pen tests overall, there are basically two types of penetration tests defined by EC-Council: external and internal. An *external assessment* analyzes publicly available information and conducts network scanning, enumeration, and testing from the network perimeter—usually from the Internet. An *internal assessment,* as you might imagine, is performed from within the organization, from various network access points. Obviously, both could be part of one overall assessment, but you get the idea.

We've covered black box, white box, and grey box testing already, so I won't beat you over the head with these again. However, just to recap: Black box testing occurs when the attacker has no prior knowledge of the infrastructure at all. This testing takes the longest to accomplish and simulates a true outside hacker. White box testing simulates an internal user who has complete knowledge of the company's infrastructure. Grey box testing provides limited information on the infrastructure. Sometimes grey box testing is born out of a black box test that determines more knowledge is needed.

 NOTE Pen testing can also be defined by what your *customer* knows. Announced testing means the IT security staff is made aware of what testing you're providing and when it will occur. Unannounced testing occurs without the knowledge of the IT security staff, and is only known by the management staff who organized and ordered the assessment. Additionally, unannounced testing should always come with detailed processes that are coordinated with a trusted agent. It is normally very bad to have a company's entire IT department tasked with stopping an incident that is really just an authorized pen test.

Testing can also be further broken down according to the means by which it is accomplished. Automated testing is a point-and-shoot effort with an all-inclusive toolset such as Core Impact. This could be viewed as a means to save time and money by the client's management, but it simply cannot touch a test performed by security professionals. Automated tools can provide a lot of genuinely good information, but are also susceptible to false positives and false negatives, and they don't necessarily care what your agreed-upon scope says is your stopping point. A short list of some automated tools is presented here:

- **Codenomicon** A toolkit for automated penetration testing that, according to the provider, eliminates unnecessary ad hoc manual testing: "The required expertise is built into the tools, making efficient penetration testing available for all." Codenomicon's penetration testing toolkit utilizes a unique "fuzz testing" technique, which learns the tested system automatically. This is designed to help penetration testers enter new domains, such as VoIP assessment, or to start testing industrial automation solutions and wireless technologies.

- **Core Impact** Probably the best-known all-inclusive automated testing framework, Core Impact "takes security testing to the next level by safely replicating a broad range of threats to the organization's sensitive data and mission-critical infrastructure—providing extensive visibility into the cause, effect and prevention of data breaches" (per the company's site). Core Impact, shown in Figure 11-2, tests everything from web applications and individual systems to network devices and wireless. You can download and watch an entire Core Impact automated testing demo online. Go to Appendix A for the URL.

- **Metasploit** Mentioned several times already in this book, Metasploit is a free, open source tool for developing and executing exploit code against a remote target machine (the pay-for version is called Pro and is undoubtedly worth the money). Metasploit offers a module called Autopwn that can automate the exploitation phase of a penetration test (see Figure 11-3). With hundreds of exploits, Metasploit's Autopwn provides an easy, near point-and-shoot option for gaining a shell on any given target.

- **CANVAS** From Immunity Security, CANVAS "makes available hundreds of exploits, an automated exploitation system, and a comprehensive, reliable exploit development framework to penetration testers and security

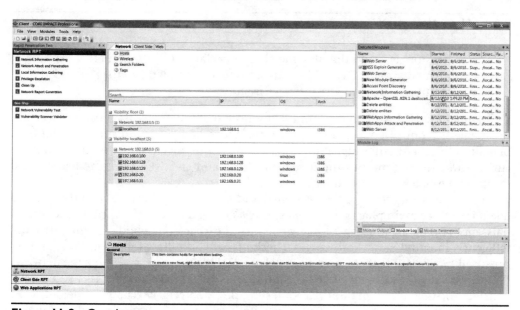

Figure 11-2 Core Impact

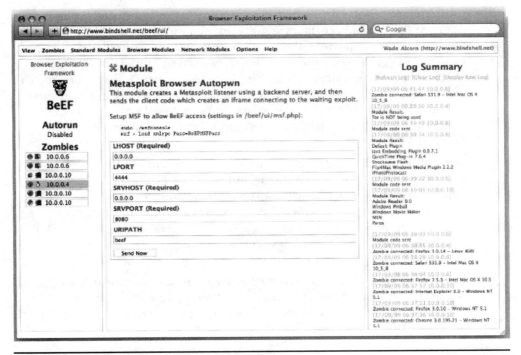

Figure 11-3 Metasploit's Autopwn

professionals." Additionally, the company claims CANVAS's Reference Implementation (CRI) is "the industry's first open platform for IDS and IPS testing." The CANVAS interface is shown in Figure 11-4.

Manual testing is still, in my humble opinion, the best choice for a true security assessment. It requires good planning, design, and scheduling, and provides the best benefit to the client. Although automated testing definitely has a role in the overall security game, many times it's the ingenuity, drive, and creativeness of the hacker that results in a true test of the security safeguards.

As for the actual test itself, EC-Council and many others have divided the actions taken into three main phases. In the *pre-attack phase*, you'll be performing all the reconnaissance and data-gathering efforts we discussed earlier in this book. Competitive intelligence, identifying network ranges, checking network filters for open ports, and so on are all carried out here. Also, running whois, DNS enumeration, finding the network IP address range, and nmap network scanning all occur here. Other tasks you might consider include, but aren't limited to, testing proxy servers, checking for default firewall or other network-filtering device installations or configurations, and looking at any remote login allowances.

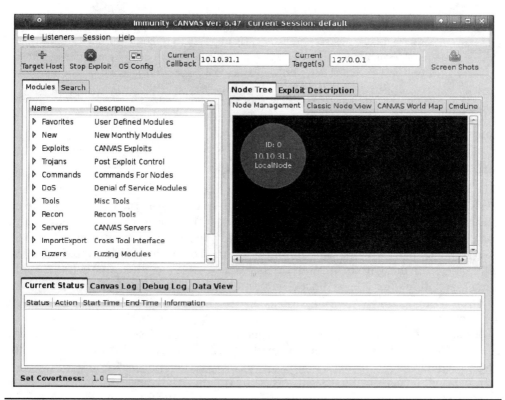

Figure 11-4 CANVAS

In the *attack phase,* you'll be attempting to penetrate the network perimeter, acquire your targets, execute attacks, and elevate privileges. Getting past the perimeter might take into account things such as verifying ACLs by crafting packets and checking to see if you can use any covert tunnels inside the organization. On the web side, you'll be trying XSS, buffer overflows, and SQL injections. After acquiring specific targets, you'll move into password cracking and privilege escalation, using a variety of methods we've covered here. Finally, once you've gained access, it's time to execute your attack code.

Finally, the *post-attack phase* consists of two major steps. First, there's an awful lot of cleanup to be done. Anything that has been uploaded to the organization's systems in the way of files or folders needs to be removed. Additionally, any tools, malware, backdoors, or other attack software loaded on client systems needs to be taken off. And don't forget the Registry—any changes made there need to be put back to the original settings. The idea is to return everything to the pre-test state. Remember, not only are you not supposed to fix anything you find, but you're also not supposed to create more vulnerabilities for the client to deal with.

NOTE Cleanup is a very difficult part of assessments. Logs, backups, and other artifacts are sometimes nearly impossible to remove. Ensuring your remote agents kill themselves off (like Core Impact does by default) can help, but if you have a client who wants manual inspection, it may become a serious cost driver.

And the second step in the post-attack phase? Well, that deals with the deliverables, which we'll discuss next.

Security Assessment Deliverables

I know you're probably going to hate hearing this, but I've got to be truthful with you—just because you're an ethical hacker performing security assessments for major clients doesn't mean you're off the hook paperwork-wise. The pen test you were hired to do was designed with one objective in mind: to provide the client with information they need to make their network safer and more secure. Therefore, it follows that the client will expect something in the form of a deliverable in order to take some action—something that will require you to practice your organizing, typing, and presentation skills. So if you thought you were getting into a paperwork-free, no-time-behind-the-desk job, my apologies.

Typically your test will begin with some form of an in-brief to the management. This should provide an introduction of the team members and an overview of the original agreement. You'll need to point out which tests will be performed, which team members will be performing specific tasks, the timeline for your test, and so on. Points of contact, phone numbers, and other information—including, possibly, the "Bat phone" number, to be called in the event of an emergency requiring all testing to stop—should all be presented to the client before testing begins.

 NOTE Some clients and tests will require interim briefings on the progress of the team. These might be daily wrap-ups the team leader can provide via secured e-mail, or full-blown presentations with all team members present.

After the test is complete, a comprehensive report is due to the customer. Although each test and client is different, some of the basics that are part of every report are listed here:

- An executive summary of the organization's overall security posture. (If you are testing under the auspices of FISMA, DIACAP, HIPAA, or some other standard, this summary will be tailored to the standard.)
- The names of all participants and the dates of all tests.

- A list of findings, usually presented in order of highest risk.
- An analysis of each finding, and recommended mitigation steps (if available).
- Log files and other evidence from your toolset.

An example of a standard pen test report template can be viewed at www.vulnerabilityassessment.co.uk/report%20template.html.

 NOTE Many of the tools we've covered in this book have at least some form of reporting capability. Oftentimes these can, and should, be included with your end-test deliverables.

And so, dear reader, we've reached the end of your testable material. I promised I'd keep this chapter short and to the point, and I believe I have. Most of the information in this chapter is a review of items we've already discussed, but it's important to know for both your exam and your real-world exploits. I sincerely hope I've answered most of your questions, and eliminated some of the fear you may have had in tackling this undertaking.

Best of luck to you on both your exam and your future career. Practice what we've talked about here—download and install the tools and try exploits against machines or VMs you have available in your home lab. And don't forget to stay ethical! Everything in this book is intended to help you pass your upcoming exam and become a valued pen test member, not to teach you to be a hacker. Stay the course and you'll be fine.

Chapter Review

Security assessments can be one of two types: a security audit (vulnerability assessment) or a penetration test. The security audit scans and tests a system or network for existing vulnerabilities, but does not intentionally exploit any of them. This assessment is designed to uncover potential security holes in the system and report them to the client for their action. It does not fix or patch vulnerabilities, nor does it exploit them. It only points them out for the client's benefit.

A penetration test actively seeks to exploit vulnerabilities encountered on target systems or networks. This shows the potential consequences of a hacker breaking in through unpatched vulnerabilities. Penetration tests are carried out by highly skilled individuals according to an agreement signed before testing begins. This agreement spells out the limitations, constraints, and liabilities between the organization and the penetration test team.

Penetration tests consist of two types of assessment: external and internal. An external assessment analyzes publicly available information and conducts network scanning, enumeration, and testing from the network perimeter—usually from the Internet. An internal assessment is performed from within the organization, from various network access points.

Black box testing occurs when the attacker has no prior knowledge of the infrastructure at all. This testing takes the longest to accomplish and simulates a true outside hacker. White box testing simulates an internal user who has complete knowledge of the company's infrastructure. Grey box testing provides limited information on the infrastructure. Sometimes grey box testing is born out of a black box test that determines more knowledge is needed.

Testing can also be further broken down according to the way it is accomplished. Automated testing uses an all-inclusive toolset. Automated tools can provide plenty of information and many legitimate results for a lesser price than manual testing with a full test team. However, they are also susceptible to false positives and false negatives, and don't always stop where they're supposed to (software can't read your agreement contract). Manual testing is the best choice for security assessment. It requires good planning, design, and scheduling, and provides the best benefit to the client. Manual testing is accomplished by a pen test team, following the explicit guidelines laid out before the assessment.

There are three main phases to a pen test. In the pre-attack phase, reconnaissance and data gathering efforts are accomplished. Gathering competitive intelligence, identifying network ranges, checking network filters for open ports, and so on are all carried out in this phase. Running whois, DNS enumeration, finding the network IP address range, and nmap network scanning are all examples of tasks in this phase.

Attempting to penetrate the network perimeter, acquire your targets, execute attacks, and elevate privileges are steps taken in the attack phase. Verifying ACLs by crafting packets, checking to see if you can use any covert tunnels inside the organization, and using XSS, buffer overflows, and SQL injections are all examples of tasks performed in this phase. After acquiring specific targets, you'll move into password cracking and privilege escalation, using a variety of methods. Finally, once you've gained access, it's time to execute your attack code.

The post-attack phase consists of two major steps. The first step involves cleaning up your testing efforts. Anything that has been uploaded to the organization's systems in the way of files or folders needs to be removed. Any tools, malware, backdoors, or other attack software loaded on the client's systems need to be taken off. Any Registry changes you've made need to be put back to their original settings. The goal of this phase is to return everything to the pre-test state.

The second step involves writing the pen test report, due after all testing is complete. The pen test report should contain the following items:

- An executive summary of the organization's overall security posture. (If you're testing under the auspices of FISMA, DIACAP, HIPAA or some other standard, this will be tailored to the standard.)
- The names of all participants and the dates of all tests.
- A list of findings, usually presented in order of highest risk.
- An analysis of each finding and the recommended mitigation steps (if available).
- Log files and other evidence from your toolset.

Questions

1. A pen test can be internal or external, and is also defined by the type of knowledge held by the tester. Which of the following test types presents a higher probability of encountering problems and takes the most amount of time?

   A. White box

   B. Grey box

   C. Black box

   D. Automatic

2. What marks the major difference between a hacker and an ethical hacker (pen test team member)?

   A. Nothing.

   B. Ethical hackers never exploit vulnerabilities; they only point out their existence.

   C. The tools they use.

   D. Predefined scope and agreement made with the system owner.

3. What are the three phases of a penetration test?

   A. Pre-attack, attack, post-attack

   B. Reconnaissance, exploitation, covering tracks

   C. Exterior, interior, perimeter

   D. Black box, white box, grey box

4. In which phase of a penetration test is scanning performed?

   A. Pre-attack

   B. Attack

   C. Post-attack

   D. Reconnaissance

5. Which type of security assessment notifies the customer of vulnerabilities but does not actively or intentionally exploit them?

   A. Vulnerability assessment

   B. Scanning assessment

   C. Penetration test

   D. None of the above

6. Which of the following would be a good choice for an automated penetration test? (Choose all that apply.)

   A. nmap

   B. Netcat

   C. Core Impact

   D. CANVAS

7. Which of the following tests is generally faster and costs less, but is susceptible to more false reporting and contract violation?

   A. Internal

   B. External

   C. Manual

   D. Automatic

8. Joe is part of a penetration test team and is starting a test. The client has provided him a system on one of their subnets, but did not provide any authentication information, network diagrams, or other notable data concerning the system(s). Which type of test is Joe performing?

   A. External, white box

   B. External, black box

   C. Internal, white box

   D. Internal, black box

9. Which of the following would you find in a final report from a full penetration test?

   A. Executive summary

   B. A list of findings from the test

   C. The names of all the participants

   D. A list of vulnerabilities patched or otherwise mitigated by the team

10. In which phase of a penetration test would you compile a list of vulnerabilities found?

    A. Pre-attack

    B. Attack

    C. Post-attack

    D. None of the above

Answers

1. **C.** Black box testing provides no information at all to the tester, thus providing more opportunity for problems along the way and taking the most time. Black box testing simulates a true outside threat.

2. **D.** Pen tests always begin with an agreement with the customer that identifies the scope and activities. An ethical hacker will never proceed without written authorization.

3. **A.** A pen test is broken into pre-attack, attack, and post-attack phases. Attacks can be internal or external, with or without prior knowledge.

4. **A.** All reconnaissance efforts occur in the pre-attack phase.

5. **A.** Vulnerability assessments (a.k.a. security audits) seek to discover open vulnerabilities on the client's systems but do not actively or intentionally exploit any of them.

6. **C and D.** Core Impact and CANVAS are both automated, all-in-one test tool suites capable of performing a test for a client. Other tools may be used in conjunction with them to spot vulnerabilities, including Nessus, Retina, SAINT, and Sara.

7. **D.** Automatic testing involves the use of a tool suite and generally runs faster than an all-inclusive manual test. However, it is susceptible to false negatives and false positives, and can oftentimes overrun the scope boundary.

8. **D.** Joe is on a system internal to the network and has no knowledge of the target's network. Therefore, he is performing and internal, black box test.

9. **A, B, and C.** The final report for a pen test includes an executive summary, a list of the findings (usually in order of highest risk), the names of all participants, a list of all findings (in order of highest risk), analysis of findings, mitigation recommendations, and any logs or other relevant files.

10. **C.** The final report contains a list of all vulnerabilities discovered on the target and is created in the post-attack phase.

Tool, Sites, and References

Greetings, dear reader, and welcome to the best appendix you've ever read—or at least the most useful for your CEH exam, anyway. This appendix is filled with all the tools, websites, and write-ups I could think of that will help you become a better ethical hacker. Keep in mind I'm not providing a recommendation for, approval of, or security guarantee on any website or link you'll find here. Neither I nor my beloved publisher can be held liable for anything listed here. For example, URLs change, pages become outdated with time, tools become obsolete when new versions are released, and so on. Not to mention that, as I clearly pointed out in the text, you need to be very, very careful with some of this stuff: Your antivirus system will no doubt explode with activity simply by *visiting* some of these sites. I highly recommend you create a virtual machine or use a stand-by system to download to and test tools from.

These websites and tools are listed here because they will help you in your study efforts for the exam and further your professional development. I purposely did not provide tools on a CD, because it is important that you learn how to find and install what you're looking for. You're entering the big leagues now, so you simply need to know how it's really done.

Vulnerability Research Sites

- **National Vulnerability Database**   nvd.nist.gov
- **SecurityTracker**   www.securitytracker.com
- **SecuriTeam**   www.securiteam.com
- **Secunia**   www.secunia.com
- **Hackerstorm Vulnerability Database Tool**   www.hackerstrom.com
- **HackerWatch**   www.hackerwatch.org
- **SecurityFocus**   www.securityfocus.com
- *Security* **Magazine**   www.securitymagazine.com
- *SC Magazine*   www.scmagazine.com
- **Exploit Database**   www.exploit-db.com

Footprinting Tools

Website Research Tools

- Netcraft   http://news.netcraft.com
- Webmaster   http://webmaste-a.com/link-extractor-internal.php
- iWEBTOOL   www.iwebtool.com
- Archive   www.archive.org

DNS and WHOIS Tools

- Nslookup
- Sam Spade   www.samspade.org
- WebFerret   www.webferret.com
- ARIN   www.whois.arin.net
- DomainTools   www.domaintools.com
- Network Solutions   www.networksolutions.com
- WhereIsIP   http://www.jufsoft.com/whereisip/
- DNSstuff   www.dnsstuff.com
- BetterWhois   www.betterwhois.com/
- DNS-Digger   http://dnsdigger.com
- SpyFu   www.spyfu.com
- Dig   www.isc.org/software/bind

NOTE   Download BIND 9 or above—BIND 9.2.1 is a 1.28MB self-extracting ZIP file. When the download completes, extract the BIND files and copy them into an empty directory. Then install BIND by running the BINDINSTALL.EXE file—dig is part of the install.

Traceroute Tools and Links

- VisualRoute Trace   www.visualware.com
- 3d Visual Route   http://3dnsmp.com
- VisualIPTrace   www.visualiptrace.com

- Trout   www.foundstone.com
- PingPlotter   http://pingplotter.com
- Path Analyzer Pro   www.pathanalyzer.com

Website Mirroring Tools and Sites

- BlackWidow   http://softbytelabs.com
- Reamweaver   http://reamweaver.com
- Wget   http://www.gnu.net/s/wget
- Teleport Pro   http://www.tenmax.com/teleport/pro/home.htm
- Archive   www.archive.org
- Google cache

E-mail Tracking

- eMailTrackerPro   www.emailtrackerpro.com
- PoliteMail   www.politemail.com

Google Hacking

- Google Hacking Database   www.hackersforcharity.org/ghdb/
- Google Hacks   http://code.google.com/p/googlehacks/
- Google Hacking Master List
  http://it.toolbox.com/blogs/managing-infosec/google-hacking-master-list-28302

Scanning and Enumeration Tools

Ping Sweep

- Angry IP Scanner   www.angryip.org
- Colasoft Ping   http://colasoft.com
- Ultra Ping Pro   http://ultraping.webs.com
- Ping Scanner Pro   www.digilextechnologies.com
- MegaPing   www.magnetosoft.com
- Friendly Pinger   www.kilievich.com

Scanning Tools

- SuperScan   www.foundstone.com
- Nmap (ZenMap)   http://nmap.org/
- NetScan Tools Pro   www.netscantools.com
- Hping   www.hping.org
- LAN Surveyor   www.solarwinds.com
- MegaPing   www.magnetosoft.com
- NScan   www.nscan.hypermart.net
- Infiltrator   www.infiltration-systems.com
- Netcat   http://netcat.sourceforge.net
- IPEye   http://ntsecurity.nu
- THC-Amap   www.thc.org

War Dialing

- THC-SCAN   http://www.thc.org/thc-tsng/
- TeleSweep   www.securelogix.com
- ToneLoc   www.securityfocus.com/tools/48
- PAWS   www.wyae.de
- WarVOX   http://warvox.org/

Banner Grabbing

- Telnet
- ID Serve   www.grc.com
- Netcraft   http://netcraft.com
- Xprobe
  http://sourceforge.net/apps/mediawiki/xprobe/index.php?title=Main_Page
- THC-AMAP   http://freeworld.thc.org

Vulnerability Scanning

- Nessus   www.nessus.org
- SAINT   http://saintcorporation.com
- GFI LanGuard   www.gfi.com

- **Retina**   http://eeye.com
- **Core Impact**   www.coresecurity.com
- **MBSA**   http://technet.microsoft.com
- **Nikto**   http://cirt.net/nikto2
- **WebInspect**   http://download.spidynamics.com/webinspect/default.htm
- **GFI Languard**   www.gfi.com/lannetscan/

Proxy, Anonymizer, and Tunneling

- **Tor**   https://www.torproject.org/
- **ProxyChains**   http://proxychains.sourceforge.net/
- **SoftCab**   www.softcab.com/proxychain/index.php
- **Proxifier**   www.proxifier.com
- **HTTP Tunnel**   www.http-tunnel.com
- **Anonymouse**   http://anonymouse.org/
- **Anonymizer**   http://anonymizer.com
- **Psiphon**   http://psiphon.ca

Enumeration

- **PSTools**   http://technet.microsoft.com
- **P0f**   http://lcamtuf.coredump.cx/p0f.shtml
- **SuperScan**   www.foundstone.com
- **User2Sid/Sid2User**   www.svrops.com/svrops/dwnldutil.htm
- **SNMP Scanner**   www.secure-bytes.com
- **NSauditor**   www.nsauditor.com
- **SolarWinds**   www.solarwinds.com
- **LDAP Admin**   www.ldapsoft.com
- **LEX**   www.ldapexplorer.com
- **Ldp.exe**   www.microsoft.com
- **User2Sid/Sid2User**   http://windowsecurity.com
- **SNMPUTIL**   www.wtcs.org
- **IP Network Browser**   www.solarwinds.com
- **Xprobe**   www.sys-security.com/index.php?page=xprobe

System Hacking Tools

Password Hacking Tools

- Cain   www.oxid.it
- John the Ripper   www.openwall.com
- LCP   www.lcpsoft.com
- THC-Hydra   http://www.thc.org/thc-hydra/
- ElcomSoft   www.elcomsoft.com/
- Lastbit   http://lastbit.com/
- Ophcrack   http://ophcrack.sourceforge.net
- Aircrack   www.aircrack-ng.org/
- Rainbow crack   www.antsight.com/zsl/rainbowcrack/
- Brutus   www.hoobie.net/brutus/
- Windows Password Recovery   www.windowspasswordsrecovery.com
- KerbCrack   http://ntsecurity.nu

Sniffing

- Wireshark   www.wireshark.org/
- Ace   www.effetech.com
- KerbSniff   http://ntsecurity.nu
- Ettercap   http://ettercap.sourceforge.com

Keyloggers and Screen Capture

- KeyProwler   www.keyprowler.com
- Handy Key Logger   www.handy-keylogger.com
- Actual Keylogger   www.actualkeylogger.com
- Actual Spy   www.actualspy.com
- Ghost   www.keylogger.net
- Hidden Recorder   www.oleansoft.com
- IcyScreen   www.16software.com
- DesktopSpy   www.spyarsenal.com
- USB Grabber   http://digitaldream.persiangig.com

Covering Tracks

- ELsave   www.ibt.ku.dk
- EraserPro   www.acesoft.net
- WindowWasher   www.webroot.com
- Auditpol   www.microsoft.com
- WinZapper   www.ntsecurity.nu
- Evidence Eliminator   www.evidence-eliminator.com

Packet Crafting/Spoofing

- Komodia   www.komodia.com
- Hping2   www.hping.org/
- PackEth   http://sourceforge.net
- Packet generator   http://sourceforge.net
- Netscan   http://softperfect.com
- Scapy   www.secdev.org/projects/scapy/
- Nemesis   http://nemesis.sourceforge.net

Session Hijacking

- Paros Proxy   www.parosproxy.org/
- Burp Suite   http://portswigger.net
- Firesheep   http://codebutler.github.com/firesheep
- Hamster/Ferret
  http://erratasec.blogspot.com/2009/03/hamster-20-and-ferret-20.html
- Ettercap   http://ettercap.sourceforge.net
- Hunt   http://packetstormsecurity.com

Cryptography and Encryption

Encryption Tools

- TrueCrypt   www.truecrypt.org
- BitLocker   http://microsoft.com
- DriveCrypt   www.securstar.com

Hash Tools

- MD5 Hash   www.digitalvolcano.co.uk/content/md5-hash
- HashCalc   http://nirsoft.net

Steganography

- ImageHide   www.dancemammal.com
- gifShuffle   www.darkside.com.au
- QuickStego   www.quickcrypto.com
- EZStego   www.stego.com
- Open Stego   http://openstego.sourceforge.net/
- S Tools   http://spychecker.com
- JPHIDE   http://nixbit.com
- wbStego   home.tele2.at/wbailer/wbstego/
- MP3Stegz   http://sourceforge.net
- OurSecret   www.securekit.net
- OmniHidePro   http://omnihide.com
- AudioStega   www.mathworks.com
- StegHide   http://steghide.sourceforge.net
- XPTools   www.xptools.net

Cryptanalysis

- Cryptanalysis   http://cryptanalysisto.sourceforge.net
- Cryptobench   http://addario.org
- EverCrack   http://evercrack.sourceforge.net

Sniffing

Packet Capture

- Wireshark   http://wireshark.org
- CACE   www.cacetech.com

- **tcpdump**   http://tcpdump.org
- **Capsa**   www.colasoft.com
- **OmniPeek**   www.wildpackets.com
- **NetWitness**   www.netwitness.com
- **Windump**   www.winpcap.org
- **dsniff**   http://monkey.org
- **EtherApe**   http://etherape.sourceforge.net

Wireless

- **Kismet**   www.kismetwireless.net
- **NetStumbler**   www.netstumbler.net

MAC Flooding/Spoofing

- **Macof**
  http://www.irongeek.com/i.php?page=backtrack-3-man/macof (Linux tool)
- **SMAC**   www.klcconsulting.net

ARP Poisoning

- **Cain**   www.oxid.it
- **UfaSoft**   http://ufasoft.com
- **WinARP Attacker**   http:www.xfocus.net

Trojans and Malware

Wrappers

- **EliteWrap**   http://homepage.ntlworld.com/chawmp/elitewrap

Monitoring Tools

- **HiJackThis**   http://free.antivirus.com
- **What's Running**   www.whatsrunning.net
- **CurrPorts**   www.nirsoft.net

- **SysAnalyzer**   http://labs.idefense.com/software/malcode.php
- **Regshot**   http://sourceforge.net/projects/regshot
- **Driver Detective**   www.driveshq.com
- **SvrMan**   http://tools.sysprogs.org
- **ProcessHacker**   http://processhacker.sourceforge.net
- **Fport**   www.mcafee.com/us/downloads/free-tools/fport.aspx

Attack Tools

- **Netcat**   http://netcat.sourceforge.net
- **Nemesis**   http://nemesis.sourceforge.net

IDS

- **Snort**   www.snort.org

Evasion Tools

- **ADMutate**   http:// www.ktwo.ca
- **NIDSBench**   http:// PacketStormsecurity.org/UNIX/IDS/nidsbench/
- **IDSInformer**   http:// www.net-security.org
- **Inundator**   http://inundator.sourceforge.net

Wireless

- **WIGLE**   http://wigle.net
- **AirPcap**   www.cacetech.com
- **Madwifi**   http://madwifi-project.org
- **Kismet**   www.kismetwireless.net
- **NetStumbler**   www.netstumbler.com
- **AirMagnet WiFi Analyzer**   http://airmagnet.com
- **Airodump**   http:// Wirelessdefence.org/Contents/Aircrack_airodump.htm
- **Aircrack**   http:// www.Aircrack-ng.org

- **AirSnort** http://airsnort.shmoo.com/
- **BT Browser** http:// www.BluejackingTools.com
- **BlueScanner** http://sourceforge.net
- **Bluediving** http://bluediving.sourceforge.net
- **SuperBlueTooth Hack** www.brothersoft.com
- **KisMAC** http://kismac.de/
- **NetSurveyor** http://performancewifi.net
- **inSSIDer** www.metageek.net
- **WiFi Pilot** http://cacetech.com
- **OmniPeek** http://wildpackets.com

Web Attacks

- **Wfetch** http://microsoft.com
- **Httprecon** www.computec.ch
- **ID Serve** www.grc.com
- **WebSleuth** http://sandsprite.com
- **BlackWidow** http://softbytelabs.com
- **cURL** http://curl.haxx.se
- **CookieDigger** www.foundstone.com
- **WebScarab** http://owasp.org
- **Nstalker** http://nstalker.com
- **NetBrute** www.rawlogic.com

SQL Injection

- **BSQL Hacker** http://labs.portcullis.co.uk
- **Marathon** http://marathontool.codeplex.com
- **Havil** http://itsecteam.com
- **SQL Injection Brute** http://code.google.com
- **SQL Brute** http://gdssecurity.com
- **SQLNinja** http://sqlninja.sourceforge.net
- **SQLGET** http://darknet.org.uk

Miscellaneous

Pen Test Suites

- **Core Impact** www.coresecurity.com
- **CANVAS** http://immunitysec.com
- **Metasploit** www.metasploit.org
- **Armitage** www.fastandeasyhacking.com
- **Codenomicon** http://codenomicon.com

Extras

- **SysInternals** www.microsoft.com/technet/sysinternals/default.mspx
- **Tripwire** www.tripwire.com/
- **Core Impact Demo** https://coresecurity.webex.com/ec0605lc/eventcenter/
  recording/recordAction.do;jsessionid=l2T1N8Lc1nQ6HHsxy0qcv8NxyFT2kV
  GvBB5LJq6c2mM6X9v2Q9PK!1120902094?theAction=poprecord&actname=
  %2Feventcenter%2Fframe%2Fg.do&apiname=lsr.php&renewticket=0&renewt
  icket=0&actappname=ec0605lc&entappname=url0107lc&needFilter=false&&is
  urlact=true&entactname=%2FnbrRecordingURL.do&rID=12649862&rKey=ab
  1a8bb5a77fe5d3&recordID=12649862&rnd=7966714724&siteurl=coresecurit
  y&SP=EC&AT=pb&format=short

Linux Distributions

- **Distrowatch** http://distrowatch.com
- **BackTrack** www.remote-exploit.org/index.php/BackTrack

Tools, Sites, and References Disclaimer

All URLs listed in this appendix were current and live at the time of publication. Mc-Graw-Hill makes no warranty as to the availability of these World Wide Web or Internet pages. McGraw-Hill has not reviewed or approved the accuracy of the contents of these pages and specifically disclaims any warranties of merchantability or fitness for a particular purpose.

About the CD

The CD-ROM included with this book comes complete with MasterExam and the electronic version of the book. The software is easy to install on any Windows 2000/XP/Vista or Windows 7 computer and must be installed to access the MasterExam feature. You may, however, browse the electronic book directly from the CD without installation. To register for the bonus MasterExam, simply click the Bonus MasterExam link on the main launch page and follow the directions to the free online registration.

System Requirements

Software requires Windows 2000 or higher and Internet Explorer 6.0 or above and 20MB of hard disk space for full installation. The electronic book requires Adobe Acrobat Reader (included on the CD).

Installing and Running MasterExam

If your computer CD-ROM drive is configured to auto-run, the CD-ROM will automatically start up upon inserting the disc. From the opening screen you may install MasterExam by clicking the MasterExam link. This will begin the installation process and create a program group named LearnKey. To run MasterExam, use Start | All Programs | LearnKey | MasterExam. If the auto-run feature did not launch your CD, browse to the CD and click the LaunchTraining.exe icon.

MasterExam

MasterExam provides you with a simulation of the actual exam. The number of questions, the type of questions, and the time allowed are intended to be an accurate representation of the exam environment. You have the option to take an open-book exam (including hints, references, and answers), a closed book exam, or the timed MasterExam simulation.

When you launch MasterExam, a digital clock display will appear in the bottom-right corner of your screen. The clock will continue to count down to zero unless you choose to end the exam before the time expires.

Electronic Book

The entire contents of the *Exam Guide* are provided in PDF. Adobe's Acrobat Reader has been included on the CD.

Help

A help file is provided through the help button, located in the lower-left corner of the main page. An individual help feature is also available through MasterExam.

Removing Installation(s)

MasterExam is installed to your hard drive. For best results removing programs, use the Start | All Programs | LearnKey| Uninstall option to remove MasterExam.

Technical Support

For questions regarding the content of the electronic book or MasterExam, please visit www.mhprofessional.com or e-mail customer.service@mcgraw-hill.com. For customers outside the 50 United States, e-mail international_cs@mcgraw-hill.com.

LearnKey Technical Support

For technical problems with the software (installation, operation, removing installations), please visit www.learnkey.com, e-mail techsupport@learnkey.com, or call toll free at 1-800-482-8244.

802.11 Wireless LAN standards created by IEEE. 802.11a runs at up to 54Mbps at 5GHz, 802.11b runs at 11Mbps at 2.4GHz, 802.11g runs at 54Mbps at 2.4GHz, and 802.11n can run upwards of 150Mbps.

802.11i A wireless LAN security standard developed by IEEE. Requires Temporal Key Integrity Protocol (TKIP) and Advanced Encryption Standard (AES).

Acceptable Use Policy (AUP) Policy stating what users of a system can and cannot do with the organization's assets.

Access Control List (ACL) A method of defining what rights and permissions an entity has to a given resource. In networking, Access Control Lists are commonly associated with firewall and router traffic filtering rules.

access creep Occurs when authorized users accumulate excess privileges on a system due to moving from one position to another; allowances accidentally remain with the account from position to position.

access point (AP) A wireless LAN device that acts as a central point for all wireless traffic. The AP is connected to both the wireless LAN and the wired LAN, providing wireless clients access to network resources.

accountability The ability to trace actions performed on a system to a specific user or system entity.

acknowledgment (ACK) A TCP flag notifying an originating station that the preceding packet (or packets) has been received.

active attack An attack that is direct in nature—usually where the attacker injects something into, or otherwise alters, the network or system target.

Active Directory (AD) The directory service created by Microsoft for use on its networks. Provides a variety of network services using Lightweight Directory Access Protocol (LDAP), Kerberos-based authentication, and single sign-on for user access to network-based resources.

active fingerprinting   Injecting traffic into the network to identify the operating system of a device.

ad hoc mode   A mode of operation in a wireless LAN in which clients send data directly to one another without utilizing a wireless access point (WAP), much like a point-to-point wired connection.

Address Resolution Protocol (ARP)   Defined in RFC 826, ARP is a protocol used to map a known IP address to a physical (MAC) address.

Address Resolution Protocol (ARP) table   A list of IP addresses and corresponding MAC addresses stored on a local computer.

adware   Software that has advertisements embedded within. Generally displays ads in the form of pop-ups.

algorithm   A step-by-step method of solving a problem. In computing security, an algorithm is a set of mathematical rules (logic) for the process of encryption and decryption.

annualized loss expectancy (ALE)   The monetary loss that can be expected for an asset due to risk over a one-year period. ALE is the product of the annual rate of occurrence (ARO) and the single loss expectancy (SLE). It is mathematically expressed as ALE = ARO × SLE.

anonymizer   A device or service designed to obfuscate traffic between a client and the Internet. Generally used to make activity on the Internet as untraceable as possible.

antivirus (AV) software   An application that monitors a computer or network to identify, and prevent, malware. AV is usually signature-based, and can take multiple actions on defined malware files/activity.

Application layer   Layer 7 of the OSI reference model. The Application layer provides services to applications, which allow them access to the network. Protocols such as FTP and SMTP reside here.

application-level attacks   Attacks on the actual programming code of an application.

archive   A collection of historical records or the place where they are kept. In computing, an archive generally refers to backup copies of logs and/or data.

assessment   Activities to determine the extent to which a security control is implemented correctly, operating as intended, and producing the desired outcome with respect to meeting the security requirements for the system.

asset   Any item of value or worth to an organization, whether physical or virtual.

asymmetric   Literally, "not balanced or the same." In computing, asymmetric refers to a difference in networking speeds upstream to downstream. In cryptography, it's the use of more than one key for encryption/authentication purposes.

asymmetric algorithm   In computer security, this is an algorithm that uses separate keys for encryption and decryption.

asynchronous   The lack of clocking (imposed time ordering) on a bit stream.

asynchronous transmission   The transmission of digital signals without precise clocking or synchronization.

audit   Independent review and examination of records and activities to assess the adequacy of system controls, to ensure compliance with established policies and operational procedures, and to recommend necessary changes.

audit data   Chronological record of system activities to enable the reconstruction and examination of the sequence of events and changes in an event.

audit trail   A record showing which user has accessed a given resource and what operations the user performed during a given period.

auditing   The process of recording activity on a system for monitoring and later review.

authentication   The process of determining if a network entity (user or service) is legitimate—usually accomplished through a user ID and password. Authentication measures are categorized by something you know (user ID and password), something you have (smart card or token), or something you are (biometrics).

Authentication, Authorization, and Accounting (AAA)   Authentication confirms the identity of the user or device. Authorization determines the privileges (rights) of the user or device. Accounting records the access attempts, both successful and unsuccessful.

authentication header (AH)   An Internet Protocol Security (IPSec) header used to verify that the contents of a packet have not been modified while the packet was in transit.

authorization   The conveying of official access or legal power to a person or entity.

availability   The condition of a resource being ready for use and accessible by authorized users.

backdoor   Whether purposeful or the result of malware or other attack, a backdoor is a hidden capability in a system or program for bypassing normal computer authentication systems.

banner grabbing   An enumeration technique used to provide information about a computer system; generally used for operating system identification (also known as fingerprinting).

baseline   A point of reference used to mark an initial state in order to manage change.

bastion host   A computer placed outside a firewall to provide public services to other Internet sites, and hardened to resist external attacks.

biometrics   A measurable, physical characteristic used to recognize the identity, or verify the claimed identity, of an applicant. Facial images, fingerprints, and handwriting samples are all examples of biometrics.

bit flipping   A cryptographic attack where bits are manipulated in the ciphertext itself to generate a predictable outcome in the plaintext once it is decrypted.

black box testing   In penetration testing, this is a method of testing the security of a system or subnet without any previous knowledge of the device or network. Designed to simulate an attack by an outside intruder (usually from the Internet).

black hat   An attacker who breaks into computer systems with malicious intent, without the owner's knowledge or permission.

block cipher   A symmetric key cryptographic algorithm that transforms a block of information at a time using a cryptographic key. For a block cipher algorithm, the length of the input block is the same as the length of the output block.

Blowfish   A symmetric, block-cipher data-encryption standard that uses a variable-length key that can range from 32 bits to 448 bits.

Bluejacking   Sending unsolicited messages over Bluetooth to Bluetooth-enabled devices such as mobile phones, PDAs, or laptop computers.

Bluesnarfing   Unauthorized access to information such as a calendar, contact list, e-mails, and text messages on a wireless device through a Bluetooth connection.

Bluetooth   A proprietary, open, wireless technology used for transferring data from fixed and mobile devices over short distances.

boot sector virus   A virus that plants itself in a system's boot sector and infects the master boot record.

brute-force password attack   A method of password cracking whereby all possible options are systematically enumerated until a match is found. These attacks try every password (or authentication option), one after another, until successful. Brute-force attacks take a long time to work and are easily detectable.

buffer   A portion of memory used to temporarily store output or input data.

buffer overflow   A condition that occurs when more data is written to a buffer than it has space to store, and results in data corruption or other system errors. This is usually due to insufficient bounds checking, a bug, or improper configuration in the program code.

bug   A software or hardware defect that often results in system vulnerabilities.

cache   A storage buffer that transparently stores data so future requests for the same data can be served faster.

CAM table   Content Addressable Memory table. Holds all the MAC-address-to-port mappings on a switch.

certificate   Also known as a digital certificate, this is an electronic file used to verify a user's identity, providing non-repudiation throughout the system It is also a set of data that uniquely identifies an entity. Certificates contain the entity's public key, serial number, version, subject, algorithm type, issuer, valid dates, and key usage details.

Certificate Authority (CA)   A trusted entity that issues and revokes public key certificates. In a network, a CA is a trusted entity that issues, manages, and revokes security credentials and public keys for message encryption and/or authentication. Within a public key infrastructure (PKI), the CA works with registration authorities (RAs) to verify information provided by the requestor of a digital certificate.

Challenge Handshake Authentication Protocol (CHAP)   An authentication method on point-to-point links, using a three-way handshake and a mutually agreed-upon key.

CIA triangle   Confidentiality, Integrity, and Availability are the three aspects of security and make up the triangle.

ciphertext   Text or data in its encrypted form; the result of plaintext being input into a cryptographic algorithm.

client   A computer process that requests a service from another computer and accepts the server's responses.

cloning   A cell phone attack in which the serial number from one cell phone is copied to another in an effort to copy the cell phone.

CNAME record   A Canonical Name record within DNS, used to provide an alias for a domain name.

cold site   A backup facility with the electrical and physical components of a computer facility, but with no computer equipment in place. The site is ready to receive the necessary replacement computer equipment in the event the user has to move from his main computing location to an alternate site.

collision   In regard to hash algorithms, this occurs when two or more distinct inputs produce the same output.

collision domain   A domain composed of all the systems sharing any given physical transport media. Systems within a collision domain may collide with each other during the transmission of data. Collisions can be managed by CSMA/CD (collision detection) or CSMA/CA (collision avoidance).

Common Internet File System/Server Message Block   An Application layer protocol used primarily by Microsoft Windows to provide shared access to printers, files, and serial ports. It also provides an authenticated interprocess communication mechanism.

community string   A string used for authentication in SNMP. The public community string is used for read-only searches, whereas the private community string is used for read/write. Community strings are transmitted in clear text in SNMPv1. SNMPv3 provides encryption for the strings as well as other improvements and options.

competitive intelligence   Freely and readily available information on an organization that can be gathered by a business entity about its competitor's customers, products, and marketing, and can be used by an attacker to build useful information for further attacks.

computer-based attack   A social-engineering attack using computer resources, such as e-mail or IRC.

Computer Emergency Response Team (CERT)   Name given to expert groups that handle computer security incidents.

confidentiality   A security objective that ensures a resource can be accessed only by authorized users. This is also the property that sensitive information is not disclosed to unauthorized individuals, entities, or processes.

console port   Physical socket provided on routers and switches for cable connections between a computer and the router/switch. This connection enables the computer to configure, query, and troubleshoot the router/switch by use of a terminal emulator and a command-line interface.

contingency plan   Management policy and procedures designed to maintain or restore business operations, including computer operations, possibly at an alternate location, in the event of emergencies, system failures, or disaster.

cookie   A text file stored within a browser by a web server that maintains information about the connection. Cookies are used to store information to maintain a unique but consistent surfing experience, but can also contain authentication parameters. Cookies can be encrypted and have defined expiration dates.

copyright   A set of exclusive rights granted by the law of a jurisdiction to the author or creator of an original work, including the right to copy, distribute, and adapt the work.

corrective controls   Controls internal to a system designed to resolve vulnerabilities and errors soon after they arise.

countermeasures   Actions, devices, procedures, techniques, or other measures intended to reduce the vulnerability of an information system.

covert channel   A communications channel that is being used for a purpose it was not intended for, usually to transfer information secretly.

cracker   A cyber attacker who acts without permission from, and gives no prior notice to, the resource owner. Also known as a malicious hacker.

crossover error rate (CER)   A comparison metric for different biometric devices and technologies; the point at which the false acceptance rate (FAR) equals the false rejection rate (FRR). As an identification device becomes more sensitive or accurate, its FAR decreases while its FRR increases. The CER is the point at which these two rates are equal, or cross over.

cross-site scripting (XSS)   An attack whereby the hacker injects code into an otherwise legitimate web page, which is then clicked on by other users or is exploited via Java or some other script method. The embedded code within the link is submitted as part of the client's web request and can execute on the user's computer.

cryptographic key   A value used to control cryptographic operations, such as decryption, encryption, signature generation, and signature verification.

cryptography   The science or study of protecting information, whether in transit or at rest, by using techniques to render the information unusable to anyone who does not possess the means to decrypt it.

daemon   A background process found in Unix, Linux, Solaris, and other Unix-based operating systems.

daisy chaining   A method of external testing whereby several systems or resources are used together to effect an attack.

database   An organized collection of data.

Data Encryption Standard (DES)   An outdated symmetric cipher encryption algorithm, previously U.S. government–approved and used by business and civilian government agencies. DES is no longer considered secure due to the ease with which the entire keyspace can be attempted using modern computing, thus making cracking of the encryption very easy.

Data Link layer   Layer 2 of the OSI reference model. This layer provides reliable transit of data across a physical link. The Data Link layer is concerned with physical addressing, network topology, access to the network medium, error detection, sequential delivery of frames, and flow control. The Data Link layer is composed of two sublayers: the MAC and the LLC.

decryption   The process of transforming ciphertext into plaintext through the use of a cryptographic algorithm.

defense in depth   An information assurance strategy in which multiple layers of defense are placed throughout an Information Technology system.

demilitarized zone (DMZ)   A partially protected zone on a network, not exposed to the full fury of the Internet, but not fully behind the firewall. This technique is typically used on parts of the network that must remain open to the public (such as a web server) but must also access trusted resources (such as a database). The point is to allow the inside firewall component, guarding the trusted resources, to make certain assumptions about the impossibility of outsiders forging DMZ addresses.

denial of service (DoS)   An attack with the goal of preventing authorized users from accessing services and preventing the normal operation of computers and networks.

detective controls   Controls to detect anomalies or undesirable events occurring on a system.

digital certificate   Also known as a public key certificate, this is an electronic file that is used to verify a user's identity, providing non-repudiation throughout the system. Certificates contain the entity's public key, serial number, version, subject, algorithm type, issuer, valid dates, and key usage details.

digital signature   The result of using a private key to encrypt a hash value for identification purposes within a PKI system. The signature can be decoded by the originator's public key, verifying his identity and providing non-repudiation. A valid digital signature gives a recipient verification the message was created by a known sender.

digital watermarking   The process of embedding information into a digital signal in a way that makes it difficult to remove.

directory traversal   Also known as the *dot-dot-slash attack*. Using directory traversal, the attacker attempts to access restricted directories and execute commands outside intended web server directories by using the URL to redirect to an unintended folder location.

discretionary access control (DAC)   The basis of this kind of security is that an individual user, or program operating on the user's behalf, is allowed to specify explicitly the types of access other users (or programs executing on their behalf) may have to information under the user's control.

distributed DoS (DDoS)   A denial-of-service technique that uses numerous hosts to perform the attack.

DNS enumeration   The process of using easily accessible DNS records to map a target network's internal hosts.

domain name   A unique hostname that is used to identify resources on the Internet. Domain names start with a root (.), then add a top level (.com, .gov, or .mil, for example), and a given name space.

Domain Name System (DNS)   A network system of servers that translates numeric Internet Protocol (IP) addresses into human-friendly, hierarchical Internet addresses, and vice versa.

Domain Name System (DNS) cache poisoning   An attack technique that tricks your DNS server into believing it has received authentic information when, in reality, it has been provided fraudulent data. DNS cache poisoning affects user traffic by sending it to erroneous or malicious end points instead of its intended destination.

Domain Name System (DNS) lookup   The process of a system providing a fully qualified domain name (FQDN) to a local name server, for resolution to its corresponding IP address.

droppers   Malware designed to install some sort of virus, backdoor, and so on, on a target system.

due care A term representing the responsibility managers and their organizations have to provide information security to ensure the type of control, the cost of control, and the deployment of control are appropriate for the system being managed.

due diligence Steps taken to identify and limit risks to an acceptable or reasonable level of exposure.

dumpster diving A physical security attack where the attacker sifts through garbage and recycle bins for information that may be useful on current and future attacks.

eavesdropping The act of secretly listening to the private conversations of others without their consent. This can also be done over telephone lines (wiretapping), e-mail, instant messaging, and other methods of communication considered private.

ECHO reply A type 0 ICMP message used to reply to ECHO requests. Used with ping to verify network layer connectivity between hosts.

EDGAR database A system used by the Securities and Exchange Commission (SEC) for companies and businesses to transmit required filings and information. The EDGAR database performs automated collection, validation, indexing, acceptance, and forwarding of submissions by companies and others who are required by law to file forms with the U.S. Securities and Exchange Commission. The database is freely available to the public via the Internet and is a potential source of information for hackers.

Electronic Code Book (ECB) A mode of operation for a block cipher, with the characteristic that each possible block of plaintext has a defined corresponding ciphertext value, and vice versa.

electronic serial number Created by the U.S. Federal Communications Commission to uniquely identify mobile devices; often represented as an 11-digit decimal number or eight-digit hexadecimal number.

encapsulation The process of attaching a particular protocol header and trailer to a unit of data before transmission on the network. Occurs at layer 2 of the OSI reference model.

encryption Conversion of plaintext to ciphertext through the use of a cryptographic algorithm.

End User Licensing Agreement (EULA) A software license agreement; a contract between the "licensor" and purchaser establishing the right to use the software.

enumeration In penetration testing, enumeration is the act of querying a device or network segment thoroughly and systematically for information.

Ethernet   Baseband LAN specification developed by Xerox Corporation, Intel, and Digital Equipment Corporation. One of the least expensive, most widely deployed networking standards; uses the CSMA/CD method of media access control.

ethical hacker   A computer security expert who performs security audits and penetration tests against systems or network segments, with the owner's full knowledge and permission, in an effort to increase security.

event   Any network incident that prompts some kind of log entry or other notification.

exploit   Software code, a portion of data, or sequence of commands intended to take advantage of a bug or vulnerability in order to cause unintended or unanticipated behavior to occur on computer software or hardware.

exposure factor   The subjective, potential percentage of loss to a specific asset if a specific threat is realized. The exposure factor (EF) is a subjective value the person assessing risk must define.

Extensible Authentication Protocol (EAP)   Originally an extension of PPP, EAP is a protocol for authentication used within wireless networks. Works with multiple authentication measures.

false acceptance rate (FAR)   The rate at which a biometric system will incorrectly identify an unauthorized individual and allow them access (see false negative).

false negative   A situation in which an IDS does not trigger on an event that was an intrusion attempt. False negatives are considered more dangerous than false positives.

false positive   A situation in which an IDS or other sensor triggers on an event as an intrusion attempt, when it was actually legitimate traffic.

false rejection rate (FRR)   The rate at which a biometric system will incorrectly reject an access attempt by an authorized user.

Fast Ethernet   An Ethernet networking system transmitting data at 100 million bits per second (Mbps), 10 times the speed of an earlier Ethernet standard. Derived from the Ethernet 802.3 standard, it is also known as 100BaseT.

Fiber Distributed Data Interface (FDDI)   LAN standard, defined by ANSI X3T9.5, specifying a 100Mbps token-passing network using fiber-optic cable and a dual-ring architecture for redundancy, with transmission distances of up to two kilometers.

File Allocation Table (FAT)   A computer file system architecture used in Windows, OS/2, and most memory cards.

File Transfer Protocol (FTP)   An Application layer protocol, using TCP, for transporting files across an Internet connection. FTP transmits in clear text.

filter   A set of rules defined to screen network packets based on source address, destination address, or protocol; these rules determine whether the packet will be forwarded or discarded.

Finger   An early network application that provides information on users currently logged on to a machine.

firewalking   The process of systematically testing each port on a firewall to map rules and determine accessible ports.

firewall   Software or hardware components that restrict access between a protected network and the Internet, or between other sets of networks, to block unwanted use or attacks.

flood   Traffic-passing technique used by bridges and switches in which traffic received on an interface is sent out all interfaces on the device except the interface on which the information was originally received. Traffic on a switch is flooded when it is broadcast in nature (intended for a broadcast address, as with ARP or other protocols) or if the switch does not have an entry in the CAM table for the destination MAC.

footprinting   All measures and techniques taken to gather information about an intended target. Footprinting can be passive or active.

forwarding   The process of sending a packet or frame toward the destination. In a switch, messages are forwarded only to the port they are addressed to.

fragmentation   Process of breaking a packet into smaller units when it is being transmitted over a network medium that's unable to support a transmission unit the original size of the packet.

FreeBSD   A free and popular version of the Unix operating system.

fully qualified domain name (FQDN)   A fully qualified domain name consists of a host and domain name, including a top-level domain such as .com, .net, .mil, .edu, and so on.

gap analysis   A tool that helps a company to compare its actual performance with its potential performance.

gateway   A device that provides access between two or more networks. Gateways are typically used to connect dissimilar networks.

GET   A command used in HTTP and FTP to retrieve a file from a server.

Google hacking   Manipulating a search string with additional specific operators to search for vulnerabilities or very specific information.

gray box testing   A penetration test in which the ethical hacker has limited knowledge of the intended target(s). Designed to simulate an internal, but non-system-administrator-level attack.

gray hat   A skilled hacker that straddles the line between white hat (hacking only with permission and within guidelines) and black hat (malicious hacking for personal gain). Gray hats sometime perform illegal acts to exploit technology with the intent of achieving better security.

hacktivism   The act or actions of a hacker to put forward a cause or a political agenda, to affect some societal change, or to shed light on something he feels to be political injustice. These activities are usually illegal in nature.

halo effect   A well-known and studied phenomenon of human nature, whereby a single trait influences the perception of other traits.

hardware keystroke logger   A hardware device used to log keystrokes covertly. Hardware keystroke loggers are very dangerous due to the fact that they cannot be detected through regular software/anti-malware scanning.

hash   A unique numerical string, created by a hashing algorithm on a given piece of data, used to verify data integrity. Generally hashes are used to verify the integrity of files after download (comparison to the hash value on the site before download) and/or to store password values.

hashing algorithm   A one-way mathematical function that generates a fixed-length numerical string (hash) from a given data input. MD5 and SHA-1 are hashing algorithms.

heuristic scanning   Method used by antivirus software to detect new, unknown viruses that have not yet been identified; based on a piece-by-piece examination of a program, looking for a sequence or sequences of instructions that differentiate the virus from "normal" programs.

HIDS   Host-based IDS. An IDS that resides on the host, protecting against file and folder manipulation and other host-based attacks and actions.

Hierarchical File System (HFS)   A file system used by the Mac OS.

honeynet   A network deployed as a trap to detect, deflect, or deter unauthorized use of information systems.

honeypot   A host designed to collect data on suspicious activity.

hot site   A fully operational off-site data-processing facility equipped with hardware and system software to be used in the event of a disaster.

HTTP tunneling   A firewall evasion technique whereby packets are wrapped in HTTP, as a covert channel to the target.

human-based social engineering   Using conversation or some other interaction between people to gather useful information.

hybrid attack   An attack that combines a brute-force attack with a dictionary attack.

Hypertext Transfer Protocol (HTTP)   A communications protocol used for browsing the Internet.

Hypertext Transfer Protocol Secure (HTTPS)   A hybrid of the HTTP and SSL/TLS protocols that provides encrypted communication and secure identification of a web server.

identity theft   A form of fraud in which someone pretends to be someone else by assuming that person's identity, typically in order to access resources or obtain credit and other benefits in that person's name.

impersonation   A social-engineering effort in which the attacker pretends to be an employee, a valid user, or even an executive to elicit information or access.

inference attack   An attack in which the hacker can derive information from the ciphertext without actually decoding it. Sensitive information can be considered compromised if an adversary can infer its real value with a high level of confidence.

Information Technology (IT) asset criticality   The level of importance assigned to an IT asset.

Information Technology (IT) asset valuation   The monetary value assigned to an IT asset.

Information Technology (IT) infrastructure   The combination of all IT assets, resources, components, and systems.

Information Technology (IT) security architecture and framework   A document describing information security guidelines, policies, procedures, and standards.

Information Technology Security Evaluation Criteria (ITSEC)   A structured set of criteria for evaluating computer security within products and systems produced by European countries; it has been largely replaced by the Common Criteria.

infrastructure mode   A wireless networking mode where all clients connect to the wireless network through a central access point.

initial sequence number (ISN)   A number assigned during TCP startup sessions that tracks how much information has been moved. This number is used by hackers when hijacking sessions.

Institute of Electrical and Electronics Engineers (IEEE)   An organization composed of engineers, scientists, and students who issue standards related to electrical, electronic, and computer engineering.

integrity   The security property that data is not modified in an unauthorized and undetected manner. Also, the principle and measures taken to ensure that data received is in the exact same condition and state as when it was originally transmitted.

Interior Gateway Protocol (IGP)   An Internet routing protocol used to exchange routing information within an autonomous system.

International Organization for Standardization (ISO)   An international organization composed of national standards bodies from over 75 countries. Developed the OSI reference model.

Internet Assigned Number Authority (IANA)   The organization that governs the Internet's top-level domains, IP address allocation, and port number assignments.

Internet Control Message Protocol (ICMP)   A protocol used to pass control and error messages between nodes on the Internet.

Internet Protocol (IP)   A protocol for transporting data packets across a packet switched internetwork (such as the Internet). IP is a routed protocol.

Internet Protocol Security (IPSec) architecture   A suite of protocols used for securing Internet Protocol (IP) communications by authenticating and encrypting each IP packet of a communication session. This suite includes protocols for establishing mutual authentication between agents at the session establishment and negotiation of cryptographic keys to be used throughout the session.

Internet service provider (ISP)   A business, government agency, or educational institution that provides access to the Internet.

intranet   A self-contained network with a limited number of participants who extend limited trust to one another in order to accomplish an agreed-upon goal.

Interior Gateway Protocol (IGP)   A routing protocol developed to be used within a single organization.

intrusion detection system (IDS)   A security tool designed to protect a system or network against attacks by comparing traffic patterns against a list of both known attack signatures and general characteristics of how attacks may be carried out. Threats are rated and reported.

intrusion prevention system (IPS)   A security tool designed to protect a system or network against attacks by comparing traffic patterns against a list of both known attack signatures and general characteristics of how attacks may be carried out. Threats are rated and protective measures taken to prevent the more significant threats.

iris scanner   A biometric device that uses pattern-recognition techniques based on images of the irises of an individual's eyes.

ISO 17799   A standard that provides best-practice recommendations on information security management for use by those responsible for initiating, implementing, or maintaining Information Security Management Systems (ISMS). Information security is defined within the standard in the context of the CIA triangle.

Kerberos   A widely used authentication protocol developed at the Massachusetts Institute of Technology (MIT). Kerberos authentication uses tickets, Ticket Granting Service, and Key Distribution Center.

key exchange protocol   A method in cryptography by which cryptographic keys are exchanged between users, allowing use of a cryptographic algorithm (for example, the Diffie-Hellman key exchange).

keylogger   A software or hardware application or device that captures user keystrokes.

Last In First Out (LIFO)   A programming principle whereby the last piece of data added to the stack is the first piece of data taken off.

Level I assessment   An evaluation consisting of a document review, interviews, and demonstrations. No hands-on testing is performed.

Level II assessment   An evaluation consisting of a document review, interviews, and demonstrations, as well as vulnerability scans and hands-on testing.

Level III assessment   An evaluation in which testers attempt to penetrate the network.

Lightweight Directory Access Protocol (LDAP)   An industry standard protocol used for accessing and managing information within a directory service; an application protocol for querying and modifying data using directory services running over TCP/IP.

limitation of liability and remedies   A legal limit on the amount of financial liability and remedies the organization is responsible for taking on.

local area network (LAN)   A computer network confined to a relatively small area, such as a single building or campus.

logic bomb   A piece of code intentionally inserted into a software system that will perform a malicious function when specified conditions are met at some future point.

MAC filtering   A method of permitting only MAC addresses in a preapproved list network access. Addresses not matching are blocked.

macro virus   A virus written in a macro language and usually embedded in document or spreadsheet files.

malicious code   Software or firmware intended to perform an unauthorized process that will have an adverse impact on the confidentiality, integrity, or availability of an information system. A virus, worm, Trojan horse, or other code-based entity that infects a host.

malware   A program or piece of code inserted into a system, usually covertly, with the intent of compromising the confidentiality, integrity, or availability of the victim's data, applications, or operating system. Malware consists of viruses, worms, and other malicious code.

man-in-the-middle attack   An attack where the hacker positions himself between the client and the server, to intercept (and sometimes alter) data traveling between the two.

mandatory access control (MAC)   A means of restricting access to system resources based on the sensitivity (as represented by a label) of the information contained in the system resource and the formal authorization (that is, clearance) of users to access information of such sensitivity.

mantrap   A small space having two sets of interlocking doors; the first set of doors must close before the second set opens. Typically authentication is required for each door, often using different factors. For example, a smart card may open the first door and a personal identification number entered on a number pad opens the second.

master boot record infector   A virus designed to infect the master boot record.

MD5   A hashing algorithm that results in a 128-bit output.

Media Access Control (MAC)   A sublayer of layer 2 of the OSI model, the Data Link layer. It provides addressing and channel access control mechanisms that enable several terminals or network nodes to communicate within a multipoint network.

methodology   A documented process for a procedure designed to be consistent, repeatable, and accountable.

minimum acceptable level of risk   An organization's threshold for the seven areas of information security responsibility. This level is established based on the objectives for maintaining confidentiality, integrity, and availability of the organization's IT assets and infrastructure and will determine the resources expended for information security.

multipartite virus   A computer virus that infects and spreads in multiple ways.

Multipurpose Internet Mail Extensions (MIME)   An extensible mechanism for e-mail. A variety of MIME types exist for sending content such as audio, binary, or video using the Simple Mail Transfer Protocol (SMTP).

National Security Agency (NSA) INFOSEC Assessment Methodology (IAM)   A systematic process for the assessment of security vulnerabilities.

NetBSD   A free, open source version of the Berkeley Software Distribution of Unix, often used in embedded systems.

NetBus   A software program for remotely controlling a Microsoft Windows computer system over a network. Generally considered malware.

network access server   A device providing temporary, on-demand, point-to-point network access to users.

Network Address Translation (NAT)   A technology where you advertise one IP address externally and data packets are rerouted to the appropriate IP address inside your network by a device providing translation services. In this way, IP addresses of machines on your internal network are hidden from external users.

Network Basic Input/Output System (NetBIOS)   An API that provides services related to the OSI model's Session layer, allowing applications on separate computers to communicate over a LAN.

network interface card (NIC) An adapter that provides the physical connection to send and receive data between the computer and the network media.

network operations center (NOC) One or more locations from which control is exercised over a computer, television broadcast, or telecommunications network.

network tap Any kind of connection that allows you to see all traffic passing by. Generally used in reference to a NIDS (network-based IDS) to monitor all traffic.

node A device on a network.

non-repudiation The means by which a recipient of a message can ensure the identity of the sender and that neither party can deny having sent or received the message. The most common method is through digital certificates.

NOP A command that instructs the system processor to do nothing. Many overflow attacks involve stringing several NOP operations together (known as a NOP sled).

nslookup A network administration command-line tool available for many operating systems for querying the Domain Name System (DNS) to obtain domain name or IP address mappings or any other specific DNS record.

NT LAN Manager (NTLM) The default network authentication suite of protocols for Windows NT 4.0—retained in later versions for backward compatibility. NTLM is considered insecure and was replaced by NTLMv2.

null session An anonymous connection to an administrative share (IPC$) on a Windows machine. Null sessions allow for enumeration of Windows machines, among other attacks.

open source Describes practices in production and development that promote access to the end product's source materials.

Open System Interconnection (OSI) Reference Model A network architecture framework developed by ISO that describes the communications process between two systems across the Internet in seven distinct layers.

OpenBSD A Unix-like computer operating system descending from the BSD. OpenBSD includes a number of security features absent or optional in other operating systems.

operating system attack An attack that exploits the common mistake many people make when installing operating systems—that is, accepting and leaving all the defaults.

out-of-band signaling Transmission using channels or frequencies outside those normally used for data transfer; often used for error reporting.

overt channel A communications path, such as the Internet, authorized for data transmission within a computer system or network.

packet A unit of information formatted according to specific protocols that allows precise transmittal of data from one network node to another. Also called a datagram or data packet, a packet contains a header (container) and a payload (contents). Any IP message larger than 1,500 bytes will be fragmented into packets for transmission.

packet filtering Controlling access to a network by analyzing the headers of incoming and outgoing packets, and letting them pass or discarding them based on rule sets created by a network administrator. A packet filter allows or denies packets based on destination, source, and/or port.

Packet Internet Groper (ping) A utility that sends an ICMP Echo message to determine if a specific IP address is accessible; if the message receives a reply, the address is reachable.

parameter tampering An attack where the hacker manipulates parameters within the URL string in hopes of modifying data.

passive attack An attack against an authentication protocol in which the attacker intercepts data in transit along the network between the claimant and verifier, but does not alter the data (in other words, eavesdropping).

Password Authentication Protocol (PAP) A simple PPP authentication mechanism in which the user name and password are transmitted in clear text to prove identity. PAP compares the user name and password to a table listing authorized users.

patch A piece of software, provided by the vendor, intended to update or fix known, discovered problems in a computer program or its supporting data.

pattern matching The act of checking some sequence of tokens for the presence of the constituents of some pattern.

payload The contents of a packet. A system attack requires the attacker to deliver a malicious payload that is acted upon and executed by the system.

penetration testing A method of evaluating the security of a computer system or network by simulating an attack from a malicious source.

personal identification number (PIN) A secret, typically consisting of only decimal digits, that a claimant memorizes and uses to authenticate his identity.

phishing The use of deceptive computer-based means to trick individuals into disclosing sensitive personal information—usually via a carefully crafted e-mail message.

physical security Security measures, such as a locked door, perimeter fence, or security guard, to prevent or deter physical access to a facility, resource, or information stored on physical media.

piggybacking When an authorized person allows (intentionally or unintentionally) someone to pass through a secure door, despite the fact that the intruder does not have a badge.

ping sweep The process of pinging each address within a subnet to map potential targets. Ping sweeps are unreliable and easily detectable, but very fast.

polymorphic virus Malicious code that uses a polymorphic engine to mutate while keeping the original algorithm intact; the code changes itself each time it runs, but the function of the code will not change.

Point-to-Point Protocol (PPP) Provides router-to-router or host-to-network connections over asynchronous and synchronous circuits.

Point-to-Point Tunneling Protocol (PPTP) A VPN tunneling protocol with encryption. PPTP connects two nodes in a VPN by using one TCP port for negotiation and authentication and one IP protocol for data transfer.

Port Address Translation (PAT) A NAT method in which multiple internal hosts, using private IP addressing, can be mapped through a single public IP address using the session IDs and port numbers. An internal global IP address can support in excess of 65,000 concurrent TCP and UDP connections.

port scanning The process of using an application to remotely identify open ports on a system (for example, whether systems allow connections through those ports).

port knocking Another term for firewalking—the method of externally testing ports on a firewall by generating a connection attempt on each port, one by one.

port redirection Directing a protocol from one port to another.

POST An HTTP command to transmit text to a web server for processing. The opposite of an HTTP GET.

Post Office Protocol 3 (POP3) An Application layer protocol used by local e-mail clients to retrieve e-mail from a remote server over a TCP/IP connection.

Presentation layer Layer 6 of the OSI reference model. The Presentation layer ensures information sent by the Application layer of the sending system will be readable by the Application layer of the receiving system.

Pretty Good Privacy (PGP) A data encryption/decryption program often used for e-mail and file storage.

private key The secret portion of an asymmetric key pair typically used to decrypt or digitally sign data. The private key is never shared and is always used for decryption, with one notable exception: The private key is used to encrypt the digital signature.

private network address A nonroutable IP address range intended for use only within the confines of a single organization, falling within the predefined ranges of 10.0.0.0, 172.16-31.0.0, or 192.168.0.0.

promiscuous mode A configuration of a network card that makes the card pass all traffic it receives to the central processing unit rather than just frames addressed to it—a feature normally used for packet sniffing and bridged networking for hardware virtualization. Windows machines use WinPcap for this; Linux uses libcap.

protocol A formal set of rules describing data transmission, especially across a network. A protocol determines the type of error checking, the data compression method, how the sending device will indicate completion, how the receiving device will indicate the message was received, and so on.

protocol stack A set of related communications protocols operating together as a group to address communication at some or all of the seven layers of the OSI reference model.

proxy server A device set up to send a response on behalf of an end node to the requesting host. Proxies are generally used to obfuscate the host from the Internet.

public key The public portion of an asymmetric key pair typically used to encrypt data or verify signatures. Public keys are shared and are used to encrypt messages.

public key infrastructure (PKI) A set of hardware, software, people, policies, and procedures needed to create, manage, distribute, use, store, and revoke digital certificates.

qualitative analysis A nonnumerical, subjective risk evaluation. Used with qualitative assessment (an evaluation of risk that results in ratings of none, low, medium, and high for the probability.)

quality of service (QoS) A defined measure of service within a network system—administrators may assign a higher QoS to one host, segment, or type of traffic.

quantitative risk assessment Calculations of two components of risk: R, the magnitude of the potential loss (L), and the probability, p, that the loss will occur.

queue A backlog of packets stored in buffers and waiting to be forwarded over an interface.

Redundant Array of Independent Disks (RAID) Formerly Redundant Array of Inexpensive Disks; a technology that provides increased storage functions and reliability through redundancy. This is achieved by combining multiple disk drive components into a logical unit, where data is distributed across the drives in one of several ways, called RAID levels.

reconnaissance The steps taken to gather evidence and information on the targets you wish to attack.

red team A group of penetration testers that assess the security of an organization, which is often unaware of the existence of the team or the exact assignment.

remote access Access by information systems (or users) communicating from outside the information system security perimeter.

remote procedure call (RPC) A protocol that allows a client computer to request services from a server and the server to return the results.

replay attack An attack where the hacker repeats a portion of a cryptographic exchange in hopes of fooling the system into setting up a communications channel.

reverse lookup; reverse DNS lookup Used to find the domain name associated with an IP address; the opposite of a DNS lookup.

reverse social engineering A social-engineering attack that manipulates the victim into calling the attacker for help.

Request for Comments (RFC)   A series of documents and notes on standards used or proposed for use on the Internet; each is identified by a number.

RID   Resource identifier. The last portion of the SID that identifies the user to the system in Windows. A RID of 500 identifies the administrator account.

Rijndael   An encryption standard designed by Joan Daemen and Vincent Rijmen. Chosen by a NIST contest to be the Advanced Encryption Standard (AES).

ring topology   A networking configuration where all nodes are connected in a circle with no terminated ends on the cable.

risk   The potential for damage to or loss of an IT asset.

risk acceptance   An informed decision to accept the potential for damage to or loss of an IT asset.

risk assessment   An evaluation conducted to determine the potential for damage to or loss of an IT asset.

risk avoidance   A decision to reduce the potential for damage to or loss of an IT asset by taking some type of action.

risk transference   Shifting responsibility from one party to another—for example, through purchasing an insurance policy.

rogue access point   A wireless access point that has either been installed on a secure company network without explicit authorization from a local network administrator, or has been created to allow a hacker to conduct a man-in-the-middle attack.

role-based access control   An approach to restricting system access to authorized users in which roles are created for various job functions. The permissions to perform certain operations are assigned to specific roles. Members of staff (or other system users) are assigned particular roles, and through those role assignments they acquire the permissions to perform particular system functions.

rootkit   A set of tools (applications or code) that enables administrator-level access to a computer or computer network and is designed to obscure the fact that the system has been compromised. Rootkits are dangerous malware entities that provide administrator control of machines to attackers and are difficult to detect and remove.

route   1. The path a packet travels to reach the intended destination. Each individual device along the path traveled is called a hop. 2. Information contained on a device containing instructions for reaching other nodes on the network. This information can be entered dynamically or statically.

routed protocol   A protocol defining packets that are able to be routed by a router.

router   A device that receives and sends data packets between two or more networks; the packet headers and a forwarding table provide the router with the information necessary for deciding which interface to use to forward packets.

Routing Information Protocol (RIP)   A distance-vector routing protocol that employs the hop count as a routing metric. The "hold down time," used to define how long a route is held in memory, is 180 seconds. RIP prevents routing loops by implementing a limit on the number of hops allowed in a path from the source to a destination. The maximum number of hops allowed for RIP is 15. This hop limit, however, also limits the size of networks that RIP can support. A hop count of 16 is considered an infinite distance and is used to deprecate inaccessible, inoperable, or otherwise undesirable routes in the selection process.

Routing Protocol   A standard developed to enable routers to exchange messages containing information about routes to reach subnets in the network.

rule-based access control   A set of rules defined by a system administrator that indicates whether access is allowed or denied to resource objects.

RxBoot   A limited-function version of the Internetworking Operating System (IOS), held in read-only memory in some earlier models of Cisco devices, capable of performing several seldom-needed low-level functions such as loading a new IOS into Flash memory to recover Flash if corrupted or deleted.

SAM   The Security Accounts Manager file in Windows stores all the password hashes for the system.

scope creep   The change or growth of a project's scope.

script kiddie   A derogatory term used to describe an attacker, usually new to the field, who uses simple, easy-to-follow scripts or programs developed by others to attack computer systems and networks and deface websites.

secure channel   A means of exchanging information from one entity to another using a process that does not provide an attacker the opportunity to reorder, delete, insert, or read information.

Secure Multipurpose Mail Extension (S/MIME)   A standard for encrypting and authenticating MIME data; used primarily for Internet e-mail.

Secure Sockets Layer (SSL)   A protocol that uses a private key to encrypt data before transmitting confidential documents over the Internet; widely used on e-commerce, banking, and other sites requiring privacy.

security breach or security incident   The exploitation of a security vulnerability.

security bulletins   An announcement, typically from a software vendor, of a known security vulnerability in a program; often the bulletin contains instructions for the application of a software patch.

security by obscurity   A principle in security engineering that attempts to use anonymity and secrecy (of design, implementation, and so on) to provide security; the footprint of the organization, entity, network, or system is kept as small as possible to avoid interest by hackers. The danger may be that a system relying on security through obscurity may have theoretical or actual security vulnerabilities, but its owners or designers believe the flaws are not known.

security controls   Safeguards or countermeasures to avoid, counteract, or minimize security risks.

security defect   An unknown deficiency in software or some other product that results in a security vulnerability being identified.

security incident response team (SIRT)   A group of experts that handles computer security incidents.

security kernel   The central part of a computer or communications system hardware, firmware, and software that implements the basic security procedures for controlling access to system resources.

segment   A section or subset of the network. Often a router or other routing device provides the end point of the segment.

separation of duties   The concept of having more than one person required to complete a task.

service level agreements (SLAs)   A part of a service contract where the level of service is formally defined; may be required as part of the initial pen test agreements.

Service Set Identifier (SSID)   A value assigned to uniquely identify a single wide area network (WAN) in wireless LANs. SSIDs are broadcast by default, and are sent in the header of every packet. SSIDs provide no encryption or security.

session hijacking   An attack in which a hacker steps between two ends of an already-established communication session and uses specialized tools to guess sequence numbers to take over the channel.

session splicing   A method used to prevent IDS detection by dividing the request into multiple parts that are sent in different packets.

Serial Line Internet Protocol (SLIP)   A protocol for exchanging packets over a serial line.

sheepdip   A stand-alone computer, kept off the network, that is used for scanning potentially malicious media or software.

shoulder surfing   Looking over an authorized user's shoulder in order to steal information (such as authentication information).

shrink-wrap code attacks   Attacks that take advantage of the built-in code and scripts most off-the-shelf applications come with.

SID   Security identifier. The method by which Windows identifies user, group, and computer accounts for rights and permissions.

sidejacking   A hacking method for stealing the cookies used during a session build and replaying them for unauthorized connection purposes.

signature scanning   A method for detecting malicious code on a computer where the files are compared to signatures of known viruses stored in a database.

Sign in Seal   An e-mail protection method using a secret message or image that can be referenced on any official communication with the site; if an e-mail is received without the image or message, the recipient knows it is not legitimate.

Simple Mail Transfer Protocol (SMTP)   An Application layer protocol for sending electronic mail between servers.

Simple Network Management Protocol (SNMP)   An Application layer protocol for managing devices on an IP network.

Simple Object Access Protocol (SOAP)   Used for exchanging structured information, such as XML-based messages, in the implementation of web services.

single loss expectancy (SLE)   The monetary value expected from the occurrence of a risk on an asset. It is mathematically expressed as

single loss expectancy (SLE) = asset value (AV) × exposure factor (EF)

where EF is represented in the impact of the risk over the asset, or percentage of asset lost. As an example, if the AV is reduced two thirds, the exposure factor value is .66. If the asset is completely lost, the EF is 1.0. The result is a monetary value in the same unit as the SLE is expressed.

site survey   An inspection of a place where a company or individual proposes to work, to gather the necessary information for a design or risk assessment.

smart card   A card with a built-in microprocessor and memory used for identification or financial transactions. The card transfers data to and from a central computer when inserted into a reader.

Smurf attack   A denial-of-service attack where the attacker sends a ping to the network's broadcast address from the spoofed IP address of the target. All systems in the subnet then respond to the spoofed address, eventually flooding the device.

sniffer   Computer software or hardware that can intercept and log traffic passing over a digital network.

SOA record   Start of Authority record. This record identifies the primary name server for the zone. The SOA record contains the host name of the server responsible for all DNS records within the namespace, as well as the basic properties of the domain.

social engineering   A nontechnical method of hacking. Social engineering is the art of manipulating people, whether in person (human-based) or via computing methods (computer-based), into providing sensitive information.

source routing   A network traffic management technique designed to allow applications to specify the route a packet will take to a destination, regardless of what the route tables between the two systems say.

spam   An electronic version of junk mail. Unsolicited commercial e-mail sent to numerous recipients.

spoofing   A method of falsely identifying the source of data packets; often used by hackers to make it difficult to trace where an attack originated.

spyware   A type of malware that covertly collects information about a user.

stateful packet filtering   A method of network traffic filtering that monitors the entire communications process, including the originator of the session and from which direction it started.

steganography   The art and science of creating a covert message or image within another message, image, audio, or video file.

stream cipher   A symmetric key cipher where plaintext bits are combined with a pseudo-random cipher bit stream (keystream), typically by an exclusive-or (XOR) operation. In a stream cipher the plaintext digits are encrypted one at a time, and the transformation of successive digits varies during the encryption.

suicide hacker   A hacker who aims to bring down critical infrastructure for a "cause" and does not worry about the penalties associated with his actions.

symmetric algorithm   A class of algorithms for cryptography that use the same cryptographic key for both decryption and encryption.

symmetric encryption   A type of encryption where the same key is used to encrypt and decrypt the message.

SYN attack   A type of denial-of-service attack where a hacker sends thousands of SYN packets to the target with spoofed IP addresses.

SYN flood attack   A type of attack used to deny service to legitimate users of a network resource by intentionally overloading the network with illegitimate TCP connection requests. SYN packets are sent repeatedly to the target, but the corresponding SYN/ACK responses are ignored.

syslog   A protocol used for sending and receiving log information for nodes on a network.

TACACS   Terminal Access Controller Access-Control System. A remote authentication protocol that is used to communicate with an authentication server commonly used in Unix networks.

target of engagement (TOE)   The software product or system that is the subject of an evaluation.

Telnet   A remote control program in which the client runs on a local computer and connects to a remote server on a network. Commands entered locally are executed on the remote system.

Temporal Key Integrity Protocol (TKIP)   A security protocol used in IEEE 802.11i to replace WEP without the requirement to replace legacy hardware.

third party   A person or entity indirectly involved in a relationship between two principles.

threat   Any circumstance or event with the potential to adversely impact organizational operations, organizational assets, or individuals through an information system via unauthorized access, destruction, disclosure, modification of information, and/or denial of service.

three-way (TCP) handshake   A three-step process computers execute to negotiate a connection with one another. The three steps are SYN, SYN/ACK, ACK.

tiger team   A group of people, gathered together by a business entity, working to address a specific problem or goal.

time bomb   A program designed to execute at a specific time to release malicious code onto the computer system or network.

time to live (TTL)   A limit on the amount of time or number of iterations or transmissions in computer and network technology a packet can experience before it will be discarded.

timestamping   Recording the time, normally in a log file, when an event happens or when information is created or modified.

Tini   A small Trojan program that listens on port 777.

traceroute   A utility that traces a packet from your computer to an Internet host, showing how many hops the packet takes to reach the host and how long the packet requires to complete the hop.

Transmission Control Protocol (TCP)   A connection-oriented, layer 4 protocol for transporting data over network segments. TCP is considered reliable because it guarantees delivery and the proper reordering of transmitted packets. This protocol is used for most long-haul traffic on the Internet.

Transport Layer Security (TLS)   A standard for encrypting e-mail, web pages, and other stream-oriented information transmitted over the Internet.

trapdoor function   A function that is easy to compute in one direction, yet believed to be difficult to compute in the opposite direction (finding its inverse) without special information, called the "trapdoor." Widely used in cryptography.

Trojan horse   A non-self-replicating program that appears to have a useful purpose, but in reality has a different, malicious purpose.

trusted computer base (TCB)   The set of all hardware, firmware, and/or software components critical to IT security. Bugs or vulnerabilities occurring inside the TCB might jeopardize the security properties of the entire system.

Trusted Computer System Evaluation Criteria (TCSEC)   A U.S. Department of Defense (DoD) standard that sets basic requirements for assessing the effectiveness of computer security controls built into a computer system.

tumbling   The act of using numerous electronic serial numbers on a cell phone until a valid number is located.

tunnel   A point-to-point connection between two endpoints created to exchange data. Typically a tunnel is either an encrypted connection, or a connection using a protocol in a method for which it was not designed. An encrypted connection forms a point-to-point connection between sites in which only the sender and the receiver of the data see it in a clear state.

tunneling   Transmitting one protocol encapsulated inside another protocol.

tunneling virus   A self-replicating malicious program that attempts installation beneath antivirus software by directly intercepting the interrupt handlers of the operating system to evade detection.

Unicode   An international encoding standard, working within multiple languages and scripts, that represents each letter, digit, or symbol with a unique numeric value that applies across different platforms.

Uniform Resource Locator (URL)   A string that represents the location of a web resource—most often a website.

User Datagram Protocol (UDP)   A connectionless, layer 4 transport protocol. UDP is faster than TCP, but offers no reliability. A best effort is made to deliver the data, but no checks and verifications are performed to guarantee delivery. Therefore, UDP is termed a "connectionless" protocol. UDP is simpler to implement and is used where a small amount of packet loss is acceptable, such as for streaming video and audio.

Videocipher II Satellite Encryption System   A brand name of analog scrambling and de-scrambling equipment for cable and satellite television, invented primarily to keep consumer Television receive-only (TVRO) satellite equipment from receiving TV programming except on a subscription basis.

virtual local area network (VLAN)   Devices, connected to one or more switches, grouped logically into a single broadcast domain. VLANs enable administrators to divide the devices connected to the switches into multiple VLANs without requiring separate physical switches.

virtual private network (VPN)   A technology that establishes a tunnel to create a private, dedicated, leased-line network over the Internet. The data is encrypted so it's readable only by the sender and receiver. Companies commonly use VPNs to allow employees to connect securely to the company network from remote locations.

virus   A malicious computer program with self-replication capabilities that attaches to another file and moves with the host from one computer to another.

virus hoax   An e-mail message warning users of a nonexistent virus and encouraging them to pass on the message to other users.

vulnerability   Weakness in an information system, system security procedures, internal controls, or implementation that could be exploited or triggered by a threat source.

vulnerability assessment   Formal description and evaluation of the vulnerabilities in an information system.

vulnerability management   The cyclical practice of identifying, classifying, remediating, and mitigating vulnerabilities.

vulnerability scanning   Sending packets or requests to another system to gain information to be used to identify weaknesses and protect the system from attacks.

war chalking   Drawing symbols in public places to alert others to an open Wi-Fi network. War chalking can include the SSIDs, administrative passwords to APs, and other information.

war dialing   The act of dialing all numbers within an organization to discover open modems.

war driving   The act of searching for Wi-Fi wireless networks by a person in a moving vehicle, using a portable device.

warm site   An environmentally conditioned workspace partially equipped with IT and telecommunications equipment to support relocated IT operations in the event of a significant disruption.

web spider   A program designed to browse websites in an automated, methodical manner. Sometimes these programs are used to harvest information from websites, such as e-mail addresses.

white box testing   A pen testing method where the attacker knows all information about the internal network. It is designed to simulate an attack by a disgruntled systems administrator, or similar level.

Whois   A query and response protocol widely used for querying databases that store the registered users or assignees of an Internet resource, such as a domain name, an IP address, or an autonomous system.

wide area network (WAN)   Two or more LANs connected by a high-speed line across a large geographical area.

Wired Equivalent Privacy (WEP) A security protocol for wireless local area networks defined in the 802.11b standard; intended to provide the same level of security as a wired LAN. WEP is not considered strong security, although it does authenticate clients to access points, encrypt information transmitted between clients and access points, and check the integrity of each packet exchanged.

wireless local area network (WLAN) A computer network confined to a relatively small area, such as a single building or campus, in which devices connect through high-frequency radio waves using IEEE standard 802.11.

Wi-Fi A term trademarked by the Wi-Fi Alliance, used to define a standard for devices to use to connect to a wireless network.

Wi-Fi Protected Access (WPA) Provides data encryption for IEEE 802.11 wireless networks so data can only be decrypted by the intended recipients.

wiretapping Monitoring of telephone or Internet conversations, typically by covert means.

worm A self-replicating, self-propagating, self-contained program that uses networking mechanisms to spread itself.

wrapper Software used to bind a Trojan and a legitimate program together so the Trojan will be installed when the legitimate program is executed.

written authorization An agreement between the penetration tester and the client detailing the activities the tester is permitted to perform.

XOR operation A mathematical operation requiring two binary inputs: If the inputs match, the output is a 0, otherwise it is a 1.

Zenmap A Windows-based GUI version of nmap.

zero subnet In a classful IPv4 subnet, this is the network number with all binary 0s in the subnet part of the number. When written in decimal, the zero subnet has the same number as the classful network number.

zombie A computer system that performs tasks dictated by an attacker from a remote location. Zombies may be active or idle, and owners of the systems generally do not know their systems are compromised.

zone transfer A type of DNS transfer, where all records from an SOA are transmitted to the requestor. Zone transfers have two options: full (opcode AXFR) and incremental (IXFR).